Also by Donna Gaines

TEENAGE WASTELAND: SUBURBIA'S DEAD END KIDS

VILLARD / NEW YORK

A MISFIT'S MANIFESTO

THE SPIRITUAL JOURNEY OF A ROCK & ROLL HEART

* A MEMOIR *

DONNA GAINES

Library of Congress Cataloging-in-Publication Data
Gaines, Donna Louise
   A Misfit's Manifesto: the spiritual journey of a rock & roll heart / Donna Gaines.
      p.   cm.
   ISBN 0-679-46327-5
      1. Gaines, Donna, 1951–   2. Rock music fans—New York (State)—Biography.
   3. Sociologists—New York (State)—Biography.   I. Title.
   ML423.G17 A3 2003
   781.66'092—dc21
   [B]   2002024989

Villard Books website address: www.villard.com

Printed in the United States of America on acid-free paper

9 8 7 6 5 4 3 2

First Edition

Book design by Casey Hampton

FOR RAYMOND AND MY D.O.M.

Why did the soul,

Oh tell me this,

Tumble from Heaven

To the Great Abyss?

The most profound descents contain

Ascensions to the heights again. . . .

—S. ANSKY, *THE DYBBUK* (ACT IV)
Adapted and translated from the Yiddish by
Tony Kushner and Joachim Neugroschel

CONTENTS

AUTHOR'S NOTE

This is a sociological memoir of my life as a fan, the personal narrative of a damaged kid with a rock & roll heart who was saved and transformed more than once. It's also the story of my career as an habitué, a scene maker with scholarly intent. I found my epiphanies out in the street, on subway trains, in bars, in bits and pieces of places and things typically cursed, poisoned, and condemned.

For me "rock & roll" has meant all things *rockist:* guns, surfing (by Web or sea), the occult, muscle cars, tattoos, science fiction, horror gore, pornography, pizza, movies, video games, drinking, drugging, sex, hair, comic books, chewing gum, high technology, and, of course, music. Above all, rock & roll has meant coolness, emotional detachment, image as a cloaking device, protective cover, a distancing mechanism; *don't stand so close to me.* Pop culture, my unholy redeemer.

For many, music has the potential to obliterate pain, transform experience, reinvent meaning, alter feeling states. It can change personal identity and cultural history. As rock & roll turned the beat around, it freed my twisted psyche like Big Yank liberated Europe. Play it loud, the pain disappeared.

Paranoid and comatose for so many years, today I sustain the battle scars of Alloy Nation: head-banger's syndrome—a herniated disk in my neck; basal cell carcinoma from body surfing under the black-hole sun. I've lost my tweeters too—a 10-percent hearing loss in my right ear from recreational gunshot. Knee injuries from dancing in my leopard-skin spikes, TMJ (temporomandibular jaw) from the involuntary teeth grinding of childhood amphetamine addiction, and IBS (irritable bowel syndrome) from bourbon on an empty stomach. I armed myself against the terror of everyday life with an arsenal of knives, guns, and advanced degrees. And still I needed more.

Carl Jung said the greatest fear human beings have is of unconditional self-acceptance. That we might actually come to know ourselves in the context of an alienating, other-directed, consumerist society seems daunting. How do we figure out who we are? For most of my life, music was the only way to connect that wouldn't eventually kill me. Living Colour guitarist Vernon Reid once remarked, "People just say to be yourself. But if you really do that, it's the most threatening, subversive thing you can do." That's a sociological statement, a fact. Finding the courage to be yourself is a critical social act. Stand tall, do or die. Usually it hurts.

At home, in the family, and at school, we may feel pitted against the whole of culture and social structure. Sometimes everything seems designed to destroy us, to make us feel worthless. Therapeutic interventions target our low self-esteem, our "dysfunctional" families, lineages of alcoholism, abandonment, child abuse, and neglect, our damaged capacities for intimacy and basic trust. Social scientists blame it on mass culture, consumerism, dehumanization, the breakdown of the family, or postindustrial capitalism. Identity theorists may point to our blood-stained histories, our abjectification as people of color, as women, as Jews, or as queers. Strung out, hunting down redemption, I felt like shit for most of my life. Joy was ephemeral, like holy water rolling off my fingertips, quickly disappearing. And then I had to start all over again. Running on empty, looking for a fix and a kiss, I did what I had to do, filling the hole, filling the hole.

Being who we are and doing what we want is a political act. People who can't or won't get with the program get punished, labeled, beaten, jailed, or thrown in the loony bin. Any cultural outlaw or social outcast understands this intuitively, through lived experience. So, in the dark night of the soul what gets us through? What constitutes a viable God concept for these fractured times? What in our culture enhances our experience of the Divine, and what obscures it? What empowers our sacred individuality? These are the larger questions explored in this book.

Growing up, the alien child learns that nothing is what it seems. Family teaches that to be loved, we must pretend the self, swallow the truth. If you are beaten or silenced whenever your own truth is articulated, you learn to lie. After a while, you lose the capacity to hear your own voice. School teaches you to obey bureaucratic authority, to conform, to value material externals—popularity, looks, grades, and athletics—over all else. Organized religion claims to address such issues, to offer meaning, community, and hope. But we all know better. More often, religion, like the family and school, is a training camp in repression, imparting that rigidly intolerant "us and them" mentality. It teaches us who's in and who's out, how we are better than the rest. Only the chosen few are saved or blessed. To hell with everyone else—infidels, sinners.

When Jim Morrison sang, "No one here gets out alive," I thought he was talking about my childhood. Alienation empowered me as it imprisoned me. Music enveloped me and set me apart. Alone in my room, I sat smirking along to Frank Zappa's bitter condemnations of plastic people. This teenage experience of isolation was soul crushing. Yet it imparted a critical edge to my thinking. I could expose the world for what it was, and that made me feel godlike. My choice was to be either stupid and happy or smart and miserable. That's the way I saw it.

Thanks to Lou Reed, Iggy Pop, and the Ramones, we now know that growing up in a deranged family situation can set the stage for a very interesting life. Marilyn Manson, too, has shown that even as parental blunders plunder our fragile psyches, they offer great ideas for lyrics, memoirs, movies, an excuse to get high, a license to ill. Courtney Love, Ozzy, Michael Jackson, Brian Wilson, Janis Joplin, Howard Stern—all misfits, heroes, role models. Rich or poor, home may not be a sane or safe place, but it can be loads of fun. Some damaged youth long for a normal life, to be like other people. They actively seek out stability. Others feel they don't have a choice. They naturally gravitate to the vortex, proud to be guilty. Better off dead than *dead woman walking*.

Many of my rocker heroes grew up in fucked-up families, hanging out, fooling around, getting obliterated. Yes, they suffered, and some are emotionally crippled for life. But for most, having a wacko childhood proved a benefit, an advantage, not a tragedy. Yes, we are "survivors," but that seemed too boring to consider. Psychotherapy was for losers, *just gimme another drink*. The greatest gift of a lunatic family of origin is a lowering of the threshold for all things bizarre.

Of course, there are many normal people from nice families with happy lives who also love music, and they, too, follow bands with obsessive interest. That's probably most of the market share. But without that gaping hole in the soul, the *scene* probably wouldn't emerge as a person's reason to live. To those who've grown up feeling abject, strangers to themselves and the world around them, rock & roll has meant much more than just the music; it offers salvation, a new lease on life. Like Johnny Thunders's guitar, it fills the hole. Their scene becomes a lifelong commitment, complete with values, norms, and mores—a code of the road.

Music rescued me from a painful childhood. Over time, it restructured my sense of who I was and what I could be. Onward, through the years, standing in front of the stage, sounds exploding in my head, bourbon swirling, my buzz swaying, I got closer to my Lord. I despised everything else about being in the world. Music was a tricky beast; it energized the addict within as it scratched the surface of the Divine. Music became my religion, and I was orthodox, adhering to strict dogma, no tolerance for anything that "wasn't rock & roll." I condemned the rest of the world as lame or culturally retarded, aesthetically repulsive. I developed a sensibility of negation that allowed me to separate myself from the dull normal world, a hostile place that never welcomed me anyway. It situated me among an elect of *my* choosing.

Music connected me to other people like myself. Misfits, outcasts, and loners, misanthropes with rock & roll hearts. By crafting encomiums to pop culture, writing about music and the subterranean worlds I inhabited after hours, I tapped into communities of like-minded, kindred spirits. Embedded in cultural writing is a secret conversation, a dialogue with other fans—coded with lyrics, references, nuances only we understand.

In witnessing the power and glory of rock & roll, I hope to answer some larger questions, to challenge critics on the left and right who would dismiss rock's redemptive power as "banal youth leisure" or "garbage culture." I hope to negate the long-standing American tradition of adult social critics on the left and right who feel the need to repress or censor youth culture. As I have said, it saved my life—music, the scene, even the drugs, sex, and alcohol had a role in sustaining me when all else had broken down.

Heroes and villains. Where the traditional institutions—family, community, organized religion, the educational system, and mainstream culture throttled my self-esteem and shut me up, outlaw strongholds redeemed me. The good guys weren't really that nice, and the bad guys were often the heroes. Filthy treasures, guilty pleasures, *everything you say, it's the other way.*

Early in the twentieth century, misguided adults unleashed their tirades against movie theaters and dance halls. By the 1950s they sought to eliminate comic books, linking them to the "rise in juvenile delinquency." In the 1980s, witch-hunts against metal and hip-hop wasted more time and resources. In the 1990s Marilyn Manson, Goth culture, and the Internet came under siege, demonized in the aftermath of the Columbine High School shootings. And still, today, youth culture remains a powerful, meaningful force in kids' lives. Many need it to live. Sometimes it's the only thing left to hold on to.

My personal experience as a "rocker"—the impact of rock & roll on my postwar, suburban female psyche—is generationally bounded, culturally and historically specific. But the experience of human alienation is universal. It was later in life that I figured this out: Whatever has worked to defeat or destroy us—child abuse, addiction, even patriarchy, racism, homophobia—*we still have to clean up the mess ourselves.*

Yes, there are angels, guides along the way, but nobody can do it for us. Forget about the rose garden. What you'll probably get is a mop and garbage pail full of bad memories. It may take your whole life to clear it out, to get back to that feeling that you are safe, that you belong here. Sometimes, no matter how high, how far you go, you'll still carry that wound, that first, fatal betrayal.

In part, I've written this book to make some sense of myself and my life, to help me figure out why I was so fucked up and how I survived. But mainly, I wrote it to testify that it is possible to survive a childhood that teaches you self-hatred and smothers you in self-pity. Misfits are found across all categories of sex, race, class, and gender preference. Rich or poor, suburban or rural, no matter what you hear at home, at school, or on the street, you can go out in the world and find your own truth. You can find self-respect and honor. You can be loved, valued for who and what you are, no matter what.

To most people, I'm a walking, talking oxymoron, a flake stuck in a web of contrary affiliations. I'm a card-carrying member of the NRA and the ACLU, a tattooed Jew with a Ph.D. and a pistol permit. I'm the talking head on TV explaining teen violence, jackknife stuffed in my boot. I'll ponder Bourdieu while wearing Velcro rollers, write professorial entries to a textbook on deviance in a lacy tank top that says HARLEY HONEY. At the NYU conference, I'm the plenary speaker with the thickest regional dialect, the visiting professor at the Ivy League university with AC/DC blasting on my headset. I'm a New York intellectual who prefers the *Post* to the *Times*.

I joined the Libertarian party the year Howard Stern ran for president. I've never voted Republican or had sex with either a white-collar worker or a registered Democrat. I claim to be a Libertarian, but maybe all this confusion and chronic angst proves I'm really a liberal, a cultural radical who loves the police and the military, especially the army. I *like* French people.

I'm an antisocial humanitarian, an extrovert who instinctively recoils from human contact. A pro-sex feminist plotting the overthrow of patriarchy while singing Ronettes lyrics. I dream of the day I can dance at a queer wedding, consecrated by God, legitimated by the state. Pro-choice, I absolutely support every woman's right to abortion. Then I wonder. If a live lobster feels pain when boiled, what about a fetus?

Stuck between capital and labor, I own General Motors stock and I'm a member of the National Writers Union, United Auto Workers Local 1981, AFL-CIO. These are the contradictions of capitalism. At least that's what my sociology professors taught me. Or maybe Lou Reed explained it better . . . *and I guess that I just don't know.*

My spiritual journey brought me home, back to my own truth. Often it felt more like a rude awakening than a spiritual one. Mostly, it was a series of events that didn't seem to add up to anything until one glorious moment of self-acceptance. No matter how far we've been pushed away from ourselves, we cannot fight the Law of Karma. We cannot go against who we are, what we are meant to be.

And this I swear is true: You can transcend the urge to self-destruct and find the courage to be who you are. You will find kindred souls to walk with you. Whether you love show tunes or farm animals, surfing or network television, embrace Jesus or Chaos Theory, whatever calls out to you, makes you smile, this is the voice of your own heart. You don't have to kill yourself or blow up your high school to find dignity and relief. Whether you are a loner by choice or resignation, labeled an outcast or you just feel like one, you are not alone. In fact, you're among some pretty awesome folks.

PART ONE

Betty Bradley and Herbie, on their wedding day, 1949.

–1–

THE KISHKA KING OF BROOKLYN

There's an old saying, God never gives us more than we can handle. What actually happens is repression: The mind shuts down so the heart won't explode. This is the story of my mother and father.

In the classical era of swing, the late 1930s and 1940s, large jazz dance bands fused rhythm & blues and pop, generating a rich orchestral sway known today as the Big Band sound. Upbeat, even the ballads were optimistic. Like New Wave was to punk, swing was cleaner, smoother, offering wider audiences a sound more inclusive than the hot jazz of the previous decade. Tommy Dorsey, Benny Goodman, Glenn Miller, Count Basie, and Artie Shaw were the gods of the day. Vocalists smiled graciously, musicianship was critical, phrasing was everything. A music of celebration, swing catapulted the GI Generation from Depression-era scarcity to Big Yank victory, to a promised land of economic opportunity and prosperity. Pushing upward and onward, propelled forward by the Big Band sound, our parents ushered in the American dream, a paradise of big cars, interstate highways, home ownership, suburbia, television, and a big fat baby boom.

Betty Bradley was a vocalist. She told reporters she came from a show-biz family, although she was the only one who ever really made it. Her mother, Miriam, played piano for the silent theater, her aunts were original Mack Sennett bathing beauties, sirens of the silent screen. Grace was a stage actress, Ethel a drama critic, and Naomi a painter. Betty started singing in 1932. At ten, she won a spot on WINS radio. *Major Bowes' Original Amateur Hour* was one of the most popular shows in America, known for launching successful stars. With Miriam prodding her along, Betty won several talent contests in the tristate area. The first contract was with Gray Gordon and His Tic Toc Rhythm Orchestra. Her father, Willie, a civil engineer, had to sign the papers because Betty was only seventeen.

The contract included out-of-town weekly theater engagements at sixty-five dollars a week, "one-night stands" at ten dollars a night with a minimum of fifty dollars a week. Recordings paid ten dollars a day, and New York City engagements forty dollars a week. In 1939 this was nice money. Gray Gordon had a regular gig at the Edison Hotel. Betty made fun of the slow fox-trots, making silly faces onstage, and he fired her. Onstage, though, her sweet melodies were sultry, soothing, the sort that propelled fans into clouds of sentiment and feeling. Then there were the perky, upbeat tunes like "Feed the Kitty." Still, by any standard, Gray Gordon's sound was *corny.* Betty liked mischief, jazz and swing, so she moved on to bigger and better.

Bob Chester had played sax with Tommy Dorsey in the 1930s; now he had his own orchestra. Once signed to Chester, Betty sometimes filled in as emcee. Critics declared her "a honey with a sweet delivery and the kind of personality that goes all too rarely with these popular singers. She can sing 'em hot and deliver 'em tropical." The verdict: "She should go places." Betty's blues vocals had traces of Mildred Bailey, she had a "delicately husky voice of an extremely attractive quality and two of the prettiest dimples in the business, the right one slightly deeper than the left." Bradley was known for deft renditions of standards like "I Want to Get Married" and "Hit That Mess," for "I Can't Give You Anything But Love" and "Do It Again." Bandleaders knew her to be reliable; she wasn't a drunk or a junkie. And she didn't run around—she always stuck with one man.

I remember her for her ballads, for "My Funny Valentine," "Tenderly," and "Summertime." How she walked through the room like a goddess, shining so much larger than life, so powerful, seductive, awesome, and vibrant. I grew up besotted, captivated by her beauty and charm. Watching her sing, dazzled by her charisma, I hung on to her every note. I knew Betty Bradley was singing to me, straight from her heart. Every great singer has that ability to make you feel like the only person in the room. But when that singer is your mother, you know the sun, moon, and stars all revolve around you. In that moment, when she looked directly at me, I felt like the center of the universe. Music was mother's milk, nourishment my soul needed to thrive.

By 1945 Betty Bradley was hanging poolside with Sinatra in Hollywood. He and Dean Martin knew her from Florentine Gardens. L.A. critics dubbed her "the Hollywood Lush Thrush." She had already shared a bill with Martin and Jerry Lewis in Jersey at the 500 Café, with the Three Stooges at the Golden Gate. She was crowned the Queen of Mint at a University of Virginia jubilee and featured in *Downbeat* and *Billboard*. She did it all—the radio commercials, product endorsements, performing for the troops stateside.

Her clothes were fabulous: high glamour, top-shelf Hollywood. At five foot three, with a tiny waist, strong shoulders, and full bosom, she was curvy, elegantly dishy in velvet and satin. A writeup in the *New York Journal and American* described a "vivacious Betty Bradley, favored with lovely features and the oval face . . . the most beautiful in facial contour." Bradley wore her gowns trimmed in lace with feathers, elbow-length gloves, lush hair, dark like Joan Crawford's, brown waves cascading around her face. She had those dimples, high forehead with a widow's peak, cupid's-bow lips, and perfect white teeth. Above her strong chin and high cheekbones, her bright hazel eyes were boldly accentuated by half-moon brows, Bette Davis style.

Betty Bradley had her clothes made to order, suits fitted tightly around her torso and suede platform shoes with ankle straps that made her legs look longer. She starred in pictures, too. She sang "Shoo Shoo Baby" in a film called *Trocadero,* based on the club she performed at on Sunset Strip by the same name. I saw *Trocadero* on TV when I was about four. I loved seeing Mommy all dressed up and Hollywood. She was as dramatic in life as she was onscreen, stormy, raging from within, delivering it all with grace and charm.

Then there were the one-nighters with the Bob Chester Band, or else solo six-week stints, back-to-back shows, a different city every night. Betty toured America by bus, the featured vocalist, the only girl in the band. Sometimes she had a boyfriend, but she took care of herself. Other women knew not to move in on her guy; she'd fight if she had to. She was tough, but she was a lady, too.

Miss Bradley played the Chicago Theater, New York's Strand, Capitol, Apollo, the Earle in Philadelphia, the Orpheum Theater in Omaha, the Golden Gate in San Francisco, and the Club Moderne, in Long Beach, California. She recorded "Do It Again" and "Summertime" for Jewel, sharing the label with Glenn Miller, Benny Goodman, and Harry James. With a sweet French accent, she did comedy as Fifi, the singing cigarette girl, as a regular on NBC radio's Rudy Vallee's Drene air shows. In her Hollywood days Betty Bradley knew everyone from the Rat Pack to Pinky Lee.

By 1948 Betty Bradley had become a prominent radio vocalist and Milton Berle wanted her for the Latin Quarter. He fought to keep her with him. They had great rapport. Bradley was a seasoned professional, a beautiful presence with strong comedic timing. The Latin Quarter was owned by Lou Walters, Barbara's father. When Walters was signing Berle, Uncle Milty, as he was known, insisted on bringing in his own singer, Betty Bradley. Walters said no way, he was using one of his sweeties. Berle held up the contract and, waving it, said, "If Bradley doesn't sing, you have no Milton Berle," and Bradley sang.

Broadway columnists were now acclaiming Milton Berle as "the greatest all-around entertainer in the history of show business." Betty's manager was Frank Berle, Milton's brother. Around this time, Milton Berle was poised to break into television. Once a week Uncle Milty charmed the nation, and he wanted Bradley. With her looks, her voice, and her comedienne's sparkle, she was perfect. But the star had another plan. She was twenty-six and wanted to settle down. Although both Berle brothers pleaded with her in letters and telegrams, Betty Bradley

Betty Bradley in Hollywood.

had made up her mind. She was getting married. Milton Berle was livid. How the hell could she walk out at her peak, in her prime, on the dawn of a new era, "to marry the Kishka King of Brooklyn"? But Bradley was tired; she'd been on the road most of her life. She wanted a home, a family, children, so she married Herbie Denmark. Some say this decision destroyed her career, maybe even her life. But, baby, it was my big break.

A few years earlier, at twenty-four, lonely, in Hollywood, on the rebound after a stormy romance with an alcoholic trumpet player in the Bob Chester Band, Betty Bradley married her first husband. Ray Cootman was the band boy—a roadie, bisexual, a Jewish junkie. After they married, he became her manager. He worked her when she was sick and squandered her money freely. Betty had a butch girlfriend named Electra who worked the circus. They fooled around in the dressing room, held hands, and partied like real galpals. But the wild life wore on her; it wasn't really her style. So she divorced Ray and secured a *get* (Jewish divorce) for a high price. Down and defeated, she returned home to Brooklyn to lick her wounds.

Betty Bradley was restless and curious. As a child she suffered from St. Vitus's dance, a movement disorder characterized by rapid, irregular, aimless, involuntary movements of the limbs, face, and trunk. She was given to fits of hysteria and high fevers. Playful and always very dramatic, she'd dress up like a gypsy kid, wander down to Brooklyn train stations feigning a foreign accent and charming the strangers. Like any teenager, she wanted to hang out with her friends, date, and go to parties. Why did she have to go to another audition? But Miriam pushed her.

Betty had been a chubby child, and her fame brought her popularity at Erasmus Hall High School. She was gearing up to be an English teacher. She loved words, excelled at vocabulary, grammar, and spelling. But she gravitated to the limelight, went for the glamorous life instead. At sixteen she had enjoyed a fling with Herbie. He was twenty-four, a big stud, six foot two, and built. Blond, with green eyes and a strong nose, he was a manly man, not a pretty boy. Rumor had it women dropped their pants at the sight of him. Street-smart and suave, Herbie had a hot car and a backseat made for love. The first time they had sex the fireworks exploded, but Betty was headed for Hollywood and Herbie was fresh back from the army, all set to run the family business.

A playboy well into his thirties, Herbie wasn't the marrying kind. He spent his nights painting the town, days working hard at the kosher catering hall. As was the habit of the day, he lived with the family till he got married but kept a room for the broads downtown at the classy St. George Hotel. As a child, Herbie preferred the streets to the books, and was considered a *trombenik,* a fun-loving bum. His boyhood cronies nicknamed him Gyp the Blood; the family called him Hertzie.

Herbie loved the business. He dropped out of high school and went to work while his two older brothers went on to law school. Bernard and Joe read the *Times, The Saturday Evening Post,* or *Collier's.* They hung out at the family's other establishment, which Bernard managed with his sister Florence. An upper-middle-class Jewish businessmen's haunt on Ocean Avenue, the Elite Club catered to Brooklyn's prominent lawyers, doctors, judges, professional men on the move.

Herbie wasn't like his stuffy brothers. His idea of relaxation was to get drunk and get himself a broad. He was a party guy, a weekend warrior, but he never drank at home or at work. Like the rest of the family, food, not booze, was Herbie's medicine. A sharp dresser, he was a regular at the haberdasheries around town. An early Buddy Hackett fan, Herbie frequented the Rusted Cabin, the Copacabana, and the Latin Quarter, all the New York nightspots, usually with a showgirl on his arm. He partied at the Concord Hotel, where he was known as a good tipper, a loudmouth, always a great time. He had a whole crew of friends he traveled with, including Uncle Butch, the father of gay-rights activist and author Karla Jay. All aboard for funtime, the bad boys of Brooklyn would invite girls up to their rooms, strip them, and throw them out without any clothes, just for laughs. That men like Butch and Herbie should beget two such radical feminist daughters is pure Goddess power, divine justice. But Herbie was young, wealthy, at the top of his game, and that's what men were like in those days.

Herbie always did the right thing. He supported his nephews through college, took young nieces to Broadway shows and nightclubs and introduced them to all the big names. Having lost his mother at age sixteen, and then his oldest brother, Oscar, just a few years later, Herbie didn't want to miss anything. He enjoyed the high life and swore the woman he was going to marry hadn't been born yet.

Meantime, back in Brooklyn, after her Hollywood divorce, Betty ran into Herbie and that old black magic started cooking. With the clothes, the good looks, the charm, and vitality, they were charismatic, wild and sweet, two good kids, family people at heart. Herbie would give Betty a normal life, Herbie would settle down. They loved language games. Herbie was known for making up words; Betty told great jokes. Herbie had met his match; Betty had found a fun, solid guy. They preferred storytelling around a large table of friends to reading books, enjoyed live entertainment, the movies. Opera and theater were for squares. These alley cats liked the night life.

Herbie said he married Betty 'cause she was the only broad he could trust. Still, he warned her, "I don't want you any further from me than I can throw an elephant." In time, Milton Berle would become known as "Mr. Television," acknowledged as the single most critical factor in the proliferation of TV sets in American homes in the late 1940s. Although Uncle Milty's television gig would never have required Betty to be any farther than Philadelphia, Herbie issued an ultimatum. He wanted her with him, where he could see her. So at twenty-eight, at the top of her game, Betty Bradley walked out on Berle, on Hollywood, on the dawn of American television, and married my father, the Kishka King of Brooklyn.

II

And so I was to the Manor born. The Park Manor was one of the first kosher catering empires in Brooklyn. Pop Denmark, Herbie's father, emigrated from Russian Poland to America in his early youth. He worked as a dance instructor and later a horse-drawn trolley car conductor. The Denmarks were a prominent Jewish family; the name had clout. Built in 1928, the Park Manor, at 450 Eastern Parkway in Crown Heights, Brooklyn, stood majestically on that four-lane tree-lined highway. As owner of the premier kosher catering establishment in Brooklyn, Henry Denmark was seminal in advancing the concept of kosher catering in a single facility, providing everything from food served on fine china right down to the ice sculptures. Pop never remarried after his wife, Dora, died. For years, he had an "arrangement," traveling first class with a Mr. and Mrs. Vile. Henry picked up tabs, the husband looked the other way. Mr. Vile wore a glass eye monocle. The missus was tiny, dark, and with her long fingernails, often in green, she was secretly dubbed Dragon Lady.

The family itself was not kosher or religious, but the Park Manor was able to offer families a complete package for weddings and Bar Mitzvahs. The dinner always started with the band playing the national anthem and the "Hatikvah," the unofficial Jewish anthem. In the ballrooms were the American and Jewish blue star flags—the Israeli state had not yet been declared. The facility had two ballrooms, an impressive lobby with a marble floor, a grand staircase with a landing, elegant for bridal entrances, regular cotillion on Jupiter. The first-floor ballroom could seat up to three hundred, with floor-to-ceiling maroon curtains, Czech crystal chandeliers, a bridal room, and large floor fans (no air-conditioning in those days). For a wedding, a large floral canopy, or *chupeh,* was set up, and a small table with a glass wrapped in a napkin would be broken at the end of the ceremony. This was to remind us Jews of the destruction of our First Temple, of the ever-changing life cycle of joy and sorrow.

Charlie Barnow was the official bandleader for the Manor. He played everything from pop tunes like "Good Night Sweetheart" to jazz and *klezmer*-type *fraylichs*—the *hora,* all the traditional Jewish dances. Kalman Kalish was the official cantor for the Manor. If two affairs were booked, he worked both the upstairs and downstairs ballrooms. The second-floor ballroom was smaller, rectangular, able to accommodate smaller parties, up to one hundred sixty. Buffet affairs were cheaper—full tables of relishes, chicken salad and tongue, cookies and desserts. Wartime, the black market kept everyone in meats, butter, parties, and gas. A freight elevator ran from the kitchen in the basement to two pantries. Glasses and dishes were stored in the pantries, silverware and trays in the basement. Ten waiters worked as permanent staff, always in tuxedos. A woman named Rosie made all the hors d'oeuvres, and a special party man came in and made three-foot-high ice sculptures, placed along with the hors d'oeuvres trays, knishes, and drinks.

The meals usually consisted of a small green salad, baked whitefish surrounding a small piece of baked salmon covered with a light tomato sauce. The fish was followed by a vegetable soup, and then by roasted half broiler with world-class kishka—big chunks of stuffed derma, richly spicy and fatty. For dessert, Italian-style fruit ices with cookies and demitasse, a black coffee made with eggshells. At the more expensive weddings, roast beef was served instead of chicken, and sweetbreads in a light pastry shell before the main course. The most lavish affairs involved "French service," rare during the war years. Waiters wore white gloves with their tuxes and served individual portions from elegant silver trays. Each table had bread trays, relish dishes with olives, pickles, and celery, bottles of Hoffman's ginger ale, club soda, and celery tonic. The Park Manor made a special grape punch in a crystal bowl; hard liquor and wine were served at the hors d'oeuvres bar and sometimes at the tables. The whole family was involved in putting these affairs together.

When a Denmark got married or Bar Mitzvahed, it had to be on an off night, midweek, so as not to cut out a weekend booking. Betty and Herbie were married there, as were older cousins. As the next to the youngest, I vaguely remember sitting there with all fifteen cousins, posing for family photos, trying in vain to hide my fat knees. The rest of the time, we met at funerals. Bad genes. Eventually cancer claimed all my aunts and uncles and one of my cousins. The Denmarks were like the Kennedys of Brooklyn, big *Machers,* always a tragedy, but Jewish, so drowning it all in food, not booze. I barely recall my aunts and uncles. Mostly, I remember the food.

Henry and Dora Denmark had eight children: four sons, four daughters. This was a patriarchal order. When older cousins had an audience with their grandfather, it was like kissing the Pope's ring. Henry was imperious and formal with the grandchildren. You'd pay your respects and then you'd get a dollar. *Dynasty* in Brooklyn. The props and the spoils went mainly to the sons. Two of the daughters got married and moved on, but Jessie and Florence stayed involved.

Large women, heavyset, Jessie and Florence were loud like the rest of the family. Unlike their sisters, they didn't marry wealth. Jessie married a baker's son who adored her. He worked for Pop. Florence's German-born husband abandoned her with a young son. Everybody figured he married her just to get a green card. But who knows? Marrying the daughter of a powerful man is never easy. Florence had a fine operatic voice and, as hostess at the Elite Club, she served as Pop's social director. Jessie took care of Pop in his ailing years and looked after Florence's orphaned son after she died. Florence had killer cheekbones; Jessie's face was radiantly beautiful, at once sensual and angelic. By today's standards Jessie and Florence might well be considered stunning, sexy, and, at around six feet tall, statuesque. Back then, they were shamed for their size, for their genetic predisposition to corpulence, and treated as an embarrassment in a family system that viewed women as fuck dolls, trophy wives, or wet nurses. "Such a pity, such beautiful faces," they'd say.

Betty Bradley wanted to name me Louise after a lyric in a song, but it wasn't her call. All firstborn Denmark grandchildren were named after Dora. Her Hebrew name, Devorah, was Americanized as Donna. They briefly considered Deirdre, but Betty declined and later explained it would have been a bad choice for me. After all, Deirdre was a name for a petite, frilly feminine type. The women who married Denmark men were small, slender, pretty, and dark, elegant. God forbid we daughters should ever look like our aunts Jessie or Florence. Some of us did.

After they married, Herbie and Betty settled in Brooklyn and spent summers in Rockaway. When Herbie chastised his bride for not polishing the silver properly, Betty replied, "Get a goddamn maid." In 1950, eight months pregnant, Betty spent her nights sitting around a large table of bagels and lox—often until five A.M. After a night at the Manor, Herbie liked to hold court at Dubrows, an all-night cafeteria on Kings Highway. Now the Hollywood Lush Thrush sang only by request at Park Manor affairs, at weddings and Bar Mitzvahs. When he found out Betty was pregnant, Herbie decided I would be named Henry, after Pop, he was so sure I was a boy. He warned her, "When that baby is born, remember, I still come first." Betty swore they would have nicknamed me Hank, but they never got the chance.

Herbie complained of being tired, run-down, with fevers and swollen glands, and was diagnosed with the flu. By the time they realized it was Hodgkin's disease, it was too late; he was dying. Unable to eat or sleep, Betty chain-smoked and sat vigil. I was born on March 21, 1951. Herbie died in the same hospital less than one month later.

A widow at thirty, Betty was on her own, shipwrecked with no real family support. Miriam told her, "I raised my children, now you must raise yours." Willie was annoyed that he'd lost his meal tickets—first his famous Hollywood daughter and now her big-shot husband. Returning to show business was not an option. Betty had a broken heart that would never heal; she never got over Herbie.

And there I was, born on March 21, the first day of spring, the vernal equinox. Actually, I could have been born a day earlier, but Betty said, "Absolutely not!" That night, she pleaded, "I want my baby to be born in daylight!" To her, a night birth was a bad omen. Moreover, March 20 was the last day of Pisces. Betty, who had studied astrology as a teenager, interpreted the sign as fragile, weak. Whenever I cried or fretted, she'd warn me to watch my latent Piscean ways, the hypersensitivity, the defeatism. At the hour of my birth, in a scene out of *Gone with the Wind,* Betty Bradley declared, "I want my child to be an Aries. Life is hard, I want her to be strong, to be a fighter!"

And so a Klingon was born. My mother waited another whole day, till the sun moved into Aries, till two P.M. when mighty Pluto was rising in Leo. In *The Astrologer's Handbook,* Sakoian and Acker describe the person with Pluto in the first house as an "individual with intense self-awareness and the potential for developing a powerful will. . . . The early environment is often filled with extreme hardships, as a result of which the person becomes acquainted with struggle for survival at a tender age. This leaves its mark in later years when he tends to be a loner and holds his innermost self aloof from those around him. People with this position display considerable initiative but at times find it difficult to cooperate with others or to conform to traditional conduct. They have a deep occult understanding of life and consciousness."

Pluto is accidentally dignified in the first house, which corresponds to the sign Aries, also ruled by Pluto. The Aries child born at zero degrees, just minutes into the first degree of the first sign, is fearless. This is the first warrior of the first battalion, pure dynamic propulsion, like a bullet. Strong, I could take care of myself, and I walked alone. At least that was the job description.

Who cares if Pluto was later discredited as a planet some fifty years later, dismissed as a big fat rock by the Hayden Planetarium? Do we really care if our belief systems are real? Either way, we'll follow blindly along. Faith, like love, will prevail long after reason and fact have collapsed, ruled invalid. Rationality is one thing. Where we live and breathe is someplace else.

Betty Bradley required induced labor. Her uncle Johnny, Miriam's brother, was the obstetrician attending my birth. Even induced and willing, Betty was so tense she couldn't dilate, so Uncle Johnny had to pry me out. He told her I used my head as a battering ram. "You have a very brave little girl," he said. "She fought hard to get into this world." Most people want to stay in the womb; I couldn't wait to break free.

Betty took me to see Herbie downstairs in the hospital room, where he lay wasting away. They laughed at my red-fuzzed pointy head and pink crinkled face, nicknaming me Denny Dimwit. I was long and lean, a low–birth weight baby. Herbie held me once before he died. After that, Betty's milk went sour. For six months, she couldn't hold me; I would squirm and scream. In time, though, she would rock me in her arms, sobbing, singing "Summertime." In Gershwin's 1934 folk opera *Porgy and Bess,* this sweet lullaby is full of promise. A child is protected, loved, cared for until the day she can fend for itself. Though defenseless, the baby is safe, a promise is made,

Until that morning, ain't nothing can harm you,
With Mommy and Daddy standing by.

Betty's sweet contralto made me whimper. I still can't listen to ballads. She thought it was compassion and empathy for her, the Piscean residue of a cuspal birth. Maybe it was. But maybe I cried because it was so creepy. In the cosmic wheel, my birth was out of sequence. It came not as a joy, but at a time of sorrow and mourning. It contradicted Gershwin's lyrics, Hollywood, and the laws of karma and of nature.

When Betty looked into the face of her tiny baby, she saw her complete failure—a great love chosen over a brilliant career, only to be so cruelly aborted. With my features so entirely Denmark, Betty saw Herbie every time she looked at me. She would cling to me as if to bring him back to life, smothering me in the process. In turn, I swallowed my mother's grief as my own, felt her sorrow as if it were mine. I'd defer always to her pain; somehow I'd be able to make it go away. My basic needs, my life itself, seemed superfluous, trivial in contrast to her suffering.

Mommy and me at the Concord Hotel, 1955.

2

ROCK & ROLL RADIO

The first time I felt my calling, I was around seven. I craved sugar, stole candy, and gorged till my teeth rotted. This led to extensive dental work and, eventually, diet pills. I didn't know it then, but bad teeth, food addiction, amphetamines, and an AM transistor radio were all part of a larger plan.

As I sat naked on her plush queen-size bed in a bedroom trimmed in pink and green, the colors of the heart chakra, my mother looked at me and lamented, "Oh, Donna, you have the body of an old woman." I stared down at the carpet, so plush and cozy, sinking into that sick, familiar feeling, *Mommy is ashamed of me.* I withered into myself, bending over my rolls of flab, saying nothing. This was how I learned to live in the world; I would fuck up, Mommy would be upset. I'd get scolded, and then, alone in my room, I'd have to figure it all out.

When I was about five years old, Betty Bradley introduced me to Rosemary Clooney. The dazzling singer was performing at a Brooklyn nightclub. It was the late 1950s, and Betty knew Clooney from their days in Hollywood. If Betty had stayed in show business, followed Milton Berle into television, she might have been as big as Clooney or even Doris Day. She never spoke about it, though. Hollywood was a lifetime ago.

"Donna," she bubbled, enthusiastically introducing me to the star, "*this* is Rosemary Clooney!" Befuddled, I asked my mother, "Who's she?" Betty Bradley froze; Rosemary Clooney just smiled graciously. But later on, her blond mink wrap hanging over me like a noose, Mom scolded, "How could you embarrass me like that? Rosemary Clooney is a famous star!" Like why wasn't I born knowing who Rosemary Clooney was? And wouldn't any other five-year-old child in America know what to do, how to finesse the situation? For the rest of my life, whenever I heard Rosemary Clooney's name, even George's, I'd cringe. I never got angry at my mother, only at myself. After a while, I deciphered what she expected of me. How I should act, what I should feel. Like Mom's pet dachshund Judy—trained to sing for food.

Betty Bradley had been a fat child, too, and so had her mother. Stuffing food was a family tradition on both sides of the gene pool. Unable to control my eating, Mom took me to see a diet doctor in Brooklyn. Dr. Dorff put me on a program of appetite suppressants and vitamin shots.

Speeding my brains out night after night, mouth dry, teeth grinding, I counted atoms, black spots in the darkness. I had trouble sleeping, so my adoptive father, Mr. Gaines, got me an AM transistor radio, and I was never alone again. Even as I walked in the valley of the daily shadow of speed-crash death, I feared no evil. I'd lie awake all night listening to Murray the K's *Swingin' Soiree,* joined to a congregation of WINS listeners, submarine race watching off the back off my eyelids.

Ooo-eee, ooo-aa-aa, ting tang walla-walla bing bang,
ooo-eee, ooo-aa-aa, ting tang walla-walla bing bang.

Flashing lights exploded, dings and chimes rattled inside my head, the synapses in my brain reverberated, and I relaxed. Something zapped me and gave me form and direction. I'd recently had my tonsils out. They say you never forget your first high, that you spend the rest of your life chasing it down. Thanks to wacky songs like "Witch Doctor," high-pitched sounds, and erratic beats, I recaptured the ether dreams of that primordial buzz. It was right there, coded into the electronically altered voices of Alvin and the Chipmunks. I also heard it in the Purple People Eater—another alien who loved to rock. It came again in the twang of Chuck Berry's guitar, in stories of crash-burn teenage love, and the terror of seeing a silhouette on the shade.

On our trips to Dr. Dorff I'd look out the window and say, "Mommy, give me a word." It was a game we played. She would give me a new word and ask me to use it in a sentence three times. She promised, "Once you've used it three times, you'll own the word." She'd do anything to distract me from the weekly ordeal of needle injections, the torture rack (scale), and the doctor's insinuations of moral sloth. Older kids loitering around the office building made fun of me as I entered Dr. Dorff's diet slaughterhouse to get my flesh poked and prodded. "Fat slob!" they'd taunt, until my mother went after them like a panther down for the kill, snarling in their faces, "Do you enjoy pulling the wings off flies?"

Widowed with no real means of support—financial or familial— Betty Bradley remarried three years after Herbie died. Arthur Gaines was a successful Oldsmobile dealer in Brooklyn. Back in Mom's Hollywood days, my grandmother Miriam had been Betty's manager, so when it came time to find her a new husband, Miriam took charge. She escorted her beautiful widowed daughter to meet Mr. Gaines at the showroom. He was divorced, older, and very handsome. As a child I enjoyed my visits to Gaines Motors. It was a huge operation, and I was the boss's daughter, so people had to be nice to me. The salesmen's kids had to play with me. Nobody was allowed to make fun of me or call me fat.

Betty married Mr. Gaines when I was three. He legally adopted me. In 1954, without my consent, I surrendered the name Donna Denmark, the porn star I might have been. I was further diminished by this transaction; Herbie's family, the Denmarks, were descended from Levites of ancient Israel, members of the tribe of Levi who served as Temple attendants under the elite priest class, the *kohanim* (anyone named Cohen). Mr. Gaines's lineage was Israel, the congregation, the people, the nation at large. Not that it really mattered, they only tagged the males in the congregation—Eliezer Ben Chana ha'Levi.

The newlyweds decided to buy a big house in Belle Harbor, an affluent section of the Rockaways, one block from the ocean. Mr. Gaines had no family but his mother, Esther, who ignored me because I wasn't a biological child. When she died, she left me a strand of cultured pearls with a ruby clasp. I was astonished. "Mommy, she remembered me, she really did love me!" Years later, Betty Bradley informed me the pearls were not really from Grandma Goldberg. Everything she had went to her one biological grandchild, Emily. My mother bought those pearls for me so I wouldn't feel forgotten.

Mr. and Mrs. Arthur Gaines were two sad people living in suburbia trying to make a family. You probably won't know your parents are clinically depressed until the family illness directly affects you. Until then, it's just business as usual. As Mrs. Arthur Gaines, Betty Bradley went into full swing as a 1950s housewife, doing charity work and singing in local theater productions. Mr. Gaines went off to work every day, and we got two new cars every year until I was fourteen. Winter we went on nice Florida vacations, to the Shelborne and the Deauville, well-appointed hotels in Miami Beach. In the fall we went to the Catskills, to the lavish Concord Hotel. Betty often sang at charity events and family affairs. Always the same songs—"Tenderly," "Embraceable You," and "Bewitched," as if time had stood still.

A full-time live-in maid was hired to take care of me. In an attempt to call her "nursey" I nicknamed her Nizzy. Betty Bradley slept till noon; she still lived on musician time. Most of my early childhood was spent watching television and eating. In the early years before Mr. Gaines developed a heart condition, Betty Bradley didn't cook much, so Nizzy prepared huge family suppers of Southern fried chicken, sweet potatoes, and lemon meringue pie. Everyone was fat, even the dog.

Once, at night, when my parents were away, I got scared. I wasn't used to them being gone. Mr. Gaines's doctor had suggested a quiet weekend. Reluctantly, Betty agreed. In my room I saw monsters—big, dark amorphous forms—coming at me. I cried until Nizzy took me into her bed and I fell asleep. Nizzy was a fat black woman, part Cherokee, with light chestnut skin and steel-gray hair. She smelled of citrus hair pomades and spicy Tabu cologne. Every day Nizzy dressed me for school. Sometimes I was still asleep while she dragged the clothes over my body. The principal complained to my mother that I was sloppy. My clothes were dirty, and my long, stringy brown hair was often uncombed. Betty Bradley's response to this was to mimic the principal's nerdy midwestern accent, *"Dawna's slawppy."* Nothing changed. Nizzy took care of me until I was about ten, then she got sick and mysteriously disappeared.

Mr. Gaines was a prominent businessman, a Mason, quiet and retiring but savvy. My grandpa Willie had dubbed Herbie a megalomaniac, but Mr. Gaines was "the fox," quiet, cunning. He was active in the business associations of Brooklyn, in upwardly mobile Jewish men's organizations like the Forty-Six Club. He battled the unions to keep his profits up and worked the black market when he had to. Mr. Gaines was a tough businessman, but he was also a melancholy fellow. His first wife had cheated on him and his young son cried and kicked him in the shins whenever he visited, so he stopped visiting. Mr. Gaines was deeply in love with Betty Bradley, and she was very devoted too, but who could compete with the dead?

Esther and Mayer Goldberg had emigrated from the *shtetls* of Russia, settling in New Mexico. They sold fruit from a pushcart. After Mr. Goldberg died, Esther and her three sons moved to Brooklyn, the brothers obtained an Oldsmobile franchise, and they changed their name to Gaines. Mr. Gaines was the baby; his two older brothers were dead by the time I was adopted. Because heart disease ran in the family, Mrs. Goldberg warned Betty not to procreate with her only surviving son; it would be a death sentence for the child. When I was about nine, Esther Goldberg went into the hospital for a cataract operation. Two days later she snapped and jumped out a window, terrified that the Cossacks were after her. She thought she was back in Russia, in a pogrom.

Passive and aloof, Mr. Gaines would smile awkwardly whenever Mom made me "model" my Chubbette fat-girl ensembles in a humiliating ritual she probably thought would help us bond. Sometimes we did bond by playing bad piano duets and making up silly songs. We created dreamy fantasies about imaginary friends for my tape recorder. He nicknamed me *paskudnyak* (rascal, punk) and taught me the Oldsmobile theme song, "Come away with me, Lucille, in my merry Oldsmobile. . . ."

When I became sexually curious, Betty arranged for the door to their bedroom to be left open. Mr. Gaines was lying on the bed, nonchalantly, with his flaccid penis exposed. There was nothing sexual about it, just Mom's loopy way of explaining about the birds and the bees. My parents took me to nightclubs and bought me Shirley Temples. Benny Maksiks's Town and Country featured the Jewel Box Revue. A famous early drag show, the Revue starred the most gorgeous showgirls in the world. The most glamorous women I'd ever seen were actually men.

We had a beautiful home with a TV room where Mr. Gaines read the *Daily News* and enjoyed the music of marching bands on his built-in state-of-the-art stereo system. Mr. Gaines's bad heart got worse after his mother's suicide. He became even more distant. I loved him in the misty way girls idealize and romanticize handsome, remote fathers. I always called him Daddy, but I thought of him as Mr. Gaines, as a formal relation. To me, he looked like John F. Kennedy, elusive, powerful, handsome, untouchable. There was this dreamy look in his steel-blue eyes, like he was somewhere else, maybe with his dead brothers, or his parents, or a secret lover, or with his real son. Wherever he was, it wasn't with me.

Once, when I was playing absentmindedly in the street, a car came careening down the block and Mr. Gaines rushed out between me and the moving car, shielding me with his own body. In Betty's mind, that proved that he actually did love me. Whether he did or not, I had my own version of things. When I was five, my parents told me I was adopted, Mr. Gaines wasn't my "real" father, he "chose" me, they said. So I gave him a tray of chocolate pudding. I said I wanted him to be glad he chose me. But I don't think he had much choice; I was part of the package, like the mahogany bedroom set Betty brought with her from Brooklyn.

Rock & roll radio filled my nights and by day I attended Beth-El Day School. A Conservative yeshiva, it was later renamed the Robert Gordis Day School after our accomplished head rabbi. We had English studies in the morning and Hebrew in the afternoon. Or maybe it was the other way. All I know is recess came in the middle, and then lunch. I usually slept through class until the day's hit of speed kicked in. Time-released Eskatrol Spansules lasted longest, over twelve hours if boosted with Preludin. On those days of greater enlightenment, I'd rip through the hermeneutic texts; penetrating the deeper meanings of Gemara, relishing Rashi's Aramaic commentaries. I delighted in Ashkenazic folktales—*The Wise Men of Chelm,* so dense and concrete in their thinking, they tried to fish the reflection of the moon out of a puddle, convinced it was the moon itself.

The people of the book are a people capable of great abstractions. Mine were enhanced early on by ceremonial chemistry provided by Mom and Dr. Dorff. All this went on in Hebrew, the official language of the newly declared State of Israel. Although our parents sometimes used it, Yiddish was considered the tongue of oppression, humiliating, Germanic. The ancient texts of the chosen people were handed down to me via the liberal policies of the Conservative movement. Conservative Judaism allowed coeducational prayer and study. Standing proudly on the corner of Beach 121st and Rockaway Beach Boulevard—not a Jewish neighborhood by the time I got there—Temple Beth-El was built between 1921 and 1925. It was red brick with iconic columns and glorious stained-glass windows. Reformed synagogues like West End Temple in Neponsit did most of their stuff in English. Most of the men didn't even bother to cover their heads. The Conservatives broke even.

Girls sat with boys, praying together in Hebrew, facing the Ark of the Covenant. But we didn't get called to read from the Torah on Sabbath like they did. When it came to that, Judaism had a *no girls allowed* clubhouse policy.

Mr. Mirsky taught us our *Haftarahs,* the passage we would read in front of the congregation as our rite of passage—Bat Mitzvah. A girl Bat Mitzvah did a lovely reading of a Psalm, the boy Bar Mitzvah read straight out of Deuteronomy or Leviticus. Still, Mom was proud; she said I got a good tempo going by the end of the Twenty-third Psalm. But most of what I remember from those years is my teachers rudely summoning me from my dreams. I floated in and out of consciousness at Yeshivat Beth-El, my brain a murky swirl inside a goldfish bowl, random thoughts swimming back and forth, strands of associative logic without roots. After a while I was stealing extra doses and medicating myself. Stelazine, Miltown, phenobarbital, and Librium helped our mothers get through their days. *Baruch Hashem,* Mom's medicine chest was my stairway to heaven.

Early on I was labeled an "underachiever" for having tested with a high IQ yet having the lowest scholastic performance in a class of fifteen. The English teachers were female, more secular. Mrs. Fricke brought her daughter to class to play protest songs. Mrs. Diamond made us listen to Bob Dylan, while she paced the classroom like a bad detective in a Raymond Chandler novel. A windbag with brown smoker's teeth and greasy bangs, she encouraged some and annihilated others. She never messed with me. I think she was afraid of Mom. My mother once cornered a classmate who taunted me for being fat, snarling, "You're a very ugly little girl. Donna can always lose weight. What will you do about your face?" The ugly girl got a nose job at sixteen; Mrs. Diamond left me alone.

The Hebrew teachers were male, Orthodox, from Brooklyn or Far Rockaway. Mr. Kolsky was my favorite. With green-tinged skin and black kinky hair, he attacked the material with the nervous intensity of a true Torah scholar. Once, when he gave us a lot of homework, I muttered, "Well, when you're a sadist, you go all the way." He suspended me on the spot. I explained to the principal that I just liked the sound of the word *sadist,* I didn't really mean anything by it. Wasn't even sure of what it meant. I was just trying to own a new word. Playing the game Mom and I enjoyed in the car. I apologized by way of explanation and the suspension was aborted.

To everyone's shock, including my own, in the eighth grade I wrote the prize English essay, "What the Jews Can Contribute to America." I got to read it on the *bimah,* at the temple, at graduation. They told Mom I also won the Hebrew, but my grammar was wretched and, besides, the Hebrew prize always went to a boy. When Mom explained the decision to me, she expressed it with a tacit understanding; we didn't even question it, we accepted it like sunrise or sunset. After all, Judaism really was *their* religion. All the women did was hang around. Besides, I was fat, so I wasn't really a girl. It never occurred to me that the most intellectually compelling aspects of Judaism were off limits.

Our Hebrew teachers always asked us to place things on the desk, like chalk or keys, so as not to pass them directly into their hands. Just in case we were unclean that day, *niddah,* menstruating, carrying death in our wombs with our unfertilized shedding. Beth-El Day School did have other projects besides suppressing women. Students were admonished always to support Israel, to cherish the memory of Jerusalem, to mourn the destruction of the First and Second Temples of our people even on our wedding day, when the groom breaks the glass underfoot. We raised money for Israeli orphanages, hustled funds to plant trees in the holy land. We celebrated Jewish holidays with songs, honey, dances, carob, and dates. On Passover we visited clandestine matzo factories in Brooklyn and rejoiced on Israeli Independence Day.

The state was declared in 1948, three years before I was born, so Israel and I grew up together. I had long admired the tough Jews of old who stood up against the other nations. Men like Simon bar Kochba, who led our people's last revolt in Roman-annexed Judea circa A.D. 135. Old Bible stories were filled with heroes like the Maccabees or Joshua at Jericho, warriors who served an angry, jealous God. You had to obey

Him no matter what. In the magnificence of the Israeli army of modernity I saw a proud nation of manly men and fearless women. Kibbutz life heralded a robust return to the land, restoring the vigor and vitality lost in centuries of Europe's killing fields. Israeli soldiers wouldn't take shit from anybody. So inspired was I by these tales that I renamed Judy—Mom's dachshund—Judas Iscariot.

In the religion of my childhood, being able to memorize the prayers and recite them rapid-fire brought great status. I rarely knew what I was praying about or to whom. I just knew I had to say it faster, let the words ride the lightning off my tongue. My picture image of the G-d of Israel was Jackie Robinson swinging a baseball bat against a scalloped sky. In a speed-induced dyslexic brain flip I'd mistaken the word *God* for *Dodger,* so Jackie Robinson, *He was the Lord.*

At Beth-El Day School every morning began with mandatory prayers. We prayed after the lunch meal as well. I loved the Shemoneh Esre, our standing prayers, which at one point required taking two or three little steps, bowing and then doing a quick little shimmy before you really got it going. You can't move your feet once you start, so we'd sway along, *davening,* trancing out like kids at a Dead show or a rave. As the sacred Ark of the Covenant opened we stood in awe of G-d and the Law. As the *aliyah* read his portion from the holy Torah, I heard Jerry Butler's somber *bomp bomp bomp . . . wanting you . . . bomp bomp bomp . . . for your precious love . . .* Although the Hebrews have been shunned as the geek-nerds in world history's high school status hierarchy, Bob Dylan, Lou Reed, Gene Simmons, and Joey Ramone have axed the notion that a Jewish rocker is an oxymoron. But for now, yeshiva bop was as close to Philly as I was getting.

My radio nights infused my days with a joy and light not normally found in a Queens yeshiva. I watched June and Claudette, the older girls on the block, practice the lindy in bobby socks and poodle skirts. I remain forever grateful to Ritchie Valens for writing a song that made "Donna" a name with a rocker pedigree, like Maybellene, Carol, or Barbara-Ann. I blushed when the older neighbor guys sang "Donna the Prima Donna" to me, but I loved it. I was slowly becoming part of something. I know the lyrics to every doo-wop song since 1958, 'cause that's when I got my transistor radio.

In those days if you were fat or queer or if you were adopted, forget about it. If your parents were divorced or drunks, if you were an only child or interracial, you were a weirdo. Shamed, you suffered silent and alone. The wretched of the earth eventually came up for air, fighting back, speaking out, asserting alternative models of beauty, family. They banded together, organizing, creating their own notion of community in nurturing spaces that offered acceptance and love. Angry, humiliated, some misfits started killing abusive parents, schoolmates, and teachers. When I read about the slaughter at Columbine High School, the work of two outcasts, about all those perfect kids who tormented Klebold and Harris till they snapped, a twisted little voice inside whispered, "It's about fucking time."

But in the 1950s if you were abject, you just swallowed it and hated yourself. Without the radio under my pillow, there would have been no exit, no escape, no reprieve; just a lonely kid sitting alone daydreaming about having people to see and places to go. The songs gave all those imaginary people names, voices, attitudes, personalities. It made them seem like friends, situated them in a place I could visit anytime. Listening to the songs over and over again, I became part of a world nobody could take away.

To show up, I only had to turn on the radio and instantly I was there, making the scene, in with the in crowd. Always welcome, *zip-a-dee-doo-dah*, I was just like everyone else. I learned to think in rock code, weaving lyrics into sentences, subversively, to include myself and exclude others. I mimicked the DJs' play on words, incorporating regional dialect till *ragdoll* became *skagdoll, shagdoll,* or *slagdoll.*

I spent a lot of time cutting out photos of cute boys like Buzz Clifford and Bobby Rydell. But I sustained a loyal membership in the Bryan Hyland Fan Club. Bryan Hyland had a sneer and a dirty-blond pompadour. Although he was better known for his number-one hit single "Itsy Bitsy Teenie Weenie Yellow Polka Dot Bikini," I preferred "Sealed with a Kiss." It suited my mood in 1962. *Yes, it's gonna be a cold, lonely summer, but I'll fill the emptiness. I'll send you all my dreams, every day in a letter, sealed with a kiss.* He was gorgeous, and he understood the empty feeling of coming home to nothingness after a dreary day, the comfort of having someone there, even if you couldn't see him.

Yes, Bryan Hyland was all mine. I even had the photos to prove it. I caressed one copy through the plastic in my wallet. I brought it to Beth-El and stared at it like an amulet. The others were glossies pasted up on my bedroom wall. Bryan was always waiting for me, in my room.

I was so devoted to rock & roll radio that in 1964 when WINS changed format to all news, I held a private memorial service in my room. I made lists of my favorite songs, DJs, and slogans. I never lost any weight from the diet pills, but I know my life was saved by rock & roll.

II

like most addicts, I was a loner. But I did have my partners in crime, mostly younger boys from the block. After school we'd orchestrate commando raids across Rockaway Beach, striking candy emporiums without mercy. We needed a name: I opted for the Scorpions, but a popular TV show won out, and so we called ourselves the Swamp Foxes. Our gang of elementary school kids was made up of six or seven boys and two girls. Klowie, who lived across the street, was my main accomplice. I beat the shit out of him when we were little and really regretted it years later when he grew to be six feet four. The Ryans' dad was a fireman, and there were five of them. Kathy was the only girl in the family, the only other girl in the Swamp Foxes. There were Jewish girls my age next door to the left and the right, but I rarely bothered with them—they were busy with Girl Scouts and homework. We Swamp Foxes had lesson plans of our own, like fishing off Jamaica Bay. We'd bike over, catch blowfish, and toss them into Beach Channel Drive, watching gleefully as their eyeballs exploded under the tires of unsuspecting drivers.

I knew the gutters and alleys of my street like a guerrilla fighter. Swamp Fox turf was Beach 139th Street. The block just happened to have a lot of kids—Jewish, Irish, and Italian. Like the integrated doo-wop crew 5 Delights or the multicultural Ronettes, we were one of the early visible ethnic mixtures on the streets of Rockaway. I had grown up with the Ryans, the Malones, and the Monacos. Their mothers were always nice to me except once. Mrs. Malone caught us playing doctor in the basement and freaked out. Mom was cool about it, explaining, "Donna, you *know* she's a devout Catholic. They get very uptight about sex." And that's all she said. Betty Bradley was always more concerned with whether you were a Virgo or a Pisces than a Jew or a Christian.

But in the halcyon days of white suburbia, ethnicity was like the ice cream choices on the menu at our local Chinese restaurant: vanilla, chocolate, or strawberry. Today we enjoy a constellation of variety—like the flavors at Baskin-Robbins, never-ending differentiation and blending. Not so then. My neighborhood was mostly Eastern European Jews. Our parents were American-born, our grandparents were mostly European. Up in Neponsit, near the Reformed West End Temple, a handful of German Jews held court. I'd see the colored people waiting patiently, tired maids at the bus stop heading east, down to their housing projects in Hammels and Arverne. There are so few of them in the world, I thought, they must all be related. I actually expected all colored people to greet each other with a big kiss and a hug, like I did when I saw my cousins. Give or take a few Italians, in Belle Harbor you were either Jewish or Irish and that was it.

I was nicknamed Slugger by Muggs, my best friend. Only Andrew "Muggs" Malone could kick my ass. I could pummel all the other boys. I was their age but twice their size. I never fought the girls; they were too tiny and completely disinterested in gang warfare. The Swamp Foxes played everything from punchball to doctor, went out on regular missions involving window peeping and shoplifting. Best of all was the secret clubhouse. Old lady Gusterson's garage was ours, a safe place to run away from parents, homework, bullies, and bad dreams.

Periodically, some of the Monaco kids came from across the boulevard, from a big house near the beach. Frankie Monaco's family was dark, Sicilian. People whispered they might really be Spanish, even gypsies, so rare was an Italian family in our soda bread and matzo ball world. We were sure their dad was Mafia. Of course in Belle Harbor, all Irish were drunks, all Jews were rich, and all Italians were connected. But the Monacos had the double jeopardy of living among Jews and going to school with the Irish, so they became mediators, the Garibaldis of the Rockaways.

Their home was a haven for budding misfits, a day care facility for lost souls. Later on, it became a teen drop-in center. The Monacos were the first to have surfboards, hot cars, and unusual pets—snakes, ferrets. Antiques, oil paintings, tropical plants, and stained-glass windows like a cathedral. Unlike the rest of Belle Harbor, the Monacos' place had character, it was alive with activity. Mrs. Monaco was always checking the waves, kids were roller-skating across the dining room, and everywhere animals. I always felt relaxed in that house.

Once in a while on sugar missions, I let Klowie tag along for cover. Chugging down rich chocolate egg creams and Drake's Crumb Cakes, we'd linger for hours combing the candy store's magazine racks. I went for lurid pulp like *True Confessions;* while I was sucking down chocolate-covered marshmallow eggs, bad girls were getting pregnant. With each hit of M&Ms, every single Goldenberg's Peanut Chew, we consumed an equal share of Superman and Archie comics. For suburban kids, this was a first taste of pop culture.

In time, my life as a sugar addict did lead to crime. I busted into Mom's wallet at regular intervals to steal candy money with gleeful abandon. Even with a generous allowance, I always wanted more. I stole punchballs, marbles, jacks, and penknives and bartered them for jawbreakers and boxes of Good & Plenty. The grand theft was a magnifying glass useful for the Swamp Fox ritual of incinerating bugs via the death voltage of direct sunlight.

These early defects of character were usually excused as my poor adjustment to the traumatic early loss of my biological father. Herbie might as well have been Marlon Brando—an icon, a mythic figure I knew only as the great love of Mom's life. What did any of it have to do with me?

My sugar fiending required weekly torment perpetrated by Dr. Silverman. The bespectacled dentist drilled deep into my caverns of decay, never quite numbing the nerves. He would stop and start with each scream, administering ever larger doses of novocaine. Every week another tooth was sacrificed to my addiction, but even that did not curtail my cravings. In fact, I loved going to the dentist. Any diversion was a cherished relief.

Dr. Silverman's office was located ten blocks from my house, on Beach 129th Street, the Vatican City of Belle Harbor's Irish community. One day a group of girls were sitting across from me in their Catholic school uniforms. They looked like angels, so light with twinkling blue eyes, like fairies or kittens with blond silky hair. Adventurous and curious, we started talking. Turned out we had friends in common—the Irish girls knew the Swamp Foxes from St. Francis de Sales, the parochial school up the street. By the time we left the dentist's office we'd made plans to hang out.

The girls represented a cross section of Irish-American experience. Annie and her sisters lived over the stores. Mary Ellen's family was wealthy; they owned bars and restaurants. Eileen lived in a big old wooden house. They had seven kids. After school sometimes we'd come over, sit around her huge kitchen table snacking on Saltines and grape jelly. I was fascinated by the notion of multiple siblings. The mother was always racing around, cooking, cleaning, feeding. The father was outside, working with his sons. As an only child, such cooperative effort among family members was completely alien to me. I studied the way they interacted together—so casually and unconsciously. From what I saw, the Irish girls had it made.

Sometimes after the dentist's we'd migrate over to their school, hanging out on the steps of St. Francis. In those days these new friendships usually lasted until you were diverted to the next episode. You hung out for a while, then drifted apart in the natural scheme of childhood liaisons. As long as dental work was in progress, I spent quality time with the Irish girls. I remember we'd walk by the school yard, barely noticing the freckled, skinny boys playing ball. In 1962 I knew all their brothers and male cousins, but we didn't bother with them; any contact was incidental. I didn't see the Irish kids again until a few years later, when I definitely noticed those boys.

Most days after school I watched *American Bandstand*. The Philly kids looked so cool, I studied their hair and footwear. Hair and shoes, the two essential ingredients of correct rocker style. Everything else is negotiable. They sounded so authoritative and important rating the records. White, black, Spanish, clipping their words in rock & roll's standard faux-Ebonic dialect, "I give this record a ninety-six 'cause it got a real good beat." Dick Clark talked to the budding teen consumers of rock product like they were bona fide experts, arbiters of taste and style no adult could grasp.

The kids danced the Slop, the Bop, the Hand Jive, and the Stroll. I followed along in my living room. Every week they listed the Top Ten records, and I updated my stash of 45s. Mr. Gaines had bought me a phonograph, a little box that featured a turntable. I practiced the dance steps in my room—the highlight of the year was *American Bandstand*'s dance contest. I watched it every afternoon until 1963, when it switched to Saturdays. By then I was twelve; I had other things to do.

Bobby Darin, Fabian, and Frankie Avalon broke their careers on *American Bandstand,* but something else was going on. Boomer youth were emerging as serious consumers of popular culture, a market to be reckoned with. This was culture our parents did not transmit; it belonged to us. Music came to us via technology, like some simultaneous discovery on an outer planet. Radio and TV were becoming an integral part of our socialization process, linking youth in solidarity against the adult world. Even sitting alone, day after day in my big empty Belle Harbor house, I felt the pull of pop culture.

Before this, they say kids dressed just like their parents—girls in white gloves, topper jackets, swing coats. Can you imagine? They listened to the same music, too, to Teresa Brewer, or the crooners, Frank Sinatra and Vic Damone. After Elvis hit Ed Sullivan in 1956, it was all over—the season of misrule commenced. When I was four months old, a Cleveland-based DJ named Alan Freed went on the air and began rotating doo-wop and R&B for white kids, bringing street culture into suburbia. Freed coined the term *rock & roll*, black slang for sex. For white suburban boomers, rock & roll would become a sociological concept, a declaration of our unique collective experience at a specific time and place, of our moment in history. Rock & roll wasn't about harmony, rhythm, or even guitars. It was a generational statement with the power to define us against all others, linking us together and to all the artifacts of our time. For Freed's audience, rock & roll meant unity through popular culture and mass media.

By the grace of God the doo-wop sound kicked in during World War II. The Ink Spots are credited with breaking the sound. Back then the genre was lumped in along with R&B, thought of simply as "race music" or marketed as "vocal groups." It wasn't until the 1970s that New York DJ Gus Gossert started calling it doo-wop—following the "shoobee-doo-wop-doo-wah" nonsensical lyrical style that embroidered songs like "Blue Moon" by the Marcels. By 1956 many of the hits were doo-wop style, by 1958 it virtually dominated the airwaves and Freed had been brought to NYC to WINS. The Four Seasons, Jay and the Americans, and Dion and the Belmonts' tales of love, class conflict, and longing wrapped around a larger regional experience we listeners could relate to.

Throughout my suburban childhood, on family car rides through places like Brooklyn, Howard Beach, or Far Rockaway, I'd catch a glimpse of the boys-only doo-wop ensembles harmonizing in stairwells and neighborhood storefront alcoves, one singing bass, one singing falsetto, the rest weaving harmonies in a cappella. It was magnificent, but I couldn't figure out why the only thing anyone cared about in these songs was love. Across the proud boroughs, bridges, and tunnels of our land, in black leather car coats, slicked-back hair, tight pants, and knot shirts, clusters of Italian, Irish, Latino, Jewish, and African-American boys came together, a rising nation in five-part harmony.

In Chicago, Philly, Jersey, and Staten Island, too, music had the potential to break down social barriers and connect people at the level of the soul. The gospel roots, the devotional nature of hymnlike harmonies had a spiritual quality that could be readily embraced by all. This was youth-generated public entertainment, free, easy access, independent of parental supervision. Some were hitters, others were not. To my untrained eye, they just looked cool. As important as cruising or graffiti, they were a seminal part of early 1960s pop culture like Brooklyn Fox shows, tight sweaters, teasing combs, and switchblades.

Doo-wop and rockabilly were strictly Boystown. In contrast, Phil Spector's wall of sound felt like a hot, wet estrogen blanket wrapped around an erupting female libido. Critics understood it as an R&B-derived rhythm section with a robust echo, and strong choruses blending percussion, strings, saxophones, and voices. I understood it as a lesson in how to be a woman and what it meant to love "him." As nature began to torture my body into uninvited childbearing functions, the Matron Saints of Big Hair spoke to me, direct from the heart. Listening, lovesick, with a particular boy in mind, the soft strings formed crescendos of tears, a much-needed catharsis for teenage heartbreak. Then, bells, chimes, a bouquet of devotional harmonies celebrated young love, human dignity reclaimed. Your best friend might get tired of hearing you obsess over him, but the girl groups just encouraged more.

Not only was the sound emotionally raw, honest, and inspiring, but it completely reflected my own life experience coming of age in Queens. I never cared whether the music was a male-generated, socially constructed market fabrication, as some critics later decreed, or if this was the foundation of New York rock, or just a fad. I made sense of this music through the context in which I experienced it, from living in my world in a time when suburban street gangs, back-alley abortions, reform school, bad reputations, and probation officers ruled the day. When girls wore push-up bras, and smoking cigarettes made you "tough." From the first moment my eyes locked and loaded on *that handsome boy over there.*

Betty Bradley was still fixated on the Big Band era. I didn't have any older sisters, and my older girl cousins were mostly sheltered "good girls" sequestered by their parents in their bedrooms. If they were bad, they did it on the sly, like my cousin Doris, the Queen of All Sock Hops. I didn't know about her secret life until years later. Doris started in the late 1950s. At first she pursued jazz, poetry, and writing. Then came Elvis, Lenny Bruce, and the beatnik life at NYU in Greenwich Village. At one point Doris dated rock & roll radio idol Bruce Morrow—Cousin Brucie. He gave Doris her first 45 case filled with the Top 100 singles: Chuck Berry, the Everly Brothers, Little Anthony and the Imperials.

At one point, Cousin Doris arranged for my mother to give singing lessons to some kids she knew. It was a local band called the Harbor-Lites. With them gathered around the piano, Mom taught the basics of breathing and harmony, style and taste. No scales or theories; Betty Bradley was not a music teacher, she was a musician. She'd had little formal training herself. Music was instinctual, mainly by ear. I should have paid more attention because some of the Harbor-Lites later became Jay and the Americans—Kenny Vance lived around the corner.

With Cousin Doris undercover, it was the girl groups who taught me about love, cosmetology, and how to guard my turf (boyfriend). My mentors also instructed me in the rudiments of class struggle, gender politics, and intergenerational conflict. Once I got interested in boys, I transferred the devotional quality of the music from monotheism (one G-d) to monogamy (one man). I was taught that the constituent elements of true love involved absolute faith, unwavering devotion, and relentless capacity to hang in, even if he treats you like shit. Following the teachings of Harvey and the Moonglows, in 1958, I have kept "The Ten Commandments of Love" to this day.

One: Thou shall never love another.
Two: And stand by me all the while. . . .
Oh happy we will be if we keep the Ten Commandments of Love.

Like punk, rap, hardcore, and death metal, the girl groups' music was created by teenagers for teenagers, about teenage themes. The doo-wop crews taught me what to look for in a boyfriend—loyalty, a righteous heart, and tough, manly street skills. The girl groups instructed on things teenage girls cared about—parental control, boys, reputations, and marriage. Some of this music could get as melodramatic as Yiddish theater. But these were my concerns, and I heard them articulated every night, broadcast under my pillow via a transistor radio. I understood all about love at an early age.

When boomers wax nostalgically for the '60s, they usually mean the tie-dye days of Woodstock Nation, the pot, the counterculture, the blows against the empire. But not me. I idolized the hitters, not the hippies. My 1960s was rooted in the styles and subculture generated by the defiant youth of the 1950s, when adult moral panic was focused on juvenile delinquency, comic books, TV, music, and movies. I idolized the gearheads, greasers, and gang members featured in *The Blackboard Jungle*, *West Side Story*, and the closer-to-home suburban middle-class angst of *Rebel Without a Cause*.

The girl groups of the early 1960s ruled the airwaves around the time I hit puberty. They celebrated and canonized that Golden Age of the Hitters with a sensibility that has informed New York's finest bands from Blondie to Luscious Jackson. Like I said, I grew up in Rockaway Beach, Queens, the surf town later made famous by the Ramones. Summers, teenaged Dee Dee used to hitchhike from Forest Hills to Beach 116th Street to meet chicks on the boardwalk. Like the Shangri-Las and the Ronettes, the New York Dolls and the Ramones came from the boroughs and 'burbs of New York City. Intuitively, they understood the dialectic of vulnerability and guts and packed it into a perfect three-minute single. If you study Johnny Thunders's early hair, it's pure Ronnie Spector. And Joey Ramone, who sounds like Ronnie, looks a lot like Shangri-Las' singer Mary Weiss (the nose, those lips). Hair slinking over the face, like a Hollywood starlet punched out by the wrong guy at the right time.

By the 1960s, the 1950s greasers were known as *hitters*—our regional crop of bad boys and girls. The hitters would eventually oppose the hippies on all matters of music, politics, patriotism, drugs, and sex. Long hair against short, juicer versus pothead, pro-war against anti-war. The tough guys who ruled youth culture in the pre-Beatles age of grease. By 1969 a lot of that got washed away in one Big Kahuna of heroin, but more about that later.

As a young doofus in orthopedic shoes and fat-girl clothes, it was my life's ambition to be a hitter chick. Tough, cool, sexy, and very bad. The Ronettes had the hotter look—bigger hair, darker eyeliner, tighter clothes. The Shangri-Las were meaner; white ethnic girls, they never smiled, not even on TV. Their songs were schmaltzy portraits of tough girls, street queens as fearless as the wild boys they worshiped, "good-bad" rebel rocker boys who walked to the beat, singing a tune. Like Reparata and the Delrons, they were Catholic school girls lured from piety by the call of the streets. The sweet tenderness of the Blessed Virgin mixed with fierce boroughs grit as they reached out to their bad boy, unconditionally. *Dirty fingernails, tight leather pants, high-button shoes, he's always looking like he's got the blues.* He was a prize only a bold girl with a soft heart was hip enough to recognize and strong enough to handle. Known as the "bad-girl groups," they were my idols.

A generation later, when they aren't mistaken for "girl bands" like Elastica, L7, and Babes in Toyland, or blamed for perpetrating incorrect gender ideology, the girl groups are pitied for the foul social relations that left most of them penniless and washed up by the age of twenty-one. Produced by people who specifically geared the songs to a teen market, few of these entertainers enjoyed significant careers past 1965, when surf music, the British Invasion, and Motown took the market. The Beatles and the Stones were girl-group fans too, the former covered a number of girl-group songs like "Chains" (the Cookies), "Please Mr. Postman" (the Marvelettes) and "Baby It's You" (the Shirelles).

It would be a mistake to read girl-group music as anthems for Future Battered Wives of America. It may be true that the girls who grew up embracing these ideologies were ultimately rewarded with a decaying suburbia, high divorce rates, and kids who worship Satan. But we can't take any music out of context. The guys who were raised on this stuff (and boy-group doo-wop) ended up with Vietnam, disinvestment, and bad American cars. Proving only that blind faith can kill you if you let it.

My favorite girl groups came from the New York metropolitan area—the five boroughs of New York City, Long Island, and New Jersey. I was less interested in their Detroit counterparts, the Supremes, Martha and the Vandellas, and the Marvelettes. I loved the songs, but the singers themselves seemed more Hollywood, more studied and polished. But all the girls loved to sing, often with family members— sisters, cousins, best friends. Mostly black, mainly prole teenagers, they often sang in church first.

Ma-ay-be, if I pray every night, you'll come back to me.
And ma-ay-be, if I cry everyday, you'll come back to stay.
Maybe, maybe, ma-ay-be.

The girl-group sound was ushered into U.S. cultural history in 1958 with "Maybe," the Chantels' "chick doo-wop" breakthrough hit. Some of the girl groups were fans of Frankie Lymon, with his crystal-clear falsetto. Unfortunately, most of the girls couldn't really sing. They had shrill voices, articulating with what I'd call a "squelp"—a combination squeal and yelp. But it worked, because it sounded like a real teenage girl declaring her love, demanding his, defiant, standing her ground against hostile forces: the town, the neighbors, parents, rival girls. It's tough talk, visceral and raw. You know it when you hear it. It's authentic to the ear, true blue, even if nothing else about this music was. Despite the way it was written, produced, packaged, or promoted, the squelp spoke a social truth.

Actually, the god concept is only part of the equation. Religion is the opium of the people, Marxism is the opium of intellectuals, once a junkie, always a junkie. Long before my readings of Marx and Engels, the girl groups taught me the rudiments of class theory. The centerpiece of both doo-wop and girl-group music is a heterosexual love that is stronger than death. With the girl groups, class antagonisms surface often and more dramatically. Not only is she expected to love him even when he beats her and ignores her, she has another function; only a woman can offer a love that is strong enough to buffer her man against the brutalities of the workplace. In "Uptown," as written by Barry Mann and Cynthia Weil, life sucks. It's degrading and cruel, except when he goes home, uptown, to her. The world he navigates is humiliating, unbearable, but for the unwavering faith and loyalty expressed by the Crystals:

Uptown he knows that I'll be standing by.
And when I take his hand,
There's no man who could put him down.

Like her sisters in country, she's gotta stick by him. True love heals all wounds, including those inflicted by exploitative labor relations. The brutalities of her workplace aren't considered because in 1962 we were all expected to marry and have babies, which, of course, wasn't acknowledged as work—it was a nonalienated labor of love, L-U-V. Despite his degraded status in the marketplace, she will love him unconditionally. I embraced this notion as an absolute truth.

The Chantels' Arlene Smith was classically trained with a rich, disciplined voice like no other. No squelper, at age twelve she had performed as a soloist at Carnegie Hall. The Chantels were five friends who sang in the choir at St. Anthony's of Padua in the Bronx. In time, these gospel roots translated into the celestial rhapsody of girl-group music. "Maybe" was written by the Valentines' Richard Barrett as a powerful story of losing someone you adore and the despair of trying to win them back. In Arlene Smith's hands, the song sounds more like she's mourning a lapse in faith; she offers lamentations, not lyrics. Arlene Smith was sixteen when she recorded "Maybe." She once commented that what inspired her singing in "Maybe" was the love she felt *for her parents.* Even though the lyrics spoke to heterosexual love, there's a sacredness, a fierce passion for some higher state of grace that elevates the song. This was true of a lot of the girl groups' material. "Maybe" transcended human love. Smith sounds like she's singing about God, about the absence of faith. "Maybe" hit into higher ground every time.

This cherishing and striving for redemption in love was also characteristic of doo-wop. Actually, when it comes to the torment of love, the masochism and pining away, the girl groups weren't any more soppy or sentimental than the boys. Forget Judas Priest, Ozzy, and all the other metal bands crucified for their lyrics during the PMRC (Parents' Music Resource Center)–inspired witch trials of the 1980s. Doo-wop is the biggest suicide music of them all.

Some songs were morbid, but others were famous for offending the feminist sensibility and inculcating incorrect thought in young women. The Crystals' "He Hit Me (And It Felt Like a Kiss)" was a classic in female self-abnegation. As everyone knows, "He Hit Me" was written by Carole King with her husband, Gerry Goffin. The song didn't exactly reflect the norms of the day. Even in 1962 teachers didn't want the kids listening to it, and producer Phil Spector pulled it off the charts before it got near the Top 100. Barbara Alston, singing lead for the Crystals, didn't like it then either, and even Goffin himself admitted it was radical for its time.

And when I told him I had been untrue
He hit me and it felt like a kiss.

More than thirty years later, Courtney Love boldly appropriated the song for a Hole performance on *MTV Unplugged,* introducing it as a "really sick song." The song walks the fine line between generic sadomasochism and sheer male brutality. The protagonist cheats on her boyfriend, he gets really pissed off, he hits her, and then she realizes he loves her. The violence against her becomes a sign of passion, hence real caring. She is overjoyed by this act of possession, climaxing, "He made me his." Given contemporary spousal-abuse rates, there's some satisfaction in seeing guitar-slamming Courtney cover this tune. She could have really camped it up or milked it for irony, but she didn't. She took it seriously, addressing an age-old nasty logic: "If he beats me, it means he loves me." Courtney Love's version leaves us unresolved and murky. It sounds as menacing now as it did when the Crystals sang it. That we can love someone even when he doesn't love us, even when he hits us, is part of the genius that makes this music at once so compelling and so repulsive.

Class theory, street fighting, and surrender to the greater glory of love were life lessons I wasn't gonna learn at home or in school. Although they didn't hit it until late 1964 with the tearjerker "Whenever a Teenager Cries," Reparata and the Delrons started singing in 1962, at St. Brendan's, a Catholic high school in Brooklyn. The lead singer, Mary Aiese, changed her name to Reparata after her elementary school choir leader, Sister Mary Reparata. What better focus for saintly feminine devotion than the sullen "Tommy," who once treated our girl with consideration, respect, and tenderness? But then Tommy starts acting like a dick. Still, she won't give up on him. Her response to his callous indifference is to love him even more. I ached to love a boy like that, only in dreams.

> *He's not so sweet and he's far from polite*
> *Hardly ever calls me,*
> *And comes to pick me up late every night.*

Like I explained, in Belle Harbor if you weren't Jewish, you were Catholic. In the music business, the doo-wop and the girl-group sounds were usually lumped in with R&B, "colored music." Of course, many African Americans did belong to Protestant sects, but none of them lived in Belle Harbor. Because the Chantels, Shangri-Las, and Delrons were Catholic school girls, in my ignorance I assumed the street sound was firmly rooted in their religion, in Catholicism, in the Church of Rome, and that being "rock & roll" was some sacred rite of baptism, a blessing. Of course, Belle Harbor had many upstanding Roman Catholic youth engaged in wholesome activities—mowing the lawn, pondering St. Thomas Aquinas, living peacefully among their neighbors. They were not hitters. Like good kids everywhere, if they didn't make any trouble, they were invisible. Likewise, some lower-middle-class Jews definitely qualified as hitters, but with no visible street-corner society on Jewish turf, how would anyone know? In Belle Harbor, Catholic kids did hang out, so early on, in my world, rock & roll and Roman Catholicism were intertwined; they were one and the same.

By the eighth grade of Beth-El came the Bar Mitzvahs. In the class of 5724 (1964) the boys had galas, grand displays of bourgeois wealth. The girls' parties were more humble, usually catered in someone's home. Betty Bradley wanted mine to be a big bash in a hall, but I foolishly refused. I didn't want to stand out. Regardless, the parties always digressed into little spin-the-bottle and seven-minutes-in-heaven make-out extravaganzas. Eight boys and seven girls meant a limited gene pool. The sexual experimentation began as the boys got taller and the girls busted out. Voices were changing, crushes impending. The girls were following teen fashions, developing nicely. I had a smoldering fixation on the smartest boy, the one who won the prize Hebrew essay. He was a dark, brooding number, also, oddly, with green skin. But he declined my advances; the short boy, the ugly girl, the fairy among us never had a chance. Most of us had been together since we were five years old, the same fifteen kids from kindergarten to eighth grade. A safe, suffocating womb of homogeneity. Regardless of my lowly status in the sexual social hierarchy, this was not hot.

On Saturday mornings Beth-El students were required to attend synagogue services. We needed a formal note excusing us with good cause if we missed it. The Conservative temple was about a mile away and we were expected to walk 'cause it was the Sabbath. That was a real drag. But there was an Orthodox temple about five blocks away from my house, and I had a plan. Betty Bradley was always flexible about making the world bend over for my special needs, so she persuaded Beth-El to let me attend Ohab Zedek with its more rigorous *halakhic* traditions. Ironically, it was Beth-El's mandatory Sabbath prayer policy that ultimately brought my rock & roll radio world to life.

About two years after I met the Irish girls at the dentist's office, at the edge of adolescence, I would make a startling discovery. Just five blocks from the Orthodox *shul* was the bad boy I longed for, the one I imagined while submarine race watching alone in my room for all those years. He was waiting for me, right there in the school yard of St. Francis de Sales *when I saw him standing there.*

My Bat Mitzvah dress, 1964.

3

OUT IN THE STREET

Parental supervision atrophied as Mr. Gaines's illness commanded Mom's full attention. Newly teenaged, hormonal meteor showers setting in, I found I was on my own. Mr. Gaines was suffering from heart disease and was deteriorating—frail, thin, and bedridden most of the time. He needed his rest. At some point I understood it was better for me to be out of the house.

This sad situation carried an unintended consequence, an opportunity rarely afforded a middle-class Jewish girl. It was 1963–64, my last school year at Beth-El, I was turning thirteen, and suddenly I was free. Free to wander, free to roam. The benign neglect of an overburdened parent pushed me out into the street where anything was possible. Lacking the family resources most people depend upon, Betty Bradley invested her confidence in my ability to make the right choices. I had no real curfew, no set family dinner hour, only Mom's blind faith to guide me. So I ventured forth. Once in a while, I considered myself lucky.

Saturday mornings at the Orthodox services at Ohab Zedek, I flirted with pimply boys from behind a *mehitzah,* a sex-segregated partition. I watched them pray, with their hand-crocheted *yarmulkes* and blue-and-white prayer shawls swaying in the wind. By the time they hit the *shema,* they might as well have been headbangers at an Iron Maiden show. But for me, the highlight of the Sabbath was the *kiddush,* a lavish weekly wine and schnapps fiesta replete with sponge cake and all manner of treat, especially if there was a Bar Mitzvah.

Stuffed from the *kiddush,* I decided to take a slow Sabbath afternoon stroll. Bored with the more familiar surroundings, I wandered five blocks east instead of west, walking in the opposite direction of my house. I found myself loitering across the street from the schoolyard of St. Francis, on Twennyninth; Beach 129th Street and Rockaway Beach Boulevard. Though I passed by it often, I hadn't really hung out since the days of Dr. Silverman and the Irish girls. The school yard was part of a large complex involving the church, a school, a rectory, and meditation gardens. All in brick orange against luscious greenery, colors glorious like the flag of Erin.

Even with my marginal ties to Twennyninth and exalted status as a former Swamp Fox, a yeshiva girl like me had no business going there, especially on *Shabbas.* I knew it was risky. Childhood was one thing, but once you were older, you were expected to stick with your own kind. If you got along too well with the Irish kids, other Jews considered you a race traitor, a betrayal to all the kids who were getting the shit kicked out of them. It was disrespectful to our parents, to the memory of the six million, the 673 martyrs at Masada, everyone all the way back to Moses on Mount Sinai.

Mixing was forbidden and for good reason: They hated us and we hated them. But I figured that wasn't my problem. I didn't fit in anywhere. Unaccepted by either group, what did I have to lose?

Normally, historically, Jewish girls and boys would do anything to avoid confrontation with the *goyim.* We were two very different peoples, alienated from each other by distinct cultures, histories, traditions, beliefs, and values. You felt these differences as soon as you crossed over.

To the sheltered Jewish child, the children playing on *their* streets were bigger and wilder. They played harder and sometimes they were dirty. In their plaid uniforms, they looked almost paramilitary. Perpetually *farbiseneh* (pissed off), they never smiled, except right before they slammed you in the ear. The Jews dismissed most Irish as *shkutz,* white-trash barbarians, psychotic from the nuns and their drunken parents beating them up all day. In turn, they viewed us as big-nosed snobs, rich as Rothschilds, acting like we owned everything. And who did we think we were, claiming to be G-d's chosen people? What made us think we were so much better than everyone else?

Once upon a time, this is how otherness was measured in America: Miracle Whip against Hellmann's, they had cats, we had dogs. They worked on their boats; we worked on our tans. They smelled different, too—salty luncheon meats of unidentifiable origins on their breath. To them, we reeked of onions, chopped liver, and egg salad sandwiches. Only in peanut butter and jelly was there any possibility of common ground. Even if you lived on their block, grew up among them, if you looked Jewish, they'd beat you silly 'cause you killed Christ. They didn't care that Christ was a Jew or that you weren't even there when it happened. They were immune to appeals and spat upon you just the same.

If groups of Irish kids were seen roaming Jewish streets, trouble was automatically assumed; they were drunk and looking to kick ass or rob houses. Fear of rowdy *goyim* always lurked right under the surface. It was woven into our diasporic identities like gefilte fish and poppy bagels. I remember when President Kennedy was shot. Instinctively paranoid, anticipating backlash, my mother said, "I hope to G-d a Jew didn't do it."

As far back as anyone remembers, there were Judeo-Celtic turf wars in Belle Harbor and strict rules of disengagement. If you were Jewish and they knew it, walking to school through Irish streets could be a deadly proposition. You had to be especially careful on your way to the elementary school. Public School 114 was on Beach 135th Street across from Beth-El Day School, two blocks north of Ohab Zedek. Unless you claimed ties to one of Belle Harbor's famous Jewish basketball-

Kadima ("Forward"): Beth-El Day School yearbook.

playing families or knew Ernie the head lifeguard, you were cooked meat.

In the fifth grade my friend Robby was cutting out of P.S. 114 at lunch with a friend and his little sister to get pizza on Twennyninth, their mecca. You had to pass St. Francis to get to the beach, too. You walked by terrified of Christ hanging off the wall like he was gonna grab you. Then there was always a saint lurking around and Mary in her ominous hooded robes. Spooked by all these graven images so taboo under Mosaic Law, every Jew understood Twennyninth was the Celt's capital city. Irish flags hanging everywhere, all the beers, bars, and blondes. Twennyninth had street life, the Jewish part of Belle Harbor and Neponsit did not. So people knew right away who belonged and who didn't.

All the way back to school after lunch, Robby and his friends were followed by a group of Irish kids who repeatedly stepped on the little sister's heels until they'd broken her shoes. The "Jewboys," as they were called, did their best to bravely confront them, but the odds were five against two. The Irish kids were bigger, tougher, and scarier. But there was something else. According to Robby, "We knew the one truth that made us losers in every one of those confrontations. No fury was great enough to overcome what we'd been taught all our lives—to stop hitting once the opponent is down. Whereas for the Irish kids, it seemed as if it just started getting fun once you'd been knocked down. If blood wasn't drawn, it wasn't a fight. Our fear of facing that incomprehensible ethos made us almost too timid to even try and defend ourselves."

In *Tough Jews,* historian Paul Breines's examination of political fantasies and the moral dilemma of American Jewry, three modes of Jewish response to violence are analyzed. The Weak Jew didn't fight back. He passively submitted to his persecution. This was the legacy of the Holocaust, the Jew as wimpy victim. Like Jesus, the Noble Jew chose not to fight back on moral principles that eschewed violence. He turned the other cheek and walked with G-d.

Alternatively, the Tough Jew doesn't take any shit—à la Bar Kochba, he fought back, pounding the enemy until he prevailed. Breines, an anti-Zionist, feared the Bar Kochba legacy was at the root of contemporary Israeli aggression against Palestinians. Quoting authors of classic studies on European *shtetl* culture, Breines observed that physical violence was historically considered "un-Jewish." Our traditions emphasized "intellect, a sense of moderation, cherishing of spiritual values, and the cultivation of rational, goal-directed activities." Behaviors were frowned upon as non-Jewish if they placed "emphasis on the body, excess, blind instinct, sexual instinct, and ruthless force." Eastern European Jews and the more elite German-Jewish Americans held the belief that violent crimes were "not in the Jewish blood." On Twennyninth, that put Robby at a grave disadvantage.

Robby's father was a cop; they lived in the Irish part of Belle Harbor. This wasn't class warfare involving shanty Irish and a rich, propertied Jewish child of privilege. His predators were of the same or even higher economic status. As adolescents, Robby and his pals enjoyed reading a book each week and discussing it as a group, listening to a parent's cherished jazz collection, playing cards at home. Even if the valiant Robby hadn't been outnumbered and outsized, he would not have fought like the Irish kids—it would have been antithetical to his Jewish values. Breines notes most of the tough Jews of history tended to be found among lower and working classes. For that, you went to Far Rockaway.

Rumor had it that a local priest had instructed the kids to seek vengeance for the Jews' role in the crucifixion, so holidays were always the worst. The Irish boys drank heavily, then migrated uptown toward Neponsit looking for a showdown. Independence Day they'd bomb the Washington Hotel, where weddings and Bar Mitzvahs were held in the grand old style of Grossinger's and the Concord. They'd stick a lit cigarette inside a cherry bomb, leave it next to the window, and run away. When the butt burned down, the cherry bomb exploded. Halloween was the Holy Inquisition. Irish gangs would stop kids on the street asking, "Are you Catholic or Jewish?" If they got the wrong answer, they'd beat you silly. The Belle Harbor boys fought back, but like Robby, they played by different rules. Only when the police were called in and Irish parents were asked to control the situation did it stop.

But something else was going on, equally threatening though never openly acknowledged: S-e-x. The roving Celts brazenly flirted with the Jewish girls and took a special delight in romancing them away from the Hebrew men. There was even a special place for interfaith lovers who wandered—Bay 1 of Riis Park. Established early on as an outpost for pre-Stonewall queer freedom fighters, Bay 1 was strategically situated between the rigidly exclusive communities of Jewish Neponsit and Irish-Catholic Breezy Point. Breezy was the westernmost community, right over the bridge from Brooklyn. Isolated and gated by the early 1960s, Breezy was off limits, formally guarded, we understood, to keep out the Jews. If Breezy had good waves, dedicated Jewish surfers only got in on the benevolent wings of a Christian friend. In the age of hitters, beer, and zits, Bay 1 became a place of refuge, the heavy make-out spot for Belle Harbor's clandestine Judeo-Celtic couples. Nobody would ever know unless he told, and he always did.

More than a few *Yiddishe madels* became willing war brides. Imagine seeing a teenaged Matt Damon walking down your street, a Mark Wahlberg or a Kevin Bacon. Smiling broadly at you, his blue eyes twinkling, winking at you. The young Celts were dashing, charismatic, sexy, dangerous, and, above all, strictly verboten. Going with *goyim* was a *shande*, it brought shame on your family. A generation earlier, if you married out, the family considered you dead—they sat *shiva* for you. The price you paid for a taste of unkosher salami was banishment from the clan. This was enough to curtail lust among a majority of the female Semite population.

Yes, by messing with an Irish boy, a Jewish girl was defying adult authority. But thanks to my studies at Beth-El, I knew a secret. Even if the bad girl married her Celtic love god and had his fair-haired babies, she wasn't hurting our tribe. Even if she relinquished her faith, under our laws of matrilineal descent, *the children would still be Jews.* Even if their hot father was directly descended from Celtic warriors and kings, from Brian Boru himself, the kids were forever *ours.* Even if she converted, baptized them as Roman Catholics, fed them pork and shellfish, they retained the right of return under Jewish law. Moreover, such an intermarriage could improve our gene pool, help to dilute diseases of *shtetl* inbreeding like Tay-Sachs disease. In a way, the Jewish girl who surrendered to the smoldering arms of her Hibernian performed a patriotic duty for *Am Yisrael.* Unfortunately, most Jewish parents didn't see it that way.

Hear O, Israel, the Lord our G-d is One. A few years ago someone showed me a copy of the West End Temple newsletter. I noticed the names of the Bar Mitzvah kids—David Shea, Hannah O'Connor, Rebecca McNamara. It seems that in the end, the Jews of Belle Harbor got their revenge; we got their children. See! Love is all you need.

II

B y 1964 D.T.K.L.A.M.F. (Down to Kill Like a Mother Fucker) was scrawled on every soda machine, playground wall, and train station from Rockaway Beach to Ozone Park. The A train on Sixteenth travels through East New York en route to New York City, so sometimes there were regional elaborations—T.T.H. (To the Heart), T.L.A. (True Love Always), the latter tag usually wrapped around a heart with lovers' initials. My personal moniker was T.M.C.I., which I imagined described me the day I sealed my fate. When I entered the school yard of St. Francis de Sales. Trespassing on their consecrated holy ground, on Roman Catholic terrain, T.M.C.I., Too Much Coolness Involved.

A few days after my *Shabbas* stroll past the school yard, I took my vows. I made the full commitment: I grabbed the needle-sharp point of a neglected math compass and demolished my brown gum-soled orthopedic shoes. In a rage, I shredded the last in a line of tattered girdles I'd worn since fourth grade, tight white elastic shorts that never really suppressed the fullness of my belly or hips. This daily punishment of my excess only hampered my digestion, caused endless chafing and sores between my thighs. In 1964 repression of flesh and female sexuality went hand in hand. A fat girl was meant to be invisible, her body punished, scorned for her carnality, for her unbridled appetite. Food and sex, lust and longing. Rock & roll radio had offered me an alternative and it was time to seize the day.

First, I poured a bottle of straight hydrogen peroxide over my hair, teasing it into a ferocious high orange bouffant. I socked on wads of black eyeliner and green shadow, light pink frosted lipstick. Thick base and face powder to cover my zits. Eyebrows tweezed, I banished my fat clothes from Lane Bryant and opted for size 16 department store fashions designed for the full-figured female body. Trading in my frumpy plaid pleated skirts and modest pastel-colored button-down yeshiva blouses, I had a new after-school look. Skin-tight turquoise blue elastic pants, slinky floral pattern shell tops, and black pointy ankle boots with taps on the heels. The call had come and I did not tarry.

I walked back to that school yard with determination, cranked, hormones ablaze, ready for anything. And then I entered. Now I was hitterized in a Bat Mitzvah of my own design, a rite of passage from childhood misery to adolescent thrills. Sprouting boobs, a lipstick, and a comb in my back pocket, down to kill.

And *la de fuckin' da,* there they were, waiting for me. Tall, wiry, lean, lanky in Levi's and low Cons, straight hair slicked back, light brown, strawberry blond, freckles, flapping madras shirttails, gliding across the court with grace, sweaty with lethal intent, playing basketball in the school yard. Standing somewhere at the crossroads between the hitters and surfers, rock & roll in the flesh, standing before me, bad boys bopping around, blowing spit like James Dean (or at least Jim Carroll). I watched the school yard soldiers swagger, full metal jacket, masculinity in motion. They could have been Korean, Puerto Rican, or Polish, but that wasn't the demographic. They were *other,* and that meant desire. They'd fight to the death for their turf—on the basketball court or on the street. The Irish got here first, D.T.K.L.A.M.F and they'd never let the Jews forget it.

I'm not even sure how I slipped into their world. Maybe I recognized a familiar face, a brother or a cousin of someone I knew, an old crony from the dentist's office. Maybe nobody even cared who I was or where I came from. I was a new face, and that was enough. I came back the next day and every day after.

I hit the school yard like I once raided the candy store, with passion and persistence. I wanted it like I needed an egg cream. Gradually I joined the Celts at beer blasts, fraternizing out in the open, even on the streets of Neponsit. Just being around them was enough. Of course, my cross-cultural foray into the forbidden school yard of Eire proved much too transgressive for my own good. Now I would be presumed dumb, sexually active, wild, and dangerous through mere association with the Irish kids. But I didn't care.

By embracing my abjectification and formalizing my identity as an outcast, I altered my fate. I was no longer a "fat slob" shamed and rebuked. I was angry, defiant, and a new whole world stood behind me, ready to back me up. I didn't need parents, school, or the neighbors to tell me who I was or how to live. This street brought my rock & roll radio to life. The universe of doo-wop, girl groups, hitters from all five boroughs, New Jersey, and all the way to Philly covered my back. Being tall and "big boned" became an asset. People were automatically afraid of me. I didn't need my mother to fight my battles. I never beat anyone up; I didn't have to. I just looked at them and they backed off.

There, out in the street, religious passion, raging resentment, amphetamines, pop music, and teen angst coagulated, and I was formed. From that day on, I embraced the life, I mastered the fine art of hanging out. Quantities of beer soon tempered my speed jitters, a quick way out of any bad situation, a sure bet. Taste of alcohol down my throat and I felt instantly warm, beautiful, strong. I was walking tall, in charge.

I learned to navigate an ever-changing theater of activity. Fights, crushes, jealousies, the endless street banter, ear candy of dialogue and dialect, especially in Queens. By foot, on bikes, whether breaking and entering, dry-humping or huffing glue. From the school yard I'd make the scene at the stores on Twennyninth, up to Dirty Irv's back behind Neiman's pharmacy. Head down to the beach, back up to Ziggy's for a slice. Then, over to Lee's Chinese takeout. Back and forth, in constant motion, always with a plan—go get cigarettes, find a place to piss, eat, make a call, meet a friend. Sometimes I attended Catholic Youth Organization dances and basketball games at St. Francis. I joined in the prayers, hedging my bets. With green eyes, red hair, and a baby face, I always passed.

Manners especially applied on the street. In time come the rank-outs, playful put-downs, then pledges of loyalty and affection. Fights, fall outs, then a new alliance is formed. I quickly learned the etiquette of what we'd now call "old school." Don't push too hard. Be yourself and show respect. Don't talk to a group of guys unless you know one of them well. Ladies don't stare; try to meet the other girls first. Respect property rights (monogamy). You can go up to a boy alone, but never intrude on a couple. If people don't include you, keep your dignity and move on. If you like a guy and he likes you, find an empty house. Break in, walk around, make out, take inventory, but never steal; that isn't the point. These are the rudiments of street life.

Rockaway's mean streets were never very mean, except for young lovers. I saw my Tommy for the first time on that pivotal *Shabbas* day when I walked past the school yard. He wasn't shooting hoops; he was flicking butts, staring at his feet, drinking a beer. Mostly he was leaning against a wire fence, watching. He didn't say much, and he never smiled. To me, he was a walking miracle, scruffy, scrappy, mean, lean, and not too clean. Tommy didn't talk to the girls. They were all afraid of him. He was older, already seventeen.

Too shy to go up to him, I watched for a while. I found out where he lived, in a run-down apartment over the stores around Sixteenth. Beach 116th Street was a tougher part of town; people were poor and angry. Tommy was a street urchin. He went to St. Camillus, a parochial school that made St. Francis kids seem like Neponsit boys. Tommy drank beer like I ate candy—relentlessly. Sometimes I would stand across the street from where he lived, in the shadows, lurking in the doorway, hoping he'd show up, but he never did. Tommy never knew how I felt 'cause I said nothing. I just watched.

> *He's a rebel and he'll never be any good. . . .*
> *Well, just because he doesn't do what everybody else does*
> *That's no reason why I can't give him all my love.*

Following the advice of the girl groups—who were, of course, all tough and Catholic like Tommy—I understood I had to love my wild boy unconditionally. And since he was bad news, so out of control, he needed my love even more. The woman's role, as per the girl groups, was to stand as a wall of roses between her man and the world. He empowered her to resist against the parents who grounded her, the town that judged her harshly, friends who shunned her, the whole social order that rendered her isolated, invisible, and ineffectual. Her sins of passion and devotion would cost her dearly in the community, but they were sanctified for his name's sake.

Tommy had a street rep that made him even more abject and alienated than I was. This afforded me the advantage of reflected glory within the inverted status hierarchy of the hitters. By loving an outsider, I would get something for myself, too: reverberated charisma. In those days, adult fear and respect were hard to come by, especially for teenage girls. There was a real risk in openly loving the boy from the wrong side of town, running wild and free, scaring adults. He could ruin your chances at a good life. He could cost you your respectability, and the relationship could tarnish the class aspirations of an entire community. What would the neighbors think? I already knew and I didn't care.

Apparently, my freedom to move around as I pleased posed a threat to adult authority. I was big, loud, and wild. Even parents who liked me thought I was trouble. By now, Belle Harbor's *yentas* warned my friends' moms, "How could you let your daughter be seen with Donna Gaines?" I was officially branded. People felt sorry for Betty Bradley, nursing a sick husband and now this daughter out of control, running with a bad crowd, drinking, in public view.

In the end, the girl in the song must always choose between the bad boy and her parents, between middle-class security and the road. Invariably, a tragedy occurs before she has to make a choice. In the classic girl-group melodrama "Leader of the Pack," the parents make it clear: She has to break up with him. When she does, he turns and walks away, saying nothing. Then he cracks up his bike and dies. She'll never forget him, the leader of the pack. At the high school all the girls stand around her in awe, "Betty, is that Jimmy's ring you're wearing? Gee, it must be great riding with him. Is he picking you up after school?" "Uh-uh." He's dead. There was no happy ending once you crossed over.

I knew exactly what to do. I would love Tommy with all my heart and he would be mine. I was proud of him, he was my hero. I knew we were meant to be together. One Friday night I was busy getting my look together, thinking about Tommy, wondering how to hook up with him. He'd be at Brian's party. Brian was the leader of a loosely organized street gang who called themselves the Magicians. They were the older guys, the same ones I saw playing basketball in the school yard on Twennyninth the day of my holy epiphany. The last hitters on earth, always more of a writing gang than a fighting crew, except when it came to pounding Jews. The Machines in Ozone Park and the Alliance from under the el near Seaside were more serious fare. Remember, this *was* Belle Harbor.

The older girls warned me Tommy was the toughest guy of all, totally crazy if he got mad. This only turbocharged my passion. At Brian's party the girls had set it up. Janet and Linda were Jewish girls like me who had defied the norms. They always looked out for me, upheld the rules of Jewish-girl sexual conduct. They were older, sixteen, and they had devoted Irish boyfriends, hard guys with cool cars. Tall, tough-talking, with big hair, cracking gum with attitude, you best believe they could kick your ass.

I remember sitting on Tommy's lap. We drank beers all night and made out. He was shy, didn't say much, just smoked his Lucky Strikes. With his pale complexion, and black hair slicked back, I thought he was cold looking, like a reptile—though more turtle than snake. That only made me want him more. Tall and lean, with gray horn-rimmed glasses like Buddy Holly's, in his black Levi twills, sandy-colored desert boot shit kickers, navy sport jacket, and white button-down shirt, Tommy was *dressed*.

It got late, Tommy passed out. Brian suggested he get some air. "Tommy, why not walk Donna home?" Half unconscious, he stumbled down my block, into my house, and met my parents. As I explained, in my neighborhood or his, Jewish girls who dated Irish Catholic boys were whores (pronounced "who-uhs"). Mr. Gaines shook Tommy's hand as Tommy reeled, drunk and terrified. Most parents would have disowned such a wayward girl and banished her bad boy on the spot, but mine welcomed Tommy. They were different. Mr. Gaines grew up dirt poor, a first-generation Jewboy in New Mexico, fighting off tough Latino boys. Despite the suburban glaze that had fallen over her life,

Betty Bradley had seen the world. She remained oblivious to the petty status hierarchies of a town where most mothers had been boring schoolteachers prior to marriage. Still, my high street visibility caused her trouble; neighbors stepped in to control the situation, relatives urged her to send me away. Mom just made fun of them.

That night my mother offered Tommy a soda, but he ran for his life. Historically, being around parents has always creeped out teenagers. Especially alone in a neighborhood that's not your own, drunk on a first "date." The next day Tommy called me up, terse and to the point. "Meet me down the beach. I'll get a six-pack, Brian and the guys will be there." This was probably the most romantic moment of his life.

Twennyninth was his turf and I'd be totally safe with him. He was the de facto leader of the pack. The toughest guy in town. But I was afraid to meet him because I couldn't imagine that he really liked me. I was a fat girl, not obese, but big enough to know no boy would ever love me, even the biggest outlaw on Twennyninth. I was convinced he only wanted to use me. It was understood that Catholic boys thought Jewish girls were "easy." Jewish boys thought Catholic girls were whores, too, but they rarely crossed over. In those days the sanctions against Jewish men who forfeited their children's Hebrew birthright to a Gentile mother were too harsh. Someday there would be offspring enrolled at St. Francis with names like Sean Goldberg, Kevin Weinstein, and Siobhan Shapiro. But that came later, after the drugs.

There was another obstacle standing in the way of true romance: my bad reputation. By confusing myth with tradition, I made a serious blunder and was almost excommunicated from Twennyninth. Because of my faulty assumption that Catholic girls were easy, libertine about sex, I generated racy stories about myself. Besides, it was an honor to be labeled a slut instead of a fat girl. Most of all, I desperately wanted to be in with the in crowd. In my quest for self-acceptance, I misread a norm that said you could do *whatever*, but always act like you're innocent and pure.

My lurid tales of heavy breathing and make-out sessions behind the drugstore culminated in a confrontation in the girls' bathroom of St.

Francis. My name was scrawled boldly, with the word *whore*. I was devastated. At first I thought it was the Irish girls. Had I unwittingly involved someone's boyfriend in my fictional narratives of teen lust? Turns out it was the work of Janet and Linda, my trusted technical advisors. They later took me aside and explained that my stories jeopardized the status of all lost daughters of Zion. "They already think all Jewish girls are who-uhs, now look what you've done! We had to stop you!" Their sanctions were justified, so I accepted my punishment.

But my tall tales got me in even deeper shit. Now Brian's girlfriend (also Jewish) was looking to kick my ass. Carol came right up in my face and said, "Meet me after school. I got some talkin' to do." Panicked, I called Janet for advice. Carol was small but nasty, a little pit bull with dead black eyes and a big beak. So ugly and mean I was genuinely scared of her. Janet advised, "Just don't show up," and I didn't. I decided to lay low till it blew over, and after a while, I just stopped hanging out.

I never went to meet Tommy down at the beach that day. I couldn't believe that he really cared about me. I assumed he only wanted me for sex—I was a shy virgin with very little experience, despite my stories. I had only kissed a few reluctant Yeshiva boys at Beth-El's Bar Mitzvah basement sex parties. But I loved Tommy! True love had come down while we were on the phone. He was trying to talk to me. I could hear his mother in the background, yelling at him to get off the phone. He screamed back at her "Fuck you!" and then the phone went dead. This was the first time I had ever heard anybody, male or female, curse their parents. I thought Tommy was the Duke of Earl. Still, I never went to meet him. I never saw him again, though the night I stood him up, I carved his initials into my arm with the point of that same needle-sharp math compass I had used to demolish my brown orthopedic shoes. The scab lasted about six weeks, and I wore it like an Iron Cross.

Weeks later, the truth came out. Janet and Linda told me I really hurt Tommy. Turned out, he really *cared* about me. According to Janet and Linda, after that night at Brian's party Tommy considered me his girlfriend; in fact, I was his first. But when I didn't meet him down at the beach that day, he just assumed I was using him to get Brian jealous.

I cried and told Janet and Linda that I loved Tommy, not Brian, never Brian, always Tommy, but it was too late. I blew it, and now I had the pit bull after me. Meantime, Tommy had gotten arrested for brutally beating some local Jewish boys. "Split that kid's skull right open," I heard. According to lore, they left a trail of blood all the way into Bernstein's, the candy store up on Forty-fifth. At first, this episode delighted me. I knew the guys he attacked—typical Neponsit boys, snobs who wouldn't bother with girls like me. But this had nothing to do with me—it was business as usual, class war, ethnic cleansing in the Rockaways, something the boys played out among themselves. The girls never fought over anything except the boys. Our vendettas transcended any ethnic or religious ties. But this episode was especially ugly, and this time the victims pressed charges.

Tommy's family was poor; they lived over a hardware store in the "bad" part of Rockaway. He had no dad, just a fat mother on welfare and a bunch of older brothers, thugs who enforced family discipline by beating the shit out of him. The Jewish boys Tommy had pummeled lived in Neponsit, the wealthiest section of the Rockaways, in big houses with loving parents. They went to prep schools and attended parent-supervised parties. They dated refined, obedient girls in "collegiate" garb—penny loafers, kneesocks, circle pins, sweater sets, no makeup. Eventually, they went to college, where some of them smoked pot and began to question the order of things. Tommy's life followed a different story line.

Tommy was sent up to teen jail in upstate New York. When he hit eighteen, the judge offered to cut his sentence if he enlisted. Shipped off to Vietnam, he was ready for war. Tommy came out a year later on a full psycho disability. Soon after, they said "he shot a nigger up by the train station" on Sixteenth. For all I know, he's spent the rest of his life in a psychiatric prison.

I still think about Tommy now. I wonder how he is, rotting away somewhere, a wasted life, detached from all reality. In my ballad of codependency, I still believe if I had met him at the beach that day, if he had known how much I respected him, that I loved him, he might not have been so angry. Maybe if I had trusted him, had faith in myself, it might have been different. Maybe he wouldn't have beat up those guys, gone to jail and then to Vietnam. Maybe he would've seen life differently. Maybe I would have, too.

Maybe, maybe, maybe.

"My Three Dads":
Herbie (top left),
Mr. Gaines (top right),
and D.O.M. (bottom).

4

DIRTY OLD MAN

watched as Mr. Gaines waved good-bye to me from the car. Mom was driving him to the hospital in Brooklyn. As usual, I was hanging out on the corner. He was only supposed to be gone a few days, so I didn't bother to visit. Two days later, when I got home from school, my grandparents were there. All dressed up, staring awkwardly, they sat on the living room couch and said nothing. Betty's parents never visited us, so something was definitely up. I asked them where my mother was and they kept silent, avoiding eye contact. So I went upstairs, called the hospital, and asked for Mr. Arthur Gaines. After a few moments of searching, the operator said, "Sorry, there's no such patient here." I knew my father was dead.

I didn't realize when my mother drove away with him that day that he would never return, that I'd never see him again or get to say good-bye. My mother didn't tell me he was dying. She didn't want me to feel guilty for not visiting him in the hospital. Consoling me, she said, "He felt it would be too upsetting for you to see him like that." At the end Mr. Gaines was all bones, finally thin after so many years of battling weight. My parents shielded me from death as they had from the illness. To protect me, they pushed me away. I wasn't expected to participate, only to disappear quietly. All I knew about the last days of Mr. Gaines was that he wanted a Coca-Cola, a cold, sweet, brown soda in a green glass bottle. That was his last wish.

While she made funeral arrangements, Betty Bradley sent me to stay with the neighbors. Mr. Gaines had no family, and it never occurred to either of us that her side of the family, the Cretins, should somehow be involved. Betty Bradley took care of her dying husbands by herself. Shattered, hopeless, twice widowed, now my mother talked of suicide. "But, Mommy," I implored. "I need you!" I offered myself as an incentive, motivation for her to stay alive. It worked after Herbie died, so I figured it would again and it did.

The unexpected death of my adoptive father precipitated another critical life event. It was the first time I got drunk. Up to now it had just been a few beers with the Irish boys. Now I meant business. I stole a bottle of whiskey from the liquor cabinet and stumbled through the damp, chilly streets of Belle Harbor wailing, "My father died, my father died." I was fourteen.

At my father's funeral I asked one of the neighbors to walk up to his casket with me. I touched his forehead; it felt cold, like the marble sink in the bathroom of the funeral home. I no longer associated it with him. Since Mr. Gaines didn't have a son available to say Kaddish for him, I did it. Alone in my room every day, once in the morning and again when I returned at night. By summer I knew the memorial prayer for the dead by heart. I said it even when I was high, every day for one year, in accordance with Jewish law.

When I was very little, I was always surrounded by family. Eating together, laughing, carrying on. As the next to youngest of fifteen Denmark cousins, someone was always holding me. I was an only child, though rarely alone. I was part of a rowdy extended family life. I belonged to people who looked like me and loved me. But a few years after my mother remarried, my big birthday parties ended and our family ties began to fray. The Park Manor closed in the early 1960s and became a Baptist church. With the business disbanded, the family gradually moved away. Fallen from bourgeois grace, my older cousins dispersed, joined the meritocracy, and prospered. Since Mr. Gaines had no family, most of my childhood was spent with Betty's family—a treasure chest of mental decay.

Betty Bradley's father was supposedly a genius. Grandpa Willie was a Cornell graduate in civil engineering, an agnostic, a man of science. As a teenager, Betty showed an interest in astrology, but Willie dismissed it. So she challenged him and he set out to disprove its validity. He claimed he succeeded but for ten percent of the predictions he couldn't discount. This "ten percent" kept him fascinated for years. He set up a magnificent system of index cards, with astrological data meticulously filed. Willie calculated my astrological chart right after I was born, using it to explain my behavior. If I fidgeted during his long lectures on Uranus transits, he attributed this to my frisky natal Mercury in Aries. If I was weepy, it was Jupiter exalted in Pisces, willful, Mars in Aries.

Willie instructed me rigorously on the signs, the houses, the planets, and their aspects. I loved it, like biology, psychology, and sociology, astrology could explain who we are. For example, was I fated to be an addict because of something nasty in the gene pool? The result of starvation in utero—the eternal hunger of a low-weight baby? Or was it the effect of early childhood trauma—paternal abandonment and consequent maternal neglect? Perhaps my addiction was cultural, the generational sway of sex, drugs, and rock & roll? Or was it merely an ideological construct, hence meaningless?

Alcoholism is, of course, just another name for "Writer's disease." With a musician mom, it was a wrap. But according to my horoscope, my addiction was fated long before Betty's milk turned sour. Decreed the moment my soul contracted with hers to set the hour of my birth. Her will and mine, destiny, governed from afar.

I wanted answers, all the paradigms I could get my hands on. As far as I was concerned, astrology was the macro-theory mother of them all. Basically, a person's horoscope involves a unique configuration of variables—the signs, houses, planets, and then all the aspects between them. Understanding one's natal horoscope can be a guide toward greater self-knowledge and help us realize our individual potential, like studying the history of our people or our own DNA.

For some astrologers, this is predictive science, a rational causal relationship where planets have direct impact. But in the last generation, many have embraced a more Jungian approach. According to astrologer John Marchesella, "Astrology is based on the principle of synchronicity . . . the meaningful coincidence between two or more events. If one of these events can be understood, then the other(s) will be understood, too." Rather than predict and direct outcomes, the planets tell a story in symbols, in pictures, like dreams. As the planets move, our story unfolds. It develops over time, like the mind or the body.

As planets like Pluto and Venus orbit, they express their energies in each of the twelve signs of the zodiac. The horoscope is a road map for the soul, a snapshot of the sky at the moment of our birth. Planets live in specific houses, and each house is a distinctive realm of human experience—health, work, money, love, partnership, death, and sex. There are twelve houses. For example, I have the sun (personality) in Aries (first sign of the zodiac), in the ninth house (the higher mind; philosophy, religious belief, foreign travel). On the day I was born, the sun conjuncted (joined with) the planet Jupiter, which expands everything from tumors to the capacity for faith. A sun-Jupiter conjunction yields an optimistic, enthusiastic personality prone to expansion and excess. I don't know or care if any of this is "true," if karma really exists, or if there's life after death. Astronomers refuted it, scholars ridiculed it, but that never stopped me. How can faith be argued or proved? Even a godless man of science like Willie had to admit something was going on.

Willie met my grandmother Miriam on the beach. The cantor's son grew up poor on a New Jersey farm. He got scholarships and waited tables for his Ivy League education. He fell in love at the first sight of a doctor's beautiful daughter. When he was young, Willie looked like Robert De Niro. Miriam was blond, with a delicate dreamy look in her blue eyes. They were gorgeous together, but badly matched—like mineral oil and seltzer.

Cretin family life was part comic book, part horror gore, dysfunctional, completely Ramones. I remember my grandparents' modest brick semi-attached row house in Brooklyn, where Willie sat for hours playing chess with himself in Russian, getting up only to blow his nose in the sink, methodically, one nostril at a time. He drank the mineral oil for regularity, leaving a trademark silver-dollar stain on the butt of his gray trousers. He had an office in the basement and lots of engineering tools to play with. He built all the houses on Brooklyn Avenue and was involved in the initial construction of the New York City subway system. Willie swore he could have been a millionaire but decided against it. "Hell, most of it would just end up in taxes." It sounded like bullshit, even then. Betty Bradley was the only one with the clips to back up her stories.

When word got out that I was sprouting pubic hair, Willie teased me with his tweezers, threatening, "I'll pull out every hair on your pussy!" When he died, the family made sure I inherited the tweezers. Now and again he'd stroke my arm, discussing my Venus (love nature) in Taurus (earthy, sensual). He'd purr, "I could really arouse a woman like you." Like all doting grandfathers, Willie advised me about life. "When you fall in love," he warned, "make sure to do it with your brain, not your snatch."

I was never scared of Willie. I just laughed it off, till years later when he died and I learned I was descended from two generations of incest. Miriam's father, Moses (Betty's grandfather), had incested all four of his own daughters. And then, a generation later, Willie raped Betty.

My great-grandfather Moses Cretin played violin for the czar, immigrated to America, and married Rebecca, a Jewish society girl. American-born, Rebecca's family owned the Gambetta Snuff Company. The snuff shop was at 113 Division Street at Orchard. Rebecca's parents bought leaf tobacco from stands along the Bowery, ground it up, sold it, and opened the shop in 1876 with ten dollars in gold. Thirty years later, the family refused an offer of half a million for the business, which by then had branches across America. By the time the Depression hit, snuff was passé, and the business was valued at a tenth of its original worth. Today, it's a hair salon in Chinatown.

At the peak of the snuff empire, Rebecca's mother was a popular philanthropist known as the Angel of the Lower East Side. The Cretins sometimes told people they were part Egyptian or Portuguese. But there were no Sephardic traditions; they were Russians like everyone else, garden variety *Ouester Yidden*. In the early years Moses went to Columbia University Medical School, waiting tables to pay his way. Years later, after he was a respectable doctor, Moses ran into a man on the street who remembered him from the lean years. He spat at the man and walked away. After he married Rebecca, the Cretins lived on Rivington Street, though the family later denied that, too.

Miriam was the oldest of six, the caretaker for her siblings and the first to be raped by Moses, who probably thought of it as "seduction." The Cretin family was proud of their cultured heritage. Moses was remembered as a prominent Brooklyn doctor, a physician who built a hospital and fathered six talented and brilliant children. Uncle Johnny, who delivered me, also graduated from Columbia Medical. He married Maggie, a Presbyterian nurse from New England. Even though they were apologetic Jews, Anglo pretenders, the Cretins never let Maggie forget she wasn't Jewish. Aunt Maggie was an impulsive shopper who discarded some of the greatest rock & roll clothes I've ever owned. Black voile shirts, silver scarves, earrings, and fabulous negligees, artifacts from her travels—carved silver grooming tools, mirrors, jewelry boxes.

Uncle Al was the youngest Cretin. He owned a marina on Long Island, a fantastic operation on the North Shore. He had a family, a beautiful wife, a great life. But he drank too much and ran with the broads. Uncle Al died young when his heart gave out. Betty had a brother, a slightly built Sal Mineo knockoff. Browbeaten regularly by Willie, "Sal" was Miriam's favorite; Betty belonged to Willie. Around the age of ten she pulled the plug on the incest. She told her mother. Willie blamed Miriam for the activity; if only she hadn't been so frigid. It was her fault he had to go elsewhere for his pleasures. Betty figured he was just too cheap to pay for a hooker.

A few years later, when Betty began dating, Willie watched her like a hawk. He beat her with a strap when he suspected she fooled around with a handsome Polish boy. But she just laughed at him, taunting "Hit me, go ahead, beat me!" She always won. I cried when Betty told me what Willie had done to her. She was fifty-eight, and I was the first person she had ever told. Of course, Miriam and Sal Mineo knew, but they only got angry if she brought it up, like it never really happened, or it was just a play for sympathy. Grandma described her only daughter as "pathetic." Poor Betty was so needy, so eager to please.

Oddly, Betty never viewed herself as a victim. She told me she was never scared of Willie and she didn't *feel* violated. It happened in the daytime. He waited until Miriam went shopping for her costume jewelry, a frequent ritual. He took his daughter upstairs to his bed. He always used a condom and made sure not to puncture her hymen. Betty was no fool. Being Daddy's Girl had some advantages, and she milked it early on. It gave her an edge over the competition. Not only was she smarter than the icy Miriam, she was more of a woman, too. Fully matured at an early age, when Betty got tired of their little game, she called in her chips. Intuitively, she understood that incest wasn't about sex, it was about power. And that was *her* pleasure.

Willie never molested me because Betty Bradley never left us alone. In fact, when I was sexually molested, it was by a female. Like most child molesters, she was straight—she wasn't a lesbian. I was about eight, it was summertime. She was an older skank, about fifteen. I met Robin on the beach and we started talking. She, a more mature, wiser older woman, advised me that if I wanted to have big breasts someday, I should start right away with these special exercises that involved squeezing my nipples very hard.

Robin reached into my bathing suit top and pinched. After a while she suggested I go home, get into the backyard, lie naked in the mud, and let worms crawl on my body. That way the tits will grow faster. Then she asked if I would meet her and her boyfriend on the beach the next day at six A.M. He could really help me with the exercises. I said sure and went home for supper. I was genuinely intent on improving my bust, but I was scared of meeting Robin's boyfriend; he was from Brooklyn. When I told Betty Bradley, she called the police. Confused, I swore I wasn't sure who the girl was. It was dropped and my bra size stopped at a modest B cup.

With no father figure to guide me, Betty asked Sal Mineo to lecture me about not smoking. He took it very seriously. "So, you think smoking makes you tough? Don't smoke, Donna, be *reeeal* tough." He accentuated the word *reeeal* with a linguistic quirk that sabotaged the whole thing. This nuance of speech elevated the entire episode to absurdity. Betty and I repeated the *reeeal tough* until we were bent over with bellyaches. It became another toy, like Willie's tweezers. It became impossible for me to take any adult authority seriously because Betty just laughed at everyone—at Miriam's plastic flowers, the way Aunt Grace punctuated her commentaries with a haughty patrician sniff. At stiff *Herr Doktor* Uncle Johnny with his tennis regalia. Johnny wasn't his real name. Among some Jews, a "Johnny" is a goyboy wannabe who prefers no-Jews-allowed country clubs, who sips martinis and tries to affect a ruling class WASP ancestry.

The Cretins could be treacherous, like Cinderella's stepsisters. If you dared to shine, they had to snuff you. Envy has claws, a sharp tongue, and lethal intent. But Betty's humor and critical eye transformed Cretin family life into our private vaudeville. In another life she could have been Lily Tomlin or Roseanne—angry, smart, funny, and defiantly subversive. Sometimes the Cretin venom got to her, and she'd try to defend herself, writing out lengthy epistles explaining her actions. She'd pace around the house in her bathrobe, chain-smoking, drinking endless cups of coffee, obsessed, reading the unsent letters like they were transcripts from the Lenny Bruce obscenity trials. For most of her life, she stood before the Cretins like an Old Testament beggar, like something out of the Book of Judges. She honored them as wise and just, these fools and losers.

Now and then, she did see through them, and her wit transformed them into cartoon characters. Once you can laugh at someone, they've lost the power to destroy your psyche. Our private language worked like Kryptonite; it delegitimized their authority, disabling the Cretin death gaze. Betty Bradley's rituals of ridicule undermined them and immunized us.

Aunt Grace was the oracle. When she drank too many martinis, Cretin family values were revealed. "I was my father's mistress," she'd proudly proclaim, baiting her sisters' envy and shame. Dr. Cretin had studied the work of Robert Mesmer. Each seduction employed the art of hypnosis. He'd mesmerize each girl with a flickering candle, offering some brandy, inducing a hypnotic trance, chanting in the darkened room like he was the Aleister Crowley of Brooklyn. Then he'd move in for the kill.

Moses had pet names for all four daughters based on the sexual charms they displayed during their filial duties. There was Ethel the puma, Grace the tiger, Naomi the snake, and my grandma, the cow. When Betty was about five, Dr. Cretin locked her in his study. The aunts knew what was up and knocked on the door until the mission was aborted. They never discussed it. We only heard about it when Grace got drunk.

Grace Dalton had been a stage actress, on lithium since the 1930s after an alcohol-fueled breakdown during a production. Moses had forbidden her to marry her true love because he was a Christian. Incest was okay, but intermarriage was off limits. Instead, he bought her a piano and then arranged a brief marriage to a man with a fake leg. Grace spent the rest of her life drinking and playing piano. Aunt Ethel married Uncle Julius, who was supposed to advance her writing career. He was another relative Betty never left me alone with; he was always after her breasts. Uncle Julius collected reel-to-reel porn and organized little three-ways for himself and the puma, trolling Manhattan by taxi for willing hookers. Aunt Ethel always corrected my grammar and gave me kooky pocketbooks, my first taste of urban bohemia. Aunt Naomi was known as the bartering artist. She had a loft in SoHo and a dachshund named Doodles. Naomi painted morbidly dark abstracts and landscapes, bought mainly by the family. I later collected them.

When Naomi overdosed from sleeping pills, Doodles was found hovering around the body. The Cretins never discussed the event, but they did admit it was a suicide. I was told, "She was distraught, broke; she couldn't sell her work." Like this was the endgame result of any woman trying to be an artist, like Naomi was Sylvia Plath. Her suicide was read as a mythology, a boring bohemian cliché. No connection was made to family incest, alcoholism, drug addiction, and self-loathing.

Miriam the cow was considered the most beautiful of all the daughters. On her wedding day, Dr. Cretin lamented that his prize flower was going to this uncouth working man, Willie, the farm boy. In marriage, Miriam became a dulled bird trapped in a tacky metal cage. My grandmother spent her Brooklyn row house days serving her master and compulsively shopping for her costume jewelry. She surrounded herself with ceramic figurines and artificial flowers, as if anything sentient would suck whatever life remained inside. In the late 1970s, after Willie died, Miriam declared, "Marriage is disgusting!" And she lived happily ever after, alone. I got along with my grandmother when I was younger, but by the late 1960s, she banned me from visiting. It wasn't anything personal. Her only other grandchild, Sal Mineo's boy, wasn't welcome there, either. Our hippie clothes embarrassed her. You know, the neighbors.

So this was the classy side of the family: artists, actresses, drama critics, doctors, and lawyers. They looked down on everyone, other Jews, the Denmarks, Betty's husbands. The Cretins lived in New York City and frequented the theater, which they pronounced *theayta*. Always mannered, with clipped speech, faux British accents, and anglicized surnames, extending the right pinky as they lifted a wineglass. Highstrung, eccentric, always formally dressed and drinking gin, they treated their children as little adults, admonished to be seen and not heard, dismissed and discounted. We all know there are no Jewish alcoholics. Well, except on my mother's side.

Whenever someone died, the Cretin aunts flocked like ravenous crows to a squirrel carcass, frantically pecking away at the rotting remains. The Denmarks cried heartily at funerals and then they ate. All I remember of Cretin burials is the gathering of the spoils. Chinese lacquered boxes, carved ivory elephants, silk tapestries, Mexican jewelry, Austrian crystals, and Naomi's paintings. Betty Bradley was right on the job, pirating for prime booty. The others had no interest in these offbeat memorabilia; it was just junk to them. But we adored gathering the windfall, these preciosities of the clan. Betty Bradley taught me the art of the petty pilfer, pack rat hoarding. When I was younger, Betty collected clothes for charity, for rummage sales. We'd always skim the cream off the top: shirts, robes, dresses, pocketbooks, and costume jewelry.

For most of my adult life I purchased no toilet paper, pens, or pads. The big coup was to score a roll of toilet paper from a very fancy place. I'd get more points the higher up I went in society circles. If I went someplace nice, I was required to present a roll to the parents as a gesture of respect, in the name of family honor. When I spoke at a scholarly conference, did a TV spot, or met with a book editor, it was always lurking in the back of my mind, to grab some "T.P." I knew I had to present my parents with a roll, a souvenir to show that I had penetrated the upper echelons, exposed the elite. T.P. was evidence that for all their pretensions, the aristocracy sat on the crapper taking nasty dumps, just like the rest of us. Betty Bradley reciprocated by lifting every Kotex the airline lavatory provided. I never bought sanitary napkins. Always progressive, *The Village Voice* kept me in tampons for most of my reproductive years.

Growing up, everything was Hollywood. Drama, movie stars, intricate plots, cryptic dialogue rendered in shaded hues. In my early teenage years, Betty Bradley gave me permission to smoke and bestowed upon me all her custom-made showbiz fineries, including a rhinestone cigarette holder. Riding aimlessly through the Rockaways on the Green Bus Line, by fifteen I was sporting Mom's Lucite pocketbooks, beaded bags, rhinestone belts, cat's-eye sunglasses, and a fabulous green rabbit coat. Betty always took care of her things. I was a barbarian, more Holly Woodlawn than Hollywood.

How do we become what we are? From the Denmark gene pool I inherited flat feet, sugar addiction, green Asiatic eyes, and asthma. I got a fair complexion and a tall hairless body. I was sure I got the Cretin habit of extending my right pinky whenever I raised my glass until I saw Herbie do it in an old photograph, diamond ring and all. I also got his skills as a sharpshooter, a maniacal work ethic, and the Denmark nose. Miriam was so proud of my straight nose and light Aryan skin, she'd gush, "You're so beautiful, you don't look Jewish at all!"

The Cretins taught me the difference between Noritake and Limoges, Lalique, and Belleek, about opera, ballet, and the importance of cultural capital, of "taste" and "class." Matrilineally, I inherited an innate sense of superiority and entitlement, cupid's-bow lips, a widow's peak, and high-strung intensity. I got Willie's dimples, strong chin, and taste for metaphysics. My grandpa and Sal Mineo were engineers, who bestowed a flair for all things mechanical. Betty Bradley gave me the great spiritual gift of humor, a love of words, and she imprinted music in my soul.

I was in the ninth grade when Mr. Gaines passed away. Six months earlier, in the fall of 1964, the good Lord had delivered my weary soul to Far Rockaway High School. I was finally liberated from Belle Harbor's stale cocoon. I had graduated yeshiva and that was the end of mandatory prayer, *shul,* and those same stupid fifteen kids. Yes, there was life beyond Beth-El, Twennyninth, and Sixteenth, and I raced after it. My ninth grade at Far Rockaway High School was an extraordinary time. As boroughs kids we had no official school buses, so we relied on public transportation, the Green Bus Line. The ride covered the whole Rockaway Peninsula, the entire six miles from Breezy Point to Far Rockaway. It ran along Rockaway Beach Boulevard down past Rockaway Park through Hammels, Arverne, Edgemere, all the way to the Nassau County line. City transportation, the bus service ran at all hours, all the time, for just a quarter. Every stop along the way afforded new cultural possibilities; fresh air, new faces, fashions, foods, scenes, and situations. The daily ride to Far Rockaway delivered me, carried me far away from grief and sorrow to a land of infinite possibility.

The parochial schools ended in eighth grade, the junior highs in the ninth. The public school students entered high school in the tenth grade. So that first year, it was just a few motley kids from the Catholic schools and yeshivas, renegades all piling into the ninth grade. A small, residual category, left over after everyone else went to the private or parochial high schools. This experience of displacement and oddball ethnic blending made everyone slightly edgy, disoriented, and disheveled.

The great promise of public schooling is universal access. This is the centerpiece of participatory democracy. Ideally, the experience Americanizes the young, socializes us into a classless social body, bound together by shared values and common goals. In reality, Far Rockaway

High School's ninth grade was a killing floor for kids who had little experience of difference.

As a veteran of Belle Harbor's jihads, I came fully prepared. In gym class, on the bus, in the halls, making friends was easy. People said I wasn't a snob, even if I was from Belle Harbor, and that earned me points. The Neponsit lames went to their Brooklyn prep schools: Poly, Packer, Berkeley. Most of the kids I knew from St. Francis went to Catholic high schools: Stella Maris for the girls, Brooklyn Prep or Xavarian for the boys. I was glad to be rid of them all.

In the days before they built Beach Channel High School up in Rockaway Park, Far Rockaway High School warehoused all the teens in the region. Kids got bussed in from our entire peninsula, as well as the marshlands of Broad Channel, all the way out to Rosedale. The bogs of Broad Channel looked like rural Ireland, wooden houses on stilts built into the bay. For Rockaway kids, the best thing about Broad Channel were the bars where phony proof of age got you anything you wanted. Farther out east was Cross Bay Boulevard, legendary turf for drag races. The open road went clear through to Howard Beach. Once you got there, Pizza City was a major parking lot scene, gearheads galore.

Howard Beach kids didn't get zoned to our school, but Rosedale's did. Many of them were Italian, a rare breed where I came from. Catholic like the Irish, but dark like the Jews, Italians were big foodies, too—*mangia!* The girls were tough and sexy with the best hair, loyal allies in any gym class altercation. Rosedale was in the news in the 1950s and '60s, as black families migrated there in increasing numbers and locals got nasty. Many of the white families moved to the nearby Nassau suburbs. By the '80s and '90s, new immigrants arrived, almost half of them from the island of Jamaica, followed by Haitians and Guyanese. That's how it works in America. One man gathers what another man spills.

Although our high school was predominantly Jewish, among my new classmates were Irish, Italian, African, and Puerto Rican kids, too. In 1964–65, nobody was "Italian-American" or "Hispanic." You were Italian or Spanish. No blacks, no African Americans, just Negroes and colored kids. We barely coexisted, like unwilling nation-states under the American flag, still pledging our allegiance to the old country. This was the age of the melting pot, integration, long before white power and multiculturalism. We didn't get along then either, and in the ninth grade, many of us faced off for the first time. For me, it was fascinating. All these new faces and friendships offered a distraction, a daily escape. Unfortunately, just as I was settling in, my pleasure was arrested due to outside interference.

Toward the end of the ninth grade, shortly after Mr. Gaines died, the Cretins presented Betty Bradley with a plan for my future. After I had been seen sipping sodas with Irish boys at Bernstein's, the candy store on Forty-fifth, my uncle Johnny, the doctor who delivered me, convinced Mom to send me to Adelphi Academy, a private school in Brooklyn. It would give me structure, discipline, a fatherly influence. He and Aunt Maggie had been on Mom to send me away ever since Tommy. They warned the weeping widow that her only child was "acting like a little tramp," a notion that both confused and flattered me.

I pleaded for mercy, petitioning Betty Bradley, "Maybe I should quit school and get a job?" Opting for a proletarian solution was legitimate; Mr. Gaines's long illness and business debts left us with less than we'd expected. So I got a job as a packer at Waldbaum's supermarket. That lasted three days. Under pressure, Mom folded, and there I was, condemned to lockdown in Bay Ridge, Brooklyn.

But I got a break. That same year, Muggs Malone also got banished to Adelphi. Once noble Swamp Foxes, we were now certified as troubled youth, persons in need of supervision. Every day we got picked up and transported by limousine. We passed the time terrorizing the other kids until their mothers complained. Since Adelphi was in Bay Ridge, I tried to make it sound cool by telling everyone it was attended by the pampered children of top ranking mafiosi. In contrast to the sartorial fiesta offered at Far Rockaway High School, Adelphi Academy students were required to wear dreary preppy uniforms: navy blazers, white shirts, and pleated skirts. As a big girl, appropriating some funky style was my only way out of humiliation. If I tried to look normal I was doomed to failure.

But something else was at stake. In America it is essential to learn how to instantly stereotype, sort, and categorize others. In high school, once we have exhausted the critical categories of race, sex, class, gender preference, size, and disability, we learn to judge others by what they wear. How else can we inculcate the process of social stratification: the systematic practice of unequal distribution of status, wealth, and power? Are you cool or a geek? Clothes were the first clue. That first semester of tenth grade at Adelphi was a Grand Guignol where everyone, including me, looked like a spaz.

Everyone except for my geometry teacher. He looked like Frankenstein, tall with facial warts, and a hump in his back. When I didn't grasp his questions about sines and cosines, he screamed at me, called me an Amazon in front of the whole class. I cried. I wanted to die. Imagine: In those days, I actually took it as an insult.

Aside from Frankenstein, Adelphi wasn't that bad. The kids were friendly; even the principal was nice. But I longed for the profane world at the end of the Green Bus Line, for Far Rockaway. Desperate, I made my case to Betty Bradley. The Cretins' advice was typically misguided, laced with malice, couldn't she see it? Now I was suffering a second round of trauma and separation. Mr. Gaines died, now I was being punished, imprisoned in Brooklyn, away from all my friends.

Conveniently, around that time, Muggs and I got snagged for smoking in the limo. The other kids ratted us out and their parents freaked. I already had permission, but Betty finally saw the writing on the bathroom wall. Fall of 1965 I was back at Far Rock. This time, the Malone family sent Muggs to boarding school. That second semester of the tenth grade as I returned to public school, everything in my life was about change. The Cretins would forever be defeated. They would never mess with me again; I was getting a new dad.

II

After Mr. Gaines died, Betty Bradley began to disintegrate. She hated being alone and needed much more companionship than I could provide. So I urged her to go out, to start dating. I explained, "I'm getting older, I won't be home forever." First there was a swinging chiropractor, then a wealthy lawyer, then a dapper businessman, a widower with a daughter my age. He called her "Little Miss Femininity." That wasn't gonna work at all. Disgusted, Mom decided we'd take a trip to the Concord Hotel, where she hoped to meet a nice Jewish man.

For an entire first generation of American-born Yids, the Concord was the target zone for kosher matrimonial matches. The Borscht Belt offered an orgy of food, Jewish culture, comedy, and glitz. It was the prefeminist mid-1960s, when men were pigs and women were expected to smile and wait. Some hairy beef smiled at my mother, she was flattered, her heart started to open. Mr. Gaines had been sick for so long, she was vulnerable. Betty Bradley was doing laps when he dove into the water. Five minutes later, he was groping her in the swimming pool. My mother became hysterical, sobbing. But rage set in and Mom quickly rebounded. She shot him down hard: "I'd rather spend the night with my bath brush!" A few months later, D.O.M. came into our lives.

He always remembered the date because in 1956 Fidel Castro led a guerrilla force, the 26th of July Movement, in revolt against Batista. Ten years later, on a hot July afternoon, D.O.M. rang Betty's bell. Initially he just came to pay his respects. He knew Mr. Gaines, because every year he bought the Oldsmobile dealer's used car. Months earlier he had danced with Betty at the wedding of a mutual friend. Mr. Gaines teased her for dancing with the tall, handsome bachelor. D.O.M. knew Mr. Gaines had been sick for a long time and that this was her second loss. Gradually, from friendship and compassion, an attraction bloomed.

As Betty groomed for their first date, we watched him from her bedroom window. He sauntered up the walkway, cotton shirttails flopping in the breeze. We giggled. I went downstairs, invited him in, and offered him a drink. I almost killed D.O.M. with a lethal concoction similar in concept to Long Island iced tea; I poured every bottle on the bar into his glass. He politely declined and asked for a Coke. I liked D.O.M. right away. He was down to earth, tall, like Cary Grant, predating Elvis Costello with horn-rimmed glasses, a skinny tie, and a slim sport jacket. At forty-nine, he had never been married, no kids, no alimony, no child support. For my birthday, he bought me my first stereo. Best of all, D.O.M. owned a liquor store in Bed-Stuy. At fifteen, with a promising drinking career on my horizon, I fell into a jackpot.

In addition to Mr. Gaines, D.O.M. also knew Herbie, because his father, Benny, worked with Pop Denmark on the horse-drawn trolley. One was a conductor, the other a ticket taker. On a mystical night in the late 1940s Betty Bradley and my three dads were all hanging out in the same place, though not together. D.O.M. was with a date, and so was Mr. Gaines. Herbie came with Betty. All my parents at the Riviera, in Fort Lee, New Jersey, under the stars, seeing Tony Martin and Cyd Charisse.

D.O.M. became the glue that held my fractured bloodline together. He knew my two other dads from the Borscht Belt scene, from the Concord Hotel. Mr. Gaines's crew wore maroon-colored fez hats; they were sedate, rising business-class, serious folks. Herbie's boys were younger, louder; you always heard them coming. Weekends D.O.M. went up there, too, kicking back, checking out the bands, meeting ladies.

Betty and D.O.M. got married at West End Temple in 1966 with me as her maid of honor. In celebration of their honeymoon, my friends from Far Rockaway slept over. We rode the bus till all hours, drinking in the backseat like it was a private bar, puking out the window. With my parents cozy up in the Poconos, we slept on the beach, an all-night whiskey vigil. My parents weren't even mad, just a little worried. They were party people, heavy social drinkers. Sometimes, after a night of hanging out I'd come home and my parents would still be up, dancing to salsa, drinking Tanqueray and soda into the wee hours. D.O.M. was a drummer; he loved music. He'd be sitting in the den, smoking a pipe full of cherry-blend tobacco, tapping along on a snare pad. It had been a personal gift from drummer Billy Gladstone.

Growing up, D.O.M.'s family lived on Delancey Street, sharing a bathroom with four other Jewish families. My third father favored the trumpet, but the family couldn't afford lessons. It was the Depression and they were poor Jews, Austrian, or maybe it was part of Poland then; they kept no birth records. His father, Benny, came to America in 1905, at fifteen. His grandfather had been a career man in the Austrian

Army, a powerhouse who stood over six feet six. Since his last name was Kuhn, they always suspected Huns in the bloodline.

D.O.M.'s clan was tall with thick, straight hair. They were honest and hardworking. There were no secret messages; everything was straightforward with them. Benny was one of the founders of Local 1, the waiters' union, organizing guys he knew from off the boat. He worked with Governor Dewey weeding out union corruption—gangsters and their sweetheart contracts. At one point, the family had armed bodyguards outside the tenement door. They later migrated to East Harlem and then to the Bronx.

During Prohibition D.O.M. had a shoe-shine operation near the police precinct. One day a cop called him into the station, gave him a note and a small can, and told him to take it to the grocery store around the corner. D.O.M. came back with a full can, earning himself a penny. That was his second job, running beer for the police during Prohibition. The officers always watched his back so the big kids didn't snatch his earnings.

Another after-school job was target marker in the Armory on East 66th and Park in Manhattan. At fifty cents an hour, D.O.M. took home about six bucks a week. His soccer coach, a colonel in the 7th Regiment of the National Guard, got him the job. D.O.M. played soccer and baseball for DeWitt Clinton High in the Bronx and won a partial scholarship to Notre Dame. College was off limits, since the family couldn't cover the rest of the tuition. D.O.M.'s dream was to be a high school gym teacher. Instead, in 1934, he left high school a year early, doubling up on classes so he could graduate sooner and go to work full-time. He got a job as a waiter at the Stanley Hotel in Lakewood, New Jersey. D.O.M. had worked as a busboy in the Catskills since age thirteen, sending home all his earnings to the family. He watched the hotel bands carefully, and that's how he learned to play drums.

D.O.M.'s older brother attended City College. One night Uncle Irving took D.O.M. up to West 125th in Harlem where an old burlesque house was changing hands. The new Apollo Theatre was planning to book black entertainment. This was good news because back then black musicians were restricted. They couldn't play in white clubs, because nobody would hire them. On tour, black musicians were often forced to sleep and eat on the bus. They were banned from hotels and restaurants. Benny Goodman broke the color line when he put Teddy Wilson on piano and Lionel Hampton on vibes, forcing Goodman to give up contracts in the South.

By age seventeen, D.O.M. was hanging out at the Apollo whenever he could. The band played in the pit of the stage, so he could sit behind the drummer and study every move. Since most bands provided a drum kit, you didn't need any money to play. All D.O.M. had were drumsticks and a practice pad.

One day when D.O.M. heard his younger sister Rose tapping along with Martin Block's radio show *Make Believe Ballroom* he took two dollars out of his weekly allowance and located a drummer he knew from Harlem to give Rose lessons. Interviewed in Sally Placksin's *American Women in Jazz,* Aunt Rose claims she never could have done it without her brother. He was the one who thought she had talent and encouraged her. He would take her downtown or to Harlem to sit in. She was barely fifteen. "I could have never done that on my own, because this was the thirties and girls just didn't do things like that. He guided me and trained me like a prize-fighter. He saw that I listened to the proper bands and whatever he couldn't explain to me, he would take me to hear."

At the Savoy Ballroom in Harlem, she sat in with the hard-swing house band, the original Savoy Sultans. D.O.M. would hype the band-leaders into letting Aunt Rose sit in, saying how she had played with various greats. Once, at the Golden Gate, Rose got to play with Lucky Millinder in an eighteen-piece combo. The dance floor had two bandstands, Millinder performing on one, Harry James on the other. After she played, James's vocalist, Dick Haimes, came over to shake her hand. "That kid's gonna go places," he told D.O.M. Swing Street, as we know it today, was home to Nick's, Condon's, and Jimmy Ryan's, small clubs that hosted interracial jams up and down West 52nd Street. Downtown clubs like the Village Vanguard and Café Society hosted similar action. Rose was a regular on Swing Street, at Jimmy Ryan's, where she sat in with Zutty Singleton's six-piece combo. Singleton was Deep South, an old-time drummer out of the barns and rural gin mills. That's how Aunt Rose learned to play.

At fifteen, Rose entered the Gene Krupa contest at the 1939 World's Fair, drumming with the Krupa band. She came in second, after seventeen-year-old Al Stoller. A year later, Stoller was Tommy Dorsey's drummer. At sixteen, Aunt Rose sat in on drums with Jimmie Lunceford on Amateur Night at the Apollo Theatre. She started with a solo. Amateur Night had launched such greats as Sarah Vaughan and Ella Fitzgerald. At one point the sax player Willie Smith stood up and turned around in disbelief. Everyone was amazed. The girl had some beat. That night, she won.

Eventually, Rose needed more structured training, so D.O.M. tried to convince Billy Gladstone, the original drummer at Radio City Music Hall, to give her lessons. Gladstone never gave lessons to anybody, but he said he liked Rose's personality, so he did it for free. After Jimmy Dorsey heard the wholesome teenager, he said, "Miss, you're wonderful, I enjoyed your playing." Cliff Leeman was a drummer for Artie Shaw and Charlie Barnet, one of Rose's greatest inspirations. D.O.M. told Cliff about Rose and he arranged additional lessons for her at the Brill Building. On a signed photo, Rose wrote, "To Murray, may the bond between us always be as solid as Cliff's beat." Aunt Rose later became one of NBC's first female snare drummers, featured with Raymond Paige.

The first girl bands I knew about weren't the Runaways or even the Ronettes. The Big Band era had Babe Egan and Her Hollywood Redheads, Bobbie Grice's Fourteen Bricktops, and before them, Edna White's Trombone Quartet. Still, finding gigs was hard for female musicians unless they sang. Even with her talent and D.O.M.'s stage mothering, Rose had few options. Joining the huge, interracial Sweethearts of Rhythm was a possibility, but Rose was still very young and they were always on the road. Besides, interracial in those days meant segregated quarters for everyone, and that sucked for anyone.

After doing a few club dates and studio jobs, Rose hooked up with an all-female quintet known as Estelle and Her Brunettes. Represented by William Morris, they got some good bookings. But big bands usually had at least ten players, an army of jazz dance musicians. As a small combo, the Brunettes were better suited to TV, but it was too soon for that. Rose played with Slavin's crew till 1945. Around that time she fell in love with a professional bass fiddle player we called Lang because he was also named Irving, like Rose's oldest brother. A lifelong musician, Lang played every string instrument except the violin, and keyboards, too. On their honeymoon Mr. and Mrs. Lang traveled cross-country, since Lang was touring with Gene Krupa. He also played with Charlie Barnet and Lester Lannon. Like most musicians, Lang also needed a day job once they had kids. Motherhood eventually required Rose's full attention, and she left the business just after the war. She walked around the Bronx wheeling a baby carriage, wearing slacks, smoking cigarettes, years ahead of her time.

When D.O.M. enlisted in the army in 1941 at age twenty-four, he listed his occupation as "drummer," because he didn't want to say he was "just a busboy." He had never actually played with a band and couldn't read music, but he could fake it by ear. The army used music sheets; D.O.M. worked from memory. In uniform, whenever he was on pass in New York City, he'd slip into Nola Studios. Duke Ellington always closed his rehearsals to the public, but he made an exception for D.O.M.: "No, soldier, you stay." So D.O.M. hung out, saw Count Basie, got to know the bands. Once D.O.M. was drafted into the post band, he learned how to read sheets and marched with his 52nd Coast Artillery Band. He had grown up watching the parades with his mom in East Harlem. Now on Saint Patty's Day he was part of it. It was his first gig.

Stationed in Key West, assigned to coast artillery, cruising for German subs, the high-strung, heat-sensitive D.O.M. couldn't stand the humidity. So he volunteered for airborne and glider duty. He had never been on a plane before, but it was thrilling, being pulled by a C-47 tow plane, then cut loose and gliding through the air. He volunteered for extra jumps, just for kicks, even though gliders were estimated to have something like 60 percent crash rates. He missed D Day because he injured his knee in a practice jump.

D.O.M. went overseas in 1945, with the 13th Airborne Division

Band. They considered themselves soldiers first, musicians second. In Europe the band traveled to hospital and MASH tents. When the United States invaded Germany, the band drove around in the back of a two-ton truck. Seventy miles behind enemy lines, a combo of six guys—drums, trumpet, vocals, piano, guitar, and sax—in uniform riding down dirt roads, watching for landmines. They'd pull up, set up a makeshift stage or play off the back of the truck. Once the music started the GIs would begin crawling out of the woods. Within ten minutes two hundred guys came out. Using their rifles as pillows, they'd just lie back and watch. The band took requests—country for the cowboys, jump or jazz or swing for the city boys. Songs like "You're Nobody till Somebody Loves You" and Andrews Sisters' hits were big morale boosters. These are my father's gardens, guts and glory in a snare drum solo and an M1 Carbine.

One thing I learned from this father was to never let anyone put you down. Nobody is better than you, don't let them fool you. Everybody is equal. This was antithetical to everything the Cretins stood for. Even the most famous person—the Pope, the Queen—hits the toilet sometime. Social hierarchies are obliterated, humbled in the call of nature.

He could barely read music, but D.O.M. had an ear. At USO shows in France, he often played for hot acts—the Arnaut Brothers, even Milton Berle, Betty's old boss. D.O.M.'s theory: "The bigger the entertainer the less problems I had playing his act. There was this *putz* with a wife, a comedy act, the big shtick was she wore a mink stole, but when you looked twice, it was actually a dog." D.O.M. kept the beat for the *putz,* innovating where he had to. The *putz* didn't like that, so he berated him, screaming, "What? You can't even read?" D.O.M. looked at him hard and said, "You don't like it? Fire me." The lesson: Never waste time trying to impress lesser luminaries; always go right to the top, to the people who have nothing left to prove, they're always nicer. When he played for the amazing Bojangles (Bill Robinson), there were many intricate parts, D.O.M. was afraid he couldn't keep up. But Mr. Bojangles was so gracious, he told D.O.M., "Don't worry, son. Just follow my feet."

D.O.M. loved the army and wanted to reenlist, stay on as career, playing snare drums in the army band. But his father the socialist had just opened a liquor store in Brooklyn and his religious mother pleaded with him that they needed his labor. He returned home and stayed in uniform till he could afford to buy civilian clothes. Exhausted from the war, D.O.M. had a brief nervous breakdown, got out of the hospital, and went right into the store, where he remained overworked and underpaid for many years. Marx's notion of a fair exchange apparently did not apply to family members. His mother manipulated him with Jewish guilt, and his socialist father exploited him.

By the early 1950s an Hispanic migration filled the city with the sound of salsa. D.O.M. was living in the Bronx with Aunt Rose and her family. Hanging out on the corner of Davidson Avenue, he befriended a young policeman, an Officer Garcia. The two started hanging out at the original Palladium, on West 51st and Broadway. D.O.M. loved the Latin jazz-fusion sound and met a talented kid named Tito Rodriguez, a real *salsero* who also lived in the Bronx. Sometimes D.O.M. drove the young bandleader home after a show. They stayed friends for many years. He became a regular on the scene, dating pretty Puerto Rican ladies, dancing, watching Tito Puente and Machito.

The family liquor store was in the Bedford-Stuyvesant section of Brooklyn. Because he worked late, most of D.O.M.'s friends were cops, and most of them were black, members of the Guardian Association. On his one night off, he frequented the Guardian dances, enjoying the slow fox-trots and lindy hops. D.O.M. once heard Martin Luther King Jr. speak at a Guardian dance. Through Officer Garcia he also became involved in the Hispanic Society of the police department. He traveled to dances at hotels and catering halls in Queens, the Bronx, and Manhattan. After he married my mother, they would make this scene together. D.O.M. wasn't much of a dancer, but he couldn't get Betty Bradley off the dance floor. The music brought her back to life. Since D.O.M. worked a late shift, they both now lived on musician time. I don't remember seeing either of them much before noon, except at Denmark funerals.

Getting used to a new dad was a crash course in human behavior. Who knows who, asks Hegel, the master or the slave? The child of a reconstituted family must learn the new regime slowly, by watching carefully. Nobody sits you down and explains how your home, your life, your social class, your entire identity will be transformed. You just wing it, like a glider pilot. D.O.M. was a character, a quirk, an Aquarian. He wouldn't kill bugs, he didn't buy leather. He described his ideal woman as an "asshole buddy," like an army pal, a best friend except you can have sex, too. He adored Betty—unlike Herbie, he didn't view her as a possession. He understood her as a musician and, intuitively, as an abused, exploited child.

Unlike Mr. Gaines, D.O.M. had something in common with Betty Bradley. They lived for music and they had fun. In a matter of two years, in the transition from Mr. Gaines to D.O.M., we traveled from the Russian Tea Room to basement bingo and bowling. Drinking bumped eating as the family hobby, and everyone gradually deflated. The stuffy Forty-six Club was replaced by the 79th Precinct and a rainbow coalition of new friends. Most of all, the music changed. The marching bands were gone, giving way to lively salsa, Krupa, Buddy Rich, Stan Getz, and Harry James's wailing trumpet. The Big Bands were back in town, in Belle Harbor, on heavy rotation.

When she married D.O.M., Betty Bradley told a friend, "Donna finally has a father. I know if anything ever happens to me, she'll be safe." And I was. D.O.M. paid a visit to Herbie's grave and promised to raise me right. He was unlike anyone I'd ever known—a tough Jew, streetwise with a deep Bronx dialect. At six feet two, he walked with an unconscious swagger, so handsome all the fancy Belle Harbor ladies openly flirted with him. Sometimes their wanker husbands goaded him about his clothing. One kept at it till D.O.M. threatened to throw him up against a wall, then they all shut up. Today *everyone* has a stepfather, all manner of multiple parental units. Back then, it was cutting edge.

Now, in our house, once a gathering place for stuffy cigar-toting Brooklyn businessmen, vigilante justice prevailed. Summer weekends we kept our cars in the driveway, as parking was restricted on Belle Harbor streets. Periodically a hapless Brooklyn day-tripper would park and get a hefty fine. One day, after the police had ticketed, D.O.M. looked out his bedroom window and saw a guy park and then take a freshly minted ticket off another car and put it on his own windshield so police would think they already got him. D.O.M. realized the first guy would never know he got the ticket and would end up a scofflaw. This wasn't right, so D.O.M. decided to even the score. The decorated U.S. Army marksman took out his BB gun, an old Daisy, and blasted the bad guy's windshield, smashing it to pieces with one shot.

D.O.M. didn't take any shit. He always carried a tire iron and flask of booze under the seat of his car. He wasn't a bully, but if some pimply-faced Magician crossed his path, he'd have wiped the pavement with him. Soon various weapons appeared around the house—rifles, army issue, and knives. D.O.M. took Betty down to the basement of his store on Albany Avenue and taught her how to shoot an M1 Carbine. He was very serious about home safety. Having guns around the house was now as natural as car keys were during the reign of Mr. Gaines.

At their wedding, half the guests were police; Irish officers from our local Rockaway's 100th Precinct and D.O.M.'s African, Italian, and Latino buddies from the 79th. My friends and I got big teenage kicks drinking screwdrivers in front of the cops. That was life with my new dad.

After D.O.M. moved in we only celebrated the patriotic holidays— the Fourth of July, Veterans Day, Memorial Day, even D Day. My parents had switched from the Conservative Beth-El to the West End Temple in Neponsit. After Mr. Gaines died, my mother needed help. The Conservative Rabbi Gordis blew Betty off; he was a busy man with no time for widows and orphans.

Mr. Gaines believed in the G-d of Abraham, Isaac, and Jacob. My new dad said his faith in the almighty G-d of Israel went up in smoke in Auschwitz. His family had been poor, kicked around the *shtetls* of Europe. "A Jew should kiss American soil," D.O.M. explained, but we should also be armed, able to stand up for ourselves. "God?" he'd rant, "God is a bullet in the barrel of a loaded gun." Jewish history had taught him that prayer only led a Jew straight to the gas chamber.

D.O.M. embraced Jewish values—the Ten Commandments, education, family life. But he hated liberals, especially Hollywood types like Jane Fonda. He banned *The Village Voice* from the house because he was convinced the Jewish-owned paper was anti-Israel, even anti-Jewish. A great political triumph came years later when I published an article in the *Voice* about the Lubavitchers, including a photo of the Rebbe himself. I got a ton of fan mail from Crown Heights that week: "Such a *mitzvah!*"

Although he opposed the Vietnam War, D.O.M. supported the troops. We were the only family on the block to display the American flag during those years, even though D.O.M. opposed every action after World War II as "class war" and condemned all military action from Korea right on down to the Gulf War. D.O.M. was a soldier's soldier. A right-wing prole bohemian with rotted roots in socialist labor. He was cool, army macho, airborne like Jimi Hendrix. I never actually called him "Dad" or "Pop" because that was the kiss of death. But I never called D.O.M. my *step*father either. I still don't.

For his birthdays I generated homespun comic books, pictorial essays of the Cretins, including the family crest, an asshole with wings suspended in midair. I drew caricatures of all the tony Belle Harbor ladies who hit on D.O.M. and all Betty's former suitors. After a neighbor called me a "piss fart," D.O.M. adopted it as my nickname—but shortened to "P.F." because, unlike Betty, D.O.M. didn't curse.

D.O.M. was also a food narc. Betty and I had a long history. She was my first junko partner. We'd be strolling along at the grocery store, I'd spot the M&M's, she'd give me the look, and we were on it. Addiction is a private matter, a secret ritual to be hidden from the world. We always did it on the fly. Mr. Gaines was a sugar addict, too, but D.O.M. could take it or leave it, a notion that still baffles me. Like the husband of an alcoholic trying to prevent her drinking, D.O.M. never brought candy into the house. So when a dinner guest brought a gift box of chocolates, D.O.M. hid them in the linen closet upstairs. When he came home from work the next night, he heard scrambling at the top of the stairs. He caught his wife jamming a fistful of candies into her mouth, face covered in chocolate. On all fours, my mother and Judas Iscariot fought each other over the spoils. The closet floor was covered with empty wrappers and half-eaten candies. The dachshund had to be forcibly removed. I will never forgive my mother for not cutting me in.

Yes, I had to make some adjustments. It was okay to curse in front of Mom, but never D.O.M. Drinking was okay, but not eating candy. On top of this, he had a list of parental advisories he called "racks." These safety measures were meant to protect me by racking my brain. Racking me to call if I was gonna be late, racking me to point the blade of a knife downward after I washed it, to shut closet doors, and every imaginable rack related to safe driving, firearms assembly, and the wearing of gloves in winter. Having met whatever challenges the day brought, D.O.M. would proclaim victory, saying, "Everything is under control."

At home I was enjoying life in an upbeat paramilitary zone of salsa, swing, and cocktails. But there were rules. Once, when my parents caught me alone in my room, snapping my fingers to "Light My Fire," they chastised me, "Donna, please, don't do that. It's real cornball." Having hip parents was not easy. They differentiated between musicians and squares. As sociologist Howard Becker showed in "The Culture of a Deviant Group: The 'Jazz' Musicians," my parents had their own codes. As Becker explains in his 1963 essay, such people were formally within the law, but their culture and way of life were sufficiently bizarre for them to be labeled as outsiders by more conventional members of the community. Still, everybody loved my parents. They were very good people, fun, definitely kooks. And even *they* considered me a flake.

On aesthetic grounds, my parents hated the Rolling Stones, especially Mick Jagger. The bad-boy sex and drug imagery didn't bother them, though. It was his stage histrionics, the off-key singing, and garbled lyrics that riled them. "What the hell is he saying?" they'd scream. Then they couldn't figure out how to dance to Hendrix or Cream. They much preferred Sly and the Family Stone, Stevie Wonder, anything with a beat. D.O.M. decreed, "If you can't dance to it, it isn't music." But I danced to everything.

Betty Bradley always said, "G-d never shuts a door that He doesn't open a window." Although she had lost two husbands, in D.O.M. Betty had found her true soul mate, but she probably never knew it. She stubbornly adhered to an orthodox Herbiology, like Jews who vowed in daily prayer, *If ever I should forget thee, O Jerusalem. . . .* For her, Herbie was Zion, everything else was the Diaspora. Betty's parenting style was an incongruent mix of devouring need and free-spirited permissiveness. I was at once enslaved by Jewish guilt yet oblivious to any notion of adult authority. Fiercely possessive and overindulgent, neglecting and spoiling me at the same time, Betty was a pal, more like a sister than a mother. She was a sporty girl, not a fey mommy. Butch but sultry. When I was younger, she looked like Jane Russell, when I was older she looked more like Roy Orbison, smoking, in dark shades, with a cocktail in her hand, telling it like it is.

Betty Bradley and I would giggle over my grandma's fried eggs (saggy tits), her starstruck copies of *Photoplay,* and how Miriam clutched her purse whenever company came over, fearing theft. We discussed the relative penis sizes of my three dads and creative ways to give head. It never occurred to me that any of this was "inappropriate" or even a little nuts. I knew we weren't like other people. Some years after she died, D.O.M. admitted to me that my mother wasn't all there. "She was a nut—a lovable nut," he said. Betty Bradley fought back, but life slammed her harder.

In my neighborhood, Betty and D.O.M. were considered the cool parents, so the house was a hangout, a safe haven for all my fucked-up friends. I had a red lightbulb in my bedroom window; incense was always burning, D.O.M. had his loaded rifles up against the paneled den wall, lined up next to the BarcaLounger. From his throne he'd pontificate on world events. In D.O.M. I finally had a functional parent, a real family, and a shot at a normal life. Well, sort of.

D.O.M. is the only name I've ever called him, after the Fugs song "Dirty Old Man." As a teenager, I liked to wear black raccoon eye makeup, gobs of frosted lipstick, tight miniskirts, and white go-go boots. Throwing a quarter at me, he often teased, "Here, that's all I'd pay for a hooker." This wasn't a perverted Cretin move. My dirty old man was protective; he didn't want me to be vulnerable. He also didn't want to push the dad thing too hard. But he was in full parental mode, looking out for his daughter.

Adapt, migrate, or die. Maybe it's easier to adjust to a completely new parent when the original is dead as opposed to remarried with a new wife and kids. My bachelor father always tried to do the right thing. Without him, I might have made some irreversible turns. First, he instituted a family dinner hour, made me go to school, taught me how to drive, how to shoot, and later, he bailed me out of jail. D.O.M. understood that as a fat girl, I would systematically get less. At one point he sent me to Weight Watchers on a bribe: five dollars for each pound I lost. He alternated that with screaming. Today I am a Lifetime Member.

In contrast to the silently passive Mr. Gaines, D.O.M. was explosive, a little heavy-handed. I wasn't used to any paternal discipline. Sometimes the neighbors heard it and they'd take me aside. "Donna, he shouldn't talk to you that way. It isn't right." Betty said D.O.M. was just stressed out. He carried a gun to work every day, right there on the seat of his Oldsmobile, a loaded M1 Carbine, army issue. Working around Mayor Lindsay's gun control measures, he chopped the rifle, replacing the stock with a pistol grip. Many years later, waiting impatiently for my own pistol permit, I would similarly mutilate my Ruger 10/22.

On the streets of Brooklyn, community people of color were calling the cops pigs. Lindsay had curtailed the police presence in Bed-Stuy, hoping to neutralize the conflict. This left shopkeepers and neighborhood families without much protection, regardless of race. The liquor store got robbed six times in one month, clerks were getting cut, owners shot, black and white alike. D.O.M. set up cardboard boxes with peepholes, he crouched behind the boxes with the rifle, right up near the register. Finally, in 1969 he sold the socialist family's capitalist enterprise at a substantial loss. On top of all that, Betty said my new father was under pressure from the Cretins. Miriam and Willie refused to meet D.O.M.'s parents because the Cretins were fourth-generation American and the new in-laws were "mockeys"—immigrants, lower-class Jews. Miriam was exasperated—"Betty, I'm tired from all your

marriages"—and declined her invitation for pot roast dinner, the deli-
cacy my mother cooked for special company. D.O.M. flew glider air-
craft over the Rhine during the war bringing in medical supplies, but
Cretin logic flew right over his head. He translated Yiddish in the displaced persons' camps of Europe but couldn't decipher his in-laws.

Before he married my mother and moved to Belle Harbor, D.O.M.
lived in a basement apartment in Brooklyn. He had recently bought a
fancy king-size mattress, so he offered it to Betty for my teenage bedroom. Miriam heard this and flipped. Since he worked in Bed-Stuy, an
African-American neighborhood, my grandparents were certain that a
parade of black hookers had shared his bed, making it unsuitable for
their virgin grandchild. Miriam regularly browbeat Betty for her choice
of a working-class husband. She taunted her daughter as her own
mother had censured her. How dare he move into Mr. Gaines's house,
marry his widow, and raise his child? Wasn't buying his used cars
enough?

The Cretins looked down on my D.O.M. for being working class.
Matrilineal descent on the Cretin side, from society girl Rebecca on, involved three generations of daughters who systematically married
downward. From Belle Reve to bowling with Stanley Kowalski. Moses
Cretin was considered too crude for Rebecca. After he married her, he
looked down on Willie. In turn, Willie disapproved of Herbie, Artie,
and D.O.M. As for me, I never brought anyone home.

Although having three fathers was painful and confusing, somehow
shaming, it ultimately did prove to be invaluable, illuminating. Each of
my three dads represented different values, tastes, and habits. Mom, of
course, was strictly showbiz. The three distinct patriarchal regimes inculcated different ideologies, often imposing contradictory norms and
rules.

Once when I caught myself absentmindedly filing my nails, I panicked. I was sure D.O.M. was going to blow his top. It turned out it was
Mr. Gaines who couldn't stand the grating sound. D.O.M. hated hair
in the sink, so I was safe. D.O.M. had other idiosyncrasies, like shaving
his armpits to prevent perspiration odor. He would freak out if you left
the sponge in the sink. The sink was a place of holy purification. We

lived a block from the ocean and the priss never went to the beach because he hated the sand. I've always depended upon the kindness of strangers, and my family sure was strange.

Sometimes the Cretins hosted holiday soirees, family jams. On a good night Mom sang while a rotating pool of aunts and uncles played piano and mixed drinks. With D.O.M. on drums, it was a full-blown jazz-dance jubilee. Family, friends, amateur and pro alike, joined in—a guy who played sax with *The Ed Sullivan Show,* another cat on trumpet, one of NBC's finest studio musicians. Sometimes Betty Bradley would sneak off with the pros to smoke some "tea"—she called it "lighting up." She'd pull me aside, worried that her eyes were bloodshot, would D.O.M. find out? Everyone was happy, drinking, enjoying the music. Family life was *smoking.*

You couldn't stop the Cretins from hopping. Watching them, sometimes I got restless. I wanted to do something, too. I was sitting on the couch with my aunt Maggie. She noticed me fidgeting, turned to me, and smiled. "Hey, *someone's* gotta watch them." And that's what I've spent my life doing. In the beginning I was the lead singer's daughter. In time I would become a lead singer's girlfriend, his loyal companion, muse, and junko partner. Memorizing every note, every lyric, never missing a beat. I'd immerse myself in bands, as a scribe, fangirl, photographer, and guest-list, makeup, and hair coordinator. I'd forage thrift stores and boutiques for funky-but-chic rock & roll clothes. Local or world class, I lived for my bands. I was always there, at the front of the stage, sometimes dancing, always watching.

Grandpa Benny working the train to Far Rockaway, circa 1920.

–5–

FREEDOM RIDER

The appearance of a brand-new father meant at least six months' worth of forgeries, absence notes, and late passes—my ticket to ride. But everything else was changing, too. In 1966, the year Betty Bradley married D.O.M., civil rights emerged as the dominant social issue. America's disenfranchised were storming the gates, pouring in from the margins, demanding visibility and voice. And soon I, too, would be emancipated.

At any other time in history I would have been doomed. Thanks to drug culture and flower power, misfits like me had other choices. People would respect me for my street smarts, for my accumulated knowledge of toxicology and pharmacology. *Sock it to me.* Now everyone was a freak. The days of prissy girls, elite preps, and jocks would soon fade away like the smell of Mrs. Robinson's hair spray. No more bras, no shame for fat girls without Saturday night dates. The population was splitting into two camps, and that would be the order of things. Now there were just two cliques to choose from: heads or straights, freaks or lames. At Far Rockaway High School, even cheerleaders and football players were on my team.

The baby boom was ascending loud, hard, and fast. Public high school felt like the Tilt-a-Whirl at Rockaway's Playland, spinning, pinning me against my seat till I was giddy and slightly queasy. My sabbatical leave at Adelphi Academy had occurred during the critical first semester of tenth grade. In my absence, the unwashed hordes had flushed into Far Rockaway High School. So proudly they hailed from the public junior high schools. All the kids Mr. and Mrs. Gaines sent me to yeshiva to avoid were now my classmates and friends. Once I caught the bus heading east to Far Rockaway, it didn't matter where I was going. I was free, lost in the crowd, just another chunk of cabbage in a magnificent slaw of mass culture. Youth was exploding. The girdle was *off*.

Every day I shambled a little farther east until I'd hit all the candy stores and parking lots from Neponsit to Far Rockaway, drinking Colt 45, dancing to the Four Tops, doing routines to the Box Tops, sniffing Carbona by the sea. The Rockaway peninsula offered restless teens a garden of sociological delights. A key ingredient was the freedom train we called the Lowlife.

As the Lowlife lumbered onward, neighborhoods changed like the waves off the coast of Breezy Point. Every few blocks offered a completely different scenario. It seemed that as street numbers decreased, wealth diminished. Most likely, if you lived on Beach 149th, you were rich. If you lived on Beach 49th, you were not. A simple Green Bus Line ride through the Rockaways transported you up or down the economic ladder, depending upon whether you traveled east or west. With each stop along the way, a universe of new cultural experience awaited. At the end of the line you entered Far Rockaway, and that was a whole other story.

Most kids who are curious about other cultures would have just read books, novels, *National Geographic*, but I hated to read. Probably because I found it necessary to ponder each sentence, dissect every single word, like it was the Talmud. When I graduated high school in 1968, I was proud of having read only one book—*Lord of the Flies*.

My grades sucked, but mandatory schooling had nothing to do with my education. I craved the blooming, buzzing world. I needed constant motion, all the new people, places, and things that captured my imagination. There was also something illuminating in the sensation of grinding onward, of an engine gearing up, then slowing down. The rhythm of the road corresponded to each new scene, punctuating its beginning and end. If you shut your eyes too long, you missed it.

On the Lowlife I became captain of my fate, director of research with complete creative control and unlimited funds. For a quarter a pop, I had my own reality show. I learned much more about life travelling the Lowlife than I did in three years of high school. In fact, I don't remember anything about the teachers, books, classrooms, or exams at Far Rockaway High School, or the football games, school newspapers, student government, or plays. But riding that bus every day, I did learn this: The journey is more important than the destination.

Swytie dubbed it the Lowlife in the years before her father bought her the red Stingray. "James" was a wealthy industrialist married to a drunk who periodically subjected Swytie to strip searches and midnight beatings. James always disappeared into his room. We saw him only when Swytie needed a ride. James the Chauffeur would drive us anywhere, sparing Swytie the indignity of the Lowlife bus line. When her mother wasn't drinking, she made fabulous club sandwiches: Canadian bacon, lettuce, tomato, and fresh turkey. Swytie's mom mixed delicious egg creams with real seltzer and U-Bet chocolate syrup and served this to us on silver trays.

Betty Bradley extended her heart and our home to Swytie, as she did to all my friends. Once, in a blackout, Swytie's mother called the house at three A.M. accusing us of stealing her silverware, then fencing it to gangs in Far Rockaway. D.O.M. picked up, and she never bothered me again. But nobody could protect Swytie, not the neighbors, the relatives, or even the state. An only child isolated in a sick, wealthy family, who would dare to intrude?

FAR ROCKAWAY HIGH SCHOOL
DAVID GORDON, PRINCIPAL
BAY 25th STREET   FAR ROCKAWAY, N.Y. 11691

8th TERM FINAL REPORT

Donna Gaines
STUDENT'S NAME

217 Bch. 139 Street, NY.   8-3
COMPLETE ADDRESS   SECTION

G. W. BELL   June 196 8
SECTION TEACHER'S SIGNATURE   TERM ENDING

SUBJECT	GRADE	PDS. PER WK.	MARKS	
			FINAL	REGENTS
ENGLISH 8	8	5	75	73
AMER. HIST. 2	2	5	65	81
Family Living 2	2	5	65	
Hebrew 6	6	5	75	87
Trigonometry 1	1	5	55	
HEALTH ED. 807G		5	80	

Mr. D. Gordon   Mr. M. Cohen
PRINCIPAL   ADVISER

DAYS ABSENT (CUMULATIVE)	15	NEW SECTION	
TIMES LATE (CUMULATIVE)	3	ROOM	

— FLASH FORM

Report card

I met Swytie when she was three or four, on vacation at the Concord Hotel. I was a year older. They had a children's dining room and a counselor who organized activities, but I refused. I just wanted to sit in the lobby outside the main dining room and watch the adults. Betty Bradley said if I were well behaved and promised not to move so she could keep an eye on me, we had a deal. So I sat quietly and watched.

Swytie appeared, a sweet, shy, curly blond ball of smiles. The only other child in the adult dining room, she sat with her parents quietly, too scared to leave. The next day we met on the ice skating rink where

I couldn't stand up and she'd glide like an angel. I hated ice skating. I was clumsy, I kept falling, I cried, I wanted to die. But being with Swytie changed that. She made it fun, silly. I didn't see her again until she was thirteen, dating Piggy, a typical Belle Harbor frat-boy type who got fresh. When she declined, the Pig made up stories Swytie could never shake.

Swytie skipped a few grades and was out of high school by sixteen. But school wasn't really her thing; she loved clothes. If she liked a pair of shoes, she got them in every color, with shirts and bags and lipsticks to match. Our favorite activity together was shoplifting from the finest stores in Cedarhurst, one of the Five Towns that made up the JAP Empire to the east. Swytie would score solid gold earrings, never anything under thirty dollars. She'd pocket them, and when we got outside, she'd hand them to me and just smile. People always thought Swytie was high, because she was spaced out, dazed, her eyes rolling in her head, snapping her fingers, and giggling like she'd had a few too many. But she didn't drink. By the time we were adults Swytie went out to lunch and didn't come back.

People always think the town *they* grew up in is the most fucked-up place, the reason they're so damaged, why all their friends died young. When I think about Swytie that voice intrudes, "Don't go there." Time to flip the dial, turn up the volume. Was it nature or nurture? What does us in worse—a lousy home life, a crappy gene pool, or growing up in a bad neighborhood? Swytie was the first to fall, and I loved her the most. She stuck up for me when my mother's friend insulted my clothing. She made fun of anyone who bothered me. And I wonder, what did I give her in return?

When we are young we form fierce attachments, blood fellowships. We band together with people who understand and accept us for who we are. Some friendships make you stronger. They help you survive your fucked-up life until you are old enough to escape and find the person you're meant to be. Other liaisons are more like suicide pacts, tacit agreements between suffering people. So you drink together, you drug, you're numb, moving hard and fast, like it's all good. But it doesn't matter anyway, you're going to die young. Maybe you're already dead. So you cover each other, you take a pledge. You look the other way and then you die.

Swytie never blamed anybody. Rage kept me going. But Swytie couldn't hold a grudge. She never blamed anyone but herself. She never made it. Growing up there were always messed-up kids so damaged and diminished they never got a chance. Kids who spent their days and nights eating, drinking, fucking, and shooting anything they can find, anything to take them out of it. In my life, friends would come and go, in and out of view like seasonal home decorations, hollow artifacts. People rose up just to get shot down. Day by day, vibrant lives disappeared, places got destroyed, demolished, transformed, resurrected. People would drop into my system like a shot of sodium Pentothol— hard, fast, and short-acting. My deepest connections, fathers, family, friends, *here today, gone tomorrow.* So I had a choice: Live with ghosts or move forward. In each new scene, each chapter of my journey, I'd experience intense human contact and then *abort fin.* So please, don't get too attached to anyone I tell you about. I can't promise they'll stick around. Death was for certain, life was ever changing; it went from bad to worse. That was the long view from the Lowlife.

II

Three bridges connected the outside world to our "Everyman's paradise" by the sea. The Marine Parkway Bridge at Beach 169th (later renamed in memory of Gil Hodges) hooked the Rockaways westward to Brooklyn, to the high holy hitterlands of Flatbush. Near the police station at Beach 92nd Street, the Crossbay, now the Veteran's Memorial, was our gateway to Broad Channel and Howard Beach, and eventually the Belt and Southern State parkways. In Far Rockaway, the Atlantic Beach linked Queens Democrats to South Shore Nassau County. Out to Long Island, the land of the Great Gatsby, with surf havens stretching from Long Beach all the way out to Montauk.

The Rockaway peninsula was bounded by water on three sides, with the Atlantic Ocean to the south and Jamaica Bay to the north. Rock-away sat at the bottom of Queens, a magical surf city that ran about six miles long, not more than a mile wide, it was easy navigating even on foot. Henry Hudson set eyes on my perfect world in 1609 when he attempted to enter Jamaica Bay, thinking it was the northernmost great river in the area, the one that would lead him to the Orient. Some historians claim that a small tribe of Canarsie Indians who inhabited the area derived the name from "neck of the land," so as to differentiate their village from the other Indian villages, which were all Mohawk. Rockaway was known as Reckowacky, which translated to "the place of our own people." Elsewhere, Reckowacky has been translated to mean "lonely place" for its relentless isolation or "place of waters bright" for its stunning ocean.

Riding east every day, I became obsessed with the terrain. Studying from afar, I learned to differentiate the neighborhoods, cultivated an eye for scene markers. Sometimes, I'd get off the bus and just walk around, suck down a soda, and feel things out. Voices of past lives and worlds gone by revealed themselves in the deep structure of everyday objects. A metal fence, a garbage pail, a flower pot on someone's stoop. Seeing them day after day, these objects became subjects, friends, familiar fixtures, comforting, soothing. Like the trash can outside a candy store. Early in the day it was full of greasy food wrappings, dabs of butter, and crusted bread, candy wrappers, innocent things. The optimism of a new morning, another dollar, another day. By evening, the metal rim overflowed with empty wine bottles, shattered glass, cardboard, broken things. Someone was passed out nearby, the secret history of the candy store was right there in the trash can, mine to behold.

During the Swamp Fox era, Sixteenth had been a citadel of petty crime and sugar foraging. My first stop on the journey east, now it offered more sophisticated forms of intoxication and arousal. Once elegant and proud, by the early 1960s, the great hotels of Sixteenth, like Curley's, had deteriorated into flophouses. Many of Rockaway Park's finest boarding houses eventually became welfare hotels. In time they'd be transformed into junkie-hooker holes. Social workers in the alcoholism ward at Creedmore liked to joke that this was the main intake unit of Queens. Roger's Irish House, Fitzgeralds, Boggianos, Murphy's, and Connolly's. The percentage of alcoholics entering the hospital from our fair domain was notoriously high. Even now, mention you're from Rockaway at an AA meeting and they know right away—you never had a prayer. So many bars, so little time.

Christian charity made it easy enough for any young alcoholic to scam proof. Through my ties to Twennyninth, I secured a phony Baptism certificate, but I never drank in Rockaway bars. Like most kids, when I was underage, I drank on the corner, under the boardwalk or at house parties. Irish kids had a cultural tradition that included pubs, but Jewish kids had to rely upon their parent's liquor cabinets: J&B, Smirnoff, Bacardi, Tanqueray, Dewars. D.O.M. kept ours well stocked.

By the time I was of legal age to drink, it was 1969 and everyone was becoming more of a druggie. Between Boone's Farm and Southern Comfort I never gave up drinking entirely, even when booze was shunned by the counterculture, viewed as the diesel fuel of *plastic people,* hypocrites who condoned one poison but outlawed another. Alcohol was associated with cultural ignorance, with low-class hitters or uptight straights. With bourgeois adults like Anne Bancroft's Mrs. Robinson practicing adultery, perpetrating hypocrisy, sipping martinis. Adults claimed marijuana led to the harder stuff, but we knew differently. I didn't commit to a full liquid diet until I was around twenty-three, when tough Rockefeller drug laws convinced me alcohol offered an easier, softer way. Actually, I didn't hang out in bars until later in life, and then I called them rock & roll clubs.

Once smack trickled into the neighborhood, I saw my childhood companions hustling quarters on Sixteenth, bringing smelly old men into the seedy hotels for a bag of dope. Swytie had a friend named Bonnie, whose father died when she was young, and her older brother was a tough guy, a gearhead. We blew our first joints together, getting silly in the back of somebody's car. Bonnie was beautiful, petite, with curly red hair. She got into the shit before any of us. They said her boyfriend

Josh hit her up, then turned her out. His mother had been my piano teacher.

By the time Bonnie was sixteen she was deep into the life, a must to avoid. Bonnie was the first heroin addict I ever knew, a Jewish junkie, and female. By twenty-five she looked forty-five, battered, hardened, scarred, with a broken nose and dead eyes. There were always rumors; Bonnie went to jail, she had a kid, then we heard she died. When the Belle Harbor boys started having their bachelor parties, they hired Bonnie to give blow jobs in the men's room, even though they all knew her from P.S. 114. She didn't care anymore.

Years later I wondered why our teenage drug and alcohol rates had been so high, even by '60s standards. On a visit back to Rockaway I asked my mother's rabbi why we didn't have a teen center, someplace for kids to hang out besides the streets. He said adults worried about fights, drinking, and there was liability to consider. They feared attracting "the wrong element" (people of color). So I asked him what should the kids do instead. He suggested, "They can read a book."

Why were half the people I grew up with dead before they were twenty-one? Maybe it was because we didn't read enough books. Or maybe it really was our crazy families, or coming of age in "the '60s." Perhaps it was the demographics, the genetic predisposition to alcoholism and melancholia inherited by some, assimilated by others. Some believed it was the isolation of living on a stinkin' peninsula, with fuck-all nothing to do and the death pull of the ocean. If only we could get out of Rockaway, the curse would be lifted and we'd be fine.

Stuck in the middle of nowhere, halfway between the decaying boroughs of New York City and the glistening suburbia of Long Island always left us feeling vaguely stranded, in a state of existential despair. Pinned between the crummy old world our parents left behind and a shiny new one that seemed always out of reach, it was important to find distractions, and so we did.

My magic bus traveled on, past Sixteenth, through Seaside, home of the notorious Irish Circle bar on Beach 102nd, pulling in to Rockaway's Playland at Beach 97th Street. This extravaganza was two blocks from St. Camillus, Tommy's alma mater, where grimacing kids in uniforms flicked lit cigarettes at anyone walking by. With sixty-five rides, games, and attractions, by 1971 they estimated that 180,000 people had visited the famed amusement park by the sea. My shooter's eye was a sure bet for a shimmering goldfish in a plastic bag. The fish always died the next day, but they always had more.

Everyone looked a little mutated in the carnival light, especially at twilight. Spanish boys from the projects, and Chinese too, up close for the very first time. Boys appeared from places we never heard of as make-out sessions wedged themselves between target practice and ring toss. Swytie had the reputation, but I usually went in for the kill. Bagging a cute guy was like stealing candy, literally. Chocolate-covered burly boys from nearby Howard Beach hammered the jackpot to prove their love. Italian boys flexing olive-toned muscles in their white guinea T's (T-shirts). Miraculous metals, sweat, and Vitalis. Big brown eyes, cracked front tooth, throbbing gristle.

Originally known as Thompson's Amusement Park, Rockaway's Playland was owned by LeMarcus Thompson. Thompson invented the modern roller coaster, the one first featured in nearby Coney Island. The roller coaster, formally known as the Atom Smasher, stood on the left side of the park. The sign boasted "Family Fun Since 1901." The Cyclone's whiplash ride, the fun house, and an Olympic-size swimming pool drew people from all over. With all the bars, clams, custard, cotton candy, and saltwater taffy, perpetual party time. As Rockaway's popularity as a beach resort dwindled, and folks began migrating farther east to Long Island, Playland deteriorated. By the 1980s the monster amusement parks had drawn most of the visitors away. Increasing violence, drinking, fighting, drugging, weapons, and an increasingly "bad element" made it unsafe for families. In 1987 the roller coaster was demolished and the party was over.

Rockaway's splintered boardwalk was the foot soldier's link to all points east. It ran parallel to the Lowlife, extending seaside from Beach 126th in Belle Harbor all the way to Beach 9th in Far Rockaway. The boardwalk was my second home, from 1964 to 1969 my very own

7-Eleven. Anywhere you'd step onto it, day or night, you'd stroll along, meet friends, relax with a knish, a frank, a slice of pizza, or an Italian ice.

Under the boardwalk was the after-hours club for nocturnal teens. That's where you'd go to find your own truth, then sleep it off without interference. Squalor motel, a free bed-and-breakfast for nomadic youth. Whatever other kids did up on the roof and in the backseats of cars, we did under the boardwalk. Cool by day, it offered shelter from the swelter; at night it blocked the wind. Even with the scent of piss and sea sludge wafting, it was a better place to hide than the Swamp Foxes' clubhouse in Mrs. Gustersen's garage, because it went on for four miles.

The ocean gave the whole place a mystical, soggy feel. At once soothing and menacing, it was a healing source with lethal intent. The sea air ruined our hair, ironed straight every day to look like Cher's. But we were powerless against a foggy humidity that condemned us to ringlets. With a joint and a cheap jug of wine, sometimes you stepped on glass, or found yourself sitting on a used rubber. Now and then a rat scurried by, a syringe washed up on shore, or you collided with a ship-wrecked Tampon or a clump of dog shit. This was New York water, dark and murky. When I was young, the water was clear. There were seashells and tiny sand crabs, captured and sentenced to die in our sand pails. If you smashed one with a shell, it bled bright orange.

Eventually, the ocean turned gray from the pollution, and I couldn't see my feet anymore. Then the sand crabs disappeared. Skeevy as a city sewer, the sea carried us off. The rhythm of the waves imprinted itself into the unconscious in a sway of primordial bliss. So tiny we stood against it, fearless yet trusting. It offered refuge, our great mother. But the ocean was also an angry spirit, fierce, terrifyingly vast, all-powerful. The great Neptune bestowed life and took it away—rolling thunder, waves, undertow. In a split second, the swimmer vanished. The sea was our center, our home; we would have to be near it always. On a south-east wind the waves crashed with the sound of the blues. On a day like that, you knew it for certain; Rockaway was the piss end of the world.

Riding east, Hammels came up right after Playland, at Beach 86th

Street. The British Invasion always boarded the Lowlife at Hammels. Carlos and Richie were the Johnny Thunders and Jerry Nolan of Far Rockaway High School. Well, let's just say they had a *look*. There's a very big difference between a look and "fashion." It's the difference between Keith Richards and Donna Karan. Having played in Rockaway bands since the seventh grade, Carlos had the best hair on the peninsula, long, black, straight, unlike any other. He was always cool, always *dressed*, dapper in footwear extraordinaire. He traveled all the way to New York City, to McCreedy & Schreiber to get 'em. First came a pair of regulation Beatle boots, then he segued to a flatter heel. Carlos was formal, innately aristocratic. Richie was more school yard, sweetly boyish, really more Richard Hell than the rough-trade eleganza Jerry Nolan—cute, scrappy, casual in low Cons, button-down shirt, and skinny tie.

The British Invasion lived in the projects, they played in bands like the Beatles 5, the Footsteps, the Pathfinders, and the Wildcats. The tenth-grade public school influx to Far Rockaway High School had burst open the floodgates of rock. The Beatles 5 had been local Junior High School 180's first rock & roll band. They formed in 1964, and despite their name, they mainly did Stones covers. Most kids didn't know the Stones material, so everyone thought the band did originals. Back then most bands just did cover songs, but we didn't call them cover bands.

At the junior high, Principal Feldman had instituted a dress code involving ties. The class president would organize a show, sometimes the WMCA Good Guys would officiate and bands would perform. Once, in the middle of a school play, everything stopped and the Beatles 5 performed. They showed up in sport jackets with dickies, mock turtlenecks, and revolutionized the dress code. Their look became the new uniform, Dave Clark Five style. No more ties, no complaints. Before the band, kids wore stovepipes, button-down shirts with sweaters, and penny loafers. The music changed that, too.

Made up of a group of Belle Harbor jazz combo kids who had already been playing out and members of the school orchestra, in time the Beatles 5 splintered into other bands. But the guys played every weekend, one or two gigs, making fifty to sixty dollars a guy, Sweet sixteens, PAL shindigs, school dances, and galas at the YMHA. Before they were old enough to drink they were touring the bars on Sixteenth and the Irish Circle—the Bay Lounge and McNulty's, where, in 1966 the Lovin' Spoonful appeared.

Once the Beatles 5 got better, they changed their name to the Footsteps. The Wildcats were older, but they started their band later. The lead singer worked in the Clothes Closet, a fashion gold mine on Mott Avenue in Far Rockaway. His Belle Harbor mom knitted outrageous mohair sweaters he wore with jeans and black blazers. Bold colors with silver streaks, funky but chic, Queens boutique. Today there is a Museum of the Rockaways, and those mohair sweaters surely do belong among the great artifacts of our past.

Meanwhile, Cardoza, the "tougher" (more prole and racially mixed) junior high school to the east had its own entrees to Far Rockaway High School's music subculture. From the projects of Arverne and Edgemere came bands like the Lafayettes and the Detours. From Far Rockaway came the Germs and a surf band called the Sundowners. The Sundowners were older and had real paying gigs, so they were everybody's heroes. Part of the Wind was an all-girl band, a collaboration of Far Rockaway girls and a few hip Five Towns ladies who hated their Jappy, preppy high school. The girls met up at school dances or in town, at the beach or on the boardwalk, looking for adventure, for older guys with motorcycles and names like Shaggy, Muck, and Meatball. Part of the Wind shopped at Paraphernalia, bought Twiggy eye makeup, and played at all the dances. They looked like models, but they knew their rock & roll.

Some of these musicians became lifers. By 1967 Carlos was ready to move on. He'd been spending time at West Village clubs, seeing Richie Havens, Blues Project, and the Paul Butterfield Blues Band. Since he was always touring, Carlos blew out of Far Rockaway High School and enrolled at Quintanos, the unruly high school for performing children near Carnegie Hall. The school was a big hangout spot for all sorts of characters like Joey Ramone and Janis Ian. Also, Syl Sylvain and David Johansen, Johnny Thunders's bandmates in the Dolls. Thunders had begged his mother to send him there and then quit school at sixteen.

Quintanos was a bona fide high school, but students were mostly touring or jamming. At one point Carlos sold a guitar to Johnny Thunders. Where is that guitar now? Sometimes I think my life's purpose, my entire spiritual journey has been the search for Johnny Thunders's guitar. To understand what he was saying in those sloppy leads, in the riddles, those ruptures we call chord structures. Anyway, Carlos and Richie were the first rock stars I ever knew, so that made Hammels the rock & roll capital of Rockaway.

The Hammels Houses were part of a New York City public housing project built in 1955, low income, mostly people of color. The rest of the area was old Irish, working class, and poor. But for all Rockaway youth, Hammels remains sacred ground for another reason. In addition to Carlos and Richie, legend holds that this is the spot where surfing got started in the Rockaways. When Duke Kahanamoku, three-time Olympic swimmer and the father of modern surfing, came here from Hawaii in 1912, he landed in Rockaway without a board. So he got into the water and body surfed. They say the locals named a street after him, but now nobody can agree on where it actually is.

Like motorcycle culture and car mania, surfing came to New York in the late 1940s with the soldiers returning home from the war. Some guys who had been stationed in Hawaii brought back very long, heavy boards. But it didn't catch on right away. Surfing got a boost through music innovated by Dick Dale and the Del-Tones.

Although Dale was playing the stuff back in the 1950s, the Southern California surf music sound wasn't unveiled till the early 1960s at weekend dances at the Rendezvous Ballroom in Balboa. Stratocaster master Dale began working closely with Leo Fender, the manufacturer of the first mass-produced, solid-body electric guitar, aiming to improve the amplification and reverb that ultimately gave surf music its signature fuzzy sound. By 1961, Dale's "Let's Go Trippin'" was in the Top Fifty. In 1962 his classic instrumental "Misirlou" hit the airwaves.

By 1963, Capitol had signed the King of the Surf Guitar. Surf music and beach culture came flooding in.

The impact on New York rockers was everlasting. We hear it in Johnny Thunders's cover of the Chantays' "Pipeline." He always opened with the turbocharged instrumental, blowing all that light, airy, intricate SoCal sweetness right out his ass. For years, every New York kid with a guitar would torment friends with covers of "Wipe Out" by the Surfaris, and "Walk—Don't Run" by the Ventures. Throughout their twenty-year career, the Ramones acknowledged New York's surf culture by covering such classics as "Surf City" by Jan and Dean and "Surfin' Bird" by the Trashmen. I remember hearing the original sun-drenched surfers humming these tunes on Sixteenth, buying smokes up at Admiration.

Turn-of-the-'60s beach movies like *Gidget* and *A Summer Place* appeared. *Beach Party, Slippery When Wet* followed, spreading surf culture to noncoastal New York towns, to landlocked places like Levittown and Massapequa. The Beatles may have bumped our beloved Beach Boys from the top of the charts, but surfing was here to stay. By 1963 everyone was in madras Pendleton shirts, sandals, and tight, cropped Levi's. Good-natured moms across suburbia loaded huge, heavy boards on top of their station wagons. In 1966 a film called *Endless Summer* captured the life. Some Rockaway diehards traveled to see the NYC screening, met Duke Kahanamoku himself, got Duke T-shirts, and became fan-club members. Today *Endless Summer* is a classic; there's even a sequel, and first- and second-generation surf punks are still watching it, especially those exiled inland or to urban dry lands.

Where family, religion, school, and community inculcated fear and hatred of the *other*, surfing, like music, sex, and drugs, ultimately unified all the youth of Belle Harbor. The Jewish kids first began experimenting with bongs, filling water pipes with wine and tobacco. When they switched over to pot, the Irish kids were appalled. It was evil, sick, you were definitely going to hell.

But when the Hebrews turned them on to uppers, it was like they'd found the Holy Grail. Eat some pills, drink beer forever. You'd never pass out. Angry Sons of Erin cranked on speed and Budweiser were like young Crays running wild in swinging London. This was a turning point in Judeo-Celtic relations, after the speed, the Irish thought the Jews were cool. Reefer and acid, too, solidified interfaith relations and life was never the same.

In the beginning, only the lifeguards went surfing. Eventually, as it caught on, the churches organized trips to Puerto Rico, Catholic priests aided Christian youth in their search for good breaks. There were trips to Cape Hatteras, day excursions to Gilgo, and treks to Montauk. One guy rented a room at the East Deck, fifteen crashed out, surf all day, party all night.

As the spirituality of surfing took hold, Catholic and Jew became one, united by the new chemicals in our blood. We celebrated our unity at interfaith beach parties, gathered around bonfires, sharing communion in garbage pails filled with fruit juice and alcohol, joints, and three-day acid runs. Lasting love affairs and lifelong friendships followed. It would take the Vatican another thirty years, an entire generation for Pope Paul to make an amend to the Jews, to apologize for two centuries of Roman Catholic intolerance. But under the Church of the Blue Sky everyone stood together in God's grace. One race, soul surfers, walking on water, catching the waves. In fact, guys just five years younger than me have no memory of the bloodstained days of Judeo-Celtic combat. Interfaith lovebirds now consorted freely, no more who-uhs or race traitors. After the drugs and the waves, it had become a thing of the past, like *West Side Story.*

Praised be our rocks and jetties. Depending on who you talk to and the weather that day, the best waves were on Beach 139th, on Beach 121st, or Beach 111th, at Chicken Bone Beach at 92nd, on Beach 88th, or around Beach 39th. Bay 1 of Riis Park had decent breaks, too. A legendary outpost for pre-Stonewall freedom fighters, strategically situated between uptight Breezy and stiff Neponsit, on weekends, upstanding residents would meander down to the beach and ogle the gay and lesbian couples and nude bathers. As surfing became more popular, the city began restricting access to the water. At one point they banished all the surfers to Bay 1, pitting sun-drenched longboarders against an emerging queer nation, two subcultures of undesirables juxtaposed. Surfboards didn't have leg-leashes back then, so if a renegade board washed up to shore, terrified Rockaway surfer boys ran quick to grab them, fearing the helping hands of the friendly naked gentlemen.

In the psychedelic era Bay 1 became known as a safe place to trip. Twelve hours hassle-free—a scenic interlude off the beaten path. Eventually this stronghold of cultural radicalism became part of Gateway National Park. In the 1980s residents took Gateway to court; nude sunbathing was okay, but public sex on the beach had to stop. Local parents had documentation, photos, their children were at risk. Imagine this paradise of outlaw culture—homosexuality, interfaith sex, race mixing, LSD, Sapphic love, and surfing—just ten blocks from my house.

In Belle Harbor, from Memorial Day to Labor Day, you couldn't surf until the lifeguards went off duty. In Far Rockaway they ticketed you, charged you with "disorderly conduct." After hours, the ocean was yours. Kids carried forty-pound, nine-foot-plus longboards on their bikes or their heads. Some innovated carts to tote them around. Lifeguards who worked at private beach clubs had more influence, and were able to liberate beaches for surfers. In 1968 Rockaway's seminal watermen protested a ban on surfing at local beaches. They wanted designated surfing beaches open to surfers only. Long Beach instituted it, but like most things in Rockaway, it never quite happened.

In the early days before the famed Full Moon Surfboards and Tommy Sena's Rockaway Beach Surf Shop up on Sixteenth, kids innovated gear out of diving suits and plastic and duct tape. Soft, flexible foam bodyboards like Tom Morey's Boogie Boards were preceded by old canvas air mattresses and swim fins. Surf-punk progenitors had other hobbies, too. Early skateboarding involved a wooden plank, a two-by-four, bolted into a pair of old roller skates—metal death wheels, not sweet urethane. No suspension system; you hit something, you bled hard. Baby carriages and shopping carts were transformed into go-carts, street motion near the ocean.

There were no real surf shops, so loving parents drove kids to places like Emilio's Ski Shop in Forest Hills, or to the diving shop in Sheepshead Bay. For under a hundred bucks you could buy a bottom-of-the-line Duke Kahanamoku "pop-out" board. Made by machine, they sized them according to your weight. Some kids got Hobies, at one hundred forty dollars. That was considered pricey. Custom boards from better materials like balsa and redwood were built from scratch, like Challenger Eastern. But that came a little later. You could specify everything from thickness of rails to the width of the nose and still not pay more than one hundred fifty dollars. Surf lingo, the clothes, the life depicted in Beach Boys tunes were enticing to young boys. But you had to make your own baggies, loose-fitting cutoff jeans almost to the knees, and shirts to avoid sunburn. Your badge of honor? Knobs on your knees from paddling out. If they stuck out half a notch, that was even better.

By 1965, all the Swamp Foxes were in the water. Nobody taught them how to surf; they just watched the older guys. They liked the way the girls flocked around the lifeguards and their fiberglass boards. Because Beach 139th Street had great breaks, over time, we had an instant streetcorner scene of muscle cars, drug dealerships, and surfing. The Monacos, Carbones, and Ryans all had huge families. Younger siblings stole boards from older ones, and two or three girls surfed, too—they even stood up. I was a strong swimmer, an able bodysurfer. I loved the water and was fearless against it. But in those days, I mostly watched and made beach jewelry. Intricate beaded necklaces I sold to the tourists—the Brooklyn day-trippers and the polite, friendly gentlemen up at Bay 1.

Rockaway was a Neptunian land of dreams, some aquatic, some narcotic. New York produced Rick Rasmussen, the local boy who won the East Coast Surfing Championship in 1974. In 1981, Rasmussen was shot and killed in a smack deal gone mad somewhere down in Alphabet City. Likewise, as the subcultures evolved, some watermen became surf-shop entrepreneurs. Others became notorious drug smugglers, stashing thousands of doses of Sunshine inside handcrafted boards, shipping them off to Puerto Rico. Head shops sprung up as former members of the Magicians became major hippies, hitchhiking back and forth to the West Coast, mellow at last.

Some surfing drug entrepreneurs got murdered; others got drafted and died in Vietnam. Then there were the flea-bitten junkies, wastoids. A chosen few did devote themselves completely to surfing, viewing it as a lifelong spiritual practice—the rhythm, the natural high from breathing, meditations on the waves, the wind, the direction of the current. Paddling out flushed the toxins out of the body and kept even the most burnt looking lean and mean. After an all-night drug run, sunrise surfing reaffirmed that God's light wasn't just chemicals, it was real.

Now, once the Lowlife passed Beach 79th, you were out of Hammels and on your way into Arverne. You knew it from the old wood houses, the churches and synagogues, grand and splendid porches that wrapped around like weeping willows. The city's solution to the post-World War II housing shortage of the early 1950s had been the construction of apartment building complexes, middle-income housing projects. The Edgemere projects ran along the bay side of Beach Channel Drive to Alameda Avenue. The older Arverne Houses ran from Beach 56th to Beach 54th on Beach Channel Drive to Rockaway Beach Boulevard. More affluent Arverne dwellers lived in Nordeck, a cooperative that started on Beach 58th and ran to Beach 60th Street on the beach side. All the city projects were racially mixed, but more Hispanic and African-American families lived in Hammels, and the Redfern Houses in Far Rockaway. We mainly went there for parties. That's how I learned Spanish.

For a while I had a friend from Arverne, Michelle, whom I met in gym class. Before Janis Ian sang about it, Michelle crossed the color line for the love of a tall basketball hero. But Mr. Hoops had other plans. He asked the precocious fifteen-year-old to pull a train—to fuck all his friends—and that broke her tender heart. One night I got ready to meet Michelle. I ate a tab of blotter right before I weighed in. I left the Weight Watchers meeting at Temple Beth-El's community room and hopped on the Lowlife; told Betty Bradley I was sleeping over Michelle's that night. I got off at Beach 54th went up to her apartment, and drank tea with her European parents—out of a glass, sucking the liquid through the sugar cubes between my teeth, Russian style.

Looking at her older sister's Far Rockaway High School yearbook, the faces started looking a little distorted. Soon I felt I could see through all of them, like I knew who they really were behind their idiotic happy smiles. Acid, like pot, afforded an instant ability to deconstruct and decompose the prevailing truth, to expose it. It made me feel powerful. But I was never quite sure what to do with all this outlaw knowledge.

To get revenge against the snarky Hoops, Michelle hooked us up with two older guys, hippies from Far Rockaway. Mine had a Jewfro, curly hair. He was older, boring, always talking about the government and the war. In a flash, Day-Glo posters appeared to us against the sky. This was my first glimpse of collective consciousness, cartooning on the posters. We had walked all the way to Far Rockaway on the beach and ended up in somebody's backyard. The funky smell under the boardwalk that night was bad for the trip, and shaky, we headed toward peaceful lands. This was somewhere deep in Bayswater. The houses were bigger, it was safe and easy to hide. It wasn't the home of anyone we knew, but we slept there till it was light out.

Step by step, stop after stop, one stop at a time you got there. At the end of the line, after you'd traveled through everywhere else, the Lowlife entered a place that felt like no other. In *Tropic of Capricorn*, Henry Miller describes it: "When I say that I was at Far Rockaway, I mean that I was standing at the end of the earth, at a place called Xanthos, if there be such a place and surely there ought to be a word to express no place at all." As Miller explains, this is the end of the known world; you're thoroughly alone here, but you're not frightened. In fact, you rejoice, "because at this dropping-off place you can feel the old ancestral world which is eternally young and new and fecundating. You stand there, wherever the place is, like a newly hatched chick beside its eggshell." According to Miller, "This place is Xanthos, or as it happened in my case, Far Rockaway."

It wasn't just my imagination or Miller's. This easternmost part of the peninsula adjacent to Nassau County was also dear to Neil Simon, Woody Allen, and Allen Ginsberg. Xanthos was a space where old-world Jewish ideas mixed with shiny Americana, Indian burial grounds bubbled up mixing in a funky casserole of jazz music, fog lights, stink of mildew, *shimmy shimmy ko ko bop*. Once the Lowlife deposited you at Xanthos, there were no gimmicks. It was like, "Get here, we'll do the rest." Far Rockaway was as far away as I could get—from home, from Belle Harbor, from myself, from anything or anyone I was expected to be. It was the end of the line and the beginning of all great things.

Belle Harbor and Neponsit were richer, more elegant, with nicer homes and newer cars, but the place radiated no soul, with or without the dope. As we all know, the cultural rebellion of the hippies called for social justice, personal freedom, authenticity, meaning, and truth. Creative Belle Harbor kids generated counterculture in their bedrooms and basements. Their rebellion happened internally, underground. But Xanthos was a gaping existential space, at once filled with adventure, enchantment, and desperation. *Radio Days, Brighton Beach Memoirs.* It was a lesser Coney Island of the mind, but Coney Island had no waves. Far Rockaway had waves and *neshuma,* Jewish soul.

Although it ran from one end of the peninsula to the other, and it was technically Edgemere, when Far Rockaway people talk about "the boardwalk," they mean the one by Beach 35th—the stretch of concessions that ran from Beach 32nd to Beach 36th. All walks of life, always energizing, always something to do. The Lowlife stopped right on the corner. You disembarked and headed toward the beach. One block south and you were already buzzed, a few hits of a joint, a Marlboro, you were now entering Xanthos. This was as far, as high, as deep as you could go.

Jewish working-class families had been coming to the boardwalk since the 1930s, finding a safe summer haven from the sweltering Bronx. Playing miniature golf, frolicking in the Kiddie Park, watching the fireworks—always held on Wednesdays because Friday night was *Shabbas.* Now hungry freaks with dollar bills crumpled in their hands gobbled Jerry's Famous Knishes, kasha with a cream soda. At Lenny's

Fascination, where everyone is a winner, wasted kids gambled dope money on the roll of a ball. The lights were so bright on Beach 35th that the surfers used it to guide them home in the night waters.

Friday after closing, the game got serious. Teenage poker dons played grumpy old wiseguys for high stakes. I was better at Skee-Ball—collecting the coupons, I'd cash them in for *tchotchkes* at the end of the season. There was archery for young amazons and Paul's Bumper Cars if you wanted some heavy-metal thunder. Snack bars, watering holes, fresh Italian ices, custard stands. There was even an outdoor movie theater and the live entertainment ran all night.

The mighty Lowlife transported Rockaway youth to a nightly happening. You never saw Belle Harbor kids hanging out. In winter the boardwalk was a dead zone where empty bungalows became free motels, shooting galleries. Off season, this was the poor side of town, where families struggled to pay bills. By summer it was carnival time: drinking beer, dancing, smoking a joint, looking for love. As the 1960s exploded into a collage of music, surfboards, muscle cars, flower power, and drugs, kids came from the east, from the Five Towns into Far Rockaway. Richer, glitzy, they crossed over the Nassau County line looking for pleasure and danger. They were seekers, too. There were no JAPs on the entire peninsula until the princesses descended from the east, rich girls from Hewlett and Woodmere, beautiful, well groomed, in shiny cars. Tennis courts, swimming pools, wealthy beyond anything we'd ever seen in Neponsit or Belle Harbor.

The royalty came to date rough, invade our parties, and pair off with a guy. We smiled at them graciously, then winked at the guy. Behind closed doors we ransacked their pocketbooks. Mary Quant, Yardley, all the best new lip glosses and eye shadows, pastels, shimmering shades. Original product, not the cheesy knockoffs we lifted from the shlock stores on Central Avenue. We never took their money. We didn't even hate them. We did it for kicks. Far Rockaway guys were edgy, tough, *and* Jewish. They dressed sharp, played in bands, sparred with boxing gloves. The boys in our high school were junior wiseguys, football heroes, surf gods, pillheads. Boys from the Five Towns usually stayed at their private beach clubs, places where Rockaway boys got jobs as lifeguards, including access to private beaches and unregulated surf. It was only the foxy ladies who ventured forth, to the edge of Queens, in search of manly men. Like my early adolescent trolling of the school yard at St. Francis, Erin Go Bragh. Who could blame them?

And how could anyone resist Far Rockaway? From wealthy Bayswater to the Redfern projects, it was a parallel universe where *Jewish kids* were hip. There was streetlife, public culture, something to do all the time. Winters, when the boardwalk was closed, you walked into town, up Beach 20th past the pool hall toward Gino's where twenty-five cents bought you a slice of pizza and a Coke. Far Rockaway hitter chicks had much bigger hair than anyone on Twenny-ninth or even Sixteenth. Sitting around quietly fading into cultural history, they cringed at their boyfriends' descriptions of psychedelic excursions. Deep Queens dialect, she's filing her nails as he's dragging a Kool, "I just don't get it, what's so great about seeing a flower explode off the wall?" *Well, fuck, if you had to explain it . . .*

In a pedestrian's chess game Benny the cop would bust you for jaywalking, shuffling you from a pretzel and a cherry Coke break at the Pickwick over to the music store. After a while you just gave in and ducked into Carvel. There was Woolworth's for a quick lipstick fix. Two popular lipstick shades were Michelle and Nicole, so creamy, slutty French, and frosty sounding. We pocketed them and headed north, to the bowling alley, a fast-fading teen-culture relic. The bowling alley was the hitters' last stop before army induction. Everybody bought pea coats at Morton's Army & Navy and inserted loose-leaf rings in the lapels one year, baby pacifiers the next. Cold outside? No place to go? You'd hit the movie theaters—the old Strand, Pix, and the RKO. Or check out the action at the State Diner. Nightfall, you'd hitch a ride into Nassau County and find a party. By June, the streets were empty, everyone was back at the boardwalk.

Peak freak year: 1967. Most everyone I knew was high, but not yet wasted. There were no fights, no ugly scenes. Even the gambling and drug dealing were done quietly, discreetly. Kids in army surplus played folk music from acoustic guitars: Dylan, Woody Guthrie, earnest and angry. Longhairs talked of politics and culture deep into the night. Surf it deep by day, nod by night. High school kids, teenyboppers, sluts, and old ladies with small children—anything goes. Some guys got drafted, shot down, others got strung out. The boardwalk the old Jewish families remembered so fondly peaked in the 1950s; by 1971 it was all over.

First, a series of fires demolished key concessions, and the pizza place was lost forever. Before that the fruit market and a series of smaller stores in the area. They were never rebuilt because the city took over. Under the laws of eminent domain, buildings were cited, condemned, then bulldozed. The population was poor and underorganized, unable to resist, and very little compensation was offered. Under Mayor John Lindsay New York City officials targeted the area for urban renewal in 1964, citing urban decay.

A combination of economic setbacks and developers who pulled out left sixty square blocks of prime waterfront property in a state of desolation. One of the largest undeveloped urban oceanfront lots in the nation became an empty gaping hole in our local psyche. By 1971, all the structures south of Rockaway Beach Boulevard, virtually everything between Beach 32nd up to Beach 84th Street had been obliterated. Periodically there were plans to rebuild. In 1989, an Arverne-by-the-Sea apartment complex. In 1997, Destination Technodome, a $1-billion sports, entertainment, and hotel complex. Gambling casinos, too, were considered—a move that would have brought Native peoples back to Reckowacky, where Mohawk tribes once roamed. Even now, there are plans for one- and two-family houses, midrise apartment buildings, a retail center, and a school. But our city was gone.

The Shangri-Las understood *you can never go home anymore,* and with the boardwalk demolished, only Xanthos remained. A memory, a state of mind now archived in time. A few brave surfers by day, and crack viles, hookers, empty streets, a must to avoid after sundown. Ghosts fill the benches, strung-out veterans of undeclared wars, bad dope, overdoses, blocked arteries, heart attacks, Jewish junkies, dancing to Spencer Davis one minute, comatose in a vacant lot the next.

When Henry Miller used the word *Xanthos,* he didn't know whether there was a real place called Xanthos or not. He didn't care; he speculated it was in the Grecian Islands. But I know Xanthos was right there, a splintered boardwalk in South Queens. A shoreline refuge where today, weary surf gods roam barren wastelands eternal. Calling us home from shattered rock piles, from the jetties, the wailing walls of the sea.

Everyone says it started in the mid-1960s with reefer. Older kids swear Xanthos was heroin infested as early as 1962. By the time *Sgt. Pepper's* was on the turntable, it was all laid out. The football team won the city championship in 1968. By then our finest athletes were getting wacked—Nembutals, Seconals, Tuinals. Lunchtime, they dismantled pharmaceuticals, pulling pills apart then dumping the powders into wholesome orange drinks. After school, Tuinals with cookies and milk. Jackpot, a forgotten one found crumbling in the lining of your safari jacket, just enough to tide you over. It was as easy as buying a knish; walk up to the boardwalk and hang around, you'd always find something.

Some kids got jobs as lifeguards, at Playland, or as parkies, cleaning the beach for a few hours then they'd fuck off, get high, go surfing. Then came the works, they started shooting Tuinals, crushing up the pills, abscessing. Gamma globulin shots warded off hepatitis. The ones that didn't die right off would waste away later, long after they were clean and sober, their blood already stained. The ones who survived had nothing to say. They got married, they had jobs and normal lives. Mostly *they never wanted their kids to know.*

By 1970 heroin replaced barbiturates as the preferred method of destruction. In a matter of weeks nice Jewish boys became junkies, street people, disappearing into the bathroom after *Shabbas* dinner to get high. As it progressed, the nice boys stole from parents, from friends, from friends' parents, and from parents' friends. To see how it all ended, simply log onto the Rockaway Beach New York Official Reunion Web Site and locate the Memorial Pages.

Kiss the boys and watch them die. The football players, the surfers, the swim team, then their sisters. Lowlife comrades and all the quiet ones you never even suspected were using. Every three weeks another overdose.

Jewish guilt saved me from it. If anything happened to me, how would Betty Bradley live through it? After losing two husbands? "You'll kill me!" were the magic words that kept me alive. Okay, I did snort the stuff once, and I swear I only did it for science. Just a few lines till it made me feel queasy. It was around 1980. I was an empiricist trying to understand what it was like. What had the power to turn sane people into pincushions, to collapse their veins and keep them puking till that last unlucky shot? This was the second wave of heroin addiction, all the white punks on dope, strung out in the Lower East Side of Manhattan. There would be a third wave in the 1990s and it wasn't gonna be the last.

From Xanthos to CBGB's to Seattle, the description was always the same: "Heroin feels like pure love." It made you feel godlike. You puke, in a rush there's a warm, endless hug, an unconditional surrender. Others swore it zapped all their creative juices, sucked the light right out of them, but they did it anyway. Thank God I hated the high. It made me feel morbid, cranky, even more empty and wretched than usual. They say it's only like that the first time, but I wasn't playing. So I just sat there for a while, swooning. Then I got up and fixed myself a cocktail.

Some escape plans end up killing us, others open up brave new worlds. The years I spent riding the Lowlife were not wasted. Restless, irritable, and discontented, I found myself pleasantly distracted, fascinated, and reconstituted. Drawn out of my head and into the world, my stomach cramps disappeared. As I left my body, myself, and my life behind, I was renewed. My travels across the Rockaways calmed my thoughts and quieted my soul. And they ultimately paved the way for a slamming career.

D.O.M. always said, "Book smarts are nothing without street smarts, but the combination of both is a winning ticket." In my escape to Xanthos I was increasingly drawn to the study of people, places, and things. I was curious, completely fascinated by the structure and content of new situations. Each new vista offered a portrait, a snapshot of time stopped cold, perfect, unique, complicated, a jigsaw puzzle that lasted for days. The Lowlife transported me to where biography met history and I was an observer, a beholder of many splendid truths. The rest of the time, I was probably in my room.

1967: My peak freak year.

6

IN MY ROOM

met Marr while I was throwing up in the bathroom of the Hartman YMHA. I was facedown, praying to the great white porcelain god when she asked if I was okay. She offered me a comb and a lipstick and after that, we were best friends. Saturday dances at the Y in Far Rockaway featured local bands like the Sundowners and the Pathfinders doing endless covers of "In the Midnight Hour" and "Gimme Some Lovin'." Through album-oriented radio, an emerging rock press, and places like the Electric Circus and Fillmore East, music was taking over the socialization process of America's young. But as with many alienated suburban teenagers, the counterculture was mainly happening in my room. I spent hours up there, alone or with a friend, stoked out on Fantasy Island, door shut, *grooving.*

Innovations in Betty Bradley's home pharmacy accentuated the beat. If Marr was speeding and I was on the nod, we were perfectly in synch. I was hyper; I never stopped talking, smacking my gums at 78 rpm. I was afraid if I shut up, people would disappear. As long as I kept chattering, they were obligated to stay and listen. Once I stopped, I'd be

alone again and that terrified me, so I kept on yapping. Even under se-
dation, I was a chatterbox. Marr was the opposite. She didn't drink or
smoke pot, and she hardly spoke.

With thick black hair like Frank Zappa's and big brown eyes, Marr
was always watching. She was a lurker, astutely quiet, even when
cranked on crystal meth. The oldest daughter of a flamboyant shlock-
store mogul, Marr was extremely independent and action oriented. Her
father's rag emporium kept us in fabulous imported madras bedspreads,
mirrored bags, peasant blouses, batik scarves, silk kaftans, and brass incense burners. But a khaki green safari jacket always topped off any ensemble; we needed lots of pockets.

A barrier of contempt and self-doubt set us apart from the more
conventional habits of our gender. Instead of grooming and preening
for potential dates, we spent our time foraging for pills and rags. Showing any interest in boys was considered a serious loss of dignity and integrity. Mercilessly we made fun of girls who pined away for the mere
mortals—we called them H.U.B.s (Hard Up Bitches). We played for
much higher stakes. In my room, Michel Polnareff's French rock-blues
songs transformed us into sexy Parisian chicks. *Ooh la la,* we imagined
ourselves in tight black skirts, with striped polo shirts and royal blue
silk kerchiefs tied around our necks. Short perky haircuts finished off
the fantasy. We smoked heavily, our cigarettes dangling from dark red
lips, vintage Betty Bradley.

On a slow weekday afternoon in Belle Harbor, we peered out from
under imaginary black berets, phonetically lip-synching French lyrics
off this obscure promo album salvaged by Mom. Maybe it came from
Aunt Naomi–the-artist's estate? Or a midnight garbage run through
Belle Harbor, or some thrift store. Mostly French, our favorite cut was
"No No No No No (La Poupée Qui Fait Non)," a sweetly melodic
song, more folk than rock, but it worked. We'd imagine dashing young
beaus on shiny black mopeds, meeting for espresso and Pernod down at
the bistro. But it would only be us and John and Jimmy.

Always there, our two orange metal poles, John and Jimmy lived in
the back of my closet. They stood about four feet high and two inches

wide. We painted faces on our alloy puppet boyfriends and playfully called them our dildos. Desperate living in suburbia; we gave them voices, carved out personalities, invented situations. John was Irish, he was all mine, always brooding, he said very little. Jimmy was Spanish, more outgoing, romantic, and gallant. Through his thick black mustache he whispered, *"Marrraleeen, Marrraleeen . . . "* incessantly at Marr. John and Jimmy never cheated on us; they were always there for us. To this day, we know they're the only men who ever really loved us.

Once, we did cheat on John and Jimmy, but it was only because the nonsentient beings didn't have the lung capacity to get wasted with us. We knew these two guys from Far Rockaway. They were not our boyfriends, just our drugging buddies, close friends and business partners. Sometimes I distributed reefer for them, so there was mutual admiration and respect. Our buddies were idolized by cute younger girls we casually dismissed as teenyboppers. Marr and I didn't have time for boyfriends; we had to be at the boardwalk every night. Getting H.U.B. over anyone would have distracted from our more important work of making the scene and getting high. Besides, we had John and Jimmy.

Our two Far Rockaway associates were your typical petty thieves, good at burglaries and bad dope deals. Though they broke many hearts, we knew them only as solid guys. For a while the thieves rented a furnished room in Belle Harbor, holing up, hiding out, busy with product distribution. One Saturday afternoon we stopped by and had a party.

First we soaked the brown paper bags with a few tablespoons of Testors, pouring it like honey over fresh pretzels. Then we held it to our faces. Soon the rhythm of our breathing transformed us into rollicking Buddhas. Drooling, laughing, we ran after it, chased down the buzz like hungry dogs. I found myself pressed against the horny teenage boy. Did I grab him or did he snag me? Hands groping my tits, I'm creaming my jeans. *Yeah . . .* I'm in real time now, flying high with ugly monkeys from *The Wizard of Oz,* soldiers marching toward the castle of the Wicked Witch. Mean monkeys climbing down the tower in perfect military formation. Bouncing back and forth off the tower wall, then back into the buzz wheel again and again. Dark graphic chunks rotate with the clanging of bodies against steel walls. It's erotic and nauseating, the smell of sweaty pussy, semen, and glue in a shabby rented room. So degenerate, so sleazy, and then it fades and I come to.

I felt sickly satisfied, there on the floor with the doomed thieves, empty tubes and the rolls of flesh. Glue still stuck to my face, saliva running down my shirt, drool from him and me. The thieves never told anyone and neither did we. We probably forgot. Sex was just something we did to boost the solvent high. Drugging became an unconscious activity, like eating. A shot, a bag, a beer, a guy, a smoke, a slice, and a Coke, then back to John and Jimmy. Everyday life in our Shangri-la by the sea. Like most of the boys, the thieves eventually upgraded from solvent to poppy and died too young. Right there, in Wavecrest, the thieves were among the first soldiers of Xanthos to fall.

Today when I smell the fumes from my tiki torches, if I'm sitting on a peaceful beach at dusk, or late at night at Hess, filling my car with high octane, I'll remember. I'll catch the tail end of an old dream. I don't regret it, but sometimes I wonder, if I hadn't been such a ravenous huffer, maybe my Ph.D. would have been in physics, not sociology.

I was a teenage garbagehead. My tastes ran toward central nervous system depressants, reliable and conservative measures. I was too lazy to go out and cop. Pot made me paranoid, dope could be cut with bad shit, you never knew how strong it was. Coke could be a setup of caffeine pills and baking soda. But booze and pharmaceuticals I trusted. I had a flair for alchemy dating back to the days of making stink bombs with my chemistry set. Mind-expanding drugs like acid offered an altered state that wouldn't go away. After about three hours I got bored with tripping, I wanted it to be over. But I never tired of solvent abuse.

Generally considered the lowest lowlife, glue sniffing was viewed as a desperate measure, like shooting lighter fluid or wine 'cause you ran out of dope. Most veterans of the life won't even admit to it. Kids have always liked it 'cause it's cheap and easy. Obviously, I had other choices, unlimited resources, free access to any drug. Between my parents, Xanthos, and the thieves, I had my pick. And still, I chose that brown paper bag filled with Testors. That is, before manufacturers blocked the road to paradise with mustard seed.

While the Ramones have given glue sniffing its proper due, they created a controversy in the song "Carbona Not Glue." Not only wouldn't the record company release the song for many years, but the declaration in favor of cleaning fluid caused quite a stir in the solvent-abuse community. In the end, da bruddahs swore they never did it. Well, not that much, they said. Not like you'd think.

Like the tattooed, all the people in the world who have ever sniffed glue have, um, a bond. The act itself tells us something about one another. Back then, it separated the men from the boys. Glue sniffing is rare among intellectuals, especially you girls. To this day, I'm suspicious of a guy my age who says he never sniffed glue. Like he has no real balls, just a pair of raisins between his legs. But if he did huff a bag or two, trust me, the sex will be very, very hot. OKAY, I ABSOLUTELY DO NOT ADVISE ANYONE TO DO IT—*hey ho, Alzheimer's.* But if you want to peek, I would direct you to the Chambers Brothers' "Time Has Come Today."

By now everyone knows the song from the soundtrack of *Girl Interrupted. Tic toc, tic toc.* It starts ominously, *koo koo.* Slightly more edgy and less self-serious than the Byrds' "Eight Miles High," "Time" fused psychedelia with Afro rhythm calls in a funk fondue. "Time," this song about social displacement and anomic drift expressed both the terror and thrill I felt facing each day, lost out at sea with no reliable guidelines. *The rules have changed today, I have no place to stay.* Social upheaval at home, out in the streets, at school, even on TV—nobody knew what the fuck. The drugs gave me a goal, something to look forward to, an activity, boundaries. The music directed all the ensuing chaos into an orderly direction, a pattern I could follow. It gave everything a name. Nothing else was making any sense.

The Chambers Brothers started out in gospel, in Missouri. The drummer was a white guy. First there was a call, a holler, *"Oh lord, time has come today."* Time came in cowbells that echoed as the harmony increased. Pounding forth, it wasn't sex, it was death. The music, the glue, rising together in high-pitched sounds—you didn't know how far it would go. You held tight for that guitar riff, the familiar comfort of linearity. Or was it the sound of history unraveling? A fast train coming, or Armageddon? Settling into the buzz, reverb, gentle drumrolls, you rode the calming scales, sailing away in soft echoes. You felt safe until the screams and laughter whacked you in bidirectional drilling guitars, pecking at you, building up like that final roller-coaster ride at Rockaway's Playland. *Smash me, God is dead. Long live God.* Hit the brick wall and die. Okay, now you're born again.

This secret information about the universe gleaned in music excursions and drug runs gradually upstaged anything my parents could teach me directly. All they could tell me was lose weight, go to school, make your bed, get married, watch your mouth. I learned nothing in high school except new ways of perfecting the art of the scam. Friends, music, and pop culture soon displaced the educational functions of mandatory schooling. Of course, I wasn't the only one who figured that out.

Post-hippie, the freaks pursued sex, drugs, and rock & roll as the ends, not the means to liberation. Forget Chairman Mao and Woodstock Nation. The promise of utopia was in the next buzz. Defiant, degenerate, the freaks brought the struggle for social justice and honesty home, to everyday life. If I went down to the demonstration, it was strictly to look for guys, to make the scene. More often, my politics came down to conversations with Frank Zappa, in my room.

According to the Mothers of Invention bandleader, "On a personal level, *Freaking Out* is a process whereby an individual casts off outmoded and restricting standards of thinking, dress, and social etiquette in order to express CREATIVELY his relationship to his immediate environment and the social structure as a whole. Less perceptive individuals have referred to us who have chosen this way of thinking and FEELING as '*Freaks.*'" Zappa expounds upon the emancipatory potential of the freak-out gathering at a collective level, "The participants, already emancipated from our national *social slavery,* dressed in their most inspired apparel, realize as a group whatever potential they possess for *free* expression [italics and caps his]." The first Mothers of Invention album spelled it all out for me. It gave me a working critical theory in a language I could metabolize.

Smoke some killer weed and freak out the straights. Expose and undermine the falseness, obliterate the myth of the "natural" order. Long before I grasped the Frankfurt School's critical theorists and the meaning of reification, freaks and reefer convinced me reality was a socially constructed scam. "They" (the power elite, the Establishment, the Man) might be invisible, but you knew there was an agenda. A song like "Help I'm a Rock" expressed every feeling I had about my life in a language nobody could teach me. Even now, I can't properly explain it, but if you listen, you'll see.

Perpetrating a freak-out in Belle Harbor involved dressing up in drag, using the name Johnny McNulty, after my beloved orange metal dildo pole. I'd convince younger, impressionable neighborhood boys to cross-dress with me. We'd walk around arm in arm, strolling down the tranquil streets. I'd monitor how people reacted to us. Did we make them notice? Were they uncomfortable? Any disruption, any blow against the empire was considered a victory. Goofing on people, playfully teasing, blowing their minds. Why bother engaging straights in a direct political argument? We were well past playing their language game.

Considered the most caustic iconoclast of the rock & roll era, Zappa mixed silly frat-boy scatological lyrics with brilliantly eclectic musical experimentation. I also credit him for turning me into a lifelong noise-head. In an age when plastic people in brown shoes ruled the land, Zappa railed against hypocrisy and made nonconformity his credo. At a time when any "incorrect thought" was outlawed at home, forbidden at school by authoritarian warehousing technicians (teachers), and blocked by mainstream media running dogs, Zappa was obsessed with free speech.

A latent anthropologist, the Greek-Sicilian-American composer deciphered the nuances and textures of American society like no other. In the days of the Soviet clampdown, Zappa's music inspired the Czech underground. They tried to make him an ambassador, but the U.S. government declined. Zappa later challenged the PMRC on behalf of music, and according to my sources, he once dated feminist icon Barbara Ehrenreich.

Blasted or not, Zappa's music provided a much-needed intellectual base for my personal alienation. I could tease out the rebel yell in other music, but the Mothers served it up like a dirty hot dog. I sat smug in the knowledge that if I was in fact different, it made me feel superior and I knew I wasn't alone. The freaks were not the imaginary friends from the radio under my pillow. No longer a school yard intruder or a slumming interloper, as a *head* I was legitimately "part of." Included, accepted, I shared a vision with an entire universe of twisted kids. Across America, kids were freaking out *in Minnesota, min-mini-mini-so-ta.* In my room, in my head, even in Belle Harbor. It wasn't just me, it was everywhere. This was the power of subculture to permeate an empty life and to offer instead a world full of meaning.

Like all boomers, I listened to Hendrix obsessively and entered into lengthy debates comparing and contrasting the guitar gods—Clapton, Page, who rules? Who cares? Zappa's music was something else entirely. Serious and silly, critical and retarded all at the same time. Zappa allowed me to place sock-it-to-me pop culture against a serious yeshiva backdrop. Some people got the truth from Dylan. But Zappa's music provided the high-pitched tonal qualities I needed to metabolize the message—like the chimes and bells I first heard in "The Purple People Eater" and later in "Time Has Come Today." A song like "Who Are the Brain Police?" released the flow of *something* chemical—even when drugs were not involved. I carried this wisdom everywhere—at Cretin soirees, on the Lowlife, at school.

Thanks to all those horny GI dads returning home after the war, Far Rockaway High School was so crowded, so infested with boomer youth that we had to be placed on triple session. That meant thousands of kids constantly shuffled in and out, making it easy to slip away unnoticed. Getting up at six A.M. to be bussed for school, I had ample time to smoke my first joint of the day in the basement without intrusion. I was still high for English class at seven forty-five.

Eventually the youth quake festering around my high school required police presence. The kids in the housing projects had come of age and white suburbia saw the seeds of H. Rap Brown and Eldridge Cleaver germinating in their eyes. The actual minority presence at the high school was extremely small. Some kids of color were visible as athletes, musicians, or popular personalities. Most were hardworking and family oriented. They sat quietly on the Lowlife, well groomed and serious. But a growing fear of encroaching darkness and youth in general was taking hold, so we had the police.

The best thing about Far Rockaway High School was that they left me alone. Like I said, I never joined any clubs or teams or made any honor societies. Absolutely nothing is written under my name in the 1968 yearbook. It is an empty space, reflecting what I contributed and what I got back in return. I liked going to school, because after the initial rush of the Lowlife, it was an easy escape. At Beth-El if you wanted to remove yourself, you had to space out. I had a highly developed capacity for out-of-body experience long before I hit high school or the solvents.

Far Rockaway High School offered me a brand-new portal. Physical escape was simple if you knew the exit plans for the day. When that seven-minute bell rang, you ducked into the ladies' room for a quick smoke, then you hit the staircase. When the final bell rang, you made your move, hall monitors be damned. Then, anything was possible. On those days I went to school in an alternative arts program funded by the A train and the City of New York. The application process involved a subway token and a dream.

The Imperial Miss of the Earring Business sold handcrafted jewels on the beaches of Belle Harbor. She was older, more beatnik than hitter, although like any adventurous Jewish girl, she too knew the Irish boys. Miss hated everyone and everything; her rants were withering tirades in the tradition of latter-day misanthropic lit, prefiguring Lydia Lunch. Miss was my primary connection to Greenwich Village. She frequented the cafés and knew all the cool stores. She took me to the Conrad Shop on MacDougal Street to get my ears pierced. Conrad looked like Curly from the Three Stooges, but he was mean. He would puncture your lobes for free if you bought a pair of earrings. As he rammed the gold spike into my virgin flesh, he kept yelling, "Stop moving your fucking head!" We called him Conrad Sadist 'cause he really enjoyed his work, making little hippie girls bleed.

While I was still teasing my hair, the culturally progressive Miss was stomping around Belle Harbor, her head wrapped up in a kerchief, big silver earrings, strumming Buffy Sainte-Marie on her acoustic guitar. She always carried it on her back, her pearls before swine. Miss was the first bohemian I ever knew; she eventually moved to Forest Hills and majored in accounting. She retired at thirty, went to live in the tropics, and never returned.

I met Miss years earlier when we were children on the beach with our mothers. According to Betty Bradley, the moms figured since both of us were fat, we might as well be friends. But we didn't really click until the banana peels. In a doofus attempt at early drug addiction, we'd bake the banana peels and then scrape off the insides and smoke it, following Donovan's lead. Donovan's electric folk music worked well against the idyllic backdrop of Belle Harbor. Fauna, flora, *mar y sol,* we could imagine ourselves somewhere in the hills of England. Meantime, my basement was full of bored suburban teenagers just trying to get a buzz. The baked peels were supposed to get us all mellow yellow, but nothing ever happened except a big mess in the kitchen and lots of choking. I don't exactly recall where or how we located real marijuana, but Rockaway was always a land of milk and honey when it came to finding drugs. After one of the thieves got busted, he asked me to hold his stash. I sold off some clumps here and there, sent the thief his cigarette money, and kept my commission.

I was able to use my influence as a small-time pot dealer to lure young Belle Harbor boys up to my room. I never thought of them as sex toys, boyfriend material, or even as guys, except once. He was tall, dark, handsome, moody, and depressed. We called him the U.L. (Unsuspecting Lame) because he seemed so clueless. Smitten, I sacrificed my virginity to the unworthy cad. Little did I know that the shy, quiet U.L. had systematically deflowered us all. He was like the slimy protagonist, Telly, in Larry Clark's chicken-porn fiesta *Kids.* Good talker, so sweet and sullen. Meantime, he was worming into your pants.

U.L. was a few years younger than me; scandalous in the age of Mrs. Robinson. Because of my long-standing notoriety as a large, outrageous girl, U.L. treated me like a filthy treasure, keeping our affair a secret. He was as ashamed of me then as I am of him today.

Nights were much too busy for homework, and by day I had other plans. Head into the city, dashing out of a side door at the high school, I'd hole up at Ellie's candy store right near the subway. Ellie's was the truant's safe house, a sanctuary, an after-hours alternative high school. Tuna on white toast and a Coke, some candy and a pinball game; that was social studies. Pick up the A train to Times Square, play more pinball, hit the Village, smoke cigarettes, and talk to black guys; that was anthropology class. Measure the week's dope, sell off a few nickels; that was calculus.

Miss never played hooky or sniffed glue. She was brilliant, secretive, and unusually high-minded. We only got along when we were stoned, which was most of the time, so we were good friends. After a while we spoke in cryptic reefer-coded rhyme. As we all know, pot does make people very stupid. Since I was tall and she was short, we crafted a little jingle for whenever we were gonna smoke: *"Gigantor and Minute, encountering some poot."* That was English class. Then we'd bust out with some ice cream, bagels, fries, and Cokes. As any real woman knows, pigging out is a form of sex education. I used to think women overate because of our sexual repression as females. But maybe the reverse is true. We have sex to suppress our real desires, to stop ourselves from thinking about ice cream, cake, and cookies.

Geography class involved compulsively hitchhiking around Xanthos, destination anywhere. To the Five Towns, to Brooklyn, anytime with anyone, blindly trusting in the earth's good bounty, always feeling protected. We'd pile in a car with some cute boys. The ride itself was the high, sick kicks, top down in winter, screaming obnoxious teenage girls. We ended up at parties in strange neighborhoods, fearless, invincible. We only had trouble once, when I invited my friends up to my neighborhood.

The night my boardwalk associates and I hitched back into the arid lands of Belle Harbor, the Celts were on the warpath. They bombarded us in a presexual courting ritual involving egg throwing and ambushing us on lawns. The Far Rockaway girls found this exhilarating, not frightening. So it escalated, moving farther into Neponsit, careening toward date rape. We took swift refuge in the basement of a mother who recognized me. Two kids my age sat sedately subdued in the family room, astonished. The Neponsit mother looked after me like I was one of her own. She protected and sheltered us till it was safe. There was a bottom line: Even a wild girl who imported her thrills from alien subcultures and distant geographic terrain remained part of the tribe. Sometimes these mothers did cut me slack; after all, Betty Bradley was in show business. So I got special consideration.

Betty Bradley was a great believer in letting me learn life's lessons from personal experience. My art teachers had told her I had great freedom of expression and a strong color sense. I had a sculpture on display at Lever House, a landmark of modern skyscraper architecture in New York City, another fluke, like the prize essays at Beth-El. My potential as a talented artist lead to a brief summer job cleaning paintbrushes for the watercolor class at the beach club at Breezy Point. I finally had my ticket in. The Breezy matrons were very friendly; they thought the art teacher was Italian.

The promise of going to art school to become a great painter like my aunt Naomi excused all manner of deviant behavior in the name of my budding creativity. I was lazy, undisciplined, couldn't draw a straight line. My paintings made Betty Bradley think I was suicidal like Aunt Naomi. But I milked it. For example, my musician parents knew we were "lighting up" and "smoking tea" in the bedroom. They could smell it coming from the basement and the bathroom, too. I guess they figured we'd get over it. Some of us didn't.

Maybe they even noticed Muggs nodding on the floor after the spike in his vein took all feelings away. As musicians in suburbia, my parents were the inverse of new immigrants trying to negotiate the old-world values in a new country. They were hip, the rest of the world was not. They relied on me like a newly Americanized first-generation Korean-American devoted daughter who helps her traditional parents understand the ways of the new culture. They depended on me to explain the norms of suburbia and to regulate myself accordingly. Mom had Librium, D.O.M. had a liquor store, and I was stoned. *That* was high school.

Still, I loved my parents deeply and took pains never to do anything too sick around them. I didn't want to hurt them, not ever. I only fucked that up once, when I came home tripping in the middle of summer. I crawled into bed, fully dressed. I was freezing. I pulled all the blankets over me, ninety-five degrees outside, the lights still on. I just sat there grinning. The ceiling was a multicolored paisley swirl of colors, high-gloss wallpaper. The walls had been painted hot pink to cover the India ink. India ink had been used in a mural, a bedroom art project that involved depicting Muggs heroic with the needle amidst terrifying beaks and claws, remnants of psychic debris from previous trips. Bad trips always ended with the birds. Now they were crashing through the paisley ceiling. I should have known better and buffered the dose with antihistamines.

Or maybe file a class-action suit, *Boomers vs. the Estate of Alfred Hitchcock*. After *The Birds* I was phobic about anything with wings. Earlier that evening I'd been walking through Neponsit, tripping, heading toward Riis Park. The acid was bad, black beaks and busted wings bled through the sky, obliterated by rocks, smashing against them. Bumming, I went home to forage for sedatives, anything to shift the chemicals. I got into bed, but the birds came back. I was fighting them off when Betty Bradley came into my room and saw me swaddled and grinning.

The Hollywood lush thrush started freaking out, screaming that I was going insane, I was gonna jump out of a window like Art Linkletter's daughter. Why was I doing this to her? Then she made me take her pulse. See? I was giving her a heart attack. Now, tripping my brains dry, barely able to function, I had to comfort her. The GI Generation never comprehended acid, and Jewish parents always made everything seem apocalyptic. And like most of Jewish history, it usually got worse before it got better.

"1969"

7

THREE DOLLARS AND A PRAYER

The Mamas and the Papas said the darkest hour is just before dawn. Just as I was beginning to see the light, I'd get blinded by it. I'd soar and kiss the sky. Then I'd nosedive hard, wallow in misery, only to resurrect myself and repeat it all again at a later date. It always happened like that. In time I came to understand it as a karmic law, a phoenix rising, the governing rhythm of my life. And so it went.

The phoenix appears in many forms. In the myths of ancient Egypt, the phoenix represents the sun that dies at night, reborn in morning. It appears as a god of Phoenicia, a sun god, a combative male symbol. Early Christian traditions adopted it as a symbol of immortality and resurrection. Eternal, in metaphysics the phoenix represents the spontaneous regeneration of spirit and matter. Astrologers relate this continuous cycle of birth, death, and rebirth to the influence of the planet Pluto prominently placed in a horoscope. It is associated with individual transformation, purification, and strengthening of the soul by fire. Thanks to Betty Bradley's merciful reconfiguration of my birth time, I got the power.

FOR Donna L GAINES   26901

No. 26

PAID AUG 12   19 70   1-337/260

PAY TO THE ORDER OF CHAMBERLAYNE JR. COLLEGE $ 3 00/xx

THREE   00/xx   SEP 2 1970   DOLLARS

The Amalgamated Bank of New York
11-15 UNION SQUARE
NEW YORK, N.Y.   1-0337
0260

Donna Gaines

⑆026⑈033 7⑆   07⑈5700 70⑈   ⑆0000000 300⑆

"Three Dollars and a Prayer."

It's hard to remember when the image of the phoenix rising entered my imagination, probably in my room, off *Abraxas,* the Santana album. Today a phoenix flies opposite my dragon, next to my Japanese fighting fish and lotus blossom, all part of a half-sleeve tattooed on my left inner forearm. The left side of the body corresponds to the right side of the brain, the creative place where dreams are born.

My first epiphany came right after high school. I had graduated at seventeen with a seventy-five average. The fact of an academic diploma made me a noted scholar among my peers. In the '60s, getting a college education was a very different proposition. Today, middle-class kids start squaring off for grades in pre-K as parents scramble to hire tutors. Back then, school was cheap, a rite of passage for slackers. Of course, there were always serious, upwardly mobile kids working hard, trying to break out of poverty, young Republicans gearing up to take over the family firm, disgruntled draft deferment slaves, or movers and shakers. But for a whole class of mid-range boomers, college was a place for social experiments, anomic drift, sexual and chemical adventurism, and above all, "finding yourself." Few are willing to admit to this now, but being a fuckup in those days was de rigueur.

In practical terms, going to college meant you dropped out a few times, changed your major, took a year off, and then you somehow "got it together." By 1969 I was a two-time dropout and I wore it like a badge. I too was part of the revolution, fighting the Establishment.

First came Rider College, Trenton, 9, New Jersey. America didn't even have zip codes then. I spent two months hanging out with the other art majors and drama kids, seeing Tommy James and the Shondells and Ravi Shankar. One night I forfeited a free Donovan ticket to study for a biology exam. A month later I dropped out.

Rider College was full of fun-loving Jersey kids, party people who commuted from places like Piscataway and Elizabeth, great cars, shiny Trans Ams, Dodge Chargers. But I had trouble eating and sleeping, I couldn't concentrate. I had to get back to Belle Harbor. I was afraid of life and I wanted to go home. I told Betty Bradley I wanted to drop out.

The whole idea of going to college in the first place had come up as an afterthought. Like, "Oh, so high school is over? Well, now what? Why not go to college!" Like we ran out of ketchup, so why not use mustard instead? There was no discussion or consideration of what to do with my life, what college I should apply to, what to major in. Betty left that stuff up to me. Now the mustard was tapped, but Betty Bradley had a plan. I should go talk to the school shrink, set it up so it looks like I'm having a nervous breakdown. To Middle American parents, therapy was more evil than Hanoi Jane (Fonda). "They just take your money and turn kids against their parents."

This visit to psych services was not for therapy. Mom figured I should get something medical on my record, just to cover myself. That way, if I ever wanted to go back to school it wouldn't look like I was a fuckup. I would just look fucked up. Medical excuses for anything were like amnesty against life, a furlough from one's worldly obligations. For example, I had been able to avoid swimming at Far Rockaway High School by getting a note saying I was allergic to chlorine. I was also allergic to amphetamines, but that never stopped me. I loved swimming, but I didn't want to be bothered changing in the middle of the school day. It would have ruined my hair.

So I went to see the Rider College psychologist. I told him I was depressed. Why? Well, you know, my father died. That excuse had worked for everything from nail biting to shoplifting. I explained, "I just don't feel right." In fact, I had never felt right. That much was true. The shrink looked at me and said, "It doesn't have to be that way." He was taking me seriously. I stared back at him blankly. *Oh no, I don't want to go there, I just want to go home.* So I thanked him and formally withdrew from school. For years after, I remembered what he said but never understood what he meant.

Back in Belle Harbor I decided to get busy constructing a plan of individualized study. I advised my mother I would be continuing my schooling at the public library, learning Spanish, biology, and reading art history books. Mostly, my lessons included stumbling, puking, and passing out cold. I'm alive today only because Pablo walked me along the beach for hours making sure I didn't overdose. A Neponsit doctor's son with chestnut ringlets and pale green eyes, Pablo came calling for me nightly, around two A.M. He threw tiny pebbles at my window— that was the signal. As parents slept in master bedrooms with private baths, thick wool carpets, satin curtains, and fine mahogany bedroom sets, we prowled the Rockaways foraging for cigarettes. The bar at the Newport Inn near Twennyninth was always open and the cigarette machine never ran out of Kools.

Window peeping between the trees, the night quiet and misty, talking with Pablo I recognized for the first time that I had a brain. Revving the gray matter, I realized I had been sleepwalking all these years. When we talked, I suddenly became alert. It was like speeding, but my thoughts were clear, clean, pure energy flowing through me. I was totally straight, no drugs, no booze, all this bliss from just *thinking.* Nothing had ever made me feel this buzzed, this alive. The brain riffing was a pleasure that lead to joyful communion with Pablo. I don't recall what we talked about. We probably didn't discuss books or art, because I never read and I hated art. We'd weave narratives, silly stories, fantasies about our family and friends. The linear collapsed into the associative and synchronicity obliterated chronology.

Our repertoire, our reading of Rockaway was our art, a private local stockpile of *Zap Comix.* Oral culture, folklore, social truths were revealed in a chorus of absurd humor, at once playful and hard-hitting. With Pablo, the teenage Swamp Foxes became the Cronies, Frankie Monaco was crowned Emperor of Cronieland, annoying Swamp Fox girlfriends became Cronie-Femmes. Pablo's cat Tiger was a Zen master lurking in the shadows quoting *The Kama Sutra.* Pablo dubbed the Un-suspecting Lame "Unsuspectos," thereby avenging my honor, dissolv-ing my obsession absurdo-reducto. In time, we had codified all of Belle Harbor. Pablo was my lover, but not my boyfriend; we were consorts, collaborators, colleagues. Pablo became the prototype for all the true loves of my life: Aries, arty, electric, arrogant, loony, and tender.

Pablo adored me at any size, on any drug, in any decade. Enough to make sure I had a place to sleep off my trip. Enough to rescue my dig-nity from jerks like Unsuspectos. Enough to hear D.O.M. screaming at me and to understand immediately, that it *never happened.* These episodes usually ended with me shattered, crying in my room, hands shaking, stomach churning, heart pounding. I was terrified, humili-ated, and trapped. Their house felt so big, cold, and empty. Tumbling, I had no center, no place in the world. It took me hours to calm down. Sometimes my mother intervened. "Donna's a good child," she'd whimper in my defense. Mostly, she took his side. He did it because he cared. It was for my own good. I needed discipline.

Once, Betty Bradley tried to reconcile us by threatening suicide, leaving a note, "No love in my life, nothing to live for . . ." A vial of pills was strewn across her desk. I took regular inventory of the drama queen's stash; she wasn't gonna overdose. But if I pushed the point, she'd ask me to consider how she would survive without D.O.M.? Did I want her to be alone? So I shut up.

A nuclear family blitz could erupt at any time. Maybe I left hair in the sink or misplaced his comb. Maybe I interrupted one of his tirades, challenged his assumptions on race, sex, or politics. The argument would quickly turn into a personal attack. D.O.M. would trash my credibility, calling me a worthless parasite. What did I possibly know about anything? After a while I got smart, I kept my mouth shut. I agreed with anything he said, no matter how ludicrous or foul. I just laughed or changed the subject.

When D.O.M. got angry, he talked to me like his father talked to him, like I was dirt. At eighty-five he would still be brokenhearted that his father never saw him play soccer, that his socialist parents ex-ploited him as cheap labor in their crummy liquor store. That it didn't even occur to him to stick up for himself, to ask for what he wanted. Bitter and frustrated, he'd say, "People stink." Like my parents, I was the victim of victims. But time was on my side. As sick as they were, my parents gave me much more than what they'd been given. Maybe that was the true measure of human evolution: how much *less* we hurt our kids in each successive generation.

As we all know, rape isn't about sex, it's about power. Well, parenting isn't always about love. More often it's about control, about having the power to establish what is the truth, what constitutes "reality." As such, any dissenting opinion can be perceived as a threat to that authority. And if the parents are really damaged, it constitutes an assault on their essential worth. The manifest function of the family is to provide socialization and nurturing for the child. The latent function is to drive us nuts.

Betty Bradley took a completely different approach. If I disagreed with her—about marriage as the ultimate life goal, civil rights, music, or even makeup—all logic broke down. She became a victim and I was a "piece of shit." By the grace of God she was short. I was tall. By age twelve I was big enough to stop her from slapping me. She was headed for my face, for my left cheek when I intercepted, grabbed her arm in midair, and held it hard. That was the last time. So now she controlled the situation through covert manipulation: How could I do this to her? Didn't she have enough with losing two husbands? She had to be constantly reassured that I loved her. It ended with my unconditional surrender, with a declaration of affection and loyalty. When she finally did die, I had no feelings at all about it. I didn't cry, didn't even miss her. I felt relief.

Besides the next-door neighbors, Pablo was the only person who knew about my parents. How they could be so insane one minute, then loving and compassionate the next. When my cat got feline leukemia, they spoon-fed him homemade chicken soup. About ten years after I'd moved away, Pablo got sick with a rare blood cancer. D.O.M. offered to drive him for his chemo treatments. Pablo withstood heavy doses of experimental drugs, suffered prolonged agony, and then died.

In teenage Pablo I began to see the possibility of bypassing the traditional role of female. At eighteen, I vowed never to marry. Feminist scholars would provide a generous political and analytic framework to explain my choice: Simone de Beauvoir, Shulamith Firestone, and Germaine Greer. Without them, I would have been classified an eccentric, a spinster, an old maid. I would have had no road map for an independent female life.

I loved boys and makeup, but that was as far as it went. I was a tomboy then and I guess I still am. Shortly after Herbie died, in my baby book Betty Bradley made a telling entry under the category "Baby's Likes and Dislikes." She noticed when I was almost two, that my four-year-old cousin Bobby was my favorite playmate. Bobby was the younger brother of Doris, Queen of All Sock Hops. My mother wrote, "I believe she prefers boys and men to females, probably because she's around women so much." Then years later, when I listed my favorite bands as Metallica, the Stranglers, and the Ramones, a perplexed female music editor asked if I was "male identified."

Well, let me see. I can't cook, and little kids really annoy me. I'd rather spend the day in jail than sitting through a bridal shower. I hate shopping, so I buy what I need at street fairs. I can spend hours at a computer show or in a record store, but spare me even ten minutes at Bloomingdale's. Even now, at a normal size with disposable income, I'd rather be cleaning my rifles. Coats, boots, hair, and eye makeup—okay. *That* was rock & roll. The rest was for Barbie dolls.

Growing up fat made me feel genderless. Maybe, too, it was safer to be a boy in a family with two generations of incest. Maybe I'm secretly a homo locked in a woman's body. After all, Betty Bradley was such a *diva,* like Judy Garland, Streisand, or Cher. But no, that wasn't it. In the days before sports bras and soccer cups, from the Swamp Foxes on down, I wanted to be where the boys were 'cause *they always had more fun.*

Yes, my will to stay free was based on more than gender politics. Iggy Pop said it best: "I don't need no heavy trips, I just do what I want to do." In between fathers, I had nobody telling me what to do. The autonomy I experienced was precious, rarely available to a woman at any age. Being alone, solitary, I was free to wander in peace and quiet.

Through a series of events, circumstances beyond my control, I had been granted a vision of an emancipated life. Who would willingly forfeit this gift, this possibility of freedom, for a dull normal life of secure detention under patriarchal house arrest (marriage)? No, I would be married only to myself.

I even had my own name. Derived from *Goldberg,* the name *Gaines* was a social construction to begin with. Although my anglicized adoptive surname was a by-product of American anti-Semitism, in feminist terms, I was freeborn. *Gaines* was not a branding name of female slavery. Mr. Gaines wasn't my real father, and *Gaines* wasn't his real name. *Gaines* had no meaning other than what I made of it. Besides being the given name of disco queen Donna Summer, "Donna Gaines" was an empty canvas. It's been my life's work to maintain that open space.

II

Teenage Wasteland, 1969. During the wasted years, a private art school was in progress on my street corner. The tsunami of heroin that had buried Xanthos now swept over Belle Harbor. Sons of Jewish doctors were stealing Demerol, practicing intravenous archery. Taking control, former Swamp Foxes became key players in the drug scene. They patrolled Beach 139th Street in Olds 442s, Mustang Mach 1s, and Plymouth Road Runners. Streetside, we traded cigarettes for rides in Ford Falcons, Dodge Chargers. Mopar cars ruled the boulevard. If you banged on the roof of Steve's 442, the smoke puffed out, and you got a free hit.

In the age of eight-tracks and collapsed veins, the Monaco home became a teen center: pool table in the basement, surfboards everywhere, a soda machine, weights table, and bowling games. Mrs. Monaco looked out for us. Sometimes Muggs slept in the Monacos' basement, in the back room. One night he turned blue and the Malone family sent him away again. Places like Phoenix House, Synanon, and Daytop Village were becoming the finishing schools for Belle Harbor's wasted youth.

Blackouts against blue skies, unconscious amidst such a beautiful landscape. Spoiled kids on 'ludes cracked up cars, and Dad cleaned up on the insurance. "Concerned" parents became antidrug vigilantes. They spied on us from their rooftops with binoculars; then campaigned to send us all to rehab. Surf Yippies-in-training thanked them with beach wall graffiti DON'T TREAD ON ME MOTHERFUCKER. The evil ringleader was the same *yenta* who had once warned Belle Harbor mothers not to let their daughters be seen with me. Now she had an entire population of misfits to malign. Whenever the ringleader approached us, we'd signal by pointing to our rings—code name the *Ring*. Lord of the Rings, the biggest *yenta* in town.

First came the intentional suicides, unhappy teens alone in their rooms, friendless and forlorn. Then came the secret deaths from anorexia, private girl worlds of pain. The parents were clueless, powerless to stop any of it. They kept crying and blaming the drugs. It took a few heroin overdoses for everyone to wake up. Some switched to pills, others surrendered to drug treatment. The lucky ones left town, followed the wild surf, out to California or Florida looking to start over. The rest, like Pablo, went to college and never returned.

School was always the place you told your parents you were heading if you could just get yourself together. Now everyone went around saying, "I'm so fucked up." I had plenty of company. Every night, cotton balls. By three A.M. a crusty white gunk had usually settled into the corners of my mouth. Slinking around for zero-hour joints, I was selling beaded jewelry and candles on the beach. This was my look: long, sun-bleached stringy Janis hair wrapped in a kerchief, enamel-painted earrings dangling, homespun beads draped over a purple Danskin leotard. Ratty and frail from speed, greasy, so skinny my jeans hung down almost to my pubes. A strip of embroidery meticulously mapped out was sewn down the left leg of my raggy bells, fruit of an all-night Cream-fueled crank ritual.

Painting lurid, dark imagery by day, hanging on the corner by night, I was a resident scholar, part of the residue freak population. But something was in the air and it was gonna hit hard. I felt it dragging me out like riptide, so far offshore I couldn't see my markers. I couldn't get back, couldn't catch my breath. I kept tumbling in the waves, each one pulling me farther and farther out.

I had a boyfriend, a hardcore Brooklyn hippie I'd met on the beach. Fuzzball was a Deadhead with a VW bus. He was older, and he took me to all the shows, but I quickly forget them. I couldn't pay attention. I was busy jamming in my head, jumping in my own skin, worrying about my parents, about what to do with my life, rehashing everything I said that was stupid, whatever I did wrong, always feeling guilty, wound up, and tense.

By September I had enrolled at Chamberlain Junior College in Boston, majoring in interior design. After two months in a zombie zone, I contracted pleurisy, probably on purpose. Fuzzball had dropped out of the community college near his house in Brooklyn, started working construction, and joined the union. He quit his job and moved to Boston to be with me. That lasted a week because he couldn't find work and I realized I had no compelling interest in interior design. Again, I wanted to come home.

My devoted parents drove eight hours in a blizzard to come get me, with D.O.M. screaming at me for forgetting to get Betty Bradley something for Mother's Day, rehashing a blunder I'd made six months prior. They pressured me to dump the Fuzz. They scrutinized me from head to toe, accusing me of being too thin, of having a lantern jaw. Then, over dinner, they cautioned me about gaining weight. When I didn't, they said I looked run-down. I had no sense of myself inside or out. I would be body dysmorphic for the rest of my life.

Back in the 'hood, D.O.M. wouldn't let Fuzzball in the house—hair, odors, politics. My dad was constantly ranting against the hairy college kids like he was Archie Bunker. "Look at them, spitting on the flag. I've watched boys die for that flag, lose their arms and legs. What do these filthy bastards know? Daddy is paying their tab while they screw around like animals."

Most of my friends thought my father was a reactionary fascist. D.O.M. was an angry white male. He had a broken heart and some anger-management issues. Mostly, he hated the world for not being a better place.

Meantime, Fuzzball had pipe dreams of splitting for the coast or else making the B.T.E. (Big Trip East—to India). He wanted me to go. I said, "I'm not leaving the corner and I can't leave my mother. I'm an only child. She would die." It was unthinkable for me to leave her, ever. Not for school, not for love, not even to live my own life. Symbiotically enmeshed, I needed her, too, desperately. Somewhat confused, Fuzzball wondered, "Uh . . . Donna, you're over eighteen. How long does this *bond* continue?" Ugh! He understood nothing.

I had followed the Fuzz to Dead shows. I enjoyed the rapture of shake and bake, swaying to the music as it tickled and teased the flow of cosmic light within. I even snuck off with him to the festival of peace and love. The only girl wearing eye makeup at Woodstock, a maroon nylon miniskirt, and a push-up bra. Anxious and apart, dazed and disconnected from a nation of peers, by now reefer made me paranoid. It was impossible to tolerate without the covert aid of central-nervous-system depressants. Some nights I rode the subway alone, from Flatbush Avenue to New York City. Passed out on bourbon and Tuinals, I woke up in the arms of strangers; I trusted anyone.

A few months before I met the Fuzzball, I had been arrested. I subsequently developed cratophobia (fear of the State), a condition that generally affects anarchists and libertarians. Being detained against my will for the ridiculous charge of "Loitering with Intent Narcotic Purposes" didn't get me scared straight. It got me pissed off. That night I saw the horror firsthand, the potential power of the State over the individual. Banal, capricious, and arbitrary. I was a middle-class white girl, I had a good lawyer and bail. I was arrested on Long Island, where even the jails were clean and nice.

My prison notebooks: One night Miss of the Earring Biz dropped by. She knew some guy from Long Island, he was friends with some college kids from C. W. Post. They were having a party. I was already in my pajamas watching TV. My parents urged me to go, after all, they argued, I'm young, why sit home alone on a Saturday night? We crossed the border into Nassau County. At a lovely house party in Valley Stream, people were flirting, nothing heavy going on. But there was clandestine activity in the back room, the police had been watching the guy. They entered the house like an army, arresting everyone in typical late-'60s antidrug overkill. Just as they were busting in, the guy I was hanging out with came on to his trip. I was straight that night, so I was his guide. Now in handcuffs, we were all going to jail.

When I got arraigned the next morning, Betty Bradley started sobbing, a performance she probably figured would soften the judge. D.O.M. was pissed off that the bail was set so high, at five hundred dollars. "What a scam," he ranted on. "Corrupt bastards." In those days the Republicans made the rules, set the terms of patronage, bribes, payoffs. I spent the night in a Mineola jail cell—me, the demure Miss, and ten yapping Long Island JAPs. Once upon a time Miss and I swapped Nancy Drew books and experimented with orange blush-on. Now we were in a jail cell in central Nassau County with a bunch of whiny Long Island bitches. The lames kept threatening the cops, "Do you know who my father is?" Luckily, the police did know some of D.O.M.'s *salsero* buddies, so they were very nice to me. They even let me keep my earrings.

Miss and I sat there, tired, the whiny girls driving us nuts. We tried to play it cool. After all, we were decorated soldiers of Xanthos, veterans of the life. We knew to sit quietly. Ugh! Long Island girls with their blue eye shadow. We only wore brown. In the back, on the bench with us were three middle-aged black women. Bloody, beaten, charged with assault and battery, they sat quietly, looking things over.

Next day I was released into D.O.M.'s custody. The charges were eventually dropped. The law itself was later declared "unconstitutionally vague." This experience paved the way to a lifetime of libertarian convictions. I would become fanatical about civil liberties, would fight to keep the State out of my gun collection, my uterus, and my porn collection. This was my battle cry. By 2001 I would be an invited speaker at the annual convention of the Libertarian Party of New York, presenting my thoughts on "Women's Rights, Gun Rights, and Columbine." Party Chair Richard Cooper later asked if I'd be interested in seeking the party's nomination for governor at the 2002 convention in Rochester, but I humbly declined. Formal politics, even the Libertarian brand, was too scary. All this, thanks to a party in Valley Stream, on a slow Saturday night in April 1969.

After Mineola, I returned to street corner patrol, except now I had a probation officer. Miss McGurk drove all the way from Nassau County to Belle Harbor to interview me. Betty Bradley made her a grilled cheese sandwich. I staged a visit by one of the Swamp Foxes. He dropped by with a Hobie under his arm saying, "Hang ten, Donna. Surf's up!!" I figured the sun-drenched surfer image would make me look wholesome and clean-cut. By now some of Belle Harbor's surfing vanguard were on their way to becoming America's most notorious drug smugglers, but the Beach Boys had everybody fooled.

Miss McGurk was matter-of-fact, no bullshit, solid, a straight shooter. Something about her stuck in my mind. I figured maybe someday I could be a probation officer, too, be like Miss McGurk, helping messed-up kids. I even thought about applying to John Jay School of Criminal Justice. And some years later I did get there, an invited panelist at an international youth conference. A generation later, all the kids were fucked up and by then I was an adult, an expert on youth violence. People would interview me, quote me, hire me as a consultant. From Germany to the Navajo Nation, parents, educators, lawyers, clergy, and police would ask me why the kids were killing themselves, their parents, and one another. And I'd be able to explain. But so much of what I'd care to know about America's teenage wastelands wouldn't come from things I'd learn at school.

A year after my arrest, Betty Bradley got breast cancer. She was one of the pioneers, back in the days when breast disease was a private matter. No pink ribbons, no celebrities. It was not yet a feminist issue, just humiliation and subordination to callous bureaucratic medical care. Betty's Yiddish name was Basha, it meant daughter of G-d. That's what D.O.M. always called her. She called him Moishe, by his Jewish name. The daughter of G-d had two radical mastectomies and thirty-six cobalt treatments. Then false alarms, tears, and nightmares for another eighteen years. When Moishe brought her home from the hospital, still bandaged and newly breastless, the first thing he did was make love to her. She told me it brought her back to life, gave her the will to survive.

At a certain point, you know your parents think you're a loser. Long gone are their greater hopes and dreams. Now they only pray you'll stay alive and out of trouble. It was hot outside, a grimy July day in Brooklyn. D.O.M. was driving back from the hospital, where I was born, where Herbie died. I could see the windows where my deranged Russian grandmother Goldberg jumped, fleeing the Cossacks. Here, where Mr. Gaines died, Betty Bradley was now recovering from surgery. When I thought about her dying, I'd freeze out. Family policy: Don't ask, don't tell. So we said nothing, we just kept driving. D.O.M. stared straight ahead, I kept chattering, warding off my fear. What will I do now? September was coming and, as usual, I didn't have a plan. I was nineteen, a two-time college dropout.

The only safe place left was to cave in on myself. Now, only narcissism held me together. I was so different than he was at my age. Moishe was a *mensch,* already supporting his parents and baby sister on a waiter's salary. I was incapable of doing anything right. I didn't even try. I would just cringe and cry. Breast cancer just four years after their marriage, and the Cretins were circling around like sharks, cries and whispers, speculations. "You think he'll get all her money?" That same week, D.O.M.'s father, Grandpa Benny, was dying of colon cancer in a hospital in Far Rockaway. D.O.M. was flipping out, and I was on ice, useless.

D.O.M. had always advised me to go civil service; it was secure, good benefits, decent work. When he was growing up, respectable Jewish working-class kids from the Bronx trained at some place called Delehanty's in Manhattan. The Delehanty Institute specialized in preparing people for civil service exams. Driving home from the hospital, losing patience, D.O.M. turned to me and barked, "Well, you better go down to Delehanty's and take a course in filing." He paused and stared at me. "Donna, you have to do something with your life."

I was stunned. This was the first time any adult had ever discussed my future with me. And this is all he thought I was capable of? I sud-

denly realized I had only been fooling myself. What evidence did anyone have of my alleged "great promise," all that untapped potential I'd
smugly hoarded in my career as an "underachiever"? Unless I made a
move, all the world would ever know about me is that I was spoiled,
dumb, passive, intermittently fat, lazy, and unable to do anything right.
That would be my life story. The end.

I couldn't hold a job, I even failed as an Avon Lady, buying more
products than I ever sold, spending more money than I earned. I lasted
less than a week selling lingerie at Martin's, a department store in
downtown Brooklyn. Four days working on the 1970 census, a mint
job that involved sitting in the community room of a housing project
in Arverne translating Yiddish and Spanish for elderly Americans. I
was fired after I left the job site to make lunch for Fuzzball and forgot
to return.

It wasn't a game anymore, I was a bona fide fuckup. Overprotected
and spoiled, pampered and neglected. Half the time I was daydreaming, I never understood what people expected of me, I couldn't follow
directions, I didn't even know how to sweep a floor. I failed my driving
test so many times D.O.M. finally had to teach me himself, army style.
He actually wore a hard hat, like a construction worker. I passed.

The truth hit hard, like an iron butterfly. But tough love worked. I
had a challenge. I needed to show D.O.M. I could be something more.
He had to take care of my mother now, I couldn't be a burden to them
anymore. I had to grow up, prove to them, to the neighbors, to the
Cretins, to the world and to myself that I was not a piece of shit, a pathetic loser.

My more exalted class privileges had long been forfeited. Yes, I was
to the Park Manor born, expected to marry well, select a china pattern,
have a maid, get my hair done. Then Herbie died. The Gaines Empire,
too, crumbled. Betty needed care, now she mostly spoke to D.O.M. in
baby talk, shell-shocked, suicidal again, depressed. She needed constant
companionship, supervision. D.O.M. sold the liquor store, taking care
of his one true love, keeping her alive for another eighteen years. That
was his calling.

III

I was nineteen and my parents had effectively disappeared. Now, only the meritocracy awaited. My professors would parent me from here on in, restore me to my rightful path. In the end I will have exceeded my class of origin. I will fly high above anyone who ever judged me. I will be an intellectual, a scholar. But first, I must humble myself. I must ask for help.

Bottoming out always meant revelations, and this was a big one. A rude awakening led me to compulsive practical action. Stirring from the ashes, I shifted gears and moved forward at warp speed, a one-track mind in overdrive. I asked my father for a check for three dollars. That would cover the transcript fee and transfer my three credits from Chamberlain, in painting and drawing, my only completed grade, B+. I would be paying for school myself now, with a little help from the welfare state. Mr. Gaines was a veteran, I was still a minor. As a surviving child and college student, that entitled me to Social Security benefits and then some. That would set me up in a tiny studio apartment on Ocean Avenue, for $57.50 a month. From Betty Bradley I got Cheryl, a 1965 metallic green Olds 88, my first car, the last remnant from the Gaines Oldsmobile dynasty.

At nineteen, I left home for good. My bohemian love pad was in Brooklyn, near Kings Highway, just a few blocks from where Herbie once held night court at Dubrow's, Betty in tow, me in utero. One block from where the Denmarks hosted at the Elite Club. Artie Gaines's car on Herbie Denmark's turf; it was a safe place. I would make and sell beads, candles, and elaborate macramé belts to subsidize my resurrection. In time I'd sell antique clothing and jewelry, too. Rag picking with Betty Bradley had trained me well.

Scholarships and scams would keep me in school for a long time, until everyone had to call me Dr. Gaines. As one door shut, another opened. As the economy shifted and markets rose and fell, I would switch careers many times—photographer, social worker, journalist, youth activist, author, consultant, sociology professor. Someday I would truly love myself and my life. But right now, all I had was a three-dollar check from D.O.M., the promise of universal access to higher education, and a prayer.

I applied to Kingsborough Community College of the City University of New York, in Brooklyn. This was the school the Fuzzball dropped out of, in Manhattan Beach, not too far from Brighton Beach and Coney Island. Situated right on the water, the school was a hearty paddle out north from Breezy, bounded on three sides by the waters of Sheepshead Bay, Jamaica Bay, and the Atlantic Ocean. Sixty-seven acres at the bottom of Oriental Boulevard, misty, damp, barges. A seawall held the waters back, and the students got wasted there. Wafts of reefer clouded the student lounges, T-1 and T-2. Sometimes Kingsborough felt just like Xanthos: hip, scrappy kids everywhere, buzzed, teeming with life and the great expectations of American working families—the hope for a better life.

Today Kingsborough is a showcase among community colleges. Back then, in 1970, the buildings were mostly prefabs, trailers, old army barracks. The campus was part of a public university, higher education for the masses. It was not a pretty place. By the grace of God and the open enrollment policies of the State of New York, I got in.

Portrait of sociologist August Comte.

8

THE PRINCIPLE OF LOVE

s I entered the pearly gates of Kingsborough, I walked with God, pressing onward past the old rusting guardhouse toward enlightenment. Maybe sociology is now just an artifact of the '60s, obsolete like tie-dye, water pipes, and dreams of social justice. But once upon a time it was the queen of the sciences, *the* hip major, soaring high above all others.

Crack open the back door to the early 1970s, our professors were kooks; all fired up, angry, hairy, fusing social theory with breathtaking visions of emancipation and transformation. Sociology was sex and drugs and rock & roll rolled up and stuffed into a spicy, chunky burrito. Our educators were freshly minted feminists gorging on Brownmiller, de Beauvoir, and Millet, New Left utopian socialists who quoted Marcuse, Fanon, Cleaver, and Laing. Others were former priests and nuns who left the church after Vatican II, hoping to serve God in the secular world. In us they saw magnificent possibilities of transcendence, American youth were viewed as harbingers of social change. They listened to us, denied us nothing, they took us seriously, never punished, humiliated, or belittled us. They loved us *historically.*

Kingsborough was a benevolent parent, indulgent and generous, nurturing in every possible way—emotionally, financially, spiritually, and mentally. In the second semester I got money from the school to organize the Arts and Crafts Club. I ordered a full array of supplies—beads, brass belt buckles, rings, cord, candle wax, wicks, scents. All the supplies we'd ever need to make and sell our wares on the streets and at flea markets. As we all know, college radio has spawned some of America's greatest talent. Indie music itself got started with restless coeds playing disc jockey, scamming free rock product. At Kingsborough I did an occasional radio show called *Women in the Blues* in memory of Janis Joplin, who had died earlier that year. With a few phone calls and an official letterhead, I secured an entire library of Bessie Smith, Ma Rainey, and Big Mama Thornton recordings, courtesy of what was once Columbia Records.

Then came the Famous Flying Panzinis. Masquerading as a street theater troupe, we performed a deranged circus act that traveled all over the City University circuit, to Brooklyn College, Staten Island. As Angelina Panzini, I introduced my brothers, acrobats Vito, Guido, Tito, and Bruno. The Famous Flying Panzinis had convinced the theater department to create a course to teach us acting. Though technically an independent study, this was actually the first of many academically based drinking-club memberships.

Kingsborough offered education as a sacred trust. It was also my first positive experience of self in the legitimate world. Here I encountered adults in authority who treated me like I knew something, like I had something to offer. I read all the books, then asked for more. I spoke up in class, and after. I soon entered into a sociological loop, everyday life and formal knowledge, ideas and experience, theory and praxis. I took every sociology course I could, and it did not end there. I would spend the rest of my life slumming for sociology, searching for truth, plundering for meaning, a momentary connection, a reprieve. I would find joy where only misery was promised. Slowly, I came to believe that this was my calling.

Tricks of the trade, tools of craft, sociological concepts clarified so many things. My career as a teenage misfit and an outcast was dignified through the study of *deviance*. My identity as a "problem child," an "underachiever," was vindicated by *labeling theory*. My early forays to Twennyninth, Sixteenth, and Forty-fifth were *ethnographies, community studies,* albeit exploratory. The initial research findings of a lonely planet girl were further illuminated by theories of *race and ethnicity,* by *stratification* and the study of *demography*. I had felt like a vapor for most of my life, and even this was explained. In fact, vast bodies of knowledge addressed it. It was called *alienation*.

The idea that human interactions were governed by norms, and that we paid a price for violating them, clarified childhood experiences like the sex party in Mrs. Malone's basement. Growing up, I learned about social norms mainly by busting them, by trial and error. Nobody explained anything, so unless I understood something intuitively, I was in for a big surprise. So at five or six, in Mrs. Malone's finished basement, showing my stuff to my friends, I had already learned an important sociological principle: Deviant behavior *defines* the norm.

When conducting fieldwork, the researcher rarely has the opportunity to ask directly about norms, role expectations, and taboos. So sociologists who engage in participant-observer research generally rely upon an informant. The informant is an insider who coaches you on the unspoken rules of conduct, deeper meanings, and shared values of the group. This is crucial to the research process because unchecked, our researcher biases can lead to misinterpretation and misinformation.

As a teenage hitter wannabe on Twennyninth, I had two outstanding informants. Janet and Linda were wise women, generous and protective. They coached me in the ways of Jewish womanhood, and checked my behavior when it violated role expectations. By assuming all Catholic girls were *who-ahs,* I based my actions on a racist-sexist stereotype. I ended up chastised and temporarily excommunicated. This fiasco demonstrated that before any action is taken, a sociologist must check with an informant. All fieldwork should begin with a thorough review of the existing literature regarding the group's values, history, norms, and mores. And when in doubt, do nothing, take no action. Keep your mouth shut.

It was my introduction to formal sociology that made me feel ironically grateful for a ruptured childhood. Exposure to four extended family groups hand-fed me social class and cultural process as lived experience. The artifacts, linguistics, and manners of the Cretins were entirely different from D.O.M.'s family, the Denmarks, or the associates of Mr. Gaines. In less than twenty years my family of origin had undergone more upheaval than many nation-states. Sociology made me realize this chaos could be an asset, a blessing.

Having three different fathers catapulted me into an *anomic* state. Although painfully confused, normless, and clueless, I became flexible, immunized against any one regime of truth. I understood that the order of things could blow up at anytime, so I learned the power of faith. I was also exposed to a variety of myths and representations of masculinity—chauvinistic (Mr. Denmark), passive-aggressive (Mr. Gaines), paramilitary (D.O.M.), political (Grandpa Benny), and soul-killing (Moses Cretin and Grandpa Willie). Given this stellar array, how could anyone take patriarchy seriously? The doors of perception opened wide to feminist thought.

Whenever I smoked pot I always ended up thinking everything was bullshit. Sociology proved me right. The sociology of knowledge exposed even the notion of self as socially constructed, ideological, historically determined. Over time, I stopped taking things at face value, rejecting the assumption that relations or conditions were natural or given. Sociological knowledge exposed the doctrine behind the veil; it questioned the "taken for granted" world. Everything was placed under suspicion. Paranoia wasn't mental illness, it was the highest form of cultural criticism.

I read the great ethnographies, *Tally's Corner, Blue-Collar Marriage, Street Corner Society,* immersing myself in the lives of jazz musicians, pool hustlers, and taxi dancers. Street-based pleasures such as "hanging around" and "making the scene," done purposefully, were actually useful and established methods of sociological analysis. I had long ago cultivated the fine art of hanging out—traveling the Lowlife to Sixteenth, past the Irish Circle, Hammels, and on down to the boardwalk. Time spent on street corners, in train stations, and in candy stores of Rockaway Beach had not been in vain, the wasted years of a useless life; it had been fieldwork. I was a participant-observer, a voyeur for science, and I had a job to do.

My "freak-out" experiments—dressing up in drag and walking around Belle Harbor—were really early unguided attempts at *ethnomethodology*, the study of how people invent and convey shared meanings in everyday routines. My earliest critical thinking had been stimulated in turntable dialogues with Frank Zappa, on midnight promenades with Pablo, and speed runs through long yeshiva days. Sociologists claimed that there had always been marginal people, individuals and small groups who couldn't or wouldn't fit in. Juvenile delinquency was a social problem as well as an oppositional discourse. When I read C. Wright Mills's declaration that "personal troubles" were "public issues," I was sold.

Even now, like most people, I sleepwalk through most of existence. I do what I do, not what I say. Even educated and enlightened, I'm still irrational, emotionally retarded, lost in a fog like a drunken monkey. Yet, as I began to understand myself as a member of a race, a sex, a class, a generation, as a creator and consumer of culture, I saw that my personal experiences were both political and sociological. I understood from my professors that no matter how hip or smart I thought I was, social roles, rules, norms, mores, and rituals bound me too.

As sociological thought began to formalize my life into a coherent and manageable package, things started making sense. Even the most subjective experiences, like love, could be understood as sociological phenomena. In 1970 we lived in *the now*, traveling down the golden road of sunshine and unlimited devotion to sociology. The pleasures of discovery overshadowed goal attainment. We never worried about what we could actually do with all this useless beauty. Having a career or even getting a job rarely crossed anyone's mind.

Sometimes, there's a moment of enlightenment, a tweak of the psyche when the world suddenly makes sense and you feel part of it. You know you are being called back home. This exuberance is akin to falling in love at first sight, or a first shot of hard liquor, or the first three notes of a cherished riff. You don't know where it will take you, but it belongs to you, it feels so right you'll follow it against all odds. You really don't have a choice. So this was their gift. In passing sociology on to me, my professors handed me the keys to my own freedom.

Born on January 19—same birthday as Janis Joplin and Herbie Denmark—in 1798, August Comte was the French philosopher who coined the term *sociology* to describe his naturalistic science of society. In his early years at school, Comte was known to be a leader, a fierce republican and son of the Enlightenment. Disorderly, insubordinate, he was insolent toward school authorities. Like all the great sociologists that followed, Comte was a wacko. Throughout his career, he suffered depression and was hospitalized for a nervous breakdown, diagnosed with "mania," discharged but declared "not recovered." Comte even attempted suicide, throwing himself into the Seine. In his most productive years, he was troubled financially, had marital problems, and experienced ongoing academic rejection. He was often isolated, ridiculed by colleagues for his off-the-wall scholarly ambitions.

Comte forged a complex blueprint of the "good positive society of the future, a society directed by the spiritual power of priests of the new positive religion, and leaders of banking and industry." Basically, he argued, sociology would replace organized religion. Comte's scientific sociologist-priests would be, as their Catholic predecessors in the theological age, the moral guides and censors of the community. They would lead using the force of their superior knowledge to recall men to their duties and obligation. Comte's new positivist order would have love as its principle, order as its basis, and progress as its aim. The self-anointed Pope of Humanity yearned to see science—as practiced through sociology—displace theology, thereby anointing it the religion of the secular age.

Like Comte, all the great dead white guys of the discipline were passionate men in their time, psychos for truth and justice. Marx, Durkheim, Weber, Simmel, as Lewis Coser has shown in his *Masters of Sociological Thought.* Some drank too much and had love problems. Like most creative types, they were often volatile, unstable, except, of course, for Durkheim.

In his methodological masterpiece *Suicide,* Durkheim found the highest rates of suicide among unmarried men and the lowest among unmarried women, thus further convincing me, in a feminist leap of logic, that marriage kills women. Many of sociology's seminal dudes were maniacal, deeply engaged and absorbed in the world around them. After all these years, even in translation, the intensity of their work bleeds off the page.

Max Weber admonished us to embrace a value-free sociology. In "Science as a Vocation" the nineteenth-century German idealist and comparative historian warns us not to overlook "inconvenient facts." For example, if we find the by-products of Marxism and feminism as repressive as fascism and racism, we gotta say so, even if it ain't the party line. Incorrect thought can lead to higher truth. Unfortunately, the notion of value-free sociology was vulgarized long ago to legitimate sociologists not getting involved. Like if we do science, we don't have to give a shit. We can hover above the dirty world without making any intervention, as if science itself absolves us of social responsibility. Weber himself was very involved in the political life of his times. He admonished his students in a series of lectures to be vigilant, to be reflexive at all times.

C. Wright Mills was the Hunter S. Thompson of American sociology. A two-fisted man of letters, always marginal, Mills has been described by biographers as a flamboyant individualist. He died in 1962 at the age of forty-five. To students of my day, Mills was a mythic cowboy on academic sociology's arid playing field. A morally charged, high-powered radical polemicist, Mills died too soon, anointing him in our pantheon of '60s heroes—Janis, Jimi, and Jim, the Kennedys and Reverend King. Like Marx's ideas, Mills's had the potential to change the world. These radical social theorists seemed like rock stars to me, a suburban girl sitting there at Kingsborough on the seawall, playing air guitar. Like Patti Smith watching Keith Richards onstage, I wanted to *be* them.

My world was transforming into a lotus blossom unfolding with infinite intellectual delights. Mentors appeared everywhere—in the classroom, on the library shelves, and out in the streets. Sociology was gradually seducing me away from my parents, from Rockaway, from my neighborhood friends. I embraced my new deities with all the fever and faith of the newly converted. I had a mission. And so I went out into the world in search of sociological truth.

Today, most people don't even know what sociologists do. They think we are census takers, welfare examiners, or head shrinkers. Back then, who could imagine sociologists reduced to their current role as bureaucratic functionaries, lackeys serving some lame corporate university regime? Our heroes were not downsized "managed intellectuals," "knowledge workers" unfulfilled, neutered into submission, in retreat from the world. They were intellectuals, men and women of ideas, crusty, lusty, and mad.

Today, over thirty years after I cracked my first textbook, sociology has become a profession, a job. Life in academia sucks. I've met more drunks there than at rock & roll clubs. Failing to apply the very theories they posit, lacking imagination, many graduate programs continue to steer students into university positions even though jobs are scarce and pay is low. The tenure process annihilates the spirit in brutal ways and still they persist. The best and brightest are encouraged to labor for love of the career, for the vita, the department, for tenure and promotion. Avoiding engagement in the outside world, embracing banality, the gatekeepers reproduce their own oppression. That's sociology the profession, Sociology with a capital S.

But for so many more, sociology with a small s remains a spiritual practice, a vocation, a calling. I discovered it on the streets of Rockaway, and again, at Kingsborough. In time, I would formalize my vows and serve with unwavering devotion. Sociology would replace religion, illuminate truth, explain the ways of the world and my place within it. Despite the historical and structural conditions that periodically beat us down, most sociologists continue to labor for one thing only—for love of the world.

And, honey, that *is* the principle of love.

PART TWO

"Donna is . . . a punk rocker."

9

SLUGLAND

Hey Jawn-ny, wuh coluh are huh eyes?
I dunno, she's oh-ways wearin' shades.

had forgotten about the Shangri-Las until one night, when I found myself standing at the foot of the stage in a drunken haze at some New
York City hole like the old Ritz or the Peppermint Lounge. It was the
late 1970s and the Heartbreakers were careening through another fuck-
brilliant set. I was with Nick, my junko partner. Inseparable, we never
missed a show. Our day usually started around ten P.M. We'd get up and
have a cocktail; dressing took hours. Lean and mean in tattered shades
of black and blue, we headed into New York City, careening hell-bent
out of Long Island, past Queens, over the Williamsburg Bridge, destination *Downtown*. Blasting the Pistols or Television, a flask of cognac
in one hand, a Beck's in the other, steering with my knees. At the end
of the journey stood our great dark man, Johnny Thunders, cranking
his lead, Walter Lure on rhythm, bantering back and forth, in deep-
Queens dialect.

The Dolls had covered the Shangri-Las' "Give Him a Great Big Kiss" too, paying homage to three glorious hitter chicks from Cambria Heights, Queens. All douched with the grease-and-glamour hairdos, frilly blouses, and a sneer, what were the New York Dolls anyway but a girl-group tribute band? The first time I saw the Heartbreakers play, I was home. *L.A.M.F.* was the title of Johnny Thunders's first Heartbreakers album. I had bought the album in some shabby Lower East Side record store before I'd ever heard of Thunders, the Dolls, Ramones, or punk. I looked at the cover, the smirk on Walter Lure's face, and I knew it was important. New York City punk-glam fashion had appropriated a fair share of post-Elvis, pre-Beatles regalia; black leather motorcycle jackets, scruffy engineer boots, tight black twill jeans, dark runny fishnets, spike heels, hair teased and sprayed, and gooey white slut lipstick. "When I say I'm in love, you best believe I'm in love: L-U-V!"

Before I met Nick, I was a woman with a purpose. I embraced the typical ambitions of a middle-class baby boomer: to uplift the race, to give something back, to make a difference. True to the ideologies of my social class and generational project, I wanted to repair the world, *tikkun olam*. Since my resurrection at the pearly gates of Kingsborough, I worked very hard. My personal motto, Beauty fades, love is everywhere, but the career endures. I was twenty-eight, building my empire, I didn't have time for relationships. I had a mission.

While completing a master's degree in social work at Adelphi University in Garden City, I had received a fellowship for 1976–77. In a training camp for intuitive healers and petit bureaucrats I demonstrated superior analytic skills. As the first recipient of this award, I was the parameter of the population, little Miss Chi Squared.

My specialty was evaluation research. In the next few years I would work with administrators, designing and conducting formal studies to determine whether social service programs were working or wasting scarce funds. I'd establish objective criteria for the measurement of social work interventions. During the 1970s, as programs were slashed and burned, the job of a good evaluator was to help rescue the good ones and kill the rest. I was a market researcher for the helping profes-

sions. The work was detailed, pristine, and anal. Integrating and soothing for a person with plodding Saturn in prissy Virgo in the third house
(which governs the mind). I read Fred Kerlinger's *Foundations of Behavioral Research* with a passion, soaked up books on unobtrusive measures and nonparametric statistics and invented games for generating
random samples.

In April 1979 my first publication appeared in *The Journal of Addictions and Health*. It was titled "Female Alcoholics: The Men They
Marry" and coauthored with two practitioners in the field of alcoholism treatment. I was hired to design the instruments of measurement
(questionnaire, interview schedule) and perform statistical analyses. In
1979, few things had been written about female alcoholism and male
codependency. Our study found that men married to female alcoholics
were nurturers, devoted husbands who tried in vain to control their
wives' drinking. Often, the husband blamed himself for his wife's problem, as if her alcoholism was caused by something lacking in *him*. One
day, I would understand all this, firsthand.

After working in and around Child Protective Services for a few
years I convinced a nonprofit family-services organization to let me organize high-risk mothers into mutual-aid and self-advocacy groups.
"Preventive services" were cost-effective and they made sense. Adjudicated abusive and neglectful by Family Court, the mothers typically
needed help with addiction, parenting skills, money management, self-
esteem, and most of all, socialization. Many lived in isolation with no
family support and no means of transportation. They were poor,
stranded with their kids in a sprawling suburb.

Foster care sucked and it was costly to the county. I figured if we
gave Mom a hand, the kids had a better shot. In 1980 I coauthored "Involving the Parents of Children at Risk" in *The Many Dimensions of
Family Practice,* published through Family Services of America. In it, I
argued for more supportive services for families, especially mothers. Recruiting moms for the program involved hanging out on the streets in
the poverty pockets of Hempstead, Roosevelt, and Freeport. Given
Long Island's de facto apartheid, the only visible white people in these
towns were hookers, junkies, social workers, or cops.

White mothers of brown babies had settled there, too, cut off from their own kind as well as from their black neighbors. My groups consisted of mothers of all colors, angry women, wounded daughters who themselves suffered the longitudinal effects of family addiction, mental illness, and poverty. Their kids were trapped in a "cycle of abuse," where Mom grows up in a fucked-up family and then passes on what she knows. That's all she's got. Generations of kids get kicked around and forgotten, but they are still expected to be good parents. Nobody ever bothers to show them how to do things differently. We still assume women are born knowing how to deal with this stuff. I didn't know much about raising kids, but neither did the State.

Social service programs were caught in a cycle of abuse themselves. Every few months another service was cut back, defunded; clients were dropped, staff laid off. Once the mothers' program folded, I went back to the public sector and helped develop reimbursement systems between Nassau County and New York State. I constructed operational definitions for the most subtle and intimate forms of human interaction, quantifying phenomena such as "parent-child contact," "supportive services," and "affective behavior." I'd summarize my findings, report the result, and provide anecdotal examples along with statistical outcomes. I lived off the left side of my brain.

Although anecdotal evidence was generally considered the lowest form of proof, it grabbed the reader's heart with real people's real lives. I always included some ethnography, too. Because this was "science," we were forbidden to write in the first person. The dry, bureaucratic language of statistical reporting was as far away from human experience as you could get. But it was a welcome relief from strip-searching kids and asking them where Daddy touched them. That was my day job.

After hours, I kept moving sideways, stuck in a horrid mid-'70s music loop. The radio offered only punishment—California retreads, the Eagles, Linda Ronstadt, the Doobie Brothers, and America. In fact, I was so desperate I went to jam sessions with my parents, listening to jazz. That was a sure sign of death—their boring old-fart music. Isolated out there on Long Island, who knew that just twenty miles away a brave new world of punk rock was exploding with the Ramones, Patti Smith, the Voidoids, and Talking Heads?

I did like Donna Summer's "Love to Love You Baby" because the music simulated female orgasm, but I hated the disco scene. The clubs were lame *and* exclusionary. You needed expensive clothes to get in, and then you had to deal with polyester, bad drugs, and arrogant dicks commandeering velvet ropes. This was the antithesis of punk.

Disco music was sweet, celebratory, conciliatory, bliss based, and that made it terminally boring. During the "disco sucks" wars, charges were hurled against the rockist resistance: Hating disco was latently racist and homophobic. In suburbia, like America, most people are racist and homophobic. But that wasn't why we hated disco. In 1978 your average resistor knew nothing about disco's "subversive" cultural roots. In the rocker imagination, the genre was not identified as either black or gay. Disco was viewed as elitist (jet set) or reactionary— *Saturday Night Fever* Guidos.

Either way, disco sucked. The dancing fools banished the guitars, appropriated all the venues, displaced our bands, and relegated us to the margins. They sent us back to the basements and garages, to the old-man bars. And that was exactly where Nick hung out.

When I consider my life before Nick, I see my soul as an amorphous blob, weaving and bobbing, unformed, aimless, dulled by its surroundings. Here and there a glitter of light, a flicker of truth, but no clear vision. I was ambitious, competitive, trying to be normal, but with no sense of my worth, my needs, or myself. Although I had a career, goals, and objectives in the outside world, inside I was empty, disengaged, bored. I needed attention, divine intervention, and there he was.

On the night of March 16, 1978, I was coming home from a classical music concert. Mostly strings, it was a fund-raiser for the Levenstein Fellowship in Research. After the concert, I stopped off for a beer at Trimbles, a local tavern in Sea Cliff. I started talking to a local guy named Silk. He mentioned a St. Patty's Day party around the corner, and we decided to check it out. By three A.M. I had ditched Silk and I found myself alone, ranting and raving for more beer. Starting in about the music, I screamed, "This sucks! Get this fucking disco off! Put on the Sex Pistols!" The first Levenstein fellow had never actually heard the Sex Pistols. Before Nick, I had never heard of the New York Dolls, and I barely knew about the Ramones or the Clash. In fact, I was only wearing black that night because it was slenderizing, a concern even then, at a stringbean size. Drunk and disorderly, I raged on about the sucky disco music until he popped out of the corner like Al Pacino in *Cruising,* like Trent Reznor, and I was stunned. A punk angel, a warlock, Nick asked me darkly, sweetly, "You like the Sex Pistols?" And I lied, I said, "Oh, yeah!" *Sure, babe, anything you say.*

I was just a boring suburban social worker, a closet nerd, but he thought I was a slinky punk-rock chick. I figured him for a rich Roslyn boy, working for Daddy like all the rest. I was busy looking out the window for the Porsche. But Nick was a teamster, half Italian, half French, almost Corsican. Tell me, what could be hotter? He was a pool shark, a portrait artist who dropped out of college at nineteen and got a day job to support his calling. Everyone was always nagging Nick to go to art school because he was supremely talented, but he hated the thought of it. Besides, he had other plans. He was in a band. In 1978 everyone was in a band. But the Slugs were good.

As we exited the party, Nick put on his dark sunglasses and a long black leather trench coat. He smiled at me at the doorway and sealed my fate. As I walked through that door I said good night to that guy Silk. Good-bye to all the Silks of the world who thought I was just a girl, someone sweet to marry, have their baby, and live in a big house. Someone pretty to look at, willing to honor and obey. When I said good-bye to Silk, I said good-bye to any lingering desire for a "normal" existence, to being like everyone else. Nothing would ever be the same. Nick would be my soul mate for life. Welcome to Slugland.

On our first date we went to see Television at My Father's Place in Roslyn. We met at the bar. Cocktails always kicked off the evening. Nick drank vodka with a twist, I preferred Jack and Ginger. We smoked cigarettes and favored corporate drugs over the outlaw powders. I bit my nails, so I usually had a bleeding cuticle. Nick took the blood and slowly wiped it across his neck in an erotic, demonic minuet. *With this ring, I thee wed. With this ring, I thee bled . . .* these were our wedding vows, declaration of our eternal symbiosis.

In order to accomplish our soul union, it was necessary to expunge our former selves, to obliterate past identities and rebirth. That meant we had to change our names. I liked the way "Nick" sounded. Macho, sultry, and butch, it fit him. It was grittier than his Christian name—some garden variety saint. In turn, Nick never called me Donna. Too bland, he said. Instead he baptized me Tessa, later tattooing the name on his arm. Tessa was an obscure nickname I'd acquired briefly during my college years. Nick heard it once and never let it go.

Although it's always been my byline, even today, there are clusters of friends who never knew my name was Donna Gaines or that Donna Gaines was Tessa, the rock & roll girl they knew from the clubs. Donna Gaines was a successful, attractive, socially acceptable white-collar worker. Tessa was exciting, cool, sexy, and edgy, was always on the guest list, knew the bands, made the scene. Donna had strong convictions, commitments to social justice, and she worked hard. Tessa was amoral; she just wanted to have fun—anything goes, anytime. Tessa and Donna Gaines were discontinuous identities. I wasn't hiding anything. My two worlds just never collided. And back then, I couldn't image how to integrate them.

Nick and I worked late shifts so our jobs wouldn't interfere with our more important work. We lived together in the two back rooms of an old Victorian in Sea Cliff, on the North Shore of Long Island. In 1978 the scenic town was a fading bohemian enclave, full of mad Russians, aging hippies, artists, musicians, and junkies. Sea Cliff was magnificently serene, lush with trees, sunshine, birds singing, and children laughing. We hated it.

Over the years Nick and I made frequent urban excursions to see the Deadboys, the Clash, Lou Reed, David Johansen, Poly Styrene and X-Ray Spex. We became regulars at the Mudd Club and any show involving spinoffs of the Dolls, Heartbreakers, or Sex Pistols. We made fun of pretentious Patti Smith but loved Klaus Nomi and never missed

James Chance or the Stranglers. The Slugs played at most of the clubs, so we always got in and often drank free. Eventually, punk rock had its own brand of velvet ropes: the right look.

Nick named our living quarters the Emporium, a space cluttered with decapitated dolls, photos of band members, Nick's artwork, a jungle of plants, and wicca nonsense—black candles, incense, and Tarot cards. The dainty chandelier was festooned with multicolored plastic enema parts, gifts from Donnie, the Slugs' bass player who worked in an enema factory. With intrusive daylight blocked out by heavy velvet curtains, the Emporium was faux medieval.

Then there were the cats. Unlike dogs, they knew how to navigate a chaotic rock & roll landscape. They'd curl up, pass out, and still manage to look fabulous. First was Divonia Rose, black as night, rescued from a Dysoxen hole on Christopher Street, only to be run over on a Sea Cliff side street three months later. Helen was an Xmas kitty Donnie had found abandoned in the enema factory warehouse. She was presented to us live at the Rock Pub, the old man's bar where the Slugs performed every weekend. Later that week we also got Dennis, with his own set of Depression china, the gift of his doting godfathers, Rudy and David. Festo was a feral psychopath, a stray my parents pawned off on us in an attempt to gain custody of Dennis. Dennis died of feline leukemia shortly after Rudy died of AIDS.

And then there was Sarah-Ann, a Burmese we adopted from an ad Nick spotted in *The Pennysaver*. He liked the fact that the animal sounded a little off, high-strung. "Pedigree, must be in a home with adults only." We drove out to Kings Park, near the psychiatric hospital, and rescued the unstable beast from a suburban hellhole of noxious infants, toddlers, and canines. Our brown girl survived fourteen years of us, mostly sleeping on my lap as I sat at the keyboard, writing. She died at nineteen. Six years later, I would still carry her photo in my wallet.

Nick loved words. When he wasn't writing lyrics, he was drawing or solving crossword puzzles, palindromes, and anagrams. He read five newspapers a day, and his spelling was meticulous. Nick hated babies, my plants, and anything having to do with the occult. Dismissive whenever I sought to discuss such matters, he'd reply, "Tarot cards do not predict the future, planets do not influence our behavior, dreams have no hidden meaning, and there are no past lives." Burned out from years of Catholic school, Nick was an atheist. He forbade the Doors and outlawed the Grateful Dead on our turntable. He hated hippie music. I was gold lamé and rococo all the way, Nick was stainless steel and gray. I found his grim intolerance amusing, even sexy.

Symbiotic and reclusive, Nick and I gradually constructed a private linguistic system. Exponential meanings, tangential, cross-referential—even we can't remember the point of origin. After a while we communicated in idioglossia. And we only referred to ourselves and each other in the third person, even under duress. "He won't be going" (I am not going to that party) or "She was the one who went to the beach!" (You went to the beach without me). Speaking in the first person was too intrusive, too terrifying. It would have left us no boundaries at all.

We had a pact: Whatever was said or done while we were high would be forgiven, no questions asked. In the old days everyone was too drunk to fuck or to remember it if they had. By the time we got over that, twenty years had passed. As we know from Durkheimian sociology, the whole is always greater than the sum of its parts. Moreover, for some forms of social interaction, we have yet to construct the proper categories. Sometimes I called Nick my husband, but that was just to protect our air space, to avoid getting entangled elsewhere. Above all, we wanted room to move, to do whatever we wanted—alone or together.

For a long time I tried to explain our relationship, but it always kept changing. I had a one-track mind; one man, one God. Nick was more easily distracted, his sensibilities more diffuse. He didn't embrace monogamy or monotheism. He thought the former was unnatural and the latter illogical. After a while if people asked about our relationship, I just said, "It is what it is."

For the first ten years, I locked him into my car when he passed out. I couldn't carry him up the stairs. Some nights I'd put a pillow under his head as he slept on the cold, damp bathroom floor. The second ten years, he was the codependent caretaker who begged, "Tessa, please don't drink tonight." But I always did, and he always made sure I was breathing. In the morning I'd have to ask him what happened. Why did I have blood on my clothes? What had I done, where had I been? He drank more but held it better. Nick remembered everything; I never did. When I finally stopped drinking, it was for him.

Years after our unification, we were riding in a taxi, going from the rock & roll club to the after-hours bar, or the other way around. By then, punk music had evaporated into the New Wave: Police, Cars, Blondie, X. Selling out seemed inevitable. I wondered if maybe we, too, could go "New Way." Clean up our act, make ourselves more acceptable, like New Wave had prettified and mainstreamed punk. We'd get radio airplay, get signed, live a straight life, *be normal.* Crashing, on the downside of a buzz I would sometimes fantasize that I could have a normal life. But Nick knew better. He said, "Forget it. It's too late." I kept peeking, but he never looked back.

Nick opened the door to the life I have today. He was the first person I loved unconditionally, and he felt that way about me, too. Under the laws of rock & roll, the good girl will support and plug the band until the end of time. Even today, I still believe in the Slugs. Long after we have broken up and Leatherboy has started listening to Cole Porter, Rufus Wainwright, and k. d. lang, I've kept the faith. Years after I have parlayed my hobby into a career as a rock writer and Nick prefers the theater, I'm still on him. He's not even my boyfriend anymore; he hasn't been for years. But here we are, in a new century, and I'm still scheming, still hoping he'll get signed, and he is embarrassed. He hates that I mention any of this.

From the day we met, I took band photos, cut their hair, never missed a show, not even a band practice. I knew every word, every chord change. I was the Yoko in the studio, the singer's girlfriend, soul mate, and muse. Up until that point my sole ambition was to be a social worker, to protect kids, help mothers, conduct survey research, and do program evaluations. But that wasn't the plan. In spite of myself, God had something else in mind, and Nick was sent to deliver the news.

And so it began, my life as Tessa. One night in Sea Cliff, walking down Destiny Street, drunk at a jock-driven party, looking for more beer. There, in 1978, my entire future standing before me, eyes like deep dark chocolate moons, overpowering, charismatic yet so shy, smiling, asking if I liked the Sex Pistols. You see, serendipity was the first prophet.

||

Slugland fell over me like an Ethernet, covering me from head to toe. I surrendered immediately. I can still feel it, the stiffness of the K-Y Jelly we used to spike our hair in the days before all the groovy gels. The tight black clothes—ironic, contradictory, half hitter, half glam. Frilly, tattered, and dirty. Black leather coats and boots, dark shades, long earrings, amulets, spikes, ruffles, track marks. White punks on dope. I can still feel the booze settle in as the band tunes up. How the riffs warp after the coke is gone, how the toilet paper sticks to my seat. What's that smell? Blood, semen, urine, and booze, smoke rings wafting around my dark, lean sweaty boy, Newport dangling, his perfect ass bent over the table in an endless pool game. Nick gives me change and asks me to put on music. He keeps my glass full. I can taste it even now, in all the cocktails I still dream of. So many years after, Sluglife lingers in all my senses.

Nick first read about the New York Dolls in the *Daily News* as a teenager, a kid in the basement of his parents' suburban home. The writer described the New York City underground scene as somewhere between Keith Richards and Marc Bolan. Bad-boy rocker imagery subversively mixed with gala glam. The lead singer, David Johansen, was a Jagger knockoff, and guitarist Johnny Thunders was an edgy mutation of Keith Richards. They looked like transvestites, some mutant strain of the Jewel Box Revue I saw as a kid. But they were locals, kids from Queens, Staten Island, "bridge and tunnel" just like us. Nick didn't see the Dolls live till they played on Long Island, right there at My Father's Place, in Roslyn.

Quaaludes, pot, alcohol, and barbiturates. The mainstream rock establishment hated the Dolls, said they couldn't play, thought they were queer with all the hair, makeup, platform shoes, and sequins. But Nick loved everything about them. The heavy sound, the exaggerated Stones influence, the great songs and their sound, so powerful and raw. He bought their first album the day it came out. After the first show he followed the Dolls everywhere, to Coventry in Queens, and the Valentine's Day Massacre show at the old Academy (later the Palladium). Eventually, he was hanging out at CBGB's, checking out the bands. He befriended a waitress. She had a crush on him, so Nick was on the house list indefinitely.

Like most young suburban fanboys living at home, Nick's clothing was modified. An accessory or two would find its way into his wardrobe—a piece of jewelry, modest platform shoes, slightly longer hair, but nothing too outrageous. He came from a strict working-class family, Blessed Virgin in the backyard grotto, papal blessing on the bedroom wall. Nick hated sports. He was an artist. That automatically made him a misfit, case closed. Wearing anything more excessive would have caused big problems.

Like his father, Nick liked to play pool and he did it well. That's how he met Donnie, in 1973, hanging at the East Hills Tavern. Tall, thin, with long hair past his shoulder, Donnie always wore shades, even at night. He came from Cambria Heights. His parents had moved to Long Island as the old neighborhood turned color. White flight, white heat. At first Donnie hated Nick because "he was like Mr. Cool and shit." The Tavern had two pool tables. Sometimes they played all night, drank together, and talked about music. They weren't yet twenty, but back then the drinking age was only eighteen so the Tavern was theirs. Donnie had an acoustic guitar and a van, so they hung out in the bar's parking lot, too, in the van, doing dope.

One Saturday afternoon at the East Hills Tavern, Nick tried heroin in the van. The first time, it wasn't that good. But the second time it was a full-on frontal assault. Still, it wasn't his drug, Valley of the Dolls—pills all the way. For Donnie, it was different. His parents were very strict, "very Catholic," and totally devoted to their son. A top student at Archbishop Malloy, Donnie didn't start snorting dope till after high school. He met a guy at a car dealership who was on a methadone program. The two Long Island teens took periodic runs up to Harlem, hung around by the FDR Drive for a guy in a Galaxy to come around. Back then you could buy dope for four dollars a bag. Donnie mostly snorted until 1978 and then gradually started shooting. That was the year I met Nick.

A few days after the party in Sea Cliff, Donnie and Nick invited me to band practice. It was the beginning of my descent into suburbia's rehearsal underground studios and a long-lived devotion to local bands. Down in a basement studio across from My Father's Place in historic Roslyn, with its quaintly aristocratic duck pond, clock tower, and landmark buildings, I walked into an explosion of energy like nothing I'd ever felt. Nick and Donnie were both Aries, so the high energy was infectious, electrifying. The sound was initially more R&B than power chord, but aggressive in some spots and endlessly diverse. I needed nothing else. *In the beginning G-d created the heavens and the earth, and the earth was topsy-turvy.* This was creation, Genesis.

Imagine if you grew up in Australia. Your older brother works in some warehouse and he knows a guy named Bon Scott. One Saturday you're bored, so you end up at a dingy rehearsal space with a bunch of rowdy guys just fucking around. Drinking a Foster's, munching chips, passing a joint. How would you feel if you happened to stumble upon the formative moments of AC/DC? You're just there on your instincts, now you're tracking every innovation, noting musical influences, nuances, all at the very moment of conception.

Or say you walked into CBGB's on a blind date and you just happened upon four hyper kids from Forest Hills onstage chopping through thirty songs in fifteen minutes. Temperamental, cranky, upbeat, they're stopping and starting in fits. Fighting and screaming at each other, walking off the stage, then coming back for more. The sound is fresh and raw. Nobody has to pull you aside to tell you, "Excuse me, that's the Ramones. They're great. They will transform rock as you know it." Nobody has to draw you a diagram. You just know it. You don't need critics or DJs or record companies to sell it to you. That's how I felt seeing the Slugs that day.

The two suburban pool sharks had been friends for five years, and already their band had been through a variety of incarnations. Nick had pulled straight A's as an art major at C. W. Post, but after a year of college, he dropped out. He hated it. He had no interest in the courses and had already started fucking around with bands. Art school dropouts becoming rock stars (John Lennon, Joe Strummer) is all part of the mythology, up there with doomed couples (Sid and Nancy) or dying too young (Jimi et al.). It's the dark side of *that* American dream. So Nick got a part-time union job loading trucks, and that was good enough. Gas money, change for cigarettes and beer.

Initially, Nick started fooling around with some childhood pals, guys he knew from Catholic school at St. Mary's. They called themselves the Cheerleaders and favored sleazed-up, fattened, speeded-out covers of Stones, Dolls, and Chuck Berry. The drummer was a volunteer fireman so they practiced at the firehouse. The firehouse had a beer bottle machine. Twenty-five cents a bottle, cleared it out every night.

After a while the Cheerleaders rented a rehearsal space and began writing their own stuff. At first they played a party, then they booked a gig at a small bar right there in historic Roslyn. The guitarist was a guy named Tony who had a great look. Streaks in his hair, and oh, such clothes—coats and boots galore, but he froze up whenever he had to play live. He even bought Donnie a black Fender Precision bass. Tony was the heart and soul of rock & roll, but he couldn't play out, so Donnie replaced him with Matt, a Cambria Heights buddy. Gradually, all the Long Island boys were expunged except for Nick.

Matt had gone to Christ the King High School, notorious by the eighth grade for drugs and hitters. He had two brothers, one a surfer, the other a hitter. Matt was asked to choose, are you a surfer or a hitter? So he decided to become a musician. Matt gave the band a stunning rock & root pedigree, thanks to the hitter brother—a member of a gang called Lil' Renos. Matt swears one of the Lil' Renos dated Shangri-Las tough-girl lead singer Mary Weiss, and I have to believe this is true. Cambria Heights is the town that gave the world its two greatest Caucasian girl groups: the Shangri-Las and Reparata and the Delrons.

One day Matt was at the Billiards Hall and his bad brother whispered to him, "See that chick? That's Reparata." Matt was stunned. Everyone in Cambria Heights knew who Sister Reparata was. That nun was tough as nails. But the little girls adored her—that's why lead singer Mary Aiese had taken her name, Reparata. *Rain falling from the sky, bluebirds they don't cry,* Reparata, hanging out at the billiards hall with the Lil' Renos.

Matt and Donnie both happened to be altar boys at Sacred Heart. In the sixth grade the nuns asked for volunteers to play music at a folk mass. So Matt and Donnie became guitarists at thirteen, playing "Kumbaya" in their Sunday suits. By fourteen, they were riding that Night Train, flying high on Mad Dog, drinking sacramental wine, munching the host. The two hung around the Boys Club up on Linden and 225th, a place designed to get kids off the streets and away from drugs. Of course, like all adult-sponsored teen centers, this was the main place in town to score. In the swansong years of grease, as the Lil' Renos battled the Bridge Boys, Donnie and Matt formed a band of their own, right out of folk mass. You see, organized religion does play an important role in society.

Eventually the delinquent altar boys played shows at college coffee houses, and wine and cheese bars. Mostly covers, Crosby, Stills and Nash, and Donnie's favorite Beatles tunes. He loved those harmonies. By 1969 Cambria was turning black, and white flight was in motion. The hitters were becoming extinct—in jail, drafted, dead, or defected to hippiedom. Donnie moved east to Long Island and discovered heroin. Matt went west, to California. That's where he, too, stumbled on poppy.

As the Slugs generated spontaneously from the rotting carcass of the Cheerleaders, they needed a new drummer. So they brought in Scott, a Jewish boy who lived two houses away from Matt. With the addition of these two Cambria boys, the Cheerleaders became the Slugs. Nick wanted a name that was short, sounded tough, and had more than one meaning. The wormy garden slime, the bullet that doesn't really kill, Slug 'em all and let God sort 'em out.

Now, with the Cambria Heights connection, the Slugs lineage could be traced directly back to the original hitters, to the girl groups and doo-wop crews of my youth. To Twennyninth, the Magicians, bad boy Tommy, my pink frosted lipstick and signature metal teasing comb. Nick's compelling interest in the Dolls, Pistols, and Clash infused the band with a menacing edge and opened up endless new grooming possibilities. Donnie was never the same after Nick played him the Sex Pistols. Since he wrote the music, everything changed. With the Slugs, the roots of New York punk had come full circle. As in the Ramones, Blondie, and Heartbreakers, the hitter legacy was recontextualized in punk, with irony, humor, grease, and glamour. *Of course,* this was gonna be my band, my reason to live. Did I have a choice?

Donnie never had any money, but he was always lucky. A guy he knew from the enema factory had robbed his own parents' house. The guy was so nervous about it, he had to confess and it had to be quick. He ran into Donnie in the bathroom at work, dragged him into the stall, and handed over eight hundred dollars cash, half the money he'd stolen. "I just had to tell someone," he cried. So Donnie took the money and got a ride with Scott over to Sam Ash in Hempstead. He was going to buy a bass amp. That's where he met Louie, white snakeskin boots and all. The boots went all the way up to his knees. Long Island could be a scary place.

Punk faux pas like Scott's mustache and Louie's cock-rocker boots were enough to drive the Slugs' fascist axis (Donnie and Nick) off the beam. Nick was strict about dress codes, overseeing everything. No facial hair, no ponytails. No bells, ever. Keep it simple. When in doubt, paint it black. Button-down shirt, boots, skinny tie, dark jacket. Sneakers, preferably Converse. Work boots, engineer boots. No sandals, and never, ever wear Capezios. Wondering what his bandmates might wear the night of the show caused Nick great anxiety. Bad stomach often ensued. Unless he had a few beers, Nick lived on Pepto-Bismol.

Donnie was no fashion plate either, with his tortoiseshell aviator glasses. But he was tall, innately toughboy, and rockist, so he always looked cool. Born on Hitler's birthday, he could be a bully. Nick was more subtle. You didn't realize he was totally controlling your life until it was much too late. If you didn't stand your ground, Donnie and Nick ate you up alive.

Most people fell into Slugland innocently. Unless you were drunk, breeding, or working on a Ph.D., being part of a band was the only antidote to life on Long Island. Without it, you were a walking zombie. But boredom had its rewards, and inciting innovation was one of them. Louie was younger, a nice middle-class Jewish boy from Baldwin. Prior to the Slugs, he listened to middle-of-the-road American rock— Foreigner, Cheap Trick. He always liked guitar-god leads and eventually he left the Slugs for a heavy-metal band. Louie had taken some music lessons as a child, played in elementary school bands, but nothing serious. He was a college dropout who worked in a factory. His parents had some money, and Louie had a van. Donnie wasn't stupid. The van was quickly put to use moving equipment to gigs and rehearsals. Within months, Louie was taking rides to Harlem looking for that Galaxy. The white boots had disappeared.

Although there were punk and glam influences, the Stones were the Slugs' controlling metaphor for sound, style, attitude, and habits of the band. Role models, you might say. As he Slugged out, Louie started looking like Bill Wyman, Donnie was the affable junkie scumbag Keith, and Nick an imperiously eleganza Mick. Brian Jones and Anita Pallenberg worked their way into the Slugs mythology too, but that came later, after we met the CorpseGrinders.

Once Louie was in the band, the Slugs' lineup was complete. Louie and Matt were rivals, two lead guitarists in a chronic pissing contest, spiteful, malicious. Scott was a pothead. They eventually threw him out because he refused to shave his mustache.

An entourage naturally developed—a roving tribe of Slugwives, family, felines, and incidental friends. There were people who took photos, copped dope, worked the sound board, moved equipment, brought in new blood, hosted parties, and made the scene. Sluglife retained many traditional suburban rituals, among them, the family barbecue. Donnie's parents always opened their home for soirees. His mom was a sweet Irish lady who made knockout whiskey sours. Shamrocks, lace, and strong Irish coffee filled the air. We were always welcome, included at any family meal no matter how skeevy-chic we looked. Donnie's father was fondly known as Mean Mr. Drill. He was a tough teutonic guy, a trucker who drank with us and adored his only son. Donnie Drill once said his dad was his whole life, the only reason he survived. Having a strong father in your life can make a big difference. Especially for a dope addict.

In between gigs, band practice was High Mass. Rehearsal studios form the foundation of a thriving rocker subculture on Long Island. Some are regular dirtbag estates, stink holes with ratty couches, mildew, and bad sound systems. Others are lavishly high tech, professional, sterile. At first we practiced at the Bay House in the swamps of Rosedale. This was just a guy's house: old, big, surrounded by trash, flies, mud, and weeds. The Slugs had recruited Tommy Rosedale on sax, he was a virtuoso who played everything. All I remember about trips to Rosedale were fantastic photo opportunities near the marshlands. Slugs piled on my car, rockerboys posed amidst every manner of filth and wreckage in high-contrast black and white. I also remember endless pool games at local bars. Nick bought me drinks and kept me in quarters. I worked the jukebox, baby. An unexpected by-product of wasted years in seedy bars, clubs, and studios was beautiful skin. I never went out in the sun, rarely even saw daylight.

Eventually Louie got us set up at Babyface Studios. The south shore of Long Island was more demented, a perfect spawning ground for rock & roll. Joey Buttafuoco, Howard Stern, the Baldwins, and the Stray Cats prove my point. Babyface Studios became a suburban drug cartel in no time. It was right next to the Long Island Railroad station, an easy hop into the city. The proprietor, Blizz, was a studio stud, real old-world Long Island. Horrible white Capezios, red spandex cock-rock leggings, long curly hair, and lots of coke. If you didn't have money, he didn't want to know you. He had hidden cameras to videotape him fucking all the blond teenage vixens that passed through, young pretty girls searching for the glamorous life, barely of age. Then he'd preview his home videos for the band while they all got high.

In the age of the hippie, coke was the rock-star drug, for special occasions only—it was too expensive for the masses. Ten years later cocaine was a big disco drug, a yuppie taste treat. Widely available, it covered the nation like a blanket of snow, seeping into everyone's lives, even those of people who were married, with children. Eventually Blizz started dealing and coke became part of rehearsal, like the butts, the beers, the sound board, or Marshall stacks. One morning Blizz woke up with a gun to his head. The Feds busted him with three ounces of coke. He was arrested several more times on drug charges. When he wasn't in jail, Blizz spent hours compulsively vacuuming the studio carpet.

Once I was with the band, I always had something to do. I had a place, a role, an identity. Sluglife was a social group, a unit with the band at the core and a peripheral army of at least fifty more associates. Tribal, we created a community. It was also sex segregated. Nick referred to this gender culture differentiation as the Penis Parlor and the Cunt Club. At parties, the Penis Parlor (guys) went off to jam or talk about band stuff. The Cunt Club congregated in another room to discuss grooming, metaphysics, work, cats, or family. Even Louie's guitarist girlfriend didn't play with the guys. In the late 1970s, on our Long Island, the idea of women in rock was unheard of. But we couldn't care less. We had careers, cars, and nice furniture. We were looking for adventure. The guys were peacocks, trophy boys—this made us feel powerful.

People always asked me how I survived living in suburbia. Well, first off, I had the band. Then, I was drunk most of the time. And when I wasn't, I was busy calculating z-scores, contemplating intervening variables and spurious relationships. For a long time the only two places I felt safe were at the foot of the stage and in a university library, trolling the stacks for social science. Pouring bourbon or poring over microfiche. Thanks to the Slugs, I had a home, a family, a band, people who watched my back, cared about me, loved me no matter what I did or said. Forgive and forget, those were the bylaws.

Domestic bliss with Nick: Cocktails usher in the grooming ritual. Ongoing battles over who will wear Aunt Maggie's black voile shirt, who needs the mascara at that very moment, who is hogging the mirror, the blow dryer or bullying the turntable (always him, still). Several lethal fruit daiquiris later, we're sitting around the Emporium, *done.* The best thing about a rocker boyfriend is he's probably more interested in sneaking off with your accessories than doing your girlfriends. Regardless of how butch, how homophobic, or how misogynistic, he'll still let you dress him up like a pretty boy doll. They love to primp and preen.

Fusing Johnny Thunders's early hair with vintage Ronnie Spector, I hit the bottle. Administered L'Oréal Preference Soft Black number three, then tinted in some Crazy Color, usually cyclamen. I set it with fat rollers, sprayed and teased it all the way back to 1965. Nick slicked his into a DA, rockabilly, sideburns, old school, Vitalis forever. Maroon sharkskin tux jacket with black piping, silver crucifix dangling over his hairless, wiry torso. We generally skipped dinner, so our pants would fit better. Besides, an empty stomach always delivered a harder-hitting buzz. No matter how raunchy or rude, our deluded parents always thought our punk look was glamorous, like Hollywood.

"You never fuck me and I always have to drive." The best line in *Drugstore Cowboy* aptly describes Slug marriage. On Long Island it was typical to see a very attractive guy in his early twenties being driven everywhere by a pretty girl. When I first moved out there, I wondered what was wrong with all these hot macho guys, why couldn't they drive? By eighteen Nick was already a DWI outlaw. Multiple charges for drunk driving, car accidents, near-death experiences that resulted in provocative scar tissue. Donnie had warrants. They all had something. Back then, police were less likely to stop women. So we drank and I drove, and then we passed out. Sometimes we pulled off to the side of the road off the Northern State Parkway. The police were usually very understanding. They'd grown up on Long Island, too, been there, done that.

One summer day in scenic Sea Cliff, Nick and I organized a "punknic" at our lovely country house. As the band's self-appointed Ministry of Culture, we decided the only way to enforce correct dress code was to inculcate it subconsciously, while our friends were wasted. I regularly raided thrift stores for spectacularly sick garments and trash accessories. It was easy to dress people up while they were high, convince them that their new look was "totally committed" and easy to maintain. All manner of leopard-skin regalia, silver chains, and hair spray. Massive amounts of heroin, booze, coke, and pills accompanied a menu of Spam cutlets on polka-dotted white bread, and blue Jell-O molds covered in green-tinted Cool Whip. Nobody ate. We just liked the food coloring. I ended the evening passed out in a field across the street. How I got there, I still don't know.

Unfortunately, most of our friends failed to grasp the campy subtext of the punknic. This was 1979 and Sea Cliff was still clinging to the tattered remnants of hippiedom. At my social work job I took an immediate stage dive into the black and out of the blue. I was the only staff member wearing straight-leg jeans to work. Half curious, half condescending, they'd interrogate me, "Why are you wearing black?" The only thing they knew about punk was what they saw in *The Rocky Horror Picture Show.* These people were wearing brown clogs, peasant blouses, and denim bell-bottoms. They probably still are.

The enema factory Donnie worked at was near the turnpike town of Westbury. Making plastic butthole surfboards for a living wasn't very interesting work, just a way for young guys like Donnie to pay for beer, booze, and drugs. The company made bags, tips, and related accessories, items I quickly integrated into a little punk-rock belt. The company had a promotional giveaway they called the Penema, a Bic pen subversively inserted into a real enema tip. They also had a workplace slogan, "With friends like you, who needs enemas?" and unsubstantiated rumors—one of the vice presidents was testing out different models of enema tips on attractive employee volunteers. Still, the highlight of the workday was sneaking off to get high, and that's how Donnie discovered the Rock Pub.

During lunch, Donnie would buy a slice and then hit the old-man's bar on Post Avenue. The Rock Pub had a pool table, pinball machines, and cheap beer. Lunchtime, Donnie started bringing in friends from work, stopping by again after work for cocktails. He convinced the owner to book him for an acoustic set Friday nights. "Music is a big draw, it'll fill the bar," he explained. Donnie could talk anyone into anything. At first he played the mellow stuff, crowd pleasers like James Taylor, the Beatles. One night he brought Nick down to do harmonies. Scott soon showed up with bongos, and eventually Matt picked up as second guitar. Friday nights quickly evolved into full-tilt electric shock syndrome and this went on for years. The Rock Pub started booking other bands, but the Slugs ruled the house.

Donnie had a drinking buddy, a guy from work named T-Bone, with a full-blown mullet haircut. He was the godfather of flips, the one hair abomination every serious rocker dreads. But T-Bone had a sister named Lizzie who also worked at the enema factory. She ran the computer room, self-taught. She was smart and tough—Teutonic. You couldn't get close to her right away. Donnie's first impression—"She has great tits and she drinks like a fish." We knew it was true love. Donnie was always more interested in playing pool and getting high than having sex. It took a real woman to distract him.

Lizzie was a disco girl, I remember the day I met her. She showed up at the punknic in a shimmering green dance skirt and top, high heels, and sparkles. She got over *that* real fast. We all did. Once you entered the vortex, Slugland was a permanent commitment. With all the zeal of the newly converted, I had zero tolerance for anything that "wasn't rock & roll." I was usually the only girl—at the rehearsal studio, in the record store, at the Max Weber conference, in the backroom at the video store. Now I had all my sisters and me. Slugwives, right up there at the front of the stage. We were the first to get up and dance, cheerleaders for our conquering heroes. It always got the room moving.

The Slugs appropriated the Rock Pub for their own private party. They brought girlfriends who brought sisters who invited friends from work, then roommates, college buddies, and parents, too. Some guests showed up in mink coats, pumps, and pearls, others in suits, sweaty work clothes, or workout gear. But everybody danced. We kept inviting people until every show was packed.

Unless we had invited you personally, you probably hated the band. Typical night: Donnie sitting at the bar, all stoned up on dope, drinking quarts of milk to coat his stomach, smoking cigarettes, puking. You knew he was high because he wasn't drinking. And because of the milk. Nick was quiet and grumpy till he'd had a few, then he was Mr. Personality, outgoing, gregarious. He hated the clientele. They were always cursing and heckling the band. But the hostility egged him on; he hissed and snarled like Johnny Rotten. He loved it. One minute he was a squirming Iggy, then a regal Bryan Ferry or a seductive Jim Morrison. Moments later, manic Manson (Charles).

Wasted on booze and 'ludes the Slugs usually played five or six hours, experimenting, abusing the audience with sick lyrics and riffs. Chemical activity in full swing, wheeling and dealing, someone always had to make midnight runs to cop. The Slugs enjoyed a lovely buffet at the Rock Pub, a smorgasbord of elixirs, boobs, brawls, and drugs.

I took endless photographs. As keeper of the mailing list, I also played hostess, making sure our guests were having fun. But my main job was watching Nick, carefully scrutinizing any impromptu innovation in lyrics or riffs. After the show, we would discuss the set in full detail, like it was *Mishna Torah*. I had to pay attention. You were not allowed to bother me while Nick was singing. I felt that way about every band I ever loved. I hated any distraction. Just me and the band. It was much more important than the guy or even the booze.

Although they were endlessly prolific, Slugs did many covers: Bowie, Stones, Dolls, and Lou Reed. As hopeless Lynyrd Skynyrd–Doobie fiends, the Rock Pub regulars probably couldn't distinguish covers from originals anyway. Nobody listened to the lyrics, and that gave Nick a free reign of terror. "Disco Bash" was an antidisco tirade. Disco bashing was a popular punk theme. *They got white suits, cowboy boots, and pockets full of cash, a very healthy trust fund and a manicured mustache. A fashion consultant so their colors won't clash, and a brand-new BMW they're bound to crash down at the disco bash.* "Sex Toy Blues" was a humorous accounting of male sexual obsolescence. One day a guy realizes he's been displaced by more sophisticated technological devices. How can he compete? *She's got a custom-made ten-speed vibrator with a monogrammed carrying case. An extra large, supercharged jism mechanism that's all in questionable taste . . . sex toys . . . sex toys.*

Each song was a story, crafted wordplay that left you guessing. I was always looking for absolute meanings, objective truths, but Nick's lyrics taught me the difference between art and science, between aesthetics and politics. Although the structure was perfect, he always left the meaning vague, nothing more than an impression—the rest was up to you. If the music was good, it didn't matter what you were saying. Left-leaning critics readily embraced punk as the voice of disenfranchised working-class youth. The music held the promise of liberation. But punk rock was never anyone's new historical subject. A few years later, when I was sitting in a graduate seminar, Advanced Topics of Marxist Analysis, the professor asked, "What happens when the *proles* accumulate surplus capital?" I knew right away, so I raised my hand, "They go out and buy new guitars!" Above all, Slug music was *fun,* the category most often overlooked by intellectuals. You could dance to it, make out, or just stand around and watch. That was liberation.

One summer night Nick and I showed up early, before Donnie got there. This was somewhat risky, since he could blend in, but we could not. We were in our own orbit. I was wearing a black miniskirt, four-inch spiked leopard-skin heels from Frederick's of Hollywood, and a coral tank top. My hair was blue-black, piled high. Most of the punk-rock girls on the Bowery looked like hookers. They called it the slut look. In fact, that's how Deborah Harry got the name for Blondie, from a truck driver thinking she was a prostitute, screaming out, "Hey, Blondie!" Some punk girlfriends did work in the sex industry, mainly as dancers. So there was some fashion crossover. But if we *really dressed* on Long Island, we were doomed.

In my spike heels, I hit over six feet. I've always looked gender-fucked. I have an angular face, broad shoulders, narrow hips, and I've never been more than a B cup. Nick wore regulation skintight black jeans from Trash & Vaudeville, black eyeliner, and a purple silk shirt opened to the waist, silver crucifix dangling like a Corsican pimp. We walked into the bar, hand in hand, the punk-rock lovebirds of the Rock Pub. Some guys started screaming at us, "Queers!" "Faggots!" They thought I was a transvestite on a date with my homo lover. At first, Nick and I were very flattered, like they thought we were Lou Reed and his beloved Rachel. But the Slugs' audience was not so amused.

To them we were drug-addicted pansies, twisted low-life scum. All night they kept screaming *"Whew!!"* (the *"Yesss!!"* of the 1970s) and throwing things at the band. By closing time, I had a fat lip and the windshield of my cherished Slugmobile was smashed in. They demolished Lisa, my 1964 baby blue F85 Oldsmobile with the Slug logo boldly painted on the front door. Broken glass everywhere: all over my shrine to Nick, on the dash, showering his teamster buttons, my Ramones stickers, slivers and shards. They barely missed the red parrot hanging from the rearview mirror, a relic from Rockaway's Playland.

There was always something going on, police coming in every hour ordering the band to lower the volume. Five cops barging through the back door to stop the music in the middle of the set. Arms got broken, ribs smashed; this often happened on Long Island. People really hated punk. The Slugs never made more than a hundred dollars, but they didn't care. They got free drinks all night, all the drugs in the free world, and an endless party. Life on Long Island was good. They had no plans to take it any further. And then we met the CorpseGrinders.

Rick Rivets with his arm around Johnny Thunders.

10

VALLEY OF FEAR

I'll never stay in the valley of fear,
I won't decay in the valley of fear,
You die every day in the valley of fear, oi!!

© JALBERT/RIVETS

ick and I were fighting, so I stayed home and he went to his cousin's graduation alone. Meantime, Stripe called about a party. The Brats were supposedly playing. The Brats in Sea Cliff? I ran out, leaving Nick a note to meet me there. I had befriended Stripe one night at a bar called U.S. Blues, where he was a DJ. The Cheerleaders had been an anomaly among Roslyn's pathetic rock-culture industry—a declining empire engineered by a handful of bloated, shaggy, coke-infested '60s retreads. This was Grateful Dead territory.

Stripe was a Deadhead, too, hair to his waist, but he had harder roots. He was a dedicated Mopar man, a gifted gearhead and notorious bad boy. Sea Cliff elders swore Stripe hadn't missed a vein since his ele-

mentary school days at St. Boniface the Martyr. He was up for any-
thing, so I asked him to play the Clash on the U.S. Blues sound system.
He got fired that night, cut his hair short, and started hanging with the
Slugs.

Stripe was a sloppy drunk, a mess of cross-addictions, breaking bottles, starting fights. He was a loyal friend and faithful comrade in arms,
but bad news when it came to the ladies. He was so gorgeous they all
fell in love with him. Of course, it always ended in a disaster involving
me in endless hours of teary phone conferences with his victims—social
workers, lawyers, strippers, beautiful women, all dropping like flies.
After a while whenever a new girl came around I'd issue an all-points
bulletin. Stripe is most famous for his romance with the girl Sid Vicious
"dated" briefly after Nancy died. The girl had been Sid's mother's idea,
not his. The romance never took off, but it made her a minor celebrity.
And even *she* couldn't deal with Stripe.

Stripe was late for the party, so I was there on my own. Standing at
the foot of the staircase, I spotted a tall, lean girl in black, with silver
amulets and black hair. She could have been my sister. Sue was actually
there with her real sisters. Long Island girls always traveled in sibling
sets. Lizzie had her sister crew, too, but they were mainly party girls, out
for fun and games. Looking for boys, trading makeup secrets, sipping
vodka gimlets. If the Slugs had been a reggae band, that would have
been just fine with them. The Mordred sisters were different.

I'd never met more serious fangirls on Long Island. They loved cute
boys, but they knew their rock & roll. Three devoted Catholic daughters of an Italian mom and a Scottish dad, they attended weekly family
barbecues. They were *good* girls. On Long Island that means remaining
loyal to family and sticking close to the nest. Superstitious, interested in
the occult—spells, tarot cards, the runes—the Mordreds dreamed of
moving to the country, to the woods to practice the craft. Having female friends to share my interests was a rare joy. On Long Island most
females just wanted to get married. At work, the bell-bottom brigade
was still rotating Fleetwood Mac and Billy Joel. It wasn't my scene.
Standing around, always holding a beer but never too drunk, the Mor-

dreds knew all the bands on Long Island. Their brother played guitar. Eventually they introduced me to the Chiselers, Sea Monster, In Cold Blood, and Rosary Violet.

The Mordred sisters started hanging around Coventry when Sue was sixteen. They had to sneak her in and hide her in the basement when the cops came. Her sister was dating a guitarist. Sue asked to meet George, and they started dating. She was young and sweet, so he took her home to Long Island after shows and kissed her good night. Then he'd head back to New York City to see his other woman, Connie Gripp. Connie had also been Arthur's girlfriend, but her claim to fame came as Dee Dee Ramone's psycho girlfriend, the inspiration behind the song "Glad to See You Go" on *Leave Home,* the Ramones' second album. A serious junkie hooker, Connie eventually hit a hard street death.

Eventually Sue and George got married and moved to a South Shore Long Island town. They visited Sea Cliff often, mostly to hang out at Trimbles. When Nick finally showed up at the party, he was introduced to Sue's husband. After that day, life was never the same.

We always called him George, but he was better known by his professional name, Rick Rivets. Rivets, his high school buddy Arthur Kane, Johnny Thunders, and drummer Billy Murcia were the founding fathers of the New York Dolls. Within months of conception, David Johansen had replaced Thunders on vocals and Syl Sylvain ousted Rivets from rhythm guitar. Although the Dolls didn't break up until 1975, Rivets lasted less than a year. He was booted out in 1971, before the first album.

Since the Dolls were Nick's favorite band, Rivets's involvement in their lineage was very compelling. Besides, Rivets was a powerhouse on leads; critics considered him a guitarist in a class with Thunders and Walter Lure. Like most of rock & roll's greatest talent, Rivets was a grade-A fuckup. But that didn't diminish the importance of his contribution; it authenticated it.

After he left the Dolls, Rivets and a Sea Cliff drummer named Kenny Donovan started the Brats. By mid-1972 the glam band was holding rent parties in huge Downtown lofts. Some nights Wayne County headlined and borough boys Kiss were also on the bill. Members of Aerosmith and the Dolls attended, too, and periodically the Brats opened for the Dolls. There were shows at Coventry every night for four months. Like most bands, the Brats never got signed, but they did put out a few 45s. The Brats didn't break up until the 1980s, but Rick Rivets got thrown out around 1977.

After Arthur's post-Dolls adventure as Killer Kane fell apart, he and Rick reunited. They hooked up with an old high school buddy named Stuie and Jimmy Criss from Teenage Lust. They named their new band the CorpseGrinders after a cheesy horror flick. In the Dolls, with his platforms, everyone said that Arthur looked like Frankenstein. The flamboyant Kane was one of a kind, a real character, and a top-notch bass player. Onstage, Rick and Arthur scaled six feet six, a mutant Aryan army from the hills of Transylvania. The CorpseGrinders aimed for a ghoul-fueled, neofascist motif that never quite caught on, at least not in America.

Placing an ad in LI's legendary rock rag, *Good Times,* they soon replaced Jimmy Criss with Tongue Blaccard, the drummer from Fats Deacon. The band had booked a Fourth of July show on the beach at Long Beach, but Arthur refused to do it. It wasn't enough money, and he said he didn't want to end up like the Monkees. But above all, he was an ex-Doll; he just couldn't stoop that low. Arthur was skittish after the demise of the Dolls. He assumed everyone was out to burn him, and he started to flake out. Stuie was increasingly too fucked up to play. He was stealing and not showing up. So after an album, some gigs at CBGB's and Max's, and a tour of the biker bar circuit, the Corpse-Grinders blew up. By 1978, Rick Rivets needed a new band.

On this summer day in 1979, at yet another pivotal party in Sea Cliff, destiny would be forever altered. Nick invited George and Sue to the Rock Pub, and in a matter of days, the seminal New York Doll was in the Slugs.

The Slugs had their dreams of stardom, but they were mainly out for fun. Although Donnie and Nick wrote constantly, they never really worked the room or hit the City clubs hoping to make connections or promote the band. Whatever came their way was good enough. After George, it got very serious. Now it wasn't just about free beers and a few lines in the back room.

Because of punk's DIY (do it yourself) ethic, new bands were erupting by the thousands. Everywhere kids were writing songs, rehearsing, booking shows. Fans in the audience one night were onstage the next. Friends took photographs, designed logos and album covers, set up independent labels, and transformed themselves into desirable rock product. Fresh crops of contenders rose up in every city, borough, and 'burb, in small towns everywhere. Young people dreamed of being their heroes—the Stones, the Heartbreakers—of walking onstage like gods of the underworld. Underlying all the claims of "never selling out" were traditional rock dreams of fame and glory, the glamorous life. Even if you just tasted it, almost made it, were almost famous, that was better than nothing.

Punk was a populist eruption that promised anyone could rule for a day, even as the best of breed remained relatively marginal, like the Pistols, the Dolls. New York bands were gritty, brilliant, and obscure. The Ramones, Kiss, Blondie, and the Velvets were among the few to break. For the rest of the kids, it was just something to do besides work in a death-zone factory or as a boring social worker. In the words of the Professionals, Steve Jones and Paul Cook's post-Pistols ensemble, *I thought I was a champion, but I found instead, it was just another dream. . . .*

Hope was alive, the New Wave was upon us. Blondie was crossing over and more polished acts like the Cars, Police, and X were getting airplay. Radio stations were changing format. In New York Vince Scelsa was rotating the Ramones on WNEW. Denis MacNamara on Long Island's WDRE (now WLIR-FM) "dared to be different" with the Pretenders, the Clash, and Blondie. In L.A., KROQ's Rodney Bingenheimer had a punk show, *Rodney on the ROQ.* His first guests were the Ramones. *End of the 1970s . . . end of the century,* the Slugs had a shot.

The Slugs sound gradually transformed from more up-tempo Stones-based R&B to full-blown power-chord, buzz-saw brutality. With Louie's metallic leanings and George's lead lust, this was a much more aggressive band. Now they *looked* like rock stars—hardcore, virulently sexy, and mean. Sometimes they booked as Slugs, sometimes as CorpseGrinders featuring "original members of the New York Dolls and Slugs." There wasn't much logic to it—whatever got them on the bill.

Although they continued to cover classics like Chuck Berry's "Carol," the Stones' "2000 Man," crowd pleasers like Bowie's "Jean Genie" and Lou Reed's "Satellite of Love," they also included Dolls originals, Heartbreakers material, and mixed medleys involving all of the above. But they specifically avoided early CorpseGrinder material. Anything from the original Kane lineup with the exception of an occasional nod to the quasi-hit "Mental Moron." The original Corpse-Grinders had played the City circuit for about two years, but their shtick as "zombified storm troopers in chalky makeup and black armbands" was off-putting and dated. Lacking the ironic brilliance of Dee Dee Ramone's German fixation (e.g., "Today Your Love, Tomorrow the World") or the Sex Pistols' anarchistic appropriation of swastikas, the neofascist pretenders never cut it. Nick adamantly refused to cover songs like "Rites 4 Whites." Not because it was politically incorrect, but because it was embarrassing.

After Stuie left the band, George asked Nick to sing on the second CorpseGrinder album. They released it in 1984 on New Rose, the French label that had issued their first album a year earlier. The latter-day CorpseGrinders included George as Rick Rivets, Blaccard, Nick, and a hideous drum machine. George played bass, but put his guitar and the drum machine on the same track. This was a primitive eight-track recording, so Blaccard had to play over the drum machine or they'd lose the guitar. On top of this, executive producer Rick Rivets stubbornly insisted on a bat-cave revival theme. It was his project and he wanted to do the makeup like the old CorpseGrinders, with the same idiotic whiteface and black eye sockets, complete with Nazi armbands and a circle with a lightning bolt—the logo tattooed on both Arthur and Rick.

I took the cover photos in a buggy South Shore swamp covered in empty beer cans and crusty tires. Nick was perched in a tree in a cutoff leather jacket, featuring every rock bride's dream—the tattoo of my name on his arm, prominently displayed. The ghoulish bat-cave look was achieved with the help of Queen Helene Mint Julep Mask. The album boasted two precious Stones covers, "Please Go Home" and "Miss Amanda Jones." The originals were a mix of stripped-down hard rockers, bittersweet ballads, and a touch of rockabilly. Still, the second album never sold quite as well as the first. Probably because of that drum machine and bat-cave look.

In the transition from capitalism to socialism is the period called alcoholism. Cultural critics have described the 1980s as the decade of greed, *the worst years of our lives.* But the view from the bottom of my glass was looking mighty sweet. After George and Blaccard came, Scott and Matt were out. The New York Dolls upstaged the Cambria Heights girl groups and spit them out. Louie, Donnie, and Nick were core Slugs; George and Blaccard the principal CorpseGrinders. This world-historic meeting of the minds led to over a decade of pirate love, suburban marriage, burglary, heroin addiction, death, methadone, star fucking, recording contracts, photo opportunities, and radio airplay. Success was in the air, these were days of ascendancy.

The merger also precipitated a parade of hapless bass players, drummers, and entrepreneurial producers. Rick Rivets was easygoing, but he adamantly refused to play in a band with a guy with a mustache. Scott was permanently banished, and Blaccard was in. For a while the Slugs caucus decided they hated Blaccard's drumming. But, really, I think he didn't fit in because he didn't get high. So they got James from an ad in the *Voice.* We never knew his last name. He showed up in a van one day with all his belongings, including an entire drum kit. He was touring from the South, living in his van. He joined the band and moved in with Donnie and Lizzie and her sister. They all lived in a Cape house in a tree-lined street in Westbury.

Except for the disaffected Nick, all my friends were registered Republicans. Most of this had to do with politics and power in Nassau County, with shady party patronage systems and access to county jobs. Still, the house in Westbury was the model of Middle American domesticity: bowling leagues, heroin, family barbecues, stolen bass amps, Tupperware parties, semen-stained wood paneling, a sewing machine, the *Joy of Cooking*, and sex toys.

James stuck around for a few gigs but eventually left to play with Black Oak Arkansas. He probably caved in from the pressure of horny Slugwives constantly hitting on him. Another famous Slugs drummer was Billy Rogers. He'd played with the Senders and Heartbreakers and recorded with the Ramones on *Subterranean Jungle*, most impressively, on their psych-o-delic cover of the Chambers Brothers' "Time Has Come Today." Billy almost became a Ramone, but heroin addiction got in the way. In Slugland, it was an asset.

Rick Rivets and a dedicated fanboy named Andy Doback had a small record company. Typical of early indie upstarts, Whiplash allowed Andy and George to produce, record, and distribute noncommercial material, all the bands they liked. Label mates included the Brats, the Killer Kane Band (featuring Blackie Guzman, a.k.a. Blackie Lawless of W.A.S.P.), Sweet Tarts, and two slamming 45s by the Slugs. They also distributed the New Rose releases of the CorpseGrinders, albums one and two.

At one point goodfella gangsta Henry Hill expressed an interest in managing the Slugs, but it was short-lived. With other pressing obligations, Hill disappeared. The unwritten history of an unsigned band often includes the false promise of a big break aborted by bad faith. Producers, promoters, managers, parasites. Amateurs at the mercy of scammers. Axl Rose was nobody's fool when he advised small-town boys and girls to take business courses if they wanted to become rock stars. Few are as vulnerable as kids blinded by the possibility of rock stardom. Over the years I've seen some of Long Island's best bands get taken down hard.

One such episode of doom involved the Slugs and a guy I'll call

Jack. Donnie and Nick were songwriters, not producers. Louie played around but never finished anything. He's been "working" on some Slugs studio tapes now for over twenty years. George was a legend, but Blaccard was the businessman. He hired a lawyer and set up the deal, laid out all the money himself. Jack had managed some minor talents and had ties to CBS. He was able to secure free studio time at Carriage House Studios, Kingdom Sound, and Secret Sound. Through Jack, the Slugs got access to top-quality engineers in a professional studio environment. There was also a tentative deal set up with Chrysalis: The label would front $20,000 for a three-song demo. All the band had to do was show up and play.

This particular venture involved core Slugs, Blaccard, and a guy named Mike on bass. Blaccard paid for the masters, hired the lawyer, did his drum tracks, and went off to a car show in Vegas. According to him, the band blew all the studio time "being creative." Songs never got finished. "Too many cooks, they just ran out of money." Jack needed more cash to get the songs finished, but he couldn't raise it, so he held the Slug tapes. Or the studio held the tapes. Or Chrysalis held them. Or Louie. Or Blaccard. We'll never know for sure.

Of course, the Slugs have a different version of this story, a tragic tale of rock & roll labor exploitation and cocaine addiction. Jack had strictly forbidden the band to drink beer because urination would have cut into valuable recording time. The efficiency expert wanted to maximize the labor process by eliminating all nonessential bodily functions. Arty and smart, the Slugs were also disciplined factory boys: tough, obedient to the rhythm of the assembly line. Union men, proud American labor, they worked hard, they showed up. Sometimes they got too loose, but they always got the job done. According to the Slugs, the problem was Jack. They swear the studio money went right up his nose.

During lull periods, side projects, rehearsals, and house parties kept Sluglife afloat. Between 1979 and 1982 the band played all over Long Island, Connecticut, and New York City. The Continental, CBGB's, Max's Kansas City, Nightingale's, Zone DK, Club Hollywood, and places I'll never remember. They booked at Long Island spots like

Sparks, February's, and the Right Track Inn, legendary suburban dives that kept us dead and alive for years. The Slugs performed at biker benefits out east, an act of community service every legitimate Long Island rocker is proud to provide. They competed in the Battle of the Bands for K-Rock at My Father's Place, losing out because they sounded "too New Wave." On jukeboxes at Bar and Nightingale's, airplay in Paris, France, and French-speaking Canada. It was big points back then to say you copped or got high with Johnny Thunders, a top prize in the inverted status hierarchy of Downtown's junkie punk rockers. The Slugs scored dope alongside the best boys of 1979, sharing bags, needles, and connections.

The night of a show, the band descended on the club like leather-clad locusts, a tribe of amoral predators, tall, lean, dope-cranky, and tough. Guitars, belts, hair, chains, spike heels, and a whiskey swagger. Coventry was a club that had seen better days. After the gig, Slugs got frisky and trashed the basement, then took photos. But that wasn't the problem. The management found a set of works stashed inside the toilet tank and said the band couldn't play there anymore. Slugs on a rampage, ripping up couches, pouring booze and beer everywhere, breaking chairs, adding to the filth and fury of Coventry's broken pipes, rust puddles, and piss pockets.

Every punk club was a squalor motel, especially the bathrooms. Punks, too, were crude and rude, probably because of the drugs they took. Heroin makes you nasty. Some of these people had no manners. Periodically I had to discipline the little bitches when they pushed too hard. Punk boys didn't scare me either. My years on Twennyninth taught me the meaning of courtesy.

Female Alcoholics: The Men They Marry. Slugwives liked to kick it, too. The Slugs played upstairs at Max's. It was their first gig at a really nice club with a good sound system. People were dancing, the place was packed, I was comatose on bourbon and Valium, zonked from the pre-party party. Somebody carried me all the way up the long flight of stairs, then deposited me under the pinball tables where I passed out. Next thing I knew the set was done and we were all backstage. Lizzie was pissed off at Donnie, and she started punching. He never hit back; he just begged her to calm down. She decked him, he distracted her, and the episode was terminated.

Lizzie and I could be mean drunks. Same for Coco, Blaccard's wife. The three of us drinking together was *Lethal Weapon 1, 2,* and *3.* Coco was a chameleon, everything she touched turned to gold. One week she dressed like a Hollywood starlet, then a North Shore horsey matron. She was a gourmet cook, a *Town & Country* maven. She had a cosmetology sideline that made her a star on Long Island's rock grooming circuit. She had been a teenage throwaway, a studio moth, a groupie. She met Blaccard when they were kids. He took care of her as long as he could and worked hard to give her anything she wanted. He was a Bronx boy, old-school Italian, working on cars since he was twelve, after his dad died. He fixed her teeth, put her through school, and built her a red Corvette. She once told me that without Blaccard, she would have just been a blow-job whore. I winced when she said it. She never saw herself the way we did—so talented, stunning, and smart. Coco would have been the last to know how special she was.

City girls knew Long Island was a land of barbarians, so they kept away from our guys. I think people were afraid of us. There is wildness that comes from living near turnpikes, hearing the roar of a Trans Am in your dreams, waking up to a tattooed love boy in the stark basement of his parents' tract home. The Slugs got jovial after a few. They bonded, pledging their love in crocodile tears. The Slugwives were different. It always started out as fun, but by the third drink the rage erupted, historical bile regurgitated onto some unrelated episode that invariably ruined the night.

Who knows why we hated the world? Lizzie's parents divorced. Dad left Mom for another woman and never looked back. Mom shut down, the kids got high. Coco was the youngest of five. Her parents died when she was young and soon after, her siblings threw her out. By now, you know my story. Like Henry Rollins says, *L.S.O.* Maybe we all had Low Self Opinion, a low estimate of our worth. Like we weren't good enough. Maybe we just wanted to fuck people up. Maybe we just wanted to enjoy the feeling of power that comes with a hefty buzz. Either way, when we drank, we punished the world for whatever we were feeling.

Periodically I boosted my pleasure with a subsidiary addiction, Valium. I went to Nick's mother's doctor, an old Italian guy in Glen Cove. I said I was *nervous*. Dressed like a depressed housewife, looking down at the floor, I'd sigh, "Maybe if I had a baby." That kept me in 'scripts for years. It was a blessing for Nick, "Val & Al," Valium and Alcohol, the dynamic duo. Instead of raging, I just passed out.

The Rock Pub days also ended in a huge blast. On a Fourth of July show, the Slugs finished their set. Three carloads of guys pulled into the parking lot, somebody jammed an M80 in the tailpipe of a car and it blew up. The band threw the equipment in the car, twenty guys stormed the bar, and they started fighting. Nick got a busted lip. Stripe jumped in, George pulled out a .357 and smacked someone in the head. The cops came. Best of all, it was in the papers. It made *Newsday*.

Sluglife careened out of control. Nick and I had a falling out, then I got laid off. Social work programs were being cut, and without work to balance me, I was losing my grip. Whenever things started crashing down like this, I knew my karma was up, phoenix nosedive, time to move on. So I headed to San Francisco, hoping to sort myself out. I stayed with a friend of Nick's. Rolex was now part of an emerging yuppie class, a stockbroker with a Rolex watch who treated me like family. He loved Nick, but Nick never left Long Island except for shows. Rolex kept inviting us out to visit. Burned out and depressed, I finally went. Rolex was not a punk rocker; he liked Steely Dan and Paul Simon. Or maybe he just looked like them, I don't remember. Rolex had a great heart and a bad coke habit. Fifteen years later, the heart and the habit collided and Rolex died. He was forty-three.

Rolex's house was located in Upper Lesbia—Noe Valley, walking distance from the Castro and the Mission. At first I lived there in exchange for housecleaning. I hated California. I couldn't relate to the people. My intensity and sharp wit had been an asset on the East Coast. Here, it came off like some deep-rooted neurotic personality disorder. I barely knew Rolex. Cut off from my symbiosis with Nick, I felt out of sorts, like I was walking on a marshmallow moon, stuck deep, sinking slowly. And I hated all the fucking colors.

One night I couldn't sleep. Out of the dim, tiny black spots started hurling themselves at me, coming closer, faster. That hadn't happened since I was a small child, when my parents left me for the first time, alone with Nizzy the maid. I didn't want to wake Rolex, and it was too late to call New York. Desperate for comfort, I cried out, "Please, God, help me, I'm losing it." And that's when he appeared. To my shock and horror, it was Jesus! Jesus Christ had come to comfort me in the darkness. He sat quietly next to my bed and a calming glow fell over me. Jesus was dressed in typical white robes with long surfy hair, just like in all the portraits. Was this a visitation or a hallucination? I still don't know for sure. Except for this: The energy in that room wasn't human, it had no recognizable body temperature. It was electric, yet light as air, gentle yet intense, seamless like water, yet oddly dry. Radiating softly until all the black spots dissolved, Jesus stayed until I fell asleep.

This totally freaked me out. But who could I tell? Nick would kill me—like most lapsed Catholics, he hated religion. And what would my Jewish parents think? I agonized for days, then dismissed it as an acid flashback. Months later, I finally confided the experience to Betty Bradley. My musician mother just smiled and whispered softly, "Hey, baby, whatever gets you through the night."

As things began turning around for me in San Francisco, the memory of my Jesus experience faded. I made friends. I started studying astrology and Tarot, working at a metaphysics bookstore. I decorated my room with colorful California artifacts—peacock feathers, amulets. Within a month I was hired as supervisor of adoptions at an agency that helped place children with special needs. In a competitive adoption market, we matched couples who had various "disabilities" with "hard-to-place" kids—kids nobody wanted. Out of this, many happy families were created: a don't-ask-don't-tell single dad and a son with cerebral palsy so severe he couldn't speak, a mother and child in matching wheelchairs, interracial couples and rainbow babies. Some kids were older, stuck in foster care most of their lives, fifteen and still waiting for a family.

Others had became "special" as a result of severe abuse and neglect. One biological mother had tied an electric hot plate to her infant daughter till it burned through, severing the child's spinal cord. Thanks to her mother, she would never walk. The girl was now in the custody of the State, *in loco parentis.* The State incarcerates such parents for their crimes and releases the child to the possibility of a better life. The degree of physical, emotional, and spiritual damage doesn't always leave much hope. Severely wounded kids are not easy. If life has shattered the capacity for trust, the possibility of love can be obliterated. But special adoption is all about hope. It's like a blind date or a mail-order marriage. You set it up and hope for the best. Just when you think a kid hasn't got a prayer, love and faith prove you wrong.

I remember meeting two research scientists in the process of adopting a second daughter with Down's syndrome. When I was growing up, we called them "retards," "Mongoloids." They were beaten, spat upon by their peers. The ultimate *shamed child,* their parents hid them away like a dirty secret. The two scientists saw things differently. The adoptive mom had been born with all her reproductive organs inside out. Their older adopted daughter was named Mary Ellen. She showed up to meet her new baby sister in long blond pigtails tied with pink ribbons, dressed like a little doll. I watched her giggle as she punched numbers into a calculator. Her mom had already taught her how to multiply. She was five years old.

Eventually, I got a night job; making the scene. Like everything, this happened by accident. I met Rocco at a Noe Valley hippie-relic coffee bar where he served lovely bean sprout salads and cappuccinos, then punished his customers with a jukebox full of angry Saints, Tools, and Clash. Turned out my new pal was the West Coast correspondent for *New York Rocker.* Rocco's scene reports covered all the shows—at the Geary Temple, Mabuhay Gardens, and Target, a seminal punk video and performance studio. Thanks to Mr. Rocco, I met the Butthole Surfers and became a lifelong Flipper fan. I listened to punk radio,

KALX, and embraced the VKTMS, Nervous Gender, and a band of seething females called Wilma. Following the release of "California Über Alles," the Dead Kennedys' debut single, Alternative Tentacles Records slammed out sick product like TSOL, Black Flag, Crucif**ks, and DOA. Now I loved California. People were restless, cranky, and pressing forward. This wasn't entertainment; it was very serious.

During my months in San Francisco, I gradually surrendered my NYC slut look, trading my spike heels for combat boots. Like everyone, I was edging toward the hardcore aesthetics that would dominate the 1980s; no sex, less glamour, more rage and rigor. Buzzed on my new scene, I rarely drank, but I developed an unnatural attachment to MDC (Multi-Death Corporation, Millions of Dead Cops, Many Dying Children). Though Rolex hated punk music, my new noise and regalia amused him. Not Nick. He was *New York über alles,* thank you very much.

San Francisco was the land of the Dead Kennedys, and that year singer Jello Biafra was running for mayor. I worked the election polls, dressed in full punk regalia, purple hair, spiked, polka-dot shirt, black everything else—covert electioneering at the polls. Biafra finished fourth in the race.

Heroin was seeping into the San Francisco scene, too, but there were also traces of straightedge in the air. An antidrug movement was growing in the hardcore scene, kids who saw what getting wasted had done to their friends, to their parents. My initial commitment at the adoption agency had been for six months. After three months they offered me a permanent supervisor's position, but I was homesick. Nick had pledged his love and I missed him. I had no idea what was going on.

All of my friends are doing the same things, all of my friends behaving like wild things, most of the boys still living the wrong way, most of the girls have nothing left to say. Sue Mordred had written a song about it, and I should have paid more attention. Back in Slugland, death was coming in. It came in slowly and hit hard.

Meantime, at Rolex's job, we had access to free long distance. The phone lines to New York were heating up. In a move right out of the

Ronettes, Nick's mother warned me that a girl named Scabette was honing in on my turf. Scabette was a temp; she worked for Lizzie at her new job as a systems analyst in Midtown. Sometimes on weekends Lizzie brought her home to Long Island and she got the hots for Nick. Scabette had a psychotic boyfriend from Staten Island; always breaking up, fighting, police, orders of protection—the usual. I was busy study-ing Tarot and listening to Flipper. Meanwhile, back in New York, Sluglife was turning south of heaven.

One night the Slugs booked a show at Mr. Laff's. Scabette came down trolling for Nick. Between sets the jealous boyfriend came in, walked by Donnie, and pushed him hard with his shoulder. Donnie turned around and cracked him in the face. Another version of this story had the boyfriend missing Donnie and hitting Lizzie by mistake, giving her a black eye. Rick Rivets always traveled with his .45. James the drummer always carried a .357 because he was Southern. A bar-room brawl broke out, fists were flying, pistols whipping. The boyfriend got the shit kicked out of him, then he was thrown into the street. Someone stuck a finger in his eye. Now a piece of it was hanging out. He tried to escape in a cab, but Louie jumped on it and stopped it. The guy was arrested, another great night of rock & roll.

The next day the police drove out to Long Island and encouraged Lizzie to press charges, but she refused, afraid the guy would come after her. The cops understood. The next week Scabette told Lizzie that some cops in New Jersey had kicked the shit out of him. A month later, he was dead. Somebody shot him.

Even before I left for San Francisco, half the band was armed. Shows were crazy. There were always fights, broken beer bottles, heckling. Club owners treated bands like shit and offered no protection. Luckily we had friends like Stripe watching the stage. Sometimes violence mixed with mental illness, like at the Thunders show in Brooklyn. We never a missed a Thunders gig. We saw him whenever he played, wher-ever he was, until he died in 1991. I drove in with Donnie and Nick. The Guidos hated Johnny. But the real problem was an overly devoted fan. Backstage, this girl was whining, it went on and on. We tried ignoring her and her little psychodrama. Suddenly, blood exploded all over the walls. She'd slit her wrists. We weren't sure whether it was because Johnny wouldn't talk to her or because he refused to shoot her up. She was wailing, blood splattering. Outside, somebody pulled a gun on Thunders, the owner called the cops, Thunders split.

Normally we would have laughed at this pathetic girl, but Donnie was despondent over a recent situation. He and Lizzie had been getting high one day at his parents' house. A novice, she shot up an artery instead of a vein, got a blood clot and ended up in the hospital. Her fingers started turning black from gangrene. After a few days they looked like rotting chili peppers, so the doctor had to amputate. Actually, Lizzie was lucky. Sometimes a blocked artery will kill you. When they got married, Donnie put the wedding ring on a stump. Lizzie was more willful, but Donnie had more experience. He knew better, he should have been on top of it. He felt guilty. So that night in Brooklyn, Donnie refused to leave the girl bleeding. He applied pressure to the wound. We drove her to the emergency room, and they wheeled her inside. Wasted, we took one look around and said, "Let's get the fuck out of here" and split back to Long Island.

Six months of San Francisco's scene had rejuvenated me. Spring, I was back in New York. Though 1980 promised a sparkling new decade, Sluglife now generated an odor, like an old black cloak, musty, mildewed, and soiled. I walked back into the Westbury house and into a needle exchange program. *L.A.M.F.* was on the turntable exactly as it had been six months earlier, like time froze. Everyone was sitting around, dirty hair, ripped leather, emaciated, low energy, played out. Nobody was smiling.

I felt oddly safe around heroin addicts. They're paradoxically tough and fearless, yet completely vulnerable and constantly filled with dread. Their defects of character are so obvious, you know you can't trust them at all. That eliminates the risk of betrayal. Nobody pretends to be nice, to be acting out of anything other than naked self-interest. Heroin addicts illustrate American capitalist opportunism at its purest. On top of that, they always look cool.

Nick and I stayed at the Westbury house for a month while looking for a place to live. We slept in the living room, lounging around watching TV until Nick had to go to work. One day I got a call from my parents. My mother was being interviewed on *Joe Franklin's Memory Lane* TV show. Betty Bradley was Joe's guest, so they played her records and reminisced about the Big Band era. I remembered my mother telling Joe Franklin how much she regretted giving up her singing career for marriage, what limited choices women had in those days, how different things were today, how she was born too soon. My mother on TV disseminating a pedagogy of the oppressed.

After their house in Rockaway got robbed, my parents moved out to Long Island. It was now my home, too. We enjoyed family meals at the diner and hanging out like the Mordreds, like a normal suburban family. The Slugs adored my parents. Some of my colleagues and friends at work patronized my parents, like they were Archie and Edith Bunker with the gin, the salsa music, bingo, bowling, firearms, and army reunions. Sometimes I did, too. Part of me was Cretin to the bone, upwardly mobile, arrogant, and condescending. I hated myself for it. In the professional world I aspired to, I felt marginal, "less than," like a dirty girl peeking into a fancy china shop. Then after hours, when I let my hair down, I felt like I was slumming in my own family. I wasn't like my colleagues or my parents. I was an outsider, except of course, when I was wasted.

To the Slugs, D.O.M. was a war hero, a working man, a manly man of the highest order. Betty Bradley was a goddess, a musician, *showbiz*. How cool is that? In turn, my parents loved Nick. He was protective, a stand-up guy. Sometimes, as he hit into a vibrato, he got that same wistful, faraway look in his eyes my mother had. He even looked like her, like her father Willie, like Robert De Niro. When I introduced Nick to my parents, he was really impressed with their bar etiquette. They picked him up at the plant after work. He got in the car, and D.O.M. promptly pulled out a flask from under the driver's seat and offered him a shot. Then we went to a bar. I had never seen my parents in action—they were pros.

Housing on Long Island was always a bummer, scarce and over-priced. We needed space for the equipment and privacy for our nocturnal hobbies. We rented the top floor of a small brick building in Glen Head, a tiny town adjacent to Sea Cliff. The upstairs had two cheaply furnished apartments with yellowed linoleum and splintered wood. It was perfect. George and Sue took the front rooms, we took the back. I made slipcovers out of black and turquoise fabric, huge zigzags. We consecrated the walls with Nick's artwork, Emporium relics and band posters, rock memorabilia; it was a clubhouse. Right downstairs was an infamous divey bar called the Glen Lounge, the neon sign flashed right outside our bedroom window. Our basement was a seedy gin joint full of locals, rednecks, dealers, and rummies.

By day, the Glen Lounge was full of old men, Grumman Aerospace retired labor force. By night their sons and heirs—the CorpseGrinders—took over. The bar had a pool table and weights, too. We sat there, a battalion of gentrifying junkie scum, eating bar food, chain-smoking, playing music, watching the guys play pool. After the bar closed, the band would come upstairs. Some nights I'd make a vat of spaghetti so we didn't OD. The cops would come, then we'd swear the music was from the bar. In a matter of weeks my hair went from L'Oréal Preference Soft Black number three to Blue Black number one. That's as dark as it gets.

Without the rocker veneer, life at the Glen Lounge was *Barfly* starring Sid and Nancy. At a moment's notice, everything could disintegrate into sordidness. We were misfits wherever we went. In the City, they hated "bridge and tunnel bands," viewed us as ignorant invading hordes. Even on the nod, we reeked of Lawn Guyland. Although the New York scene was built on the backs of indigenous talent from the outer boroughs and 'burbs, City people lived in terror of suburbia. We understood that; we did, too.

On Long Island we were also outcasts viewed as degenerate sleaze. Although we were mostly native Long Island kids, as pomo-boho-proles, we radiated East Village, implying deviance—race-mixing, pansexuality, bohemia, and worst of all, *dirt,* urban filth. Knowing everyone hated us gave us an edge. We enjoyed being a threat, feeling notorious. Slugwives kept to themselves, never sat at the bar without our guys. You never knew when something ugly would explode. Someone would try to break into our apartment, piss in our doorway, dump trash on our front steps, kill our cats, or start a fight.

But the Glen Lounge had many advantages. There was a dealer living right up the street. You could buy a twenty-dollar bag, go into the bathroom, and get high. When that dried up, there was always the Lower East Side. Our new homestead was walking distance from the train. For some, a weekend hobby was gradually turning into a daily habit. By day I was doing consulting work as a program evaluator; I never drank on the job. But I began stockpiling huge amounts of sugar for when "I didn't feel well" (needed a drink). I always needed candy, gum, anything sweet.

Nick claims these accounts of my past debauchery are somewhat exaggerated but excusable as dramatic license. From Xanthos to Slugland I was never quite as bad as my friends. I made sure of that. Yes, I scammed and hoarded pills, and I could never have "just one" of anything. Not one drink, one kiss, or one bite. Whenever I started going off the deep end on one obsession, I just switched to another. It took me that much longer to see the big picture, to bottom out on any one thing.

Hello, I'm Donna, cross-addicted. A bourbon-guzzling, pill-popping, penis-addicted workaholic. But above all, a sugar-fiending cookie whore. I'd almost always rather have that bag of Nantuckets. In arty circles, among musicians, writers, intellectuals, drug and alcohol addiction is expected, it's central to rock & roll, to the life. Unfortunately, *fat* isn't hip anywhere in the social order, even among outlaws.

We know the great goddesses were not two sticks with a hole, yet our divinely sensual women of flesh—Camryn Manheim, Anna Nicole Smith, Roseanne, Oprah, Fergie, and Monica—have been chronically ridiculed and condemned. Our cultural misogyny has crucified Mama Cass Elliot, Carnie Wilson, and Nancy Wilson of Heart for looking like *women*. And even now, after feminism, being a junkie still carries less stigma.

Donnie and Lizzie had a dope connection in Alphabet City, a couple named Hank and Trixie. I met them at the wedding; Nick was best man. As maid of honor, I made Lizzie's bridal shower featuring pasta primavera, crabmeat, and stuffed mushrooms. The ceremony took place at Lizzie's mom's in East Meadow, outside in their plush backyard. Her mother sewed the wedding dress from a pattern. The newlyweds rented a motel room; they were spending their honeymoon in the City. We drove them in after the ceremony. Lizzie wanted us to stop off on Clinton Street first so they could cop. After all, it was their wedding night. I was driving, I refused. Not because I wanted to save them from addiction, but I had my career to think about. I could tolerate eccentricities, but no way would I risk getting busted for somebody else's addiction. So I dropped them off and went out for cocktails with Nick.

Hank and Trixie were dealers. The four became best friends, hung out, like a family unit, similar to the bonding described by ethnographer Terry Williams in *Crackhouse*. Donnie and Lizzie would drop in, Trixie would go cop. She was Latina, grew up in the neighborhood. Hank was white, but they knew him on the street. They had kids. The two couples got high together, watched TV, ate dinner. But Donnie was very clear: "If they weren't going to cop for us, we wouldn't have even been there."

For Donnie, heroin was everything. Eventually, it took over his sex drive. Payback was a bitch, too. Everything is in pain, your whole body. Your bones hurt. You're hot, then cold. Worst of all, you can't sleep. But when he was "nice," it was the greatest drug in the world. It made him feel like a god. In freezing weather he could walk outside wearing just a T-shirt and he'd feel great, so strong inside, so good, so on top of it all. He said, "When you look at a junkie, they are just nodding, vegetating. But inside, they're completely alert." Donnie was hyper. He used dope for the same reason I liked booze—to calm down.

Drug addiction is many things: a means of acceptance, a way to cover feelings of failure or worthlessness, an escape from the truth of a dead-end life. It is a self-medicating, a drowning out of unbearable feelings, a cry for help. But it isn't all bad-evil and sick. It's also kicks, fun, an adventure, the expressway to a blissful communion with yourself.

Dope can be religious, too, a taste of God's love on the fly. If you're restless and bored, it's a colorful outlet. For some, smack addiction becomes a fashion accessory that completes the image. It goes with the
music, the clothes, the cocky look—instant outlaw. Over time top
heroin chic would be recognized as a distinctive style, fashion models
like Kate Moss would slink around with pasty pallor, sallow, rail-thin,
greasy hair. At one point, it was *the* look.

The Slugs' ultimate hero was Keith Richards, the greatest junkie of
the twentieth century, a legend, a survivor, second only to William Burroughs. We never missed a Stones tour. We all featured layered hair. If
Johnny Thunders was our Christ the Son, Keith was the Father. I guess
dope was the Holy Ghost. White punks were the New Apostles. Keith
in his glory was unknowable, but Johnny was one of us, mortal, from
Queens, a boroughs kid, a baseball freak, an American. Totally *Noo
Yawk,* Thunders was a scammer, a neighborhood fuckup in Chinese
handmade silk suits and a big black fedora. The Stones were English
rock stars; the Heartbreakers were former gang members, among New
York's original hitters. Jerry Nolan was in the Ellery Bops, and the Master Chaplans, Thunders hung with the 90th Street Fast Boys. Walter
Lure was a Green Dog. That's how they knew about D.T.K. L.A.M.F.
and what it meant out on the street. It wasn't something they read in
books.

In *Keith Richards: Life as a Rolling Stone,* the biography by Barbara
Charone, Keith Richards claims his lifelong heroin addiction began as
a way to calm down after touring, a segue back to the normal pace of
life. He explains, "It's coming off the road and dealing with the with-
drawal and expenditure of energy that does it. That absolute cutoff
after two or three months on the road is difficult to adjust to. Coming
back to a completely different rhythm was hard. And I found that
smack made it much easier for me to slow down, very smoothly and
gradually. Otherwise I'd be glad to be home, but I was still so hyper."
The one thing he couldn't handle was the sudden change in pace. He
had no brakes, so heroin became the way to stop it cold, to disengage
from the altered state of accelerated creative output. This need to cool

down after a work binge often accounts for addiction in actors, writers, and other artists. How do you calm down after you've interfaced with God? How do you get back to earth?

Thunders almost called the Heartbreakers the Junkies but he knew they'd never get the airplay. They never did anyway. Thunders's self-destructiveness became part of his shtick. He became a caricature of himself. Former bandmate and Voidoid Richard Hell once said, "Johnny Thunders is the rock & roll Dean Martin of heroin." After a while some people just came for the spectacle, to see if he'd collapse right there on the stage. Live in Sweden in 1984, he asked, "How many of you people came to see me die tonight?" Promoters capitalized on it, making him work even when he was bleeding and dope sick. We never dared to miss a show, always afraid it would be his last. We believed that for years.

Johnny fused the cold cockroach soul of the junkie with the relentless howl of the unlovable child. But the true brilliance came in his mistakes, accidents of creation never repeated. And then there was his hair. Black, long, thick Sicilian locks, teased and piled even higher than the Shangri-Las', those immortal hitter chicks from his neighboring Cambria Heights. Later on, he chopped it, popped a proud rooster in the crown, architecture of attitude.

One minute his music was suicidal and abject, then dopey and cruel—a misogynist prick. A garbage-pail theologian, within seconds he could shift into pure rapture, transcendent, sublime. A spasm of vulnerability and brutality propelled each chord into a cotton-shot reverb.

There are so many things we can't put into words, so music says it for us. If I could tell you why I love Johnny Thunders, what his music means to me, if I could actually put it all into words, I'd be the Queen of the Universe. I would know the unknowable nature of God. I would be speaking the unspeakable name in cascading thunderbolts. Some say the universe started with a big bang, one huge bolt of thunder, *kaboom, let there be life!* Who knows if Johnny Thunders was just fucked up and it was all an accident, a miracle, like creation itself?

Heroin, a love story. Heroin from A to Z. Demerol, morphine, Dilaudid, Pantopon, opium, Dolophine. Smoke it, eat it, shoot it, snort it, shove it up your butt. In *Junkie,* William Burroughs claimed opium was "profane and quantitative, like money." He noted there were no opium cults. But that was before the punks. In the beginning, Sue Mordred said dope felt "like waking up in her mother's arms." It wrapped around you and made you feel all warm. "There was this feeling in my neck, not far from the feeling of an orgasm, a rush of blood and you're in this protective place, clouded over, earthbound. Nothing penetrates it. It's total freedom, pure love. But the reverse was also true. You have great ideas, but you don't produce, you're in a safe cocoon, blinded by a false light, living in your head."

While she was high Sue forgot her marriage was failing, her husband was passed out, life was hitting a dead end. Smack made our seedy surroundings at the Glen Lounge seem beautiful and cool. Sue never got a habit and she never shared a needle. One day she just put it down, moved back home, got divorced, learned how to play bass, and started a band of her own. Sue had been writing songs for years, but she always gave her lyrics away. She was standing in the boys' shadows, hoping to overcome her pain, to get back some power by practicing the craft. At one point Sue was convinced the ghost of Brian Jones lived in her apartment. Spells and incantations, she was a total victim. Then she changed.

Years later I got to see her play at Webster Hall, singing her lyrics in her own band, in her own voice. Sue was the only other girl who survived. She swore the bass was going to be her ticket out. I always thought she meant to rock stardom. I didn't understand she meant it was her ticket out of death.

Rick Rivets's life in rock has been chronicled in several books, including *Too Much Too Soon,* Nina Antonia's fine history of the New York Dolls. For a few years Rivets worked at a guitar store, mentoring Long Island's fledgling axe gods in the ways of the craft. More recently he played with MFU (Martians from Uranus), recording and touring. Sue Mordred, moved up to the woods—her dream come true. Busy

writing songs and short stories, and studying astrology, she now orga-
nizes prayer circles for women.

Coco was a triple Gemini, easily bored and restless. At first she was
just a boozer. Then she started playing around, first with the guys, then
came the dope. Blaccard filed for divorce, and built himself a seaside
automotive empire. The last we heard of Coco she was in Brooklyn, out
on the street, hard living in Bushwick. In and out of Rikers, running
from warrants, no teeth, emaciated, stinky. She started speaking fluent
Spanish, self-taught. She figured out right away white girls are easy
prey. Coco ripped off everyone she knew, burned all her bridges, became a full-blown pincushion. Her worst fear had come true. Now she
was a blow-job whore.

Matt swore dope sapped all his creativity, but he did it anyway. By
1977 he was already up to two bags a day, every two days. He had an
apartment in Forest Hills; he drove a cab. He copped at 8th and D,
pulled over at 23rd Street by the river, and shot up. It went on like that
for a few years, with or without the Slugs.

He started splitting in two. When he was sober, he was playing guitar, music filled his soul, he was a happy man. When he shot dope, the
beauty of life dissolved, all his creativity drained away. All he could do
was light a cigarette and then do it all over again two days later. He lost
his apartment, moved back in with his parents. His mother found his
works. She confronted him and said he had to get out.

Matt answered an ad in the *Voice,* got a job as a handyman, and
moved to upstate New York. He knew as long as he stayed in New York
City, he'd be trapped in the cycle. He cleaned up, returned to the City
after a few months, and hit it one last time. But now it was different.
He saw he had other choices. He decided to go back to school for a degree in engineering and paid his own way. School was Matt's ticket out.
He also had music. But most of all, he had faith in himself, some faint
hope in the possibility that he was worth something. Sometimes that's
all that stands between an addict and death. It pulls you back from the
edge, it promises a second chance. Like Matt said, strumming away,
"Every good boy does fine."

Methadone is the gulag of heroin addiction. Some swear it kills you, others know it saved them from an early grave. Streetside, you could always sell it for dope money. Either way, you had to go to the clinic every day. If you smoked pot, drank, or took a Valium, it came up in your urine and they made you wait three hours to see a counselor. Or they booted you. Sometimes cranberry juice cleaned out your urine, blocked the quinine that cut the heroin, but not always. You also had to be careful not to eat poppy bagels, since it could throw off the test. They had counseling services at the facility, and attendance at Narcotics Anonymous was mandatory, but it wasn't for everyone. The God stuff really puts people off, especially in New York. And if you're not ready for recovery, it's just another pain in the ass. As such, NA was most useful for meeting other junkies, to make new drug connections. At one point the clinic line *was* the scene, a who's who of punk rock's finest junkies.

After her fingers were amputated, Lizzie and Donnie decided enough. They did a twenty-one-day detox at Flower Hill. Little white pills, Dolophine, they got clean, but they went out right after. By the early 1980s Donnie and Lizzie were living in Queens, so they got set up at Long Island Jewish Hospital. They heard it was a real maintenance program, long term. It was also five minutes from home. You have to show up at six-thirty A.M. every day, present your pay stub every six months. They start your dose by how much you have in your system. So of course the day before you surrender, you'll shoot up three to four bags, even do a little coke. They got on the "work program." For a while, everything was okay.

Humans are like addicts stumbling toward the light, holding on for the promise of infinite love. In "Heroin," Lou Reed's dictum, he says, *"I'm gonna try for the kingdom if I can. . . ."* We know it's a long shot but we go for it anyway. We have no choice. The Hebrews warn of the unknowable nature of G-d—we cannot see Him, so vast is His glory, we cannot even utter His name. This is why under Jewish law, G-d is never written completely lest it be destroyed, taken in vain, defiled.

Like everyone, the addict yearns for the unknowable truth. But we can't just take it on faith. We can't wait. Forget religion, prayer, or meditation. That's for suckers. We need to know for sure, we need to know now, and we always want more. The desire to merge with the Divine is so pressing, the agony of separation so overwhelming that we overwrite the buffer, blow out the fuse box. Drunken monkeys, grasping, desperate to *know*. We shouldn't hate ourselves for our spiritual hunger—a longing for God so intense it wants to kill us. But we do. Thunders understood that better than anyone.

Well I'll just tell you what you want to hear. . . . In "So Alone," recorded live in 1984 at the Lyceum in London, our St. John of the Gutter Guitar tells a universal tale of fear, self-deception, and redemption. Johnny spells out the paradox of the needy addict. As usual, we long to get close, to be near someone, but if we do, we know it will kill us. Luckily, there is a way out, one last hope. "So Alone" is the story of a young kid hustling on the seedy streets of Manhattan's West Side. The kid encounters a nasty-looking black guy, a huge man completely decked out in leather, total S&M. "Hey kid, come here," he orders, with dick in hand. The kid obliges and gets fucked up the butt.

But that's not the end of the story. Out of nowhere, this menacing black man starts sobbing like a child, *I'm so all alone. . . .* He's miserable, broken, spiritually bereft. Just as we're about to give up hope, Johnny Thunders declares, "But he's got this one thing," one thing left to redeem him. And with that, Johnny's guitar cries out for love in a roaring, bellowing rip. All tragedy and triumph resound in a momentary blast of power chords set in a blues field. Sacred thunderbolts of noise sent down to us from heaven, down to the hellhole of isolation, lifting us back up again into the light. On that note, we are saved. God's love fills the hole, at least for the moment.

Our Father who art in heaven hallowed be thy name . . . fuck you . . . oh God. Faith is like the weather in the Caribbean: It's here today, gone tomorrow. Intimacy is impossible. You are condemned to your private misery. Reach out for love, ask for help, and you'll get smashed. Maybe we learn that as frightened children, maybe we feel it as an existential terror. Maybe we are just born with it, born to lose, born too loose.

In Johnny's early Dolls and Heartbreakers songs, you hear that cock-of-the-walk boasting and preening. But in his later solo material, he's melancholy and downbeat, singing the blues. We hear the longing, for light, love, for the missing father he adored. Johnny's father cut out when he was young, left the family to run with the broads, to party and play. The little Italian boy waited every Christmas Eve, all dressed up in his finest, but Daddy never came back. The pros were scouting young Johnny for baseball, he was *that* good. But even a string of home runs wasn't gonna bring Daddy home. Nothing was enough to make Daddy stick around.

That longing never stops, not until you're comatose. And then, even after you're high, you're still gonna be waiting for the man. But Daddy's gone, he isn't coming back, not ever. You're older now, but you still think and feel like a little child, like you did when he left. He doesn't love you, that's why he isn't coming back. Not from the hospital or from heaven, from his drink or his new woman, his job or the streets. It's always your fault, your lack, your flaw. You can't even bear the thought *please, God, just to see him walk back into the room one more time.* But you're lucky tonight. Just before you crumble, Johnny's guitar kicks in.

God spoke to me every time Johnny Thunders played. It was a dark truth in an empty chasm, the abysmal, the wretched and abject. The raw wound exposed and buried over and over again in a dialectic of divinity. Light through pain, joy from suffering, clarity in misery. Buddhists understand that life is filled with sorrow, that human existence is based on a fundamental impermanence, which always means the experience of pain and loss. At the bottom is the terror of being abandoned, unlovable, unprotected. But how do wounded children make sense of *that?* We don't. We just try to fill the hole, kill the pain, stop the longing. We start doing it early on, and we keep doing it until it kills us.

If the existential truth of life's essential sadness hits you too soon, you may never learn how to walk through it. You'll spend years stumbling alone in the valley of fear. So many of my friends died in the valley, never knowing why they suffered or what they needed. The lucky few found a distraction, a temporary reprieve. For some, it was their music, for others, it was their kids. For me, it was sociology.

Donna between Lewis Coser and the Binary Boy.

11

SCIENCE AS A VACATION

For nothing is worthy of man as man

unless he can pursue it with passionate devotion.

—MAX WEBER

or most people, a graduate school education offers preparation for a career in mental labor and the promise of economic and social mobility.
But it is also a residual category for individuals hopelessly adrift, a rest
stop for lost souls to find new bearings. You hit a brick wall, you've been
laid off again. Or may be a bad relationship bottomed you out, or too
many dead friends. You're disgusted, looking for a new beginning. What
will you do with your life now? At least if you're in school, it looks like
you're doing *something.* You tell yourself you are moving forward, now
you have *goals.* There's still some hope you might become normal after
all. Knowledge workers need advanced degrees to compete in the marketplace of ideas, proper credentials, certification, legitimation.

For me, graduate school also promised a program of recovery, a one-
way ticket out of the valley of fear. Literature from Hazelden describes

addiction as "an experience that blocks our awareness, fills time, occupies attention, and has an overwhelming compulsive quality." Advanced study in sociology also fits that description. It distracted me from drinking, suppressed my appetite, and blocked any sexual desire. Graduate school involved hours of intense, obsessive activity. There is no greater outlet for the addictive personality than a career in graduate school.

In addition to retarding the process of my inevitable decline, I became computer literate, learned advanced statistics and research methods, and grappled with both classical and contemporary social theory. I became conversant with the substantive literatures regarding the professions, complex organizations, gender, race, culture, and theories of ideology. The first two years are like boot camp. You learn to make deadlines, to get the work in, no matter what. Even sick, bleeding, hung over, in mourning, the first thought of the day will be *to get the work done.*

Fear and self-loathing are your primary motivations. You know at any moment they will find out you are really stupid, defund you, and send you right back to your wretchedness and the dead-end life that brought you here in the first place. Their power is predicated on your sense of unworthiness. You know you will never pass your qualifying exams, defend your dissertation, get a good job, publish, or be tenured. The humility so necessary for scholarly rigor is gradually displaced by humiliation, self-effacement. Feelings of powerlessness result. After a few years, you realize you have nothing to offer anyone, no place else to go. You're broke, debts are piling up, you have no real marketable skills. Now they own you.

So you stay, three, five, ten years, even longer. Your marriage is over, you chain-smoke, you can't stop eating, you drink too much. Your hair is turning gray, and still, you're there. Obsequious, you cringe and grovel before your superiors. By now you have relinquished your identity. All control of your life has been surrendered, subordinated to their will. You are almost thirty, but you feel like a child with abusive parents who break your legs then chastise you for not running fast enough. Eventually, you want to kill them. Every night you dream of lining them up against the wall and slaughtering them just to end the pain. You can see them grimacing, their blood splattered all over the sterile floor tiles. Faces that once terrified you now beg for your mercy. But one way or another, you'll end up hurting yourself instead.

If you've been there, I don't have to tell you what it's like. Even as you resist, you succumb. Academic sociology promised to be a death trap even more horrific than getting married. But I see now that God had a plan for me, and once again, St. Serendipity intervened.

I got my degree at Big Science University, way out on eastern Long Island. As departments go, ours was eclectic, generous, and indulgent. A large, impersonal bureaucratic organization meant less intrusion, more room to maneuver. Big Science was known to be entrepreneurial. Like my high school, the best thing they did was leave me alone. In the days before do-me feminism, cultural studies, and identity politics, only men taught social theory. One tough-girl professor referred to it as "prick territory." So the women taught "methods." Like the early women in rock who were relegated to playing bass, we did the house-work, the gruntwork while *they* played lead. As the mules of the socio-logical universe, we were intellectually unclean, unfit for the holy texts. For all the liberal egalitarian rhetoric, it was a lot like my yeshiva days at Beth-El.

Thanks to glue-sniffing, I had piss-poor math skills. Given my level of intellectual engagement during high school, I didn't know basic al-gebra, and signed numbers baffled me. For in-class statistics exams I sedated myself with morphine and Valium and I always failed. But I ex-celled at research methods, designing and implementing instruments of measurement, conducting studies, doing the detective work to uncover the truths of the social world.

As a besotted undergraduate, I had mastered the use of the counter-sorter, a primitive data-processing machine, a predecessor of the com-puter. I had a wad of punch cards filled with survey responses I would hand-feed into the counter-sorter, hoping to generate causal relation-ships among variables. Respondents were asked questions like "How often do you go to church?" "Do you live in a city or a small town?" "Do you condone premarital sex?" Answers were cross-tabulated with race, income, sex, age. Does high church attendance influence people's views on premarital sex? What happens to positions on premarital sex when frequent church attending urban dwellers are compared to equally pious rural folk? I went at it for hours. I'd hit the big time. Graduate school meant higher technology and endless random sampling.

Research methods can be very intricate, involving long hours of perfecting and refining. Unlike Howard Stern and Joey Ramone, I don't have full-blown obsessive-compulsive disorder, but I do greatly enjoy repetitive motion. I figured that as director of research, it wouldn't matter if I was d-u-m-b in math. I'd just hire somebody to crank the numbers for me. Even today, I love that Big Science; it soothes like Ritalin. Like death metal, it slows my brain waves by speeding me up into overdrive.

Once a year you'd face the days of awe and trembling, when the department evaluated your "normal progress." If funding was tight, they dumped you for arbitrary and capricious reasons. If you didn't have a big daddy protector to stick up for you—a faculty member who had you on a grant or knew your name—you were doomed.

I met Lewis Coser the first day of school. I greatly admired his work but had no intention of formally studying with him; Coser was a theory guy. I was a vulgar positivist, determined to be a program evaluator, a Queen of all Quants. But there he sat at the head of the seminar table peering at us through a cloud of smoke, chain-smoking. In his thick German accent, Coser mesmerized us with tales of our forefathers, the masters of sociological thought. There were the Europeans, Mannheim, Simmel, Veblen, the refugees, and the Americans George Herbert Mead and Robert Park. Professor Coser placed these thinkers in the context of their time. Stories of great men, smoke wafting; it felt like a tribal campfire.

Although I was thirty-one when I started graduate school, I was as restless as a kid who needed Ritalin. To chill out, I usually sat in class writing song lyrics or making up names for imaginary bands. But Coser's classical theory course changed everything. Within weeks I developed a Max Weber fixation. I became obsessed with his theories of rationality and charisma, his comparative historical analyses of capitalism and bureaucracy, and his macho dueling scars. I idolized the hard-drinking, bearded Weber like he was Hemingway. At one point, dictionary in hand, I tried to read him in the original German, hoping to get closer to the source. I gave up by the time I hit *werbeziehung* (value-relevance). If a classmate dared "misinterpret" Weber's ideas, I'd explode with rage, "That's not what he meant!!!" Even though Weber died in 1920, our bond transcended time and space. On his birthday, I posted celebratory signs, distributed announcements, and brought party treats to class. After a while people called me "Maxine Weber."

From cosmetology to cosmology. Thanks to Professor Coser's course, the sociology of knowledge slowly lifted me up from the gutters of positivism. I departed the material world and entered the spiritual realm. Once, pointing from his office window out to the snowy walkways and trees of eastern Long Island, Coser referred to data as "anything out there." After that anything seemed possible. Once you got him started, Coser was full of anecdotes about the Frankfurt School scholars who, like him, had fled the Nazis. Theodor Adorno, Max Horkheimer, and the tragic Walter Benjamin, who, when Paris fell to the Nazis in 1940, fled south hoping to escape to America via Spain. Informed by the chief of police at the Franco-Spanish border that he would be turned over to the Gestapo, Benjamin committed suicide. It was like Chuck Berry telling you about Ritchie Valens and Buddy Holly. Coser was very tall, like Howard Stern and Joey Ramone. He always wore a suit or jacket, funky and formal like the Heartbreakers onstage, his white hair slicked straight back. For mainstream academe, Coser had a *look*. If you produced a cogent argument or synthesis of ideas, he'd say, "Splendid, my dear," sounding really German, like Nena in "99 Luftballons."

Banished from Hitler's Berlin because his father was Jewish, Lewis Coser, professor emeritus, now found himself sequestered on the ass-end of Long Island, among too many organization men, sterile thinkers, and feeble pedants. Coser seemed distracted and bored at Big Science. I wondered what went through his mind at department meetings as faculty pondered such weighty themes as the need to keep better records of photocopying, paper clips, and pens. Max Weber's notion of an "iron cage" was a world without grace, a stifling bureaucratic prison; like Reagan's America, academe in the early 1980s was surely that.

When Dr. Coser got into the elevator, nobody dared to speak. Students froze up, terrified of the great man. But a stellar scholar is like a rock star: charismatic, vibrant, drawing you closer, as if to fire. What fan wouldn't jump at a random chance to interact with a favorite singer or guitarist? I grew up on the teachings of Dylan and Zappa. If rock stars could be mentors, then the reverse was also true. In fact, the Sagittarian Coser was born the same day as Jimi Hendrix—a generation earlier. Surely it was a sign.

Starting a conversation with Lewis Coser in the elevator was like engaging Debbie Harry about fingernail polish backstage at CBGB's. Straight shop talk, gossip about Auguste Comte's wife the hooker, or Max Weber's ties to D. H. Lawrence through the Von Richthofen sisters. Like the Mordred sisters, these early-nineteenth-century literary babes knew their rock & roll. In the early days, women-in-theory were like women-in-rock, we had few role models. But I did have a spiritual advisor, one who transcended all categories.

If Johnny Thunders ushered me through the valley of fear, clarifying the relationship between abandonment, God, and addiction, Joey Ramone got me through graduate school. *D-U-M-B everyone's accusing me!* Fusing high-tone Britboy inflection with a low-rent boroughs twang, Joey delivered the Ramones' brutal truth with rapid fire. Through twenty years of touring, eighteen albums, over 2,250 shows, the Ramones offered a nation of warthogs, outsiders, pinheads, and social rejects an alternative to annihilation and self-destruction.

Unlike most intellectuals who claim to be utopians, the Ramones were inclusive and nonjudgmental. They were my band. Every song they ever wrote has been for me. "Now I Wanna Sniff Some Glue" valorized my favorite drug. Then the Ramones created a real controversy with "Carbona Not Glue." The song was pulled for fear of a lawsuit from the Carbona Products Company. Like most garbage heads, the Ramones didn't know Carbona was a corporate trademark for our beloved substance, carbon tetrachloride. "Carbona Not Glue" was eventually pulled from *Leave Home,* the Ramones' second album, and banned from UK radio.

Moreover, the Ramones canonized my birth turf, Rockaway Beach, and covered all the great surfing classics of my youth, like "California Sun" and "Surfin' Bird." They chronicled everyday life in the profane world as I lived it and popular culture as I loved it. The Ramones celebrated everything "serious" scholars were admonished to avoid. In the days before cultural studies exploded, mainstream academe was high-toned and tight-assed, shunning all that was sacred: pizza, TV, Coney Island, chicken vindaloo, horror movies, soda machines, cretin families, and the emancipatory promise of rock & roll radio. The Ramones shared my worldview and enhanced it with indigenous wit and irony.

Instead of letting the creeps get the last laugh, the Ramones fought the power. Making fun of the liars and hypocrites, they exposed our fucked-up families, idiotic government, repressive schooling, and the menace of psychotherapy. Los Ramones liberated us by laughing at our human frailties, ridiculing addictions from true love to Chinese rocks. If I liked some guy, I imagined him singing, *"Hey, little girl, I wanna be your boyfriend."* When it was over, and I hated his guts I'd blast *"I don't want you . . . anymore,"* and he was eliminated.

I was a Ph.D. lobotomy. If anyone in the department tried to put me down, Joey whispered, *"Gabba, gabba, we accept you, one of us,"* and I was safe. "Howling at the Moon" gave me the courage to resist the bullshit, to stand up for myself—*You broke the rules and won.* When I was lonely, lost, feeling useless, and misplaced, Joey had a prayer for me, *something to believe in.* As teenagers, the Ramones were awkward, they had trouble getting girls, they were disturbed, loners, misfits who turned to music as an alternative to suicide, homicide, or final surrender (being normal).

The Ramones also reminded me of my family. The original members grew up in middle-class Queens, rode the subway, carrying their guitars to rehearsal in shopping bags. Johnny and Dee Dee were obsessed with war movies. Johnny spent two years in military school. Dee Dee grew up in Germany on a military base, an army brat. His childhood pet was Kessie, a dachshund, like the Judas Iscariot of my youth.

Together, Johnny and Dee Dee made up the psycho-paramilitary faction of the Ramones. Like my D.O.M., they were fiercely patriotic, collected war memorabilia, and hated hippies. Marky's father was a longshoreman who got a law degree at night. He was a socialist, a labor guy like my grandpa Benny.

Joey's mother was a bohemian like Betty Bradley, an artist, Jewish, too. He was the world's most unlikely rock star, tall, skinny, gawky, and shy. The kind of guy that got picked on at school. If it hadn't been for a rock & roll heart, Joey probably would have blown up Forest Hills High School.

Like my psyche, the Ramones were a collision of discordant ideologies cranked at ten. Thanks to them, a world of contradictions and oxymorons made sense. I was alienated yet patriotic, arrogant yet populist. I hated the world yet wanted to save it.

Most important, the Ramones taught me something about writing. Dee Dee's Queens logic mandated that "rock & roll should be three words and a chorus, and the three words should be good enough to say it all." I hoped to apply this to social theory, to uplift academic discourse from the passive-aggressive intentional obfuscation of our professional jargon, to write important books that my parents and friends could read and understand. Ever implied in the promise of upward mobility is the severing of old ties; thanks to the Ramones, I never lost my roots.

At a time when American intellectuals were turning away from the social world and increasingly toward "the text," the Ramones demonstrated more guts than any of them. *Bonzo goes to Bitburg and goes out for a cup of tea.* When most remained silent, the Ramones spoke out against President Reagan's inconceivable betrayal, his German tour of Nazi SS soldiers' graves. In "Gimme Gimme Shock Treatment," their rant against mandatory psychotherapy prefigured radical psychiatrist Peter R. Breggin's chilling exposés of Ritalin and Prozac. Going mental, being sedated, the Ramones covered everything from world decline and personal alienation, and they made their point fun, quick, and direct.

Even with the Ramones serving as my de facto dissertation committee, I did need some additional guidance. At one point I asked Dr.

Coser to review a conference paper I was giving, a critique called "*Star Trek III* and the Ethics of Technology." I had a longtime fascination with Mr. Spock and saw in his relationship with Captain Kirk the dialectic of rationality and humanism implied in Marx's and Weber's theories on technology. With all the self-seriousness of the aspiring dilettante, I boldly stated my intention in my introduction, "The purpose of this interrogation is to deconstruct the discourse of scientism . . ." blah, blah, blah. . . . Like I knew what the fuck I was talking about. Usually a mellow guy, Coser became furious. "Look, Donna, you're a very smart woman, but this paper is *pretentious.*" Like Dee Dee Ramone, Lewis Coser had familial roots in Berlin. And following the Minimalist Master Dee Dee, Coser scolded, "The social world is complex enough. We don't need to make it worse with overly complicated writing!"

I was mortified, finished. I had been found out. Now he knew I was a fraud, it was all over. I skulked away and sought out the support of another graduate student who worked with Coser. Instead of consoling me, he congratulated me. "That's great! He takes you seriously!!" From the deep void, light appeared. Now I had protection. Coser's interest in my scholarly development meant the department had to take me seriously. They couldn't just dismiss me as a flake in tattered regalia. Once people think you're smart or talented, you can get away with anything.

Thanks to Lewis Coser, I also had a conversion experience, a paradigm shift. A career in quantitative sociology would have bestowed marketable skills that translated into a high-powered job in a multinational corporation. Today, some of my best friends from graduate school are making high six figures, riding in limos, crunching numbers, predicting quarterly profits. But it wasn't my fate. I became a writer, a journalist. No big bucks, but, hey, I'm on the guest list.

Although he himself rejected the label, Coser was considered a "conflict theorist," focused on class and power in a macro-structural framework. A student-peer of eminent sociologist Robert Merton at Columbia University, Lewis Coser enjoyed a stature in the discipline that gave the department much of its scholarly prestige. Most American intellectuals at the time seemed xenophobic, like they *hated* the USA.

But not Coser. He and his wife, Rose—an acclaimed scholar in her own right—did not look back to the killing fields of Europe, to "good old days" that were never really that great. Instead, they pushed forward, forging an intellectual bridge between the old world and the new.

More sedate in their later years, the Cosers were rebels for their time, bohemians. Every summer they went to Cape Cod to write. They took sabbatical leave in France. At Big Science, the Cosers hosted fabulous monthly soirees at their home, *salons.* I mainly remember drinking cognac and watching Tisa the Siamese cat sprawled out on the piano. Art and music filled the air. There was good food, the finest wine and cheese.

To some, Lewis Coser's conflict theory was (gasp) "not really Marxian," but mere Durkheimian sociology dressed up in lefty drag. Durkheim understood the, uh, glue it took to hold the world together. What the hell did Marx know about love? By 1986 I was so disgusted with the lack of patriotism among American intellectuals that I presented a paper at the Annual Conference on Social Theory, Politics and the Arts at the New School titled "Snobs and Slobs: Loving the Masses Theoretically." Back then I fought back through vitriolic papers, convinced that writing itself could somehow transform the world.

At least I could settle the score on outstanding vendettas. Symbolically defending D.O.M. against the Cretins, or myself against the *yentas,* I played it out my way. I couldn't understand how you could uplift the race if you held most of it in contempt. I had to purge this poison in myself and in others. That was my war, my bias, and I soon found an army of like-minded comrades. I met Anthony in the parking garage downstairs from the Social and Behavioral Sciences building. Parked, all alone, just sitting in the Ice Beast, peacefully smoking a pipe of cherry-blend tobacco, listening to Pere Ubu. A mutual friend advised that Anthony loved rock & roll. He suggested we become pals because we had so much in common. Jaded and disgusted by our surroundings, we both assumed it was something horrid and New Wave, soft like the Police or the Cars.

To test the waters, I made Anthony a cassette tape. In the 1980s tapes were a gesture of friendship, extending an invitation into your world, a way to connect or seduce. I gave Anthony a collection of favorite Slugland punk tunes, including a most subversively situated (for 1984) cut of "Stairway to Heaven." What bonded us for life was my inclusion of the obscure "Annalisa" by Public Image, Ltd. This led to a decade of noise—Butthole Surfers, Hüsker Dü, Sonic Youth, Big Black, Black Flag—then thrash: Motörhead, Metallica, Anthrax, Slayer, and Danzig. I got Anthony involved with hardcore's amazing S.O.D. (Storm Troopers of Death), he sent me copies of neo-Nazi Skrewdriver. A while back, Anthony made me buy *The Marshall Mathers LP.* Thanks to life with D.O.M., I have a high tolerance for the intolerant.

My new best friend was a 350-pound biker from the Florida panhandle who dressed like ZZ Top. Sometimes Anthony wore a powder-blue polyester three-piece suit. He often employed a hand-carved walking cane with a sterling silver handle. When we weren't shopping or drinking, we were eating huge meals at the diner: roasted Long Island duck, mashed potatoes, French fries, egg creams, buttered rolls dipped in clam chowder, cheesecake, chocolate layer cake. Once we ate so much we puked all over the parking lot.

Anthony had a secret crush on a granola feminist who later became a lesbian. I harbored a burning desire for a conservative Canadian, a mild-mannered organizational theorist. Why? Because somehow Anthony convinced me this guy was secretly Joey Ramone. We decided to take them out for dinner, to a classy Italian joint. As a test drive, we first went ourselves, got fully dressed, made reservations, picked out the perfect table, and ordered a lovely meal. But we never got up the courage to ask them out, or anyone else.

Anthony's favorite movie was *Eraserhead,* and that's how he combed his hair—a big brown fluffy muff, five inches high, until the day he shaved it off and went skin. Later, as the heaviness of the alloy 1980s kicked in, Anthony favored death and destruction nonsense—engineer boots, black leather, cutoff T-shirts, skulls, and multiple piercings. This necessitated frequent excursions to St. Mark's Place, where we enjoyed endless rounds of cocktails at the Holiday Lounge, a neighborhood bar with a good jukebox and punks on parade. Thanks to Dr. Fiend (speed), Anthony lost over a hundred pounds. After that he looked like Lou Reed's guitarist Robert Quine.

Anthony could get away with anything. Once, he beat the shit out of a hairy New Left relic who was always bossing people around. Everyone was delighted; they lined up to shake Anthony's hand. Then he shocked the politically correct "sensitive males" by bringing a porn tape to a department bachelor party. The feminists loved him for his exposé of the wimp hypocrisy. Born a Southern Baptist with an Appalachian bloodline, Anthony grew up on a farm, an active member of the local 4-H Club. Somehow, at a tender age, Lou Reed, not Jesus, came into his life. Anthony's idea of heaven was a bottle of Johnny Walker Black and an endless loop of Reed's *Berlin*.

My parents loved Anthony. He was a polite southern gentleman, and his father was a veteran, like D.O.M. At one point Anthony took me home to meet his mama, but we couldn't tell her I was Jewish. Mama had never crossed the Mason-Dixon line. Still bitter about the War of Northern Aggression, she didn't like Yankees. Mama wasn't specifically anti-Semitic, she had just never met a Jewish person before, and we were afraid to freak her out.

The Slugs quickly absorbed Anthony into the vortex, their mutual devotion to Dr. Fiend and Professor Aloysius (alcohol) yielded an immediate perfect positive correlation. They dubbed him the Genius Biker. Anthony was a quantitative wonder kid. He worked high up in administration at Big Science, where his invaluable skills made him untouchable. On the night of my statistics final, Anthony spent four hours hopelessly trying to teach me signed numbers. For his birthday I got him a tattoo of a rock & roll heart off a favorite Lou Reed anthem. For my birthday he presented me with four copies of the Heartbreakers' classic vinyl *L.A.M.F.* He was a compulsive collector of albums, T-shirts, silver rings, bandanas—whatever caught his eye. Our friendship reached its peak when Anthony gave me a copy of *Statistical Methods for the Social Sciences* by Agresti and Agresti. This was proof of the highest devotion; his holy bible, up there with *Berlin*, his favorite Lou Reed album. I still use it every day in my work. In fact, it's right here, right now, under my computer monitor, lifting it up an inch and a half so my field of vision is just right.

As the pressure of hangovers, sleep deprivation, hunger, and qualifying exams mounted, I began dreaming about Joey Ramone. Let us take a moment to explicate the concept of the imaginary friend and its role in popular culture. Everyone has one. The lefties have theirs in the proletariat. Anthony has one in Lou Reed. Other people have one in Jesus, Allah, Buddha, or the G-d of Israel. Well, I had one in Joey Ramone. My personal savior offered guidance and deliverance—about some guy, a conference, my funding, career opportunities, or a pep talk right before exams.

Even now, after the band has broken up, after Joey himself has ascended to pure Spirit, he's still here, he tells me what to do. I go to sleep, and Joey appears, we'll consult, and when I wake up I have an answer. Joey is a conduit to my higher power, a sacred connection to my own divinity. He's the catalyst for personal integration, for deep connection with the universal truth. Like every Ramones fan, I'm taking communion every time I eat pizza.

The dream was always the same: Joey Ramone sitting in the corner on a chair, arms folded, head tilted to the left, listening, digesting, calmly dispensing wisdom in holy boroughs regional dialect. As usual, Anthony twisted this all around to suggest I was secretly in love with Joey Ramone. But Anthony was dead wrong about my relationship with Joey Ramone. Rock stars were not meant to be objects of sexual or romantic love. They're spiritual guides, shaman priests. To imagine anything else is impure, blasphemous.

In his construction of ideal types, Max Weber offered an analytic device by which we might identify and measure the motivations of the social actor. It helps us to understand, for example, the individual mentality that developed as key elements of the Protestant ethic and the spirit of capitalism began to converge centuries ago. The expressed purpose of graduate school in America is advanced training, mastery of the discipline, upward mobility through hyper-credentials. But its latent function was to provide me with live entertainment. On a daily basis the department served up a cornucopia of ideal types, characters more worthy of D. H. Lawrence and Jean Genet than Max Weber or Emile Durkheim.

First there were the Great Leaders of the Revolution. By the 1980s the glory days of sociology were long gone. A handful of '60s politicos lingered on from the age of the hippie. These smelly authoritarian patriarchs with beards and matted stringy hair populated academic departments across America. Now I understood why D.O.M. hated them. Many leftists are poets, high-minded men and women who dream of making the world a better place. These engaged, practical utopians have a lifelong commitment to the repair of the world. I have seen them sustain their faith in the best and worst of times, intent upon social equality, protecting human dignity by abolishing exploitative social relations. Barbara Ehrenreich, Stanley Aronowitz—these people are my heroes. I'm not talking about them at all.

The Great Leaders of the Revolution were neither poets nor heroes. They were self-righteous power freaks who patronized you, fighting for your rights without ever bothering to ask what you wanted for yourself, always assuming they knew better. Underscored by the very same elitism that led Marx to believe *someone* had to lead the proletariat, they were forever searching for their imaginary friend, the historical subject. Judgmental, humorless, we hated them. They didn't know what to make of us. Were we reactionaries, positivists, arty, hegemonic, or what?

French political theorist Raymond Aron has called Marxism "the opium of the intellectuals," and the department sure had its share of junkies. But unlike the Slugs, these fools couldn't play bass or dance. Ironically, the professor who actually taught Advanced Topics in Marxist Analysis was a laid-back guy from California who loved to play basketball. He was obsessed with Bruce Springsteen and spent hours teasing out the critical underpinnings of the Boss's lyrics. Always enthusiastic, the Marxist Theory professor took a genuine interest in our wretched lives. Recognizing that graduate-student labor was ripe for exploitation, he did what he could to protect and uplift us. He even rescheduled the entire Advanced Topics seminar to accommodate my musician-time sleep schedule.

The Marxist Theory professor eventually married one of his students, a Long Island home girl who, like me, wore makeup in defiance of feminist decree. His young wife edged him out of his old New Left clothes and into a groovy look. After studying things like the structural embeddedness of business decisions and intercorporate relations among the capitalist class, the Marxist Theory professor began applying his analytic skills to more entrepreneurial goals. Collaborating with another colleague, he eventually became a multimillionaire—more about that later.

In addition to the Great Leaders, another specter was haunting Big Science: the Rusty Nuts. Pre-Madonna, these book-smart feminists were uptight, humorless prigs. You knew they'd squeak whenever they got screwed, just like a rusty nut. Sisterhood was a powerful tool—for career advancement, nothing more. Normal women had to lie or whisper about being married with children lest they be considered dumb, unfortunate victims of false consciousness. Nobody dared to wear makeup except the secretaries and commuter students. We were from Lawn Guyland; it was a class indicator. And all this was *before* the dreary days of political correctness.

It was the Binary Boy who first developed the Typology of the Rusty Nut. Probably from all his years at Yale, where he snorkeled around, drinking gin, wearing a Hawaiian shirt. It is very common for professors to coauthor with graduate students, chaperoning the novice into the discipline. As his faithful teaching assistant, it was my responsibility to help him refine a most important work, "Towards a Critical Theory of the Rusty Nut."

The Binary Boy was an organizational sociologist, a networking microtheorist who did his dissertation fieldwork in a mental hospital. A cultural hero of the new economy, the Binary Boy eventually appeared as a regular in *The Village Voice* in my column, my ongoing tales of computer lust, "She's Gotta Hack It." When I first met him, he was generating mathematical models in APL—A Programming Language—developed by Harvard math professor Kenneth Iverson to teach his kids mathematical concepts. At first I wasn't so impressed, but when I heard him say *Boolean,* I fell in love. Not with him, with his bloc models—a technique developed by sociologist Harrison White for analyzing complex social networks. He'd sit there socking out cluster after cluster of cells. It was breathtaking watching somebody order the universe in such abstract, discrete, perfect terms.

B-Boy got his doctoral degree at Yale, then got tenure at Big Science. Considering his fieldwork at the hospital, we can think of this as a continuum of mental illness. The B-Boy taught advanced quantitative methods. He was once an ironworker from California, the oldest son of a Mexican-American father and a mom from Wisconsin. He lost a few of his fingers on the job. B-Boy was an Aries. As a teenager in Los Angeles, he drove a '52 Plymouth. He shaved off the head with a blowtorch and upholstered it with Indian madras. In the early 1960s the Binary Boy rode the waves goofyfoot on a Dewey Weber 9' 2", alternating with a Hobie banana board. Huge rails, multiple skags, nose turned up so he didn't pearl dive. He started surfing at thirteen, at Doheny, Salt Creek, then onward to Rincon and Dana Point. Most surfers face the waves; the Binary Boy turned his back to them.

The B-Boy was the first skateboarder to go down the pipeline at Claremont and Upland in SoCal, near Angeles Natural Forest. The tubes came down into a channel four miles downhill, all this on a plywood skateboard with steel wheels. Mom was waiting on the other side with the pickup truck.

By now I almost always carried a weapon. I collected knives, switchblades, double-edged serrated, illegal, over six inches. I bought them on the street or at the Levittown Flea Market. I stashed my weapons in my black boots, along with a lipstick and a tampon. In my purse I carried a razor-sharp metal teasing comb, a relic of my hitter-wannabe youth. I also began to employ any number of protective amulets to ward off the evil vibes. Pentagrams, Bast, sacred signifiers, artifacts of a precious secret life. For the first year of graduate school I wore my social-work clothes, sedate professional-managerial garb, middlebrow, neat, and perky. I tried to be normal. By the second year, everything was tattered and worn. I'd trashed it all. Everything had broken down. Even the feminists knew something was up.

Let us consider, what kind of kook would devote an entire life to so-

ciology? Spend the better part of the decade of greed working on a doctoral degree while the rest of the world got filthy rich? Some of my
graduate school cronies had collapsed a few veins in their day. They've
had careers in everything from addiction to prostitution, outsiders,
criminals. My girlfriends in the sociology department were also high
risk-takers, deviants. As mothers, they rarely hung out after hours, and
they've asked to be excluded from any further discussion here, for their
kids' sake. Such is the labor of parenting. It forces you to become normal, lest the State intervene and remove your children.

Pinky was a union organizer, a handsome, hard-drinking lefty, but
not a pompous relic like the socially useless Great Leaders. He was a
bread-and-butter socialist like Grandpa Benny. Compassionate, he argued that even an heiress like Gloria Vanderbilt was our sister in struggle, because the social relations of capitalism degraded rich and poor
alike. Pinky also constructed a typology to help us separate creeps from
assholes. He said it was okay to be an asshole, a fool who made stupid
mistakes. But a creep was a different matter, because it implied a willful
intent to be snarky. Sometimes even we were assholes; it was part of our
humanity. But we had to watch out for the creeps.

A few years later, when I went to Bergenfield, New Jersey, on assignment for *The Village Voice* following a quadruple teenage suicide pact, it
was Pinky who explained the mean-spirited, creep-generated social relations in that town. Even after the four kids were dead, people continued to label them "dirtbags," "burnouts," and "losers." No mercy; like
Pinky said, just creeps.

Eventually, a culture of alcoholism emerged in the sociology department. We were the devoted students of Professor Aloysius of the
School of the Streets, a conceptualization lifted from another comatose
night of Johnny Thunders's stage banter. Whiskey and wine were considered original texts, and I delved into them with scholarly fury. With
my first taste, I whispered, "I'm coming home, I'm with my Lord." In
Latin, alcohol is *spiritus;* the same root word used to denote the most
sacred religious experience. Both the sacred and the profane *spiritus*
oriented the individual toward union, wholeness, merger with self,
God, and the body social. As a student of both Professor Aloysius and

Emile Durkheim, I had a compelling interest in the notion of social integration. I considered all of this scientific research in the sociology of religion.

As part of my studies, I began to collect imported china, crystal goblets and decanters, sterling silver–plated flasks, all the artifacts of high bottom drunken debauchery. I drank more in graduate school than I did in all my years as a Slugwife. In part because alcoholism is a progressive disease and the clock was ticking. But mostly because life in graduate school was deadline driven, I fell into the natural rhythm of a binge drinker. I didn't have to drink every day, and unlike most alcoholics, I could actually have "just one." And once I stopped, it was over, for good, like my cigarette smoking. They say it isn't how much you drink, it's what it does to you, and it sure did it to me. Where Sluglife debauchery was chronic, this was acute.

I developed a ritual. I cleaned the house, put on my writing clothes, locked myself up for days, weeks, working all night, getting up from the desk only to eat or empty the piss jar. Sleeping all day, phones disconnected, doors bolted, showering only after the first draft was done. Then I submitted the work. It was always on time, sometimes early. Making a deadline was followed by a drinking spree. Writing scorched the soul, stripped it dry, peeling off each layer until all protective cover was removed. This left me parched, thirsting for a drink. I needed a psychic douche: a shot, a beer, a guy, sleep it off, and then I'd start all over. That's what punctuated my life, how I marked my time. Some projects took longer, and I could go for months without a drink, without any desire whatsoever. But when the work ended, the party began. Mostly, like Keith Richards explained in his theory of addiction, I needed booze to come down off my writing high, to level myself out.

Every Friday assorted faculty, graduate students, and staff would knock off to coagulate at a bar, drinking till we went blind silly. Midweek I shared a house with Anthony; weekends, I went home to Slugland. At one point Pinky became a bartender at the Checkmate, a local gin mill where students weren't welcomed. We were delighted that Pinky was now a deacon in the Church of Al (Professor Aloysius). Anthony quickly became a regular. As acting Checkmate bouncer, he often extended protection to hapless denizens of Big Science, mediating between the two worlds. I never went to the Checkmate. Even with Pinky and Anthony at the wheel, it wasn't ladylike.

On a binge later christened the Weekend of Infamy, Anthony, and I drank straight through a three-day run. The first night, Pinky fell in love with a hippie girl at a house party and drank beer from her shoes. He followed her around until he almost got arrested. I woke up the next morning with a blinding headache and the name *Sean* scrawled on my right arm. Before we went out, I always made Anthony swear he wouldn't let me go home with any guys, no matter what I said.

Like most distinguished students of Professor Aloysius, I was prone to falling in love while under the influence. Some women use alcohol to get loose with a guy. I used guys to get loose with the booze. To me, a relationship meant one thing only: protection to drink until I passed out. It was the only reason to bother having a boyfriend. According to Anthony, we met Sean in some parking lot. We flirted, he wrote his name on my arm, and I promised to call the next day as soon as I woke up. I swore I'd meet him by the docks, we'd hang out—cocktails, candles, a night in Kashmir, then true love, teary psychodramas, orders of protection, the usual bliss of the alcoholic relationship. I vaguely remembered meeting a young kid with long blond hair and a denim jacket. I preferred younger men—more stamina, less baggage. I was on my way to becoming the Blanche DuBois of Port Jefferson when Anthony washed the ink off my arm. We know all men (and women) are gorgeous and sexy in the eyes of Professor Aloysius. But the next day, you wake up and realize your new lover was imported from the Central Park Zoo.

During my tour of duty, from 1982 to 1985, Big Science University was a stronghold for big, butch hardcore positivism. In our department, the Binary Boy was the high priest, the biggest Quant, a true Durkheimian scholar. Anthony was a Spencerian. These people see the social world in terms of physics. If anyone at school suggested a *three-way,* they usually meant a three-way analysis of variance. Night after night people sat around generating structural equation models, verimax rotations. We spent hours starved at the computer terminal, parched, waiting for the sadistically cruel Univac mainframe to yield forth our cross-tabulations. I now had the capacity to generate endless reams of meaningless data. I never got up from the terminals unless I had to pee or the system crashed, whichever came first. I was always spent—hungry, tired, cranky, and disoriented. It was awesome.

Following the work of Irving Howe on our immigrant fathers, the World of Our Mothers was a research project headed up by Rose Laub Coser, an elegant European lady, professor emeritus, and the only female faculty member who wore eye makeup. The World of Our Mothers project always had food, thanks to Rose and two generous graduate student assistants named Gladys and Kathy. After hours, any graduate department looks like the unlocked ward of a mental hospital, students laboring in obscurity, pondering the grand minutiae. Writing endless treatises on everything from pauperization to millenarianism. We knew nobody would ever read them, and if they did, they wouldn't give a shit. But it still seemed like a matter of life or death, imminent, urgent. Some people just slept in their offices; they never even bothered going home. By four A.M. the department looked like a shooting gallery, timeless shades of gray, like the Slughouse in Westbury. I felt right at home.

After long nights of drunk driving on the Univac, Gladys and Kathy offered shelter and comfort to us neophytes—coffee, candy bars, crumb cake. Childhood sugar addiction was reactivated in graduate school. I still have trouble writing without craving sweets. I'll hit a brick wall and break out the Pepperidge Farm. Ask any hacker: Junk food fuels intellect.

Graduate student members of upper cohorts always offered sisterly advice, who to work with, who to avoid, gossip, street dirt. They identified potential sexual predators among faculty, helped us select gut courses. Gladys was no different. One night after an unsatisfying computing experience, I was shot. The system was down, my run was aborted, and I was shanghaied. Holed up at the World of Our Mothers, I began rambling on to Gladys about my bands, my after-hours life with the Slugs. The guys still played sporadically, and Nick and I were still going to see Thunders. Now our pilgrimages included Anthony, the Binary Boy, Pinky, anyone in need of redemption.

Every day I drove an hour east to Big Science eating bags of Sugar
Babies, pumping myself full of power chords and noise, playing air guitar to the Clash, *I don't judge you, why do you judge me?* By the time I got
to Big Science, I was exploding with manic energy. Nobody could
touch me. As enthralled as I was with Durkheim, Marx, and Weber,
Gladys said I sparkled whenever I mentioned my rock & roll. She said,
"Donna, why don't you just study what you love?" I stared at her in
complete disbelief. Nothing could be a more alien concept. Was she
nuts?

At Big Science I loved the work, but I hated the job. Personally, I
was treated very well. There was always someone willing to support any
sick idea I came up with. The wide range of interests among faculty
meant endless resources. But I hated my lowly status, the poverty, and
lack of power. I had come into the department from a bona fide profession, from middle management, salaried with a staff. School was in-
fantilizing, and that became annoying. So I worked my ass off just to
get out. I went A.B.D. (All But Dissertation) in three years—record
time. In the beginning, my dissertation topic was "False Consciousness?: Ideological Proletarianization Among Social Workers and Engineers." I had fallen into a post-Marxian abyss, regurgitating 1972 news,
dull, mainstream. It seemed a safe bet for a tenure-track position. I
passed my qualifying exams, but I would have never finished. I would
have died first, of terminal boredom.

Nobody ever directed me to do it this way, but submission was always implied. I assumed compliance was the only way out. In my first
year I went to an outdoor concert and drank beer with two talented
young professors who never got tenured. They warned, "Unless you
make it big in the outside world first, the university will never accept
anything innovative." It was like that everywhere. So I sold my soul for
the promise of deliverance at a later date. I would defer gratification,
play the game, and someday I'd get to do what I really wanted. I just
had to bide my time.

I was convinced that if I wrote about something interesting or cool,
I would be doomed to marginality and unemployment. Gladys urged
me to write papers about popular culture, about my bands, about life

on the turnpike, but I refused. I didn't want to expose the part of myself that was sacred. I needed to keep that for myself to survive. Besides, academic discourse has the power to render anything banal and dull—including sex, drugs, and rock & roll. Writing about bands for academic sociology would be like fucking to your tax returns. I dared not violate my one true love. So I withheld my private world, fierce and tight. It was all I had left of pride and dignity.

Still, Gladys put a bug in my head. Why did I feel I had to wait for somebody else's permission to be myself? For all my rebel yell, I was really a coward, a conformist, a scared child anxious to please. I would do anything to feel acceptable, even destroy myself. I had my amulets, my bands, my weapons, my protections, but what *real* power did I have? Without my help, and against my will, I see now that God had a plan for me. Divine guidance was bestowed throughout my spiritual journey, showing me the way home. If not for these random gifts of grace, I probably would have committed suicide in graduate school instead of writing a book about it. Soon after my talk with Gladys, I started writing about popular culture.

II

In the early days before cultural studies, if you wanted to give a paper about film or music you had to do it at the American or Popular Culture Association meetings. Before the invasion of the postmodernists, these conferences were generally considered "atheoretical," not highly regarded within academic sociology. The department refused to cover your conference expenses for such trivial pursuits. They subsidized you only for the mainstream professional organizations, such as the American Sociological Association (ASA). Each branch of the discipline has a special section devoted to extensive study in that area, for example, sociology of the family, work and the professions, comparative historical, and religion.

Around 1985 I got the bright idea to organize a section on culture in the ASA. I figured that then I could give papers on movies, hardcore music, and fanzines and the sociology department would have to cover my tab. So I filed the paperwork and set out with a petition and the blessings of ASA president Kai Erikson and Lewis Coser. I drove down to Washington, D.C., with my purple hair, red-and-black-striped drinking shirt, and black leather Harley jacket. I also felt this was a chance to carve out a place for myself in mainstream sociology. I got the signatures, filed a petition, and the section was organized. I served as acting chair until we nominated someone tenured with a secretary and a salary. I was an impoverished graduate student. Today the section is one of the largest in the organization, with almost one thousand members.

It was there at the meetings in Washington that I met Stanley Aronowitz. He was widely known as a rebel, a supporter of anything cool and new. Aronowitz had been a steelworker, a New Left union guy. He was big and burly, with long black curly hair. Autodidactic, robust, and macho like Pinky, D.O.M., and Grandpa Benny, Aronowitz was a prolific writer and organizer, a bona fide two-fisted man of letters. He had earned a bad rep some years back as a womanizer, but all that was behind him. To everyone's surprise, he had settled down with the indomitable Ellen Willis, rock's first feminist critic, an avowed New Journalist.

When I met him at the ASA, in the middle 1980s, Aronowitz was busy organizing a radical program in cultural studies at the CUNY Graduate School. He invited me to sit in on study groups. Nobody in the department of sociology at Big Science was doing culture, at least not as I understood it. Stanley's students included some great minds, cultural radicals who wrote their hearts out, worked for the rights of the disenfranchised, and they could dance, too. They embraced me as their own. I convened with them at CUNY almost weekly, reading Bataille, Bakhtin, Lacan, and Lefebvre. I met righteous people like Cornel West, Andrew Ross, William DiFazio, and Lynn Chancer—urban intellectuals, scholars, activists. Afterwards, I drove back to Long Island. Sometimes I dropped Stanley off in Brooklyn, where he and Ellen lived. One day, he asked me if I wanted to meet her. After that, I was destiny's child.

Willis had been my idol ever since I was a teenager sneaking the forbidden Commie rag *Voice* into the house past D.O.M. Her writing was forceful, reasoned, and hip. But what also struck me was this: She used her own name. She didn't hide her sex as "E. Willis" or stick to "women's issues." There she was, *Ellen Willis,* feminist, rocker, smart, cool, and determined. In New Journalism, writers like Ellen Willis, Tom Wolfe, and gonzo Hunter S. Thompson dove right in. They read the social world like a Zap comic, like the Ramones. Willis wrote about the family, Lou Reed, Janis Joplin, Israel, Elvis, about everything.

When Willis opened the door, she appeared like a vision, a pre-Raphaelite goddess. Her long blond curls framed a serene, translucent, delicate face. Reading her work, I had always imagined her as someone small, intense, dark, and nervous, chain-smoking. But she was sensual, electric, and very funny. Now, finally, I could take my cues from a woman.

Nervous in her presence, I babbled on about the hardcore scene, Black Flag, the Dead Kennedys, heroin, the Butthole Surfers, Anthony, the Senders. I urged her to go see Ism, a local band who were playing a show in Queens. During the 1980s, as punk splintered off into hardcore and scenes fragmented and decentralized, you had to travel deep into the 'burbs to find the really sick music. At one point Ellen got up to get us ice cream, then cookies. Later on, Stanley brought in a pepperoni pizza with double cheese. Our friendship was sealed.

I went home and told Nick about the encounter. Then I called Betty Bradley, who quickly warned me not to buy any electrical appliances— "Mercury's in retrograde!" Having beaten cancer, my mother now devoted her time to fund-raising and public awareness, helping other women deal with mastectomies. She became a fervent bowler, winning league trophies for best score and highest game. Even though the muscles under her arms had been removed, nothing stopped her. When I told her about Aronowitz and Willis, Betty Bradley promptly inquired about their signs. So I gave her birth data for the two leftist intellectuals. Stanley and Ellen were forevermore referred to as the Capricorn and Sagittarius, respectively. Because Herbie had been a Capricorn and Betty a Sagittarius, my mother suspected I had met my true spiritual godparents. The next week I saw Stanley at the Graduate Center. He gave me a note: "Call Ellen about writing for the *Voice*," and my life as a *Village Voice* features writer began.

By day I roamed the turnpike searching for data, trawling for community, then publishing my encomiums to pop culture. I learned the purposeful use of self in the narrative. Though strictly outlawed in sociology and conventional journalism, in any rewrite, *Voice* editors urged, "Put more of *yourself* into the story!" At first I recoiled. I was trained as a positivist, pristine about data collection and fear of "contamination." Remember, formal sociology is supposed to be science—objective, neutral. Even funky ethnographers took pains not to "go native." If you overidentified with the research subjects, your findings were biased, hence useless. But the *Voice* editors kept egging me on until I had no boundaries left. I wrote about what I loved, surrendered to the field, and never returned. When done with self-discipline, the purposeful use of self in the narrative can be a useful methodological tool. Then sociology becomes a literary practice, an art as well as a science. Plus, it was so much fun.

Later on, during the Hartz Mountain days of Leonard Stern's reign, *Voice* publisher David Schneiderman hired me as a suburbia consultant. Alternative newspapers moonlighted as cash cows for advertisers. The subversive *Village Voice* was, in the end, just another media property. With an eye toward Long Island's and Jersey's hot youth markets, we conducted feasibility studies and determined that Long Island should have a *Voice* of its own.

My secret ambition was to see the names of all my friends on the masthead and our favorite bands on the cover. Long Island had an untapped market for talent. The new suburban *Voice* enlisted Rich Black from *Under the Volcano* and Arthur Stevenson from Sea Monster, fresh voices from the margins of every town. Surfers, mall rats, environmentalists, club kids, and politics, too. The paper lasted only a few years, but it accomplished my mission. In the summer of 2000, Rich Black asked me to do the liner notes for a local compilation CD, *Something in the Water—The Secret History of Long Island Punk.* Spanning 1978 to 1987, it featured rare early releases by Jimi LaLumia and the Psychotic Frogs, the Nihilistics, ISM, and Sea Monster. The *Long Island Voice* and the compilation CD proved my point: Suburban culture is not an oxymoron.

Writing about it, my life finally began to make some sense, to feel more integrated. Sluglife provided me with a blueprint for suburbia's underground music subcultures. The department of sociology at Big Science University afforded the necessary tricks of the trade, an analytic tool kit. The *Voice* gave me license to ill. I had never taken a writing course in my life, but editors like Willis and Richard Goldstein taught me how. Features in *Spin, Rolling Stone,* and *Newsday* soon followed. My life and my stories were the same. Once a lonely only child, now I poured out my heart to a million strangers.

It usually happened like this: Stop up at the *Voice*'s editorial office to pick up hate mail or just to say hello. "Hey, Donna, what's up?" Mention something demented I was doing. Editor's eyes begin to dance, twinkling with mischief. By the end of the visit, my great enabler would suggest, "I think there might be a story in it." And so my life became copy, and copy my life.

The *Voice* went through some excruciating administrative changes over the years. Each new editor-in-chief was like a new foster parent. A new regime meant heads rolled, styles changed. You lost your editor, you were banished to the margins. Some bosses preferred identity politics, others went for more hard news, less culture. For example, after Karen Durbin left, the paper's signature "confessional" style shifted to more straight "vanilla" reporting. Under her successor, Don Forst, the *Voice* effectively outlawed the use of the first-person narrative. But I didn't care. Multiculti, leftist, pomo, pander to this, then that, and back again. Long features, short ones, it was all the same; it was all about *writing.* For a multitude of talented editors and writers, the *Voice* was much more than alternative press; it was a "writer's paper," an open workshop, a nonstop crash course in cultural reporting. In fact, after she left the newspaper, Ellen Willis became a journalism professor at NYU, founding a program in cultural reporting.

I started out in the music section with a tirade against WLIR, a radio station that "dared to be different" by parading lame New Wave bands as alternative. *Voice* music editor Doug Simmons spent almost five hours editing a 850-word piece. Following Dee Dee Ramone's theory of short-and-to-the-point, it was Simmons who taught me the art of word economy, how to speed up sentences and spare the reader any flab. My next article was a cover feature. Ellen Willis literally beat the academese out of the text. I can still hear her over my shoulder, impatiently admonishing, "You're overexplaining!!! Just say it!!!"

A good editor is a combination of a shrink and a pimp. Shrink, because they force you to speak truth, to say what you really mean, what's in your heart. Pimp, because then they make you take it on the street. I found my voice at the *Voice*—the native language of my homeland, a mix of low culture and high theory, street and book, rock & roll and yeshiva. The sacred and the profane; what I learned at school, heard in Johnny Thunders's guitar and saw on the streets of Twennyninth. Now I could tell the world about it.

In January 1987 my first cover story appeared, an ode to suburbia the *Voice* editors titled "Wild in the 'Burbs." I got a whole page of letters to the editor, fourteen pieces of venomous hate mail accusing me of everything from solipsism to getting fucked in the parking lot of my local Jack in the Box. I ran under the bed and cried for three days. But then all these other writers called to congratulate me. "Donna, you're famous!" In academic circles, such negative feedback could destroy your career, shame you, shatter your life of wine and cheese forever. In journalism it made you a star.

Six months later, the *Voice* sent me out to investigate the teenage suicide pact in Bergenfield, New Jersey. I was the only street reporter they had who liked thrash metal and understood suburbia. Because of my social work experiences on the streets of Levittown, I also wasn't afraid to engage potentially suicidal kids; I *wanted* to go. After all, Bergenfield wasn't that different from where I lived, in a nonaffluent Nassau County turnpike town with strip malls, convenience stores, and hard, endless road. The *Voice* gave me all the room I needed to tell the story. But there was so much more to say, I decided to write a book.

Once I started writing features for the *Voice*, I basically forgot about my dissertation. There was always that nagging feeling, but I couldn't imagine going back to *that*. Whenever I wrote in academic discourse, I broke out in fever blisters. When I wrote in my own voice, it flowed through me like Mudhoney. When the body speaks, we must listen.

It was the Binary Boy who convinced me to make *Teenage Wasteland* my dissertation. In my investigation, I had discovered that most rare of Durkheimian types, the fatalistic suicide. I could explain the event using theories of alienation and anomie. I was adamant that sociology, not psychology, could and should explain teenage suicide. That suicide was a social, cultural, and historical phenomenon—not an exclusively medical, psychiatric one. The B-Boy read my cover story about Bergenfield and flipped. He got manic whenever he had a compelling idea, which was pretty much all the time. He began pacing, ranting and raving, "Donna, suicide is Durkheim! Durkheim is sociology! Give us theoretical and methodological appendices, a bibliography, and you are *Dr. Gaines!*" My chairman, Lewis Coser, readily agreed, as did the other committee members. It was unanimous. Unfortunately, those sweet appendices are buried somewhere in university microfilm. Nobody will ever read them because *Teenage Wasteland* was published as a trade book.

And my dissertation committee? Lewis Coser eventually retired and moved to Boston, his favorite American city. He continued to write and mentor graduate students. A few years ago, the Binary Boy, my indulgent Marxist Theory professor, and another guy set up a market research outfit. At first it was just a sideline, a devil's playground for the B-Boy to experiment. He developed some deep statistical methods and software for the entertainment industry. Most people are willing to kill or die for tenure. Big Science University tenured the Binary Boy, and then he walked, he just quit. He decided to devote himself exclusively to his bloc models. I guess those bloc models paid off, because a few years later they sold the company for millions. It was written up in *Variety*—sociology for showbiz! My dissertation committee members were proof that sociology could rock.

And so, from my after-hours life as a scene denizen, I carved out a career as a sociologist and journalist. I felt passionately about my work, and I loved writing because it was a solitary pursuit, like a drug run or a drinking spree. A Ph.D. meant I was a certified intellectual. Instead of suppressing my pathologies or denying a lifelong experience of contradictory class locations, I learned to embrace them, exploit them, celebrating it all.

Even now, everyday life presents a series of craggy juxtapositions, incongruities. Now and then I enjoy a fleeting moment of synthesis, when everything hangs together. With no formal institutional ties, no fixed affiliation or corporate workplace, I figure wherever the data are, that's where the job is. The universe, not the university, is my intellectual focus. So aimless, shiftless, rootless, I wander the wilderness on the promise of absolute truth. A tattooed Jew, an outcast among outcasts.

Maybe the parts would always be greater than the whole, the world would never be fully understood, and life would never feel complete. Maybe in every age, our belief systems would collapse and for a while nothing would make any sense. That could keep me busy for years.

For me, science was an endless vacation, a place to chill until I could figure it all out. Convinced that one field site was the same as another, and that data were everywhere, I decided to set up shop right where I was. I looked no further than my own front yard—the Jericho Turnpike. I was an organic intellectual of Lawn Guyland, a road scholar.

At home, in my Suburbia.

12

TATTOOED JEW

For fifteen years, I lived in a gas station off the Long Island Expressway, a one-bedroom in a garden apartment complex overlooking Jericho Turnpike, smack in the center of Nassau County. This is the vortex of consumerism, where the expressway, the Northern State Parkway, and the Meadowbrook Parkway intersect. My town was commercially zoned, so the landscape was redundant with gas stations, shopping centers, warehouses, and discount outlets. Roosevelt Field, one of the largest, most splendid malls in America, was less than a mile from my front door. Frontier Americana deluxe, all the love I ever needed, right there.

My living room window overlooked the Birchwood Shopping Center, a fading strip mall distinguished by Stonehenge, the C-Town monolith, mustard-colored brick against scalloped skies. I kept the windows shut if someone called because the hard sound of the road—the revving engines of motorcycles, trucks, and cars—made it impossible to hear. From my desk I saw only foliage, lush leaves on the maple trees outside the window. Periodically the sweet smell of carbon monoxide filled the whole apartment. Turnpike noise became metal machine music to my ears. Over time, I developed an appreciation for the roadscapes of suburbia.

I spent my nights in rehearsal studios, gun clubs, underground computing cadres, tattoo parlors, and adult bookstores. I hung around convenience stores, parking lots, and extended family dinners. I was mesmerized, wild in the 'burbs. I lived like a refugee, in exile. It was a perfect setup. From my marginal position peering out, pondering the neon lights outside my picture window, everything was right with my world.

I'd moved to my turnpike outpost in the early 1980s, around the time I started graduate school. Nick kept our apartment over the Glen Lounge. I lived alone. Mostly, I sat at my desk, writing, with Sarah-Ann, the Burmese, curled up in my lap. I stayed there like that until 1996. This situation baffled everyone.

Still, even now, people wonder, how could I take it all those years— the malls, the big hair, and everywhere the creepy nuclear family? Well, since I felt a little alienated everywhere, I could live anywhere and feel the same about it. Besides, was communing with attorneys and accountants in some '80s blue-chip bohemia like SoHo more socially real than the local strip mall that featured Italian Gardens? New York City's suffocating lack of drag strips and repressive gun laws didn't exactly make my planets twirl. And what was so cutting edge about sartorial stratification systems (club door policies), thirty-dollar covers, eight-dollar drinks, rude bouncers, bad music, and rooms packed for maximum profit? For several years urban artists and bohemians had been priced out, forced to spread outwards, into Hoboken, Williamsburg, and Astoria—exurbans in search of air, light, space, and affordable housing. Economically, intellectually, socially, and culturally, turnpike suburbia made my life as a freelance writer possible.

For the sociological imagination, Long Island was an entity all to itself, posing extraordinary methodological challenges. Like, how do you conduct fieldwork in a place that has no public space? No streets? No center? How do you study race, class, and ethnicity when the very premise of mass culture, of suburbia, is democratization, obliteration of difference, homogeneity? Cross-addicted, interdisciplinary, multipara-digmatic, pancultural, postmodern, my outpost was a geographic and cultural halfway house. And so I was an ethnographer of the American turnpike.

Writing requires solitude, so living in the middle of nowhere can be an asset. Loneliness too, becomes a motivational tool. Alienation warps the mundane world until it seems fascinating, and because you feel so estranged, it is. In between deadlines I saw bands and kicked it with Professor Aloysius. Although Nick lived nearby, I had limited contact with the outside world beyond my editors and a network of eccentrics programmed into my telephone AutoDial pad.

Innovations in communications technologies had transformed so-cial relations in ways favorable to asocial loners. In the age of high tech-nology we're all strangers looking in. Holed up in our hovels, rootless, floating in a cybersea of fleeting encounters, connected by discontinu-ities. Mental laborers out there on a new frontier in an assembly line di-aspora. High technology enabled optimal social autism. AutoDial, e-mail, and an answering machine permitted me to control any un-wanted input or output. This allowed me to achieve my ideal—to be left alone.

My AutoDial pad hosted an assortment of microchip fiends, misan-thropes, addicts, and bored attorneys. Nick referred to them as the Panel of Experts. My friends were just like me—loners, weirdos, knowl-edge workers under *stamonocap* (State monopoly capitalism). People I'd collected over the years; independent contractors, experts, consultants buried in the nooks and crannies of the social order. Most of us worked at home—no institutional ties, no formal affiliations, just phone num-bers and, later, e-mail addresses. Responsible adults, intelligent and suc-cessful, mostly unmarried, childless, and nomadic. Highly educated, marginally functional, we rarely saw each other in person. And some, like Joey Ramone, got voted in and never even knew it.

The Panel was dominated by atheists and agnostics; rational, edu-cated, and skeptical. They did not equate religion with spirituality, morality, or social conscience. Although Nick was my soul mate for life, he did not believe in the existence of the soul. Neither did Anthony, strictly a man of science. After graduate school, he relocated to Brooklyn to embark upon a stunning career as a statistician with the Department of Transportation. Then he moved to Boston, then Jersey. Thanks to occupational mobility, I hardly ever saw Anthony, but that was meaningless. It was no longer necessary to engage in social relations face to face. I liked that.

Over time, technology governed my primary bonds. Access to the Internet further solidified the Panel of Experts, codifying it into a buddy list of lost souls wandering aimlessly through cyberspace. The Panel of Experts convened on all matters pertaining to lust, pharmacology, hair dye, Keogh plans, family crises, mysterious infections, and the rooting of plant cuttings. Can you recommend a good microwave oven? Who does anonymous AIDS testing? Am I fat? Do I really need four-wheel drive? If I crush these pills, can I snort them? Endless discussions about real estate, condoms, and cat care.

Communing with the Panel by phone or Internet was my social life. I only went out to see bands or ravage the turnpike for data. Panel members guided me as they led me astray, often instigating forays into the dark crevices of a sordid suburban underground. With the most subtle suggestions, they'd lure me into scenes and situations no urban-based intellectual could fathom. Through the Panel, all the pleasures of suburbia would be revealed. And of course, most of it ended up in *The Village Voice*.

||

et us take a few moments to explore the caliber of kooks festering inside my AutoDial pad. The Beast was the chairman of the Panel of Experts, meaning he set the general tone. He lived in Westchester and was convinced that suburbs offered far more perversions than the more routinized and predictable hipster city life. I met the Beast during my years as an undergraduate at SUNY Binghamton. I had transferred there from Kingsborough to complete my degree in sociology. In the early 1970s my college sweetheart was an ardent Kahane supporter. Meir Kahane appealed to working-class Jews, tough Jews who felt pressed by urban crime, liberal double standards, and global anti-Semitism. Back then, D.O.M. was a JDL member, too.

Beast's hobbies included chain-smoking and flicking wads of snot at people. When we hooked up in 1972 he was wearing a black leather motorcycle jacket and steal-tipped engineer boots, and had a pierced ear. He was hung like a horse and that made him arrogant. Beast often brandished a thick metal chain, which he featured at student government meetings. He used it to menace leftist Jews who organized in support of the Palestinian cause. Liberal Jews too seemed eager to support the liberation struggles of any people except their own. Beast said they needed discipline.

On our first date he took me to see *The Wild Ones* with Marlon Brando. I dressed in my best mid-'60s hitter regalia. We drank beer and sported huge Jewish stars, calling ourselves the *Alien Yids*. Beast was always twirling his hair, compulsively, clearly a masturbatory gesture. On our second date we saw *Performance* with Mick Jagger and James Fox. That night Beast wore black eyeliner and a lace shirt. And after the movie, at the student center, he proved his love to me. He entered the sacred chambers, the women's bathroom, and pissed all over the walls. On Saturday nights he would pin me down and play hanging spit torture, dangling a wad of phlegm over my face. Sometimes it slipped. He did this on command. We stayed together for three years.

Because of these disgusting habits, I called him my Beast. That meant I was his Beastessa. After we broke up, I annulled the Beast and that's how I became known as Tessa, the name later appropriated by Nick in our punk-rock soul union.

It was the Beast who first urged me to get a Ph.D. in sociology, "That degree will be your ticket into any sick little scene—prisons, mental hospitals, sex clubs, dog shows. You name it, honey, you're in." To make his point, Beast introduced me to the newly converted Lubavitchers of Binghamton. This was back in the early 1970s, the dawn of identity politics. Brooding, serious students were returning to their Jewish roots by associating with the followers of the late Menachem M. Schneerson, the Rebbe now believed by some to be the Messiah. The Rebbe was responsible for developing an extensive outreach to lapsed

Jews. He sent out emissaries all over the world, developing Chabad Houses, outposts for learning and worship in remote regions of the world where Jews were cut off from community. Although Gay Liberation was the dominant political group at our college, the Lubavitchers succeeded in recruiting many vegans, who mixed macrobiotics with *Yiddishkeit,* mixing the yin yang in with the *kashruth.*

At one point, Beast joined a local synagogue. He told his rabbi we were married, and that scored us a huge cheap apartment in downtown Binghamton. We lived together in a bizarre arrangement as Mr. and Mrs. Beast, tucked away in a four-family wooden house overlooking a run-down family grocery. For several months I wore a *shietl* (marital head covering) and kept kosher for him. One Passover we went to Crown Heights, to an Orthodox Seder. Beast sat around the table with the men, sharing in the festive meal, eating plump roast chicken, sumptuous greens, and *tzimmis* off exquisite traditional ceramic plates. After cooking, preparing the home, serving, and cleaning up, all the women sat down together to eat. We gathered at the periphery of the room, crowding together to eat the leftover ritual eggs and matzos. The eggs were dry, lukewarm, haphazardly mashed up on paper plates. That was our ritual meal. My exalted role as a Jewish woman amounted to eating men's scraps.

Ah, but it was a full moon that night and I belonged wholly to the Goddess: I was menstruating, shedding the unclean tears of my unfulfilled womb. "Aunt Flo" was pumping heavy and some blood leaked through my black skirt. From the corner of my eye, I noticed a tiny stain on my chair. Almost invisible but forever present, this mark was clearly the revenge of an ancient, defeated matriarchy. I always bled on the full moon. I considered it a blessing. Now I had a problem. I dared not say a word to my hostess. It would have been catastrophic. And it was impossible to clean it up. It was almost invisible, soaked deep into the chair's dark, frayed fabric. So I left it behind, this secret message to all distaff *shaineh maidels,* straight from the Magna Dea.

Every Sabbath the Beast invited unsuspecting young boys to the house for *Shabbas* dinner. He cooked, I cleaned. Each week, another lost soul ventured to Leroy Street, up the stairs to our humble lair, for wine, gefilte fish, and dead bird (chicken). The men did the blessings and the prayers, discussing *Yiddishkeit* on into the night. Beast tried to cajole them into going to *shul*, to putting on *teffilin*. Never girls, never couples, always cute, always boys. He was only eighteen when I met him. I was twenty-one. Eventually I figured it out, and so did he.

A few years after Binghamton, the Beast abandoned *Yiddishkeit* for the love that dare not speak its name in most organized religions. He fell in love with a tall, handsome, pumped-up New York State trooper who eventually became my gun dealer. Together they comprised the arms committee of the Panel of Experts.

Another specimen was Donna Producer, a restless defense attorney, a trial lawyer. At the height of Nassau County's Republican era, years before Madonna's pro-sex sartorial eruption, Donna Producer appeared in court wearing slutty black fishnet stockings, spike heels, and miniskirts. Nick devised most of the Panel's nicknames, but don't ask me how or where they originated. Donna Producer's was an exception. For a month or two, the Slugs were booking shows as the Producers. One night back in '79 Donna had a fleeting flirtation with someone in the band. Nothing happened, but we kept the nickname anyway.

In the early days, the Panel was almost exclusively male. In a startling upset, Donna Producer was endorsed by Nick. He admired her exquisite rock & roll vocabulary and sharp wit. As a rule, Nick hated everyone. Although he believed women were more evolved and morally and spiritually superior to men, he thought we were basically boring. The victims of gender socialization, we were timid, limited, and dull due to our codependent fixation on other people—men and children. As such, he concluded, "Women are the appliances of the earth."

Generally, women prefer to confide in other females, yet most of my "women friends" were men. The Beast and Anthony were "supportive" and patient when it came to my emotional needs. But Donna Producer was the classic "girlfriend" to pig out with or to cry with over "him." Long after Beast and Anthony told me to get over it, Donna Producer would hang in there like the Ronettes.

Periodically, there were those psychotic episodes with my parents. Donna was a consultant, coaching me on survival techniques. "When dealing with the dysfunctional family," she advised, "set boundaries. Don't see them too much and always see them on your turf." Then, with a flick of her Rolodex (now a PalmPilot) she'd direct you to a hair colorist, a psychic, or a female gynecologist. She'd be the pal to help locate the perfect rug. Or spend hours at Mr. Cheapo's in Mineola, searching for Kinks on vinyl. Donna was as comfortable poring over contracts and dockets as she was combing the racks at TJ Maxx. Since we were always too busy working, most of these activities never transpired. But we made lots of plans.

The years passed with nothing but phone contact. Then, one time, we actually did hang out. After hearing about it on Howard Stern, Donna Producer instigated a trip to the Concord Hotel for a singles weekend. This was yet another venture I managed to get subsidized by *The Village Voice*. Being "single" was a concept I barely grasped. As a proud unmarried American, I referred to myself as "free." I didn't mind meeting Mr. Right for an hour or two, even a lost weekend, but anything more would have been an intrusion. I had important work to do. At first, this trip to the Catskills was just sick kicks. But something else was going on.

I had visited the Concord as a child and was overwhelmed by the size of the hotel. There were over a thousand guest rooms and meeting spaces for up to three thousand. The Promenade had 170,000 square feet of exhibit space, forty tennis courts, an 8,000-square-foot atrium and fitness center, indoor and outdoor pools, and three golf courses. At 24,000 square feet, the Concord's nightclub was listed in *The Guinness Book of Records* as the world's largest cabaret, seating up to 2,900 people. Clean and well maintained, the decor was fixed in the age of modernism. The logistics predated the computer age. The staff were courteous and competent, but we were always waiting on a line, making a reservation, waiting for a bill. It was as if the technologies of the postindustrial world hadn't yet kicked in.

In the glitzy traditions of my eth-class, some women were dressed for a cotillion on Jupiter. Newly rich Five Towns go-go mamas in sequins, spikes, baubles, and beehives. There were lovely women hoping to marry sober accountants and dentists, businessmen in suits, toupees, leisure suits, action wear. Sartorial statements of worth move up and down the status hierarchy of the middle class. Disaffected teenage boys who wannabe down in the hood, guys in huge gold chai medallions. Moses with the tabernacles, the Ten Commandments in diamonds, made to order. After that one, I needed air.

It was too easy to laugh at these people, to feel superior because I was an intellectual, a feminist who'd transcended such pedestrian concerns as dating and mating. But smug wasn't the story here. By now, my connections to Judaism had frayed. Sometimes I even wore a large silver crucifix earring because it looked rock & roll. My name was Tessa, but even Donna sounded Italian. *I ate traif with goyim on yontif.* I didn't live in a Jewish neighborhood and hadn't dated a Hebrew since the Beast. Even my Jewish parents spent most of their time at bingo halls, bowling alleys, and army reunion gatherings. D.O.M. despised religion on ethical grounds, and Betty Bradley went to *shul* one day a year, on the eve of Yom Kippur, to hear the mournful Kol Nidre. The cantor's granddaughter's primary connection to *Yiddishkeit* was the music.

The trip to the Concord gave me a chance to reexamine my Jewish roots. The Borscht Belt was a spiritual homeland in the Jewish Diaspora, a place where I could imagine my parents in their prime, members of New York's emergent Jewish middle class, first-generation Americans conquering a new frontier. Herbie with his feisty posse, creating tumult, chasing broads. Mr. Gaines in a maroon fez, his wealthy associates gliding through the lobby with dignity and grace. I thought of my mother's Concord experience—first as a star, then as a bride, and later as a sad middle-aged widow molested in the pool. Here, in this setting, D.O.M.'s stories also came to life. I visited Pig Alley, a place near the bar where the fat and ugly girls hung out. D.O.M. explained that at the end of the night, if a guy was desperate, that's where he went. That was the Concord in the 1950s. How much had really changed?

My weekend in the Borscht Belt reminded me of everything I loved and hated about my people—their warmth and generosity, the passionate love of the Law, the food. Then there was the judgmental intolerance, the insularity, the smothering pressure to conform, the sexism and denigration of women—exalted in text, humiliated in life. I was proud to be a Jew, awed by the exuberance of a stubborn race that refused to be defeated. Historically, the Jew was the ultimate misfit, alien, outcast. Collectively hated, hunted, haunted, yet still here, insisting on their right to be and to differ. But being a Jew also meant life as sorrow and sweetness, a bittersweet worldview. Maybe I lived my turnpike life as a repudiation of that sorrow. It seemed the further I traveled from my Jewish roots—from my dead parents, from the memory of the Cossacks, the Holocaust, and the Inquisition—the closer I felt to joy. I would always be a Jew, and I would always feel this way.

Feeding and breeding, that was the essence of Jewish experience at the Concord. First came the food, then the love connections. The dining room area was the center of life. The meals at the Concord were legendary. This was a Catskills tradition. You ordered as many entrees as you could. To an outsider it might seem grotesque, a vulgar excess, but such lavish feeding was very Jewish. In the old days, the hotels in the Catskills offered simple working people a pleasant escape from the harsh life of the tenements. The grand matriarchs—Lillian Brown, Jenny Grossinger—hosted as if they were your own mother, making sure you got enough good kosher food to eat. D.O.M. started working in the Borscht Belt as a busboy when he was thirteen. He made it to waiter, making good money during the Depression. He returned in the 1960s as a small businessman looking for pretty women. The Catskills figured into everyone's family history. At one point a Concord bellman mentioned knowing my boss, Leonard Stern, then the *Village Voice* owner. The young Stern had often visited Grossinger's with his father, Max.

By seven P.M. the festive Sabbath dinner was in progress. There were six dining rooms serving up to thirty-five hundred people three large meals a day. Donna Producer knew the ropes at the Concord. Seating at a singles weekend was strategic. You got a better table if you *shmeer,* wipe some palms with some bucks. We drank Sabbath wine and recited the *kiddush.* It was a Denmark extravaganza, Park Manor revisited, with fruit, appetizer, salad, soup, and roasts. Sweet honeydew melon, gefilte fish, matzo ball soup, broiled chicken, pot roast, corned beef, chicken cacciatore, Chinese pepper steak, broiled lemon sole, potato kugel, even a diet selection of brown rice and steamed veggies. There were five desserts—macaroons, honey cake, strudel, jelly roll, and ices. We ate them all.

The activities were endless, something for everyone. As Long Island girls, Donna and I were intrigued by the cosmetic makeover workshop. There was a wine-tasting party, tennis mix and match, nature walk, softball and Ping-Pong tournaments, religious services, Rollerblading, formal dancing, discussion groups (about singles issues), and then there were the grand events: the dating game on Friday night, and the Mr. & Ms. Bathing Beauty contest poolside, Saturday afternoon. A talent show was scheduled for Saturday night. I usually hate organized activities, but this was like channel surfing with the remote control.

After dinner we shuffled over to Forum Hall for the orientation show and dating game. Loudmouths, we became hecklers. "Hey guys, God created Adam and Eve, not Adam and Steve," says the dating game host. "That's not true," I yelled out from the second row. The contestant was a sweet young woman from Canada. She asked the three bachelors, "What movie title best describes your love life?" First answered *Ghost,* next said *Dangerous Liaisons,* the third, *Rambo.* Mr. Shy, Mr. Bold, and Mr. Asshole. Mr. Asshole was about forty, and not bad looking. There I was, sitting in the capital city of boring heterosexuality. By now the front row of ladies are booing and hissing the host and Asshole. Repulsed and antsy, Donna ended up in the game room playing pinball for the rest of the weekend. I shot hoops and swam laps. We kept eating. We swore our next trip would be to Cancun.

True love and animal husbandry were among the cultural practices of the panel membership. Originally, Donna Producer was the college friend of a high school friend of Nick's. She showed up at the Rock Pub one night to see the Slugs and hooked up with my college friend, Mr. Ace. This was a miracle; Mr. Ace and a *human* female. Let me explain.

Once upon a time in the early 1970s, Ace and I lived on a goat farm up in Binghamton. Situated three miles up in the hills of Vestal, overlooking the state university, Goatropes was our homestead. Although it was peak season for counterculture, this was no hippie commune, it was a Venus flytrap. At Binghamton University, known back then as

Harpur College, gay liberation was rampant. If you weren't at least bi-sexual, you were shunned, dismissed as hung up and repressed. Every-one was gay, everything was game.

We lived in a one-hundred-year-old one-story farmhouse with three bedrooms. Several hippie houses like this decorated Bunn Hill Road, sometimes you'd see students on cross-country skis traveling down the hill to class. Goatrope was resplendent with plum trees, wild raspber-ries, and strawberries; wild chamomile grew in the cracks of the drive-way. Goatropes grew its own food, had over one hundred acres of land and several smaller dwellings where people lived. Mr. Ace was an engi-neering dropout from RPI now enrolled at Binghamton's School of General Studies. He paid rent by fixing Saabs, Peugeots, Volkswagens, and now and then, a crusty Toyota. Offbeat funky machines from the days when foreign cars were unusual, cheap, a bohemian alternative to hegemonic Amerika's beast cars. They were bona fide hippie artifacts, like water pipes and Indian print bedspreads. That meant lots of cute boys around the property, covered in motor oil, with Ace wrenching in the barn or wanking in the goat shed.

I had my pick of car clients, Ace saw to that. He would prolong the automotive repair process until the client and I got friendly enough for all time to stand still. My rent was twenty-five dollars a month. I had my own room at the top of the stairs decorated Southern bordello style. Tattered silk scarves hung amidst moth-eaten beaded curtains, hand-dipped acrylic flowers, musty floral prints. Thrift store lace, mildew, and satin country elegance. Sunlight streaming into my lair unfiltered through the air like fairy dust. I recall my handsome knights in white satin, scent of tranny fluid wafting through an attic hothouse.

Nobody cooked communal meals or gave a shit about the politics of personal experience. The bathtub was always filled with blue food col-oring and toy boats in an effort calculated to conserve water. Ace rea-soned that if it was full, nobody would think of taking a bath. They'd shower and save on water bills. Electricity too. The television had no picture tube; it was filled with empty mackerel tin cans. Goatropes Sun-day breakfast consisted of a cold bowl of rancid buckwheat or rice and molasses. A frugal Mr. Ace always bought bulk, fifty-pound sacks of buckwheat and sunflower seeds, which meant a steady diet of the wretched gruel. The sunflower seeds sat around for weeks, even roasting them couldn't remove that smell.

On the rare occasions that housemates gathered together for a communal meal, we were usually joined by a rusted battery, a pair of jumper cables, a gunked-out spark plug or two. The mackerel filets from the cans in our TV set rounded out Mr. Ace's diet of chicken hearts and squid. Ace was often stained with axle grease. With the body of a Greek god, tall, long strawberry blond hair to his waist, chiseled features, muscular, lean, Mr. Ace was a big bargaining point in all of my negotiations. In exchange for soliciting hot car clients, I manipulated besotted coeds of varied sexual persuasions to cook us lavish meals, catering for the entire house.

On the property there was an old stone building with no roof and a shed for milking cows, although at Goatropes, we had only goats. Our smelly little friends feasted on hay and grains, Agway specials, yielding sweet milk we'd germinate into lumpy yogurt in glass jugs on the radiator. Mr. Ace cultivated a raunchy goat cheese in the basement, moldy, the outside was rotted, but the inside tasted good. Our goats were virtually house pets—Pancake, Gretchen, Bully, and later Wa-Fil, the baby.

One goat was part Alpine, part Nubian. Or maybe Alpaca and Nubian. Or Angora and Alpine. Nobody knew for sure except when it came to Bully the Toggenburg. A mean, aggro beast, the Toggenburg was always beating on the Angora, an animal so meek nobody even bothered to give it a name. Mornings when Ace went to milk the Angora, she was often bloody.

The shed where the goats lived wasn't secure; it needed rebuilding. Mr. Ace and another roommate concocted an interim plan. They'd tether the goats to an old engine block so they wouldn't run away. One night it rained so hard there was mud everywhere. The ground got soft. The goats tried to get out of the rain. Still tied to the engine block, they dragged it around in the mud. Nobody knows how it happened, but the next day the Bully goat was dead, apparently strangled in Pancake's goat ropes. And that's how Goatropes got its name.

In the early 1970s, sexual liberation was sweeping the land, at least on the fertile farmland we called home. Mr. Ace's notion of liberation extended to goats, especially Gretchen, an unfriendly, high-strung animal. He spent long hours alone in the goat shed, pulling her tail till she generated a steady, high pitched sound. At some point a jar of Vaseline appeared in the shed. Most likely, it was used simply to soothe the weather-beaten hands of working men. But it quickly led to speculation about man-goat love, rough trade in the goat shed, nocturnal submission.

Mr. Ace eventually relocated to Long Island, abandoning goats, embracing windsurfing. He was now a respected Panel member, working in the local aerospace industry. Most of my friends' fathers had worked in places like Grumman and Fairchild. But this was a new economic order. Like the Beast, Ace became a systems engineer. Donna Producer and Mr. Ace eventually got married, got miserable, and got divorced. My matchmaking skills are about as good as my cooking talents. Come over for dinner tonight. I'm serving chunky peanut butter on the spoon, want some jelly? Here's the jar.

III

When I was a bad girl, wild in the streets of Rockaway Beach, my Cretin relatives blamed my unruly behavior on my friends—I was running with a bad crowd. In retrospect, the Panel of Experts cannot be held responsible for my unsavory life on the turnpike. Yes, my hungry sociological imagination was nourished through their peculiar obsessions, but I entered into these situations willingly, eagerly. Subcultural forays instigated by my peer group often resulted in hard copy; this is the fate of the freelance writer.

As personal computing captured the American imagination, Timothy Leary suggested that it was as addictive as heroin. But did he have any idea how many computer fanatics were actual junkies, active or recovering? The explosion of such high technology gave us all an outlet and brought several panel members face to face for the very first time. I had become computer literate at Big Science, on the Univac. But if you didn't supplement mainframe time with your own personal computer, you weren't shit.

My first microcomputer was a Kaypro. Around 1983, "the complete computer" came bundled with everything. It weighed twenty-six pounds, was supposed to be portable, but I could never lift it. Sleek, dark blue sheet metal, it looked like Darth Vader's lunch pail. As a matter of punk principle, I despised IBM. Big Blue was gradually taking over major universities and bringing with it a corporate culture of beige plastic doom. IBMs ran on DOS, the Kaypro ran on CP/M (Control Program/Microcomputer), the original operating system used by machines with 8-bit microprocessors.

In its day, CP/M was the Paris Commune of operating systems, Romantic lore recalls an age of tech nerds, the computing avant garde, who sat around wiring Zilog Z-80 chips in their suburban basements. Chips were cheap and easy to obtain, and this democratized microcomputing. Everyone could have one. IBM was capitalist enterprise, hegemonic. In the years before the New Economy exploded, it was important to resist Big Blue. To a high-tech stud like the Beast, IBM was lame, mainstream. The real hipsters in those days programmed in C for Unix systems. The word on IBM: "You can buy better, but you won't pay more."

All social struggles require great personal sacrifice on the part of the individual. Software written for CP/M machines didn't run on IBM-DOS. That threw me out of the loop, so CP/M stalwarts met clandestinely, in suburbia's libraries and back rooms. I held out as long as I could, even though my Kaypro had piss-poor memory, no power or speed. Once you are sucked into the vortex of high-tech consumerism, you are always waiting for the Man, for that next upgrade kick. Anything you buy will be dated before you install the software. As with drug addiction, you cannot win. I learned this waiting for the Ultraboard, a hardcore upgrading device that promised to breathe new life into the Kaypro. But after a while, holding on to an obsolete technology is like clinging to a bad relationship or a fading paradigm. You have to face the truth and let it go. As software and schematics became increasingly rare, I was forced to surrender. In this Inquisition, I had to declare my faith in IBM or perish. A few years later, I went through the same torment with Windows, and I hate it still.

My earliest computing experiences had been pajama parties with the women at Big Science. I missed them. I didn't appreciate the way men treated computers. They let the keyboard get all gooky, banged it to shreds, and chain-smoked near the disk drives. They were too rough. But like married working women everywhere, my girlfriends also had primary responsibility for child care. They didn't have much time to play. After the kids were born, I hardly saw them.

So, as usual, it was another night in the locker room, just me and the boys—at the keyboard, gun range, or rehearsal studio. Some people have fuck buddies; I had hack buddies. This lasted for years. These were the only people who ever visited me besides Nick. Since I was always either writing or sleeping it off, a permanent sign on my door read GO AWAY! In no time, Beast, Mr. Ace, the Binary Boy, and CorpseGrinder drummer Blaccard all became part of a loosely organized computing cartel. Nick was a Luddite. I still have to program his VCR. Like millions of suburban cowboys riding randomly across the land, the cartel swapped software, cannibalized hardware, built machines, and eventually got involved with electronic bulletin boards.

With the commercialization of the Internet, boards were effectively expunged, co-opted from cyberspace. In the early years, board action was cultlike, exclusive, underground like early indie rock or college radio. Not intended for the mainstream, it was for outlaws only. Whenever I got a new machine, the cartel took over. Mr. Ace scored free software, Binary Boy insisted on installing it, usually crashing the system. But it was the Beast who got me signed on to the gay boards, lending me his password. At first I was more interested in the sociology of electronic dating. But that changed as Blaccard got in on it and set up Substation, a members-only board that served the dual purpose of selling tranny kits and posting lurid personals. On Substation, I briefly realized my true destiny as Donna Denmark, porn star of cyberspace. This mainly involved some Polaroid tit shots posted on the board by Blaccard. After three months I only got one reply, and he lived in Kentucky.

One thing led to another. Blaccard had gotten married really young, so by now he was an avid collector of fetish porn: plumper, bondage, trans, tit, and wet. Periodically he would slip me a bootleg video like *Japanese Bondage*. Here, the master tied up the slave and poured hot candle wax on her. Then he slapped her and stuck all sorts of things up her ass. The woman seemed to be crying, but it was in Japanese, so I couldn't figure the psychological dynamics. It made me sick. I wondered, Is she in pain? Is this voluntary? What kind of guy is sitting around jerking off to this? Always an empiricist, I spent hours pouring candle wax on my leg from a height of one to two feet, just to see how it felt. Slapping, ropes, clamps, and clothespins—they hurt.

As my interest in video porn expanded, I began investigating my friends' collections. Of course, my sample was restricted to all guys. And predictably, most of the narratives were banal celebrations of the cumshot. True pornography should degrade everyone equally—men, women, net of sex preference. So I asked Anthony, "What's the big deal with the cumshot?" He suggested, "The linear logic of the male orgasm is the reason men are inclined toward math and science." Anthony further asserted, "They have to learn to come to grips with the physical properties of hydraulics and propulsion." Remember, this was back in the old days when Annie Sprinkle's cervix-centric raunch-spirituality and Candida Royale's softer, made-for-women erotic videos were first breaking into the industry. These progressive women in porn were beginning to organize as pro-sex Libertarian feminists, taking back the night from men and Rusty Nut antiporn feminists alike.

Straight porn always had gorgeous women, but the men weren't very foxy—Ron Jeremy, Long Dong Silver. After the Beast advised, "Gay porn has much hotter guys," I checked out *Sex Bazaar.* It was in French, which is already hot. The story opens in an Arab marketplace. The boys are exquisitely young, handsome, muscular, and horny. It's progressively interracial, with white, black, and brown hunks sitting around fondling, sucking, stroking, and groping. In gay porn I discovered Jeff Stryker, a California Adonis who starred in a series of bisexual flicks like *The Big Switch* and *Bi-Coastal.* HeteroLadies, what would you rather do: watch two hours of cumshots slamming across Vanessa Del Rio's face or the studly Jeff doing a well-hung great dark man?

There was also a new market percolating in genuine lesbian porn flicks—real dykes who love women and understand our needs. This is very different than the pseudo girl-on-girl aesthetic that dominates made-for-guy porn. In *Erotic in Nature* I watched a wood nymph and a golden goddess frolic in a hot tub, exploring the pleasures of female. It was sultry but boring. That too would change as queer markets opened up, people evolved, and stereotypes collapsed.

My favorite of all were the Dark Bros., purveyors of porn who rose to notoriety in *New Wave Hookers.* The scandal involved actress Traci Lords, who didn't tell them she was underage and they never asked. Realizing the idiocy of porn (and sex itself) the Bros. threw it in our faces like ca-ca. Fixated, I mastered their entire oeuvre, *Black Throat* merged into *Between the Cheeks,* and *Black Chicks* became *White Chicks.* I began renting the Dark Bros. on a daily basis, sometimes watching three flicks in a row. All their sex videos have a perky little tune that sets the mood of the story. That certainly did not help my fragile emotional state. After a while, I began avoiding my neighbors, I lost interest in live boyfriends. They seemed superfluous in comparison to my private world of Darkness.

Gradually, my personality began to change. I developed a fetish for men in uniforms, caught myself flirting with the police at the Chinese takeout. I began buying sex industry rags at Metal 24, the convenience store up the road. Sometimes I dressed like a porn director in tacky Hawaiian shirts and dark sunglasses. Other times I glided across the turnpike like a porn star, rushing off to Pathmark at four A.M. for hair bleach, convinced I looked like Amber Lynn. More likely, I resembled Divine. I'd bleat out strings of dialogue I'd picked up from my adult films, hurling them at random, abusing innocent bystanders. "Oh yeah, come on, give it to me!" I'd goad the cashier at C-Town.

When Blaccard called to tell me some hot biker porn had come in, I rushed right out to Bonge's house to scoop it up. Mr. Bonge was a photographer, an artist who customized an impressive collection of Harleys and '50s automobiles. He was a friend of Blaccard's I'd met back in the CorpseGrinder days at Babyface Studios, shooting the Slugs. We'd done some photo essays for a shortlived regional magazine called *Long Island Monthly.* Mr. Bonge was inked from head to toe; having tattoos can offer a decisive advantage in street reporting, eliciting unspoken trust. Many people fear getting tattooed because it might ruin their chances of upward mobility. But in my experience, the reverse was true.

The day of the big porn score, Mr. Bonge asked me when I would be through with the Japanese bondage film. It might take time. I was still conducting my wax dripping experiments. I hissed at him, "You'll wait!! You're gonna wait a real long time." This to a man with four hundred tattoos, skulls, bikes, iron crosses—every scary thing, including many automotive tools. This to a man with a battered Barbie doll hanging from his truck's rearview mirror on thick silver chains: Barbie in Bondage. But I didn't care; porn made me invincible. It was like Quaaludes; it melted your body and your mind into a dull, juicy, erotic haze. Like everything else, I had to stop it, cold turkey.

And when it finally ended, I was left with a tit fetish, the result of too many viewings of Candy Samples's *Bedtime Stories.* Of course, once those great enablers—the *Village Voice* editors—got wind of my nocturnal remission, my spiritual journey into the world of smut was quickly transformed into copy, a feature called "Alice in Cumshotland." Thanks to my enablers, I got to meet porn legends Annie Sprinkle and Candida Royale. I even got clandestine mail from the purveyors of porn, my favorite American filmmakers, the Dark Bros.

For me, journalism was free therapy. It also helped to transform my fantasy life into reality. Living inside my stories, writing about my life on the turnpike gradually eroded any fixed sense of time or place. Everything seemed to occur synchronically, simultaneously with no past, present, or future. I was perpetually fried from no sleep, burnt, hung over. My mind was saturated by minutiae, cosmic interconnections, metaphors, and esoteric knowledge. Sometimes I'd get so absorbed by my discoveries, I had no idea what year it was. I'd have to look on the cover of whatever publication had featured my story to pin down the dates. The Panel of Experts was no help; most of them existed in a warped dimension, too.

Intoxicated, in a perpetual state of sociological euphoria, I immersed myself in each new scene like a method actor. In a Zen-like trance, I'd study the landscape, then connect it to something inside myself. I wouldn't quit until *I got it.* Bouncing around from one obsession to another, chasing down the inner aim of anything from computer lust to bondage porn, I saw it. There, in the *telos,* I'd have a glimpse of truth, fleeting contact with a higher power, a sense of the All. There I experienced a series of random epiphanies, found heroes, godz, mentors, and fellow travelers. In these transient moments of connectivity I felt whole, integrated, saved. Egoless, artless, decentered, I surrendered myself and belonged wholly to the world.

When I was younger, I lived in a dream world of doo-wop with a transistor radio under my pillow. When I hit the streets and saw those Irish boys in the school yard of St. Francis, on Twennyninth, the songs that had nursed me through long nights of amphetamine insomnia became an empirical reality. A world germinating in my head was brought to life. Now I was getting paid for it.

My career in pornography led to a lifetime supply of clandestine mailings in brown envelopes. My adventures in cyberspace were published in 1989 as "Computer Lust." This led to a column and wads of complimentary computer software. Someone had to pay for all my hobbies. With every article, subcultural bonding with like-minded souls led to friendships that have lasted years. Writing soon became the ultimate pen-pal network; with each publication, I punched new numbers into the AutoDial pad. A flow of fresh blood continued to infuse what eventually became the Panel of Experts in Cyberspace. E-mail virtually eliminated all phone contact from my life. Technology liberated me from the distraction of face-to-face social interaction.

I had one particular suburban hobby that did not interest *The Village Voice* or anyone else. Before the advent of "women and guns," the liberal press effectively censored me out of ever publishing a story about my firearms collection. City people hate guns. Ted Nugent was my only ally, and he lived too far away. My interest in guns began during latency. I was an accomplished shooter at the penny arcades of Rockaway Beach. I won bags of live goldfish at Playland, scored high points slaughtering duck decoys. I loved shooting, but it was a most painful tragedy that led me to this particular hobby.

In 1989, after eighteen years of remission, Betty Bradley's cancer came back, and this time she lost. When she died, my first thought was to raid the trash, salvage the Dilaudids. I rescued the Valium and Percodan, too. D.O.M. refused to have a funeral. As usual, he was pissed at G-d. He had taken care of her at home for several months, watched her writhe in pain, lose hope, and wither away. She died in their bed. Just a week before, she was singing their song, "Our Love Is Here to Stay." He never told her she was dying. He lied. He said the cancer was completely removed, she was cured, but recovery would be slow. He didn't tell me either, not until the end. My mother could read my face, and I'm a bad liar. He knew her. Once she realized there was no hope, she'd want out. In a subterfuge calculated to give some sense of a future, I ordered a credit card for her on my account. She signed it, and I activated it for when she'd recover.

As her body weakened and decayed, she began to figure it out. She had always counted on God to deliver her, but now she'd lost all faith. Betty Bradley, Basha, devoted daughter of God had finally given up. She whispered, "We come into this life alone, and that's how we leave it." So, taking matters into her own hands, she begged D.O.M. to smother her with a pillow, but he couldn't. He refused to let her go, he would have kept her alive forever, a brain in a jar if he could. She would've done it for him; she was tougher. So she stopped eating and refused her medication. In an unspoken agreement, my father accelerated the Dilaudid until my mother was dead. He guarded her like a German shepherd, he wouldn't let anyone near her, even me. I watched from deep freeze as the wall between her stomach and her colon collapsed and all the waste drained out of a tube from her center, from her solar plexus. The last thing she said to me was, "Take care of my little girl."

It would have destroyed him to see her lying in a casket, so we read the Twenty-third Psalm and buried her right there, in the Gaines family plot right next to Artie. The empty space on her other side was reserved for D.O.M. At one point I wanted all my parents together and planned to move Herbie in as well. But we decided to leave him with the Denmarks, a few miles away. We put Betty Bradley in the ground, in the middle of January, in Queens. It was just me, Aunt Rose, her kids, and D.O.M. Raymond and Anthony held me up as they lowered the coffin. My two best friends refused to let me drink. That night they took me to see Johnny Thunders. Then I went back to work. I still had to finish *Teenage Wasteland.*

Betty had gotten sick the week I signed my book contract. It was always like that, as my life got better, my loved ones disappeared. I couldn't figure out if I was being punished because I was happy or if I was being rewarded as some cosmic compensation for losing them. Chronically pissed off, I hated God. I hated everything. Certain I'd die young, I burned it hard.

In my mother's memory, I had a multicolored phoenix rising out of ashes tattooed on my left inner forearm. It came up from bold orange flames, like the ones Mr. Bonge painted on his cars and bikes. Guys always asked if I had any other tattoos, and women always wondered if it hurt. Yes, it did, and that was the point: to gouge the arm and *feel* something. To scorch my flesh with the pain I couldn't allow in my heart. It hurt, but it felt wonderful too. I called my phoenix Little Wing following the Hendrix song, *When I'm sad, she comes to me, with a thousand smiles . . .*

After my biological father died, my mother held me tight. After Mr. Gaines died, it was my nagging that kept her from suicide—"Mommy, I need you!" Now, after my mother died, I worried about D.O.M. He was all I had left, the parent I always felt closest to. He fell into a bottle of vodka, and I was sure he was going next. But D.O.M. snapped out of it, for me and for his sister, the drummer, my aunt Rose.

Trying to heal, D.O.M. and I began looking for father-daughter bonding activities. My parents were passionate bowlers, I had watched my dad compete in the Pro-Am tournaments in Garden City. But I hated bowling. I sucked, never cut a score over forty-two. It was gonna be that or guns, so we hit the shooting range.

D.O.M. was an active member of the 82nd Airborne Division Association. Their meetings were held at the VFW Hall in Elmont, Long Island. The association also includes paratroopers from the 13th, 11th, 101st, and 17th. Today, the 82nd in Fort Bragg, North Carolina, remains a robust, full-powered division. When Betty Bradley was alive, they went to Fort Bragg for special jump events, reunions, and celebrations.

Whenever my travels as Dr. Gaines involved flying, I took my father's glider wings with me for good luck. D.O.M. was chronically pissed that his neighbors didn't display the American flag, even on patriotic holidays. He wore an Airborne patch on his jacket at all times. The war was the defining moment of his life; that, and meeting my mother. Once a month, at the 82nd Airborne Division Association meetings, members convene to discuss upcoming parades, memorial ceremonies, and veterans' affairs. The meetings were an intergenerational summit of soldiers who served in Korea, Vietnam, Desert Storm, and Granada, as well as noncombat. The younger ones looked up to old-timers like my dad, Big Yanks from the Big One. Since most of his cohort has passed on, he mainly hung with the Korean and Vietnam vets, whom he supported but considered "too militant."

The big action at any Long Island VFW hall is at the bar, well appointed, always packed. Once D.O.M. took me to a meeting, but he banned me from the bar. He was afraid the men would be cursing. Later on, my dad led a toast, a memorial tribute to all the troopers lost in combat, men from every war who won't be forgotten as long as the last soldier stands. As part of the toast, I got to sample some Calvados, a brutal French brandy I could barely swallow. Among World War II vets, "Calvados Commandos" are famous, mainly for their drinking. Like my biological father, Herbie, D.O.M. had been a decorated marksman in the army. Since he had taught me how to drive, firearm safety was a breeze. Remember, D.O.M. doesn't talk; he barks orders. "Donna, a gun is a lethal weapon, like a car. Treat it with care and respect!"

I had bought my first gun from the Beast's lover, that New York State trooper. It was a Mossberg 500 pump action, "police riot" shotgun with pistol grip and a hot paramilitary camouflage case. In the late 1980s, people wore long, black leather trench coats. The naked Mossberg was easily concealed. When the state trooper asked me why I wanted the Mossberg, the Beast quipped, "As a fashion statement!" After the Mossberg, I did need to accessorize, so I bought some rifles. For summer wear, I favored a Ruger Model 10/22 Carbine, caliber .22. I added a stunning plastic banana clip that took hours to load and always jammed. Then I bought a second Ruger and had it fitted on a black Choate stock, transforming the simple rifle into a folding pistol grip-chopping the gun down to twenty-seven inches. That Ruger felt like a popgun, a perfect plinking toy for slaughtering soybeans and beer bottles.

I cleaned and polished my "boys" regularly, doting on them like they were my babies. I invested in all sorts of products: Hoppe's cleaning kits replete with brushes, take-down rods, tips, patches, solvents, and oils. There's always some new scope or loader to buy, a metal safe to consider, protective gear for eyes and ears, cases, ammo. I made weekly trips to all the great gun stores of Long Island, checking out bipods, scopes, and mounts. I frequented all the hot spots. The big range out at Calverton, near Riverhead, was like the Wild West, lawless. Then there are clandestine spots, private gun clubs from Floral Park to Levittown. I'd pore over *Soldier of Fortune.* It borders on pornography—all those hot weapons in the arms of sexy mercenaries. I got subscriptions to *Guns & Ammo* and read the NRA's monthly publication, *American Rifleman,* from cover to cover.

Like most shooters, I soon tired of long guns and decided to apply for a pistol permit. In a ritual cleansing of great historical significance, I returned to Mineola to police headquarters, to the very place where I had been detained following my arrest in 1969. I was required to present endless documentation, records of arrest and dismissal and pertinent testimony to my soundness of mind. I embarked upon an application process that made getting into graduate school seem like picking up a burger and fries at the drive-up window at Micky D's.

The state's decision to grant me a pistol permit constituted the ultimate proof of good citizenship. I was absolved of all prior sins against the state. To obtain a permit in New York State, you need four character references. None of your electors can have any history of drunk driving, psychiatric hospitalization, or felony arrests. Good luck finding four such wholesome citizens on Lawn Guyland. I took photos with my hair combed straight back like D.O.M.'s, his turtle-headed daughter, spontaneous military issue.

By now D.O.M. was on the Panel of Experts, too. We had become best friends. If he screamed, I screamed back. Usually, we made our peace. Sometimes we didn't. We once stopped speaking for two years. I understood that he did the best he could, and he was proud of me, too. After a while, people said I looked like him. But then, so did Nick. D.O.M. sent Nick birthday cards addressed "To my son." In our Aquarian Age of humanitarianism and universal love, true parenting isn't necessarily based on biological or even legal ties (adoption). It is a sacred social contract underscored by much higher spiritual principles. Like Mister Rogers on TV, nurturing an entire generation of kids growing up in divorced families, the Aquarian D.O.M. was the father of us all.

It took months for the pistol permit application to be processed, for my relationship with the fascist patriarchy to be formally consecrated. So entrusted, I even stopped driving while intoxicated. Gun Safety Rule Seven of the National Rifle Association says, "Don't mix alcohol or drugs with shooting," and I never did. I took my new relationship with the State as seriously as a marriage vow. The Beast agreed, eyeing his trooper with a mischievous smile, "Yes, honey, now we're *both* tricking with the State!"

In addition to daughterly affection and the pleasures of target shooting, my embrace of firearms is justified by my structural, historical position as a Jew and a woman. Between the Warsaw Ghetto and the rape camps of Bosnia, I wondered, why would any member of a minority willingly forfeit her constitutional right to bear arms? I've taken firearms safety courses and pledged to uphold the sanctity of deadly force. Even in self-defense, I would look only to disable an attacker. Criminals don't get pistol permits, take safety courses, or join the NRA.

Some people think women who love guns suffer from penis envy, like we only want that metal rod as a dick extension. Well, why wouldn't we? Historically, a penis brings with it lots of power, money, and privilege. Female sexuality is far more evolved and sophisticated. Why would any woman want to trade off an endless multiplicity of sensual delights for a dumb, linear cumshot? In the years before Title IX, before girls got to play, being "male-identified" was the only way to learn anything from the gender elite.

When they kick at your front door, how you gonna come? With your hands on your head or on the trigger of your gun? Most of my friends hate guns. They worry about their children's safety, about accidents at home and mass killings at school. Today's debates over guns in America are as volatile as the abortion wars. I understand their fears, and I respect them, as I do people who oppose abortion. Still, I'm stuck in a quagmire. The right wants to shoot down my legal access to safe abortion; the left wants to abort my constitutional right to bear arms. Neither side understands anything about popular culture, Axl Rose, Marilyn Manson, or Eminem. Like I said, I want everyone out of my life, my uterus, my gun collection, and my porn library. Don't tread on me!

In the early days of gun hobbying, D.O.M. and I enjoyed cleaning "the boys," drinking vodka, and listening to Harry James's wailing trumpet. But once I started collecting pistols, even my dad was getting nervous. At one point he called me a "gun nut," admonishing, "Just do your writing and be a lady!" But it was too late. Firearms had triggered my combative Mars in Aries into fully automatic mode. I loved everything about guns. And like everything else, they too became addictive. I always wanted just one more, then I would stop. Years have passed and here I am, dreaming of a sweet little derringer with a genuine mother-of-pearl handle. Crappy for target, but real good at close range.

My life was a continuous swirl of activity punctuated by deadlines, drinking sprees, seeing bands, and foraging for sociology. But darkness was setting in. Guns eventually took on a deeper meaning in my life. After a while, whenever I had to deal with death or loss, I'd buy a new gun or get another tattoo.

IV

Over the years, Beast and I went to Slayer shows, took trips to Mexico, and searched the night for compelling boys and cheap thrills. Beast was a *mensch*. He took care of his family and pampered anyone he loved. He had a high-powered job as a software engineer and a black belt in karate. The macho gay boy fused Eastern religions with Jewish mysticism, carving out his own temple of love and self-acceptance. But the years in the glory hole had taken their toll, and Beast was diagnosed with HIV. He began volunteering for experimental treatments, clinical trials that slowed his decline and supplied him with endless antidepressants, tranquilizers, and syringes.

Beast kept working, too, averaging ten to twelve hours a day, sometimes seven days a week. Like most tech workers, Beast loved his work. Like most greedy corporations, tech managers eagerly exploited this dedication to craft, working their engineers to death for greater profits. Where professional ideologies are strong—based on love of craft (engineers) or a higher purpose (social workers, nurses)—workers often have no sense of themselves as labor. Unionization of professionals can temper such exploitation. Ironically, Beast's grandma was a hardcore commie. She died young with a hammer and sickle engraved on her headstone. Beast never informed the team how sick he really was. Some days he started work at three A.M., anything to get the job done, to meet the deadline. In graduate school I had taken my area exams on Work and the Professions, studying the work of "proletarianization" theorists like Charles Derber and Magali Larson. I knew what these corporate dicks were up to, and so did the Beast. But he said the work took his mind off his condition. After a while, his immune system broke down.

I watched him fade away, a little more each day, emaciated, parched, sleepwalking as the dying do, into the place where the body surrenders and the spirit takes flight. Human death appears like some tragic defeat, pathetic, repulsive. One day, the Beast just fell asleep on the toilet seat. It was over, painless and merciful.

After the Beast died, as part of a memorial tribute, I secured a Smith

& Wesson Model 60 revolver, caliber .38. It was many years before I could do much more with my feelings than bury them, gouge them into my flesh, or pump them out at the range. I walked alone on life's punishing prairie. I didn't need anyone or anything. Back then, firearms and tattoos protected me.

By the early 1990s, the Slugs were sounding better than ever. They had good jobs, nice homes, wives, and periodically, they'd book a show. Louie and Matt were clean, and so was Rick Rivets. Sue Mordred had her band. Coco hit the street, but for most, heroin was in the past. It seemed dope was done killing my friends, but I was wrong. At first, Donnie and Lizzie were doing fine. They stayed clean and worked hard. They went to the methadone clinic six days out of seven. On the sixth day, they let Donnie take one dose home for Sunday, as long as his urine stayed clean. He paid fifteen dollars a week. Eventually he was able to cut the visits down to twice a week.

They both drank, but Lizzie was a bigger alcoholic. It was her primary addiction, even as a junkie, even after her artery was blocked and her fingers rotted off. After she got hepatitis, after she was on methadone, she still kept drinking. By now, Donnie and Lizzie had been on methadone for five years. Every morning before work, the counselors smelled booze on Lizzie's breath. They started giving her Breathalyzer tests, threatening to boot her if she didn't stop drinking. They weren't being mean; they wanted her to be drug free. The program won't work if you're not.

As everyone knows, methadone can be a super addiction in itself, as heavy as heroin. It gets into your bones, fucks you up bad, your teeth, everything. And if you ever wanted to detox from methadone, it took a long time, and you didn't get much support. After a while you got sick of standing on line, of watching people you know dying of AIDS and hep C. You just wanted out. But it wasn't that simple. Even if you wanted to take a vacation, you had to show your airline tickets. Touring with a band would be impossible. Once you were on methadone, the State owned your ass.

Donnie worked around all that. The night before he was getting tested, he just didn't drink, simple. He was a heroin addict, so the program worked for him. But Lizzie was truly powerless over alcohol. She wasn't going to let anyone tell her how to live. She had already lost her job and now they wouldn't medicate her. So she just said screw it; she decided to detox herself. It wouldn't have occurred to her to ask for help. She was independent, a self-made woman, she would do it herself. Lizzie wouldn't be the first addict to die trying to get off methadone, and I'm sure she wasn't the last. Unfortunately there aren't great government statistics measuring methadone's casualties, just sad street stories.

By the end, Lizzie was drinking every day. When she showed up at my fortieth birthday party, I was amazed she could actually walk, and I felt honored that Lizzie loved me enough to show up. I knew it was hard for her to be in public. She had lost yet another job, but she still had a boyfriend in the City. She'd go to meet him, they'd drink, sometimes he'd cop for her. The marriage to Donnie had long since unraveled; they stayed in different rooms, two separate lives. He slept in the living room, she took over their bedroom. Lizzie spent days alone, drinking in her room, reading trashy novels. Only Judy the cat was welcome.

A month before she died, she was hospitalized with a liver infection. They warned her that if she didn't stop drinking, she'd die. We told her we loved her, offered to take her to AA meetings, to the gym, shopping, anything to distract her. Everybody begged her, and she said, "Yeah, yeah, I know." A week later when Nick saw her on the beach, her stomach was distended, her arms and legs like twigs, her face was putty gray. She had been trying to detox herself from methadone. She kept drinking, doing dope. But her system was shot.

The weekend Lizzie died the Slugs were supposed to record at a studio in the City. Louie called Donnie in the morning to firm up plans. Donnie just said, "Lizzie's dead." Nick came over and woke me up; he was crying. He and Louie had been to their apartment to clean up. The living room was its usual mess. She died in the bedroom. The police had been there and Donnie's father. Donnie was shattered. He didn't want any help, but the Slugs insisted.

Donnie had gone out that morning to play golf. They weren't talking much anymore. He walked out without saying good-bye. He didn't check on her; he just picked up and left. If he had checked, he figured, chances were she was just getting sick, choking, in the process of dying. He felt guilty, but he couldn't deal with her, she was too far gone. The doctor at Jamaica Hospital had told him she was hopeless. We all knew it. In recent months Donnie and Lizzie had isolated themselves from everyone. He was trying to get his life together, to separate himself from her psychologically. When he came back from golf she was already dead, her liver exploded.

Lizzie was a Girl Scout; she sewed her own curtains and baked Christmas cookies every year. She got me into Clinique's Aromatics Elixir; it became our signature scent. She wasn't supposed to die like that, alone, in agony, in Queens, with Judy.

Alive, Lizzie looked like Tina Turner. Like Deborah Harry, she was sexy, tough, and pretty. She looked eighty years old in the casket, shriveled up, withered. *I'll never stay in the valley of fear, I won't decay in the valley of fear, you die every day in the valley of fear.* Everybody said she considered me her closest friend. At the wake, they wanted to know what had happened. Her mother came up to me, stunned, clueless. Why was her daughter dead at thirty-seven? Lizzie loved me and I loved her, too, but I didn't know her at all. I didn't even know myself. We hung out all the time. We had deep drunk talks, cheap emotions, but everything evaporated the next day in a hangover. We rarely spoke in the language of the heart. Mostly, we let the drugs and booze do it for us. Once, I had all my sisters and me. Now they were gone: Sue Mordred to the hills, Coco to the streets, Lizzie to the Lord. That left me the last girl standing, alone on the dance floor again.

Johnny Thunders checked out around the same time as Lizzie. He died in New Orleans on April 23, 1991. Alone, in room 37 of St. Peter House. In pain, ripped off, sick from bad drugs and lymphatic leukemia. We still don't know all the details. To the police, Thunders was probably just another dead junkie in a seedy boardinghouse. To this day, fans suspect foul play and cover-up. All his money was missing. So were the fabulous Chinese silk suits he'd had made to order during a recent Asian tour.

If Thunders hadn't become St. John of the Gutter Guitar, he would have played pro baseball. An altar boy and a scumbag, like all the punk boys from 1977, Thunders dressed to kill. Half the reason we'd go see him was to check out his look. Some said his pirate leads were sloppy, he couldn't really play. But his music generated something that kept me alive, something only a fan could hear. When I felt empty, Johnny's guitar filled me up. It gave my life its emotional center, its connection to anything meaningful that spoke to me in my own words. But I'm afraid if I have to explain it, you'll never get it.

Sure, I had my suburbia stories; there would always be the next new distraction, another "it," but *nothing* like Thunderella. Now I would be bored forever. Like all his fans, I collected portraits, band shots, stockpiled every album he ever recorded, including bootlegs, even the atrocious acoustic stuff. When he died, someone sent me a photo of his gravesite in Queens, the land of our birth, *Johnny Thunders Genzale, 1952–1991.* Thunders's junko partner Jerry Nolan died less than a year later, on January 14, 1992, of complications following pneumonia and meningitis. As Nolan requested, he was buried next to his best friend in the family plot, at St. Mary's cemetery in Flushing, Queens.

Flowers, an American flag, messages with his lyrics, the tender mercies we gathered. Long Island rocker boys still go there to pay respects, to seek John's blessings for their bands. Thunders represented a purity and realness that musicians pray for. For years after, local bands covered his songs and dedicated their sets to him. His fans carried on the faith like the Deadheads after Jerry, or Zeppelin fans after Bonham. But it would never be the same.

Slugland, Thunderella, the Beast, Lizzie, Betty Bradley. Slam-dunk, swallow hard. I had to press on—buy more guns, get more tattoos, write more stories, find new bands. I had just turned forty; I needed courage and fresh music. So I got back on the turnpike, searching for a new beginning. My suburbia was full of promise. Somehow, it gave me hope.

Dr. Gaines with "The Boys," Mineola, 1992.

13

WILD IN THE 'BURBS

loved Long Island and when I finally left, it was under extreme duress. Howard Stern's vitriolic humor exemplified the suburban sensibility at work: politically incorrect, militantly populist, and completely nuts. When I was young, everybody believed America's societal institutions— the family, school, community, church—worked. If you didn't fit in, something was wrong with *you*.

Since the 1950s, social critics had warned that suburban sprawl could be toxic to the psyche, that community was impossible, alienation inevitable, even normative. By the late 1980s, the promise of the good life was slipping away. Suburban life was obviously "in decline"— divorce, alcoholism, family violence, unemployment, incest, gangs, graffiti. Everyone knew that if you grew up in suburbia, didn't kill yourself, join a gang, or blow up your high school, you were probably in a band. By the 1990s, Johnny Thunders was dead and so was Downtown, but I found sanctuary in Long Island's vital music underground.

I spent my days hanging around mildewed basement rehearsal studios, sweaty mosh pits, cluttered record stores, makeshift clubs, and convenience stores. As I got older, the bands got younger, first five years, then ten. After a while there was a generational difference. I became a soccer mom for some of Long Island's fiercest death-metal and hardcore crews.

By the 1990s there were so many great bands, I was out almost every night. So ensconced in our local scene, I only left Long Island for Dr. Gaines business—speaking engagements, to get edited. Although I was part of a robust community of urban scholars and literary types, I had no compelling interest in anything but the local product. I didn't even bother trying to explain what I was into. It would have been fruitless.

Bands like Pyrexia and Suffocation established Long Island as a death-metal stronghold. But every town offered up a multitude of talent in punk, hardcore, rockabilly. One night the Mordred sisters took me to the Right Track Inn in Freeport to see Long Island's legendary biker libertarian surf punks, Sea Monster. With songs like "Beer & Weenies" and "Sex God Chant," they exemplified the gonzo turnpike life I loved. At one point their bondage-clad frontman, Arthur Stevenson, got profiled by *The New York Times*. Then there was NutJob's art noise and the pounding of the Nihilistics. On other nights Corporate Waste, the Ghouls, or the Chiselers, Situated Chaos, In Cold Blood, and Rosary Violet. The Slugs, too, were booking regularly at crusty old Nightingale's. Between shows I became a studio rat, preferring to see bands at point-blank range, no cover, no bouncers, and no talking during a set.

What happens when worlds collide? When all the parts of your life merge and for one moment everything is clear? Except for my clandestine hacker parties, most members on the Panel of Experts had never met face to face. But I do remember one night when it all came together—at my book party. On a tip from another *Voice* writer, I held the debutante ball for *Teenage Wasteland* at Brownie's, a punk palace down on Avenue A. Editors, writers, academics, musicians, and friends communed in an unlikely sociological ragout. I was proud that of two hundred people, only one was genetically linked to me, my favorite cousin Bobby, who lived in Jersey.

What a scene it was. Nick sitting with Robert Christgau, Barbara Ehrenreich, and the members of Rosary Violet, Ellen Willis and the Mordred sisters, Stanley Aronowitz in the same line of sight as Blaccard and Stripe. The Binary Boy was one of the few faculty members from Big Science who made the scene. Anthony brought me flowers, but he only made a cameo appearance. He hates book parties.

Meantime, Nick refused to let me go near Professor Aloysius. Here I had paid for four hours of an open bar and all I was allowed was one lousy beer. In Nick's imagination, I was a porcelain figure to be forever protected and perfected; he watched my food intake, my drinking. He approved my hair and makeup, my clothes and accessories. For birthdays, he bought me delicate Limoges boxes and Joy perfume. My co-dependent had impeccable taste. I overdid everything.

There were agents, publicists from Pantheon, and editors from HarperCollins interested in buying the paperback rights. But I could barely work the room, I was so busy fretting over D.O.M. Most people would have worried about their elderly father driving through the Lower East Side alone late at night, but D.O.M. grew up on those streets. He knew them well. Besides, he still carried a tire iron under the seat. No, I was worried about something else. What if someone cursed in front of him? Or disrespected him for saying something "politically incorrect"? I didn't want him to feel left out or too alone, to start thinking about how much he missed Betty. My hypersensitive father stood by the bar, hair slicked straight back, arms folded tight like John Gotti. He wouldn't budge an inch.

By now Mr. Bonge had his colors and was living at the clubhouse. A respected member of the 3rd Street Crew, he eventually became an officer in the club. The author of *Tattooed with Attitude* and *Marked for Life* was a distinguished photographer of hot rods, tattoos, and ladies. He traveled around the world on assignment for prestigious ink rags, rebuilt custom cars and motorcycles, displayed his wares at Beatnik Car Club extravaganzas from coast to coast. He'd had shows at spots like the Limelight and CBGB's Gallery. A celebrity biker in the fine tradition of Chuck Zito and Sonny Barger, Mr. Bonge had been in movies and profiled in print media.

That night at my book party, I took Mr. Bonge aside, explaining the situation. I prevailed upon him to make sure nobody said anything weird to my dad. Mr. Bonge was a Long Island guy, so he understood immediately. Mr. Bonge had taken a photograph of me sitting on top of a Harley in a black leather jacket, showing off my first tattoo. Parents always want us to look wholesome and sweet. But sometimes they are hopelessly blinded by love. Nick's mother thought we looked *gorgeous* in our vilest punk ensembles; the seedier and sluttier, the better. Following this same illogic, D.O.M. cherished the shot of me in leather and chains perched on Mr. Bonge's Harley. He framed it, even brought it to the bowling alley, *kvelling*, "It shows off your dimples."

At some point in edgy memoirs like these there's a life-threatening encounter with a sinister outlaw motorcycle gang. The experience is typically offered up as a measure of the writer's street creds, his or her propensity for risk-taking. Some get stomped, others gang raped. The lucky few ride reckless into the night. For me, the association worked in reverse. I have only known the New York City Hells Angels to be righteous men, dedicated fathers, loyal sons and brothers. There are more gangsters and sluts in our government. I've watched the Angels, staunch upholders of old-school American values, support each other and their loved ones at shows, funerals, and weddings. Hells Angels' women, too, are devoted, hardworking, and sincere. The merchandise support website at www.bigredmachine.com features children's clothing.

So I was counting on Mr. Bonge to make sure nobody upset my dad, to keep things "normal." On Long Island, "normal" means *no bullshit*, real. Turns out I had nothing to worry about. D.O.M. relaxed with his favorite photographer and at one point, I overheard my dad discussing the history of soccer in America with cultural studies scholar Andrew Ross.

City people always have someplace else to go, another appointment penciled in. They'll rarely hang for *la longe duree*. On Long Island, the sense of time is different; it revolves around bar closings, DWI laws, and police checkpoints. After Brownie's, Nick lifted my drinking ban and about ten of us migrated east to a bar called Alcatraz. The VIP list included assorted Slugs, the Binary Boy, and Stripe. In Slugland, the best nights ended with Stripe getting arrested. He did not disappoint. In honor of my book publication, he spent the night in jail. Some people celebrate rites of passage through weddings and baby showers. I had the book party and Stripe's arraignment.

The publication of *Teenage Wasteland* in 1991 had established me as an expert on youth suicide and anomie. When I wasn't making the scene, I spoke at universities, worked as a consultant to schools, politicians, and think tanks. I appeared regularly in print, on TV or radio. Whenever kids killed themselves, their parents, or one another, it was my job to help explain the unexplainable. California's public defenders called on me to assist in death penalty trials involving youth accused of heinous crimes. Educators, parents, and clergy sought my expertise in "reaching out" to their youth. Once, I was introduced as "the mother of all misfits." Almost fifteen years after the Bergenfield suicide pact, after gangs, after Columbine, I'm still explaining. Back then, adults denied culpability for teenage suicide; they blamed drugs, Ozzy, and Satan. Gang-related violence was subsequently blamed on drugs, hip-hop culture, and rap music. After Columbine, it was Goths, Marilyn Manson, and the Internet. S.S.D.D.: Same Shit, Different Day.

When *Teenage Wasteland* came out, *Newsday* ran a cover of me in shades and a denim jacket, big silver hoop earrings, lipstick, and a sneer. The headline read A BURNOUT'S BEST FRIEND. I was leaning against a wall in front of the 7-Eleven in Westbury. Wherever I went, Long Island local kids recognized me. They stopped me in stores and at gas stations to thank me, like I was the Margaret Mead of heavy metal. Today the alienated teens I wrote about then are in their early thirties, homeowners, mothers, career criminals, wife beaters, drunks, rock stars, and microchip masters of the universe. Some are my editors. And they still thank me for sticking up for them, for even bothering to look at what life was like growing up in Reagan's America, members of the "minority of minorities" trying to survive.

I'd had a profound, visceral reaction to the Bergenfield multiple suicide pact of 1987. It broke my spirit to see young people defeated in this way. But it also changed my life. It jolted me out of my personal amnesia. It had been many years since I was a teenage outcast in Rockaway. I had effectively *forgotten,* iced out those wretched feelings. I was always running. Like many people, I buried myself in hard work, booze, food, and sex. The only emotion I allowed myself was rage. I had lost weight, shed my fear, and reinvented myself as a winner. I had traveled far and away from the hidden injuries of my own youth. I had effectively split off from my past. But going to Bergenfield ruptured that.

Intellectually, it was my first realization of the power of history, of a new generation coming of age, bringing with it a different worldview, fresh ideas, innovations, and truths. It gave me a sense of mortality, of finite possibilities. But meeting those kids did something else: It put a fatal crack in the wall that separated me from myself.

Around page sixty of *Teenage Wasteland,* I recount the moment where the Bergenfield kids decide to engage, where they decide to take me undercover as a "burnout" so I could see for myself how they were mistreated. They instructed me on where to go, how to act, what to wear. We were standing in front of the 7-Eleven, and an interaction ensues. In the book I attributed this critical moment of bonding to the wearing of a Motörhead pin and a working knowledge of Metallica, their favorite band. I understood Motörhead as postpunk, not metal, descending from the Ramones love of speed. Lemmy even wrote "R.A.M.O.N.E.S." My enamel Motörhead pin did help break the ice, but it wasn't the whole story.

I didn't grasp this at the time: Wherever you roam, whatever you do, *if you've got it, you can spot it.* One humiliated child will always recognize another. Whether we are children of alcoholics, abused, neglected, abandoned, rejected, or otherwise devalued, we can smell each other. If you grew up feeling unloved and unlovable, it's there, always already present. It works sort of like "gaydar," as a mutual understanding, a secret code that underscores anything else you do or say. Instinctively, *they knew who I was.* I never had to explain.

Another healing occurred in Bergenfield. Frank Zappa's name came up when the Jersey kids listed all the bands they trusted. They saw Zappa as someone especially righteous. When heavy metal was condemned by the PMRC, Zappa testified before the Senate hearings and argued on behalf of the First Amendment, which '80s kids interpreted as their right to party. "He stuck up for us," they said of the transgenerational hero. After my cover story about the suicide pact appeared, several TV producers wanted to interview me and the kids. At one point I suggested Frank Zappa should be part of it, and he was very open to the idea. But I was adamant: no kids.

The Bergenfield kids had asked me to protect their anonymity at all costs. Teenage suicide was hot in the media then. I was getting calls asking me to come on TV and, oh, could I please bring a suicidal kid? Smooth and seductive, snake-oil salesmen in trench coats with cameras, the perky producers would cajole and seduce. "Donna, don't you think it would be great publicity for the book you're writing?" They were worse than strung-out junkies hitting you for spare change. Could I *please* produce a suicidal kid? Manipulative, heartless, and stupid: "Wouldn't it help the kid to share his feelings?" Fuck you very much, I regretfully declined. But I did get to thank Frank Zappa personally for his part in transporting me from my own teenage wasteland.

Late at night, returning home to Long Island from the streets of Jersey, looking for a quick sugar fix, I'd often stop in at a local convenience store I called Metal 24. The kids working there played Metallica nonstop for their entire twelve-hour graveyard shift. I recognized "Ride the Lightning" from Bergenfield, from boom boxes and car stereos. So we started talking.

Long before I got to Bergenfield I had tired of the minimalist sound of hardcore. After years of being Brunhilda of the Pit I needed to get guitar solos back in my life. For me, the sex in rock is in the lead, in the wank itself. Most people lust for the rhythm section; they want the beat, that stripping music. But not me. I need the lightning bolt channeled from outer galaxies, transmitted through a lead guitar into my brain. The electrical currents travel downward, through all my chakras, till they zap the base and I am whole. I wanted the sex back in my music. Hardcore is extremely puritanical, cranky like old-school Marxism. It was time to get rid of the Doc Martens, grow out the spiked hair, slide back into some high heels. Metallica's thrash ricocheted me right back to heavy metal, to the warped underbelly of classic rock, back to Led Zeppelin, to the music of teenage wasteland '69. Heavy metal had saved me then, and now, after I lost Johnny Thunders, it came back and rescued me again.

I hung out at Metal 24 every night, all through my fieldwork, while I wrote my book, and long after it was published. The kids in Bergenfield had changed my life. They restored my memory and my metal. Once I converted, Nick stopped talking to me. He dismissed my new bands as "goons." He left the room whenever *Master of Puppets* was playing, which was all the time. But I didn't care.

Alcohol, suicide, heavy metal, and suburbia. Today most Americans live in suburbs. Like suicide, alcoholism rates are higher in nonurban America. Heavy metal is at the heart of suburbia. Although subsidiary drugs are always involved, the primary elixir of heavy metal is *alcohol.* Bonzo, Bon Scott, Ozzy have testified to the powers of positive drinking, to the agony and ecstasy of the "suicide solution." As a leading authority on suburban life, my expertise grew in direct proportion to my own drinking. Hippies preferred pot and acid, and punks shot dope. Hardcore featured amphetamines and beer, or straightedge. But Professor Aloysius ruled Alloy Nation. He had been my main man since the days of Twennyninth. So it was like, *Welcome to the metal years!!!!*

Even now, metal refuses to die, resurfacing in every age. Like faith itself, it always returns. Plus, it's sexy fun—vulgar, excessive, romantic, populist, violent, passionate, and cheesy, just like suburbia. Like Long Island or Jersey, metal is a cultural joke and a national treasure, a sacred profanity. Heavy metal is sociologically compelling because it is cult yet mass market, consumerist yet pure. Kids find underground sanctuary in sold-out arenas, tens of thousands of head-banging lost souls, communing as one in a lead guitar solo. From Iron Butterfly to Slipknot, heavy metal and suburbia—the perfect positive correlation.

I was formally baptized in 1969, the night I saw Led Zeppelin live in Central Park with that Fuzzball hippie D.O.M. banned from the house. Summer of '69, wall-to-wall people, Zep played for over three hours. The self-righteous Fuzzball hated the crowd. Led Zeppelin's audience repulsed him. "Grippies," he declared, "greaser hippies!" Imported from the 'burbs and boroughs of New York, tough guys preening in shag haircuts and tank tops, pumped up. "Tinks" he called them, slick Brooklyn boys making the scene, loitering, waiting for their downs to synergize with the beers, hitting on all the hippie chicks.

That night Led Zeppelin offered shelter by the authority of Marshall law. It was a power much greater than me. It guided, enveloped, and protected me. In it I found a place of refuge, a music so all-consuming that it exorcised bad memories, racing impulses, and all my ugly feelings. I could feel myself and lose myself. Whenever Zeppelin played, I stopped worrying, stopped picking at myself. The committee in my head shut up. The heavy-metal thunder was stronger than all my fears. It was more immediate, reliable, and effective than the best 'ludes and shots. My spirit was wrapped in a baby blanket of noise. Mother and father, militia and messiah—all in a freshly squeezed lemonade dripping down Plant's thighs.

Justifying my passion for Zep, I remember telling Fuzzball, "Robert Plant gives me orgasms." But that wasn't what I meant at all. Their music was Tantric, but what did I know about that at eighteen? It was hopeless to explain. I was caught in the cross fire of Jonesy's strident bass run and Plant's metallic blues yodel, and I was not alone. An unpretty segment of boomer youth was in formation that night, carving out turf. An amalgam of locals, leftovers, greaser-hippies, bright-eyed flower children, earnest politicos, and a majority of marginal young people sucked up in the shaman's sway of Jimmy Page's guitar magick. Led Zeppelin's grubby velvet-ruffled sex-bombast slammed us right into the '70s. Heavy metal was ascending, claiming psychic space. Nothing could withstand the annihilating assault of Bonham's thirty-minute, whiskey-soaked, bloody-fisted Armageddon drum solos. Nothing in the entire history of the world.

Since then, I've seen heavy metal soar to world domination, nosedive into market abjectification, then come back again twice. Heavy metal is like a phoenix rising, bound in a continuous cycle of life and death. Who cares what record companies do or what rock critics say? Fans want what they want. At this writing, multigenerational arena shows like the Ozzfest and AC/DC are packed. Original Sabbath fans with their sons and daughters, two generations of concert T-shirts worn like medals of honor. AC/DC fans who remember the days of Bon Scott bring their wives. The energy current from Angus's guitar is the life force.

In the early 1990s I watched a proud Alloy Nation wither in the cruel sun of the Alternative Empire. In grunge, King Cobain's whiney legions conquered the land. Mercantile armies of destruction moved in, record companies purged their metal departments, warrior sons were dropped from labels and radio, videos fell off MTV rotation, the scene was banished from local venues. Metallica cut their hair, and rock critics spoke of precious metal no more. Since then, occupying armies of punk, hardcore, techno, hip-hop, Goth, and house have sought and failed to obliterate Alloy loyalists from suburban towns and turnpikes. Like life itself, precious metal shines eternal in the black-hole sun.

These are the laws of heavy metal as handed down to me by my friends at the convenience store. *Protect the holy music of the Creators— Hendrix, Sabbath, Purple, and Zep. Keep the flames flying high at the shrine of the N.W.O.B.H.M. (New Wave of British Heavy Metal)— Maiden, Saxon, Diamond Head, Def Leppard. Watch over Lita, Yngwie, Van Halen, Priest, and W.A.S.P. Maintain the trashing force of Metallica, Megadeth, Anthrax, and Slayer. Respect death's brutal shredders—Morbid Angel, Napalm Death, Sepultura, and Cannibal Corpse. Guard the black metal of Cradle of Filth and Zyklon-B—the extreme, the Goth, the doomed. Defend the grand hairlords Bon Jovi, Poison, and Crue. And never forget the teachings of AC/DC.*

In my life, after Slayer came death. There was no place else to go. After Slayer, all other music sounded feeble, insipid, false. Origin of the species; hardcore and thrash fused into grindcore, with British bands like Napalm Death and Carcass. Other fans will argue that the roots of death metal are in Sepultura's vocals or the music of Possessed. Some

trace it back to Black Sabbath. Then there were Tampa contenders Deicide and Morbid Angel. Some bands, like Deicide, did worship Satan.
They flat out admitted they hated Christians. Other bands were politically motivated. They'd articulate the carnage of everyday life—
starvation, war, street violence, mortal suffering.

I met Darryl when he was a teenager hanging out at Metal 24. Over
the years we went to shows—Iron Maiden, Metallica, Pink Floyd. I met
his mom, his sisters, all his girlfriends, and his daughter, too. He loved
video games and worked long hours at a bagel store. One day Darryl
declared thrash was dead, death metal would inherit the earth. And so
it began. Darryl and his friends had started listening to the sounds of
brutality in the late 1980s. By 1990, he and a guitarist named Guy had
put out an eponymously titled three-song demo called *Pyrexia*. Tower
Records in Carle Place sold this atrocity, a four-track job produced in
Guy's garage using a drum machine. But it was good enough to attract
fans. Rob, another guitarist, picked up a copy of the demo at a local
show. He contacted Darryl and Guy and started playing with them.
Eventually they brought in a human drummer, a high school kid
named Mike who was studying automotives. They did the first show
without a bass player. It sounded amazing. By the fall of 1991 they
found a bass player and Pyrexia had a full lineup. They were known and
admired on the death circuit.

By early 1992, Pyrexia had cut a four-song demo called *Liturgy of
Impurity*. With a full sound and sixteen-track recording, the demo
began making its way around the death circuit. *Liturgy* has been re-
viewed in no less than a hundred 'zines worldwide: on the cover of
Metal Age in Sweden, written up in *The Spell* in Mexico, *Ugly Zombie
Zine* in Holland, *Fatal Overload* in Singapore, *Necrobeastility* in France.
In 'zines in Poland, Finland, West Germany, England, and Kentucky.
Never large cities, mainly small ones, rural towns, and suburbs. From a
spot in the local economy of the scene to world domination in no time.

Darryl's Mineola apartment was jammed with books on virtual reality, computer manuals, a deck of Tarot cards. *Wedlock's Treasury of
Witchcraft, The Illustrated Encyclopedia of Myths and Legends,* three vol-
umes of Clive Barker's *Books of Blood,* and the collected works of Isaac

Asimov and Stephen King. Darryl had a copy of the *Necronomicon,* a relic from the Satanteen years.

Abnormal elevation of body temperature and the burning of dead flesh—pyrexia, the name for their band, in the dictionary. They quickly became part of the worldwide network of death, an underground organized by mail order, 'zines, local shows, demos, and word of mouth. Darryl wrote the lyrics, laid them out himself on an Apple using Aldus PageMaker. The first album, *Sermon of Mockery,* was released in Europe on a label called Drowned. Some guy in Italy did the cover art. I took press photos and for a short period of time, they asked me to be their manager. I never booked any shows or helped produce the albums. They had their own experts for that. It was a scam. I plugged them whenever I was doing any Dr. Gaines stuff, TV, print, or radio interviews. It made me look like I was hip and "down with the youth," and it got their name out. Or so we figured. Thanks to the perpetual indulgences of the *Voice,* I did eventually immortalize Pyrexia in the 1993 edition of *Rock & Roll Quarterly,* in an exegesis titled "For the Love of Death."

Guy convinced a local merchant to rent them some space in the basement of a strip mall on Hillside Avenue. Having your own studio space is every young band's dream, but dreams don't come true without hard work. The first thing was to clean out the trash, move out the bricks, beams, and broken fixtures, then locate electrical outlets and run lines for the equipment. The whole space ran about twelve feet wide by twenty-five feet long. If you walked down the steps to the cold concrete cellar, you'd face two doors with heavy locks. To the right was the hair band, to the left was Pyrexia's kingdom of darkness. Out of America's turnpike Dumpsters they built their temple of doom.

Pyrexia collected a few dozen plastic milk crates, heavy duty. From their parents' garages and their warehouse jobs, they located plywood, nails, and carpet samples. In the first week the stage was built. After a day's work at something meaningless—loading at a beer distributor, toxic waste removal, slapping cream cheese on a bagel—came this labor of love. Everyone donated what they could. Wallace, artist of the occult, rendered his "scriptures" on the wall—seals, pentagrams, all manner of mystical commentary. Talismans he picked up at the Magickal Childe shop, seals taken from books by Anna Riva, Egyptian amulets, ideas from esoteric readings—the *Book of Seth,* the *Book of Thoth.* Wallace designed Pyrexia's tough skeleton claw logo. He also did work on leather jackets. I picked one up for ten dollars in the parking lot of Metal 24, cut off the fringe, and handed it over to Wallace. He painted a skull entombed in bowels and entrails, a design poured right out of his mind. He also designed a special seal for travelers. That way if I had to leave the neighborhood, I'd be protected. In recent years I've used that jacket for show and tell, when discussing semiotics with students in my Worlds of Youth class at Barnard. From the turnpike to the university, it was a cultural artifact.

Nobody in Pyrexia actually worshiped Satan. They were mainly agnostics, lapsed Protestants and Catholics. Plastered on Guy's guitar is a sticker that read GOD GO ROT. His mom picked it up for him at a crafts fair, along with a handmade pewter devil's head. This was not for shock value, nor was it a trivial pursuit. Guy and Darryl were hostile to organized religion. They were men of science and metaphysics who happened to think the dark side was interesting.

Breathe the stench of discharge nurtured in blasphemous coupling/ Breast-fed fetal pus sucked in the belly of the Beast/Distended and misshapen. In death metal, the double bass lines, pulverizing guitars, and drum blasts are pushed to the extreme, harder, heavier, faster, and tighter than thrash or hardcore. Callous—no desire, no regrets. Where industrial music spoke to a process of decline, death was terminal and fixed. This world looks like an autopsy film, not a horror movie. Flesh and carnage are explicit, pornographic, detached from human pain and suffering. Stripped of emotion and sensation, death metal offers clinically precise, grim exploration of the body, the soul, and the world. It affords no refuge, no catharsis, no psychic protection. It is collective memory forged from an evil world with hateful people and dirty deeds. Every sign, sound, and sight is terminal. No remorse, no transcendence. This is the music of forensic medicine and mortuary science.

Death goes beyond metal's traditional preoccupation with sex and Satan, past thrash's fixation on social decay. If hardcore expressed bitter rage and heavy metal cried remorse and begged for redemption, death expressed the coldness of a scientific, anti-utopian, godless world. It was the perfect soundtrack for the gurgling Internet explosion. Pyrexia owed as much to Ozzy as they did to Steve Jobs and Bill Gates, to the Zilog geeks, the Microchip Masters who built America's tech empires.

Humorless, dark, determined, this was the existential truth as we understood it. Death was guts, and guts without parody or campy innuendo. It was not for tourists. For kids who understood that nothing would change, nobody cared, everything was rotting away, it offered some comfort. In death there were no more lies, no further delusions, no future betrayals. The chill of truth filled the room and there was no back door. Void of hope, joy, or light, the music seemed godless. But actually, the opposite was true.

Organized religions seek to organize truth and codify morality. Through critique, scientific inquiry, high technology, mysticism, and poetics, death metal blew the dogmatic myth systems out of the holy water. In Pyrexia's "Abominat," you die, you are drawn to the light. But you're not headed toward the light of God. You're going the other way. You've been tricked. Supreme mistrust is articulated as a given. So death metal steps in to explore whatever scientific knowledge, theology, and political theory have left out. Sitting there, night after night, cranked on Jolt Cola, I'd ponder the deeper meanings of death.

One day a couch appeared in the studio, then some chairs, a wastepaper basket. I brought in a fan. Sodas, chips, butts, and beers were scammed from work and stored in a refrigerator. By now I was down there every night, stopping in before and after any other activity. Show up at five in the morning after seeing the Waldos at the Continental. Someone would always be down there hanging out, working out a song, fixing equipment. I was always able to lure unsuspecting friends into my newest scene. But no matter how hard I tried, everyone hated death metal, even Anthony. Night after night it was just me and the band. The compulsion was overwhelming. Some nights I'd ditch

my date so I could go. Since I was the band's manager, I had a good excuse. And then I met Him.

||

swear, I never put a guy first, never let him stand between me and a
band. It was usually the opposite. I got with the guy to get closer to the
essence of the band. A groupie wants the trophy boy, the rock star. A
maniacal fan wants the band—the music, the message, the totality of
experience. Who else but a band member will share your relentless obsession? Bleat out every lyric verbatim? Tremble at each new guitar
change? Having a boyfriend in the band is the expressway to higher
consciousness. When you break up, it will be the band you miss most,
not him. Sociologically speaking, male or female, marrying into any
subculture is always the best way to get at the data. A full conversion experience is necessary to really grasp cultural process. Full surrender
means endless love.

With Pyrexia, I was gender neutral, exalted above and beyond my
sex. Only menopause promised such peaceful refuge. But I wasn't "one
of the boys" either. I became like Wallace's wall scriptures, matter
transformed into pure spirit. Women in science, women and guns,
women in rock, women and technology, women and alcoholism, a
never-ending ghetto of degradation. In death, I finally transcended my
biology.

Leaving Pyrexia for Him was the lowest thing I've ever done and yet
I have no regrets. It all started at the copy machine at Staples. The Moth
was duplicating arty flyers for his band. NutJob was playing at the St.
Mark's Bar and Grill. I asked him about the band and I was invited to
practice. A nocturnal creature who fluttered outside the door with of-
ferings of obscure tapes or flyers, the Moth had a habit of lurking. The
Moth picked me up for practice, Melvins blasting as we pulled out of
my parking lot. On the way he stopped off to pick up a friend. And
that's when I saw him, standing in his parents' doorway, sucking a
Marlboro. He was the great love promised to me in the doo-wop songs

of my childhood. So tall, dark, and sweet in his black Schott leather jacket and tight Levi's like he was Joe Dalessandro, Holly Woodlawn's costar in Warhol's *Trash*. I should have known by now that falling for archetypes always spells big trouble.

The Adontis believed we were made of the same DNA, lovers from past lives, fated for all eternity. I wanted to marry him, cook his food, wash his clothes, have his babies. He was the only man I have ever loved like that. I figured he was about thirty and he took me for the same. He looked older, I looked younger, and by the time we learned the truth, it was much too late. He was twenty-three, I was forty-one. You do the math.

He'd seen me on the cover of *Newsday*, seen my rants about suicide, Satan, and heavy metal on the TV. He figured all I needed was a good stiff one; I didn't argue. On our first date, he brought over the complete works of AC/DC, a bottle of Wild Turkey, and an eightball of coke. For my birthday he got me a limited commemorative edition of Slayer's *Decade of Aggression,* complete with a certificate of authenticity. I'd finally met my match. Before Him, nothing had ever been enough for me. I always needed *more.* But with Him, I felt complete. I'd waited an entire generation for the Right One to come along.

Adontis was the same age as the kids in my book. Consorting with any of them in such a manner was unthinkable. I viewed them as younger siblings, even sons. But he was different. If you saw us together, we looked perfectly normal. He was tall, with a full growth of stubble. Back then, I looked like your typical Chrissie Hynde "rock chick." Our respective intragenerational resentments quickly came into play. We both hated dating people our age. By the '90s too many boomer men (born between 1945 and 1964) had become yuppie scum, boring jazz-and-brunch wimps. In my Adontis I saw the lost warriors of Xanthos. All the heroes sacrificed a generation ago to Vietnam, to heroin. In turn, the Adontis hated baby-bust females (born after 1964). He condemned them as "uptight, materialistic, and shallow." They liked insipid dance music, not rock & roll. He viewed me as a free-spirited hippie type, a sexual libertine, a purist who had seen Hendrix live, and Zep too—including Bonzo on drums. Hedonism, polymorphous perversity, an intergenerational liaison rescued us both from historical doom.

Born in 1969, a year after I was graduated from high school, my Adontis came to earth in the bloodstained year of Altamont, dead rock stars, Manson, and helter-skelter. My lover was three weeks old the night I was arrested and arraigned in nearby Mineola, four months old the summer I went to Woodstock with the Fuzzball. He was playing Little League as I was completing a master's degree in social work, planning his prom as I was writing *Teenage Wasteland.* The Adontis showed me a photo of his parents. A stunning mom with a big beehive, eyes made up like Ronnie Spector's, black fishnets, riding on the back of Dad's Harley. All the doo-wop lovebirds of America had gotten married, migrated to suburbia, and begotten heavy-metal sons, the Trans Am road warriors who now ruled our turnpikes.

During my lapse of reason, Pyrexia coldly referred to NutJob as "that other band." And of course, my sweetie hated death metal. But Pyrexia understood about the boyfriend. Irrationality over sex and love was always forgiven. After all, I *was* a chick.

True Love means all the idiotic mythologies of human history suddenly come to life. Sometimes I imagined Him as a Roman gladiator, or a soldier in Caesar's army carrying me off, spoils of war from the conquest of Jerusalem. He was devoutly Catholic, Republican, and proud. But the destruction of the Second Temple paled to the crush of his arms around me. One night I told my young lover the story of Venus and Adonis, the Roman goddess of love and her young warrior. Venus and Adonis were the primary archetypes for intergenerational lovers like us. With or without cocaine, I was a real *habladora,* a chatterbox that never quit. Sometimes he wasn't paying attention, so he thought I said Venus and *Adontis,* and that's what I called him.

Good chemistry, bad karma. According to their biographers, the Ramones enjoyed hanging out near mental hospitals 'cause they figured the chicks there were easy. Well, sex between psychopaths can be very hot. Still, with all our cross-addictions and intergenerational conflicts, we did try to be normal. We went out to dinner, took idyllic strolls through Long Island's nature preserves. When he took me home for Easter Sunday, I wore a vintage white cashmere cardigan with pearls. But when his mother found out my age, she threw him out. He moved into the garage and kept on seeing me.

Long after he got an apartment, we still preferred street sex. Underneath the water tower, on the side streets of Mineola, up against the trucks behind C-Town, in his van—even if it was parked outside my front door. Sex, drinking, and fighting. Break up, go back, fight, cry, scream yell, make up. High drama, our relationship was heavy metal itself, a Wagnerian opera set against the backdrop of suburbia.

In our years together, the Adontis did every mean thing to me that a man can do to a woman. He cheated, he lied, and he hurt me, emotionally and sometimes physically. If you ask him now, he'll say I drove him to it, that the things I did to him were worse, and his friends will back him up. He'll say I manipulated him, was arrogant, never satisfied, "a bitch." My friends thought he was dangerous, "bad news." The Panel of Experts had a full caseload with this one. Constant tears, vows of "no more," only to return again and again.

One Memorial Day, to get in good with D.O.M., the Adontis got him a new American flag from the VFW hall. But my father was not impressed. He worried for my happiness. "His family will never accept you. Someday he'll want children, and you'll be too old. He'll break your heart." While I never told D.O.M. too many details, the Panel's verdict was unanimous: I was suffering from battered-wife syndrome. *But I loved him.*

One night after we'd had a quarrel, I went off to see the Slugs at Nightingale's. The Adontis showed up unannounced, drunk and bleeding. I guess I was supposed to play nursemaid and take care of him and then we'd get back together. But I was still pissed. Besides, I was doing backup vocals that night, and I had to get onstage. Tom, Nightingale's eccentric former manager, was always very indulgent of Sluglife. He loved the band, especially Nick. He'd kept their 45s on the jukebox forever. But even he banned the Adontis from the bar. Feeling victorious and self-righteous, I forgot about him and chased down my buzz.

Around four A.M., Nick and I were heading home; I had parked the car down on Avenue A. It was late, and we were fried, so we drove home, back to Long Island.

The next day I noticed all my tires were flat. Someone had let out all the air. We'd driven home on four flat tires. Luckily there was no damage to the wheels. The Adontis called and I told him about the car. He said we had to meet, had to talk. It sounded serious. Rendezvous at McGurk's Tavern, in Mineola, by the train. Always better to take my own car. He bought us drinks. Looking sheepish, he handed over a hundred-dollar bill, confessed to the tire mischief, and apologized. Of course, he claimed it was entirely my fault, that I set him up. "But you see, I'm a stand-up guy, I'm not like you." Now *he's* the injured party, and I'm evil.

It hadn't even occurred to me that he would stumble twelve blocks from Nightingale's, bleeding, somehow locate my car down on Avenue A, unscrew the tire plugs, and let the air out. But that wasn't the point. Our relationship involved an established ritual. He did something sick because I was a bitch. He retaliated, I held moral ground, I cried. He confessed, made amends, reparations, and we made up. You know what that means: twelve hours of hot sex. And then we sat around gloating over the entire episode, reliving it blow by blow, like his best championship football game in high school. We thrived on the drama.

Once, after *he* broke up with me, I started seeing the guitarist from the Nihilistics. I had known the guy for years, and everybody liked him, including the Adontis. Even though breaking up was his idea, the Adontis still accused me of cheating. His logic: I belonged to him, forever. I should have known we'd go back eventually. We always did. So that meant I was unfaithful, a slut. To confirm my infidelity, Adontis climbed on top of the C-Town supermarket across from my window, binoculars in hand, to see if I was fucking the guitarist. When he saw I had company, he came over to kick ass. Luckily, I had the music blasting so loud, we never heard the door. The Adontis left a calling card, an ominous bank deposit slip with his name on it.

Another time, we were at the Right Track Inn for a NutJob show. I got into a friendly debate with some guy over whether Gateway National Park was technically in Queens or Brooklyn. The discussion culminated in a five-dollar bet and verification via a map in my car. Somehow it turned into a bloodbath. The guy was trying to rip me off. Or he was hitting on me. Or something. But the Adontis freaked out, broke the guy's nose, then his arm. Friends jumped in, then ambulances and police reports. The kid was beaten to a pulp, but my honey never got a scratch. Still, as the Adontis pummeled away, I got hysterical. Fearing my lover would be injured, I screamed at his hapless victim, "Don't you touch him!!"

The grand finale really should have come when I went to Poland. I was on assignment for *Spin,* covering the death-metal scene that exploded after the Berlin Wall came down. It was January 1994 and my editor told me I could go anywhere in the world in search of death. A normal person would have opted for Brazil, but I loved the idea of death metal in the dead of winter, in the midst of a collapsed socialist regime: Eastern Europe, with skinheads, entrepreneurial capitalism, Roman Catholicism, and old Polish folk traditions festering beneath. I was always intrigued by the outreach programs instituted by Iron Maiden, *Behind the Iron Curtain,* and later by Metallica. Pyrexia had played with Poland's legendary Vader when they toured America, so I had a mission, overseas airborne.

Editor Bob Guccione Jr. was a benevolent sponsor who shelled out all expenses plus a two-hundred-dollar daily expense account for what was ultimately published as "Let's Gdansk." In post-commie Warsaw, two hundred dollars a day was big bucks. Sitting in the lobby of the five-star hotel, I explained the art of the scam to my new Polish friends. The rudiments of rock star capitalism: "If we don't spend it, the cash goes back to *Spin.* Use it or lose it." So we went out every night. Me, Violent Dirge, Spargmos, their friends, managers, lovers, and siblings. Twenty people ripped, night after night, on the best Polish vodka American money could buy. Polonez, and Sameach, a kosher vodka made in Bialystok, allegedly blessed by rabbis. My friends swore it had mystical properties.

My Polish informants said that whenever bands came to Poland, they always asked to visit Auschwitz-Birkenau, the concentration camps in the south of Poland. Slayer was so moved by the rooms filled with the hair, teeth, and shoes of children, they wrote a song. But Polish bands don't sing about the death camps and Majdanek, Treblinka, and Belzec. "It is too painful for us," they confided. About one-quarter of Poland's population died in the war, including almost every Jew. Warsaw, Eastern Europe, these are the killing fields where, in 1942, an entire branch of the Denmark family tree abruptly terminates. My hosts too were wounded by the brutalities of history: first the Nazis, then Communism. They exorcised their demons in music that made the ears bleed. I hadn't mentioned being a Jew until the night we were drinking Sameach. When they told me about the rabbis in Bialystok, I asked, "Are any Jews left in Poland?" My hosts said yes, there were many. And we poured another round, *L'Chaim!*

One night we were doing shots at my hotel and the Adontis called, overseas long distance. It had been a few months since we'd split. My fling with the Nihilistics' guitarist was long over. While we were apart, the Adontis had taken up with a social worker he met on the E train. Of course, the guitarist was ten years younger than me, and the social worker ten years older than he. Both in their early thirties, they were trapped in an intermediary generation, neither baby bust nor boom. Now these historical unfortunates were entangled in a convoluted sexual quagmire with the Adontis and me. I refused to sleep with the Adontis until he ended it with the social worker. I wanted us to start over, to renew our love.

The phone call to Warsaw was meant as his declaration of independence: It was officially over with her. Yes, she cried. But the Adontis was mine, and this time it was forever. So I took him back for the 666th time. When I returned to the USA I devoted myself to him completely and he to me. I cooked for him, washed and ironed his clothes like I was married. For Valentine's Day, the Adontis was planning a very special treat. He was taking me to see Black Sabbath at the Garden. We'd rent a room at the Penta Hotel in Manhattan and party all night.

For some reason, all my ex-boyfriends, including the Adontis, always took me to see the Rolling Stones. The Stones make a great date band—cute Mick for the girls and cool Keith for the guys. Or so they figured. Thanks to a series of passionate metal articles in *Newsday*, *Spin*, and the *Voice*, I had an endless supply of rock product flowing my way. At one point I even scored us tenth-row comps for AC/DC. With or without the original lineup, seeing Sabbath together was going to be really special. Maybe they would play our song, "Sabbra Cadabra" . . . *Someone to live for, love me till the end of time . . .*

The Adontis worked in the city; sorry, but I really can't say more. He was talented, successful, and very generous—more gallant and worldly than most men my age. He called to say he'd rented our hotel room, got the Sabbath tickets, too. I invited him for dinner, but he was tied up. I got suspicious. He was just going in for an estimate, he was usually in and out. What could be keeping him?

Thanks to my years of computer lust, I hacked into the Adontis's answering machine. As it played back, I heard a woman's voice, cooing, seductive. I had retrieved a message from the social worker, the one he swore he'd dumped. I knew her voice because after they broke up she still called him. She'd send him books, use any excuse to keep it going, so I always made him tape their calls. That way I could monitor the situation. The Valentine's Day Massacre went like this: "Hi, I have to ask you something. I'm making chocolate chip cookies. Do you like nuts?" What a ditz. Apparently she was planning the dinner menu for their little Valentine's Day fuck date. He had never really broken up with her! He was planning to do her the night before our special date. *Sabbath, Bloody Sabbath!* He lied, I screamed *Adonticide!*

For six weeks, the little prick was screwing us both, playing me, using her. Or vice versa. Stupidly, I blamed her. I began calling, threatening, even stalking her. I had to see her, had to hear her voice, check out her DD-size tits, her hair, everything that might have drawn him to her. He had told her all about me, the guns, the ink, the metal. She figured I was a real psycho, and by now I was.

For hours, I would sit around figuring out ways to kill him. I figured I could pipe carbon monoxide into his bedroom window. At one point,

I even purchased a .22-caliber handgun. The bullets weren't traceable; they say that's the caliber gangsters use. I would have killed myself instead, but then he'd still be out there, cheating on me. If he was dead, I could just embalm him and keep his rotting corpse in the chair next to my bed. But I knew if I killed him, I would miss him too much. So I went out to the range and shot at Saddam Hussein targets instead.

Yes, the Adontis had betrayed my faith, *but I loved him.* So instead of committing murder, I forced him to call the social worker on the phone. He was instructed to break it off with me listening in on the extension. I needed proof; these were the terms of contract, take it or leave it. *Dirty deeds and they're done dirt cheap.* So he dumped her, as far as I know.

Unfortunately, trust is like the soul. Once it leaves the body, it doesn't return. It was over. I couldn't believe anything he said anymore. *Paranoia the destroyer.* Now I suspected him of fucking everyone. Sometimes he picked me up and shook me until my arms were black and blue. He was possessive, controlling, jealous. So was I. We stupidly mistook this for passion. I once asked him what he would do if I had cheated. He replied somberly, "Oh, I'd be O.J." I was willing to take anything, but not cheating. And I'm sure she wasn't the only one. He was twenty-five when it happened. I knew the risks. I couldn't blame him entirely, but I knew my heart. I had to leave him and eventually I did. But not because of her.

A few months later, on the full moon, Nick and I went to see Freedy Johnston—one of his bands, not mine. As a singer-songwriter, Nick favored Elvis Costello and Morrissey. He refused any involvement with my goon bands, even if I had backstage passes to meet Metallica or Slayer. Nick has "critics' taste," a euphemism for *boring.* Still, I always went with him to see his bands. Always listened politely to his tapes of P. J. Harvey, Pixies, Sugar, and Blur. So there I was at Freedy, scoping out the crowd. My obsessive fact-finding missions about the Adontis's other woman generated enough data that I could recognize her on the spot. I knew it right away. That tall blonde with the funky glasses and the big tits standing by the bar with the red pocketbook was *her.* The

Adontis and I had long since parted, so I went over to apologize. I even offered to buy her a drink. Mainly so I could check her out.

The social worker was so kind and balanced, it was impossible to hate her. She, in turn, was surprised that the big-haired, gum-crackin' Lawn Guyland Amy Fisher she imagined was so polite and clean-cut. She asked about the Adontis. I told her we had broken up for good and she seemed genuinely sad. "That's a shame, he really loves you," she said. "We were never serious, just casual. If you broke up with him because of me, that's a big mistake. People don't find true love too often." I was shocked. Even the habitually disinterested Nick was astonished at her generosity.

After the show, Nick went off to Chelsea and I went to CBGB's. NutJob was playing that night, the Adontis would be there. I told him what happened, what the social worker said. I whispered, "I still love you, I want you back," and he said yeah. But first he had to take care of some business. He told me to hang out, wait for him. By four A.M. the last car was heading out to Long Island and I finally gave up. I knew he wasn't coming back. As with any suburban road warrior, a mission into the night could last for days. I never asked my Adontis where he was going or what he was doing. For a Long Island lady, that would be rude, a violation of code. He was a Wild Boy. So I just waited to hear from him, hoping he'd return safely. It was a test of my faith and devotion.

In a 1998 essay titled "Wild Thing I Think I Smell You," media critic Leslie Savan differentiates between "Bad Boys" and "Wild Boys." Where the Bad Boy is "your basic career guy schmuck," Wild Boys are "rough and tumble dudes," raw, rebellious, "primal objects of desire." Savan explains, if a Bad Boy gets you pregnant, "he'll pay for half the abortion and never call you again; if a Wild Boy gets you pregnant, he'll insist you have the baby, possibly marry you and one day go out for that pack of cigarettes and never return." No danger, no pleasure.

If I reflect back on the great loves of my life—Tommy, the Beast, Nick, and the Adontis—I've only ever wanted that Wild Boy. The Bad Boy will always be too clean; he'll eat your pussy just to be politically correct, and he'll never bleed for your love. But there's a surcharge attached to loving that unruly boy, and I paid it willingly.

During our last days, I was living on chocolate chip cookies and Valium, so depressed I couldn't get out of bed. I stopped writing, cruising the 'net, playing music, or oiling my guns. I grew even further out of touch with myself. The Panel even threatened to resign. They didn't want to hear it anymore.

Dazed and defeated, isolated from the world, I started watching daytime TV talk shows. Every day, all day long, back to back. I needed a strong woman I could bond with. I was afraid Ricki Lake would laugh at me, Sally Jessy Raphael would yell, and Oprah would just start crying. But Jenny Jones had been a drummer; she had a rock & roll heart. She'd be understanding and confrontational, too. *The Jenny Jones Show* soon became my favorite. I was ashamed to tell my loved ones how really bad things had gotten and the idea of psychotherapy terrified me. But I could tell Jenny about it every day, even twice a day, for almost a year.

One day I tuned in the story of Jan and Tyler, another hot intergenerational couple. Woody Allen, Mary Kay Letourneau, Joey Buttafuoco, and me. Luckily, rock has its own legacy of intergenerational sex and love. Twenty-four-year-old Jerry Lee Lewis married his thirteen-year-old second cousin; Bill Wyman had Mandy, his child bride; soldier boy Elvis took the fourteen-year-old Priscilla. Then there were rock's older women, our great goddesses and their adoring younger men: Tina Turner, Ronnie Spector, Chrissie Hynde, Madonna, and Patti Smith. Many have lasted long term; some are married with children. Among rock's most legendary hearts, Courtney was older than Kurt, Nancy was older than Sid, and Yoko was older than John. Hollywood women, too, have been trailblazers for May boy–December lady dyads: Cher, Susan Sarandon, Mary Tyler Moore, Roseanne. I was in fine company.

But that day, *The Jenny Jones Show* revealed something else. In Jan, I saw my capacity for sexual manipulation; in Tyler, I saw the Adontis's vulnerability. Maybe the balance of power was skewed in my favor. Maybe that's what made him so angry. Jenny and her guests ultimately convinced me that once a guy roughs you up or cheats on you, it is foolish to think it won't happen again. For months, I'd watched Jenny urging passive, defeated women who'd been cheated on, beaten, or betrayed to think about their self-esteem. I'd hear the audience label the bad boyfriend a dog. "Kick him to the curb!" they'd yell. I'd hear the bullshit stories the nasty dog would weave and realize, *Hey, that's the Adontis's game.*

Eventually I had seen enough poisoned hearts and bad relationships on *The Jenny Jones Show* to get out. Jenny Jones may have saved my life. Still, I knew I was powerless to resist him. I was hopelessly addicted to love. I couldn't imagine life without him. I couldn't even look at another guy. It was just a matter of time before I'd run into him, he'd smile at me, hold me, kiss me, and it would start all over again. There was no way out. So I took a drastic measure. I did the one thing I swore I'd never do: I moved to New York City.

And so, proclaiming *Suburbia Über Alles* until the very end, I headed west, leaving my beloved turnpike behind. Living in the city it would be harder to see Nick and D.O.M. I also surrendered my car, "the boys," the ocean, Metal 24, the microchip cartel, Slugland, Pyrexia, St. Rocco's Feast, and tattoo parlors from Bellerose to Montauk.

I packed up my books, photos, rock product, the endless files and piles of papers, all my leathers and cosmetics. I dismantled the Auto-Dial pad and my computer. I owned three oil paintings. They had followed me throughout my life, these connections to my female line: faux-antique portraits of Betty Bradley, Aunt Ethel the Puma, and Aunt Grace the Oracle. Aristocratic renderings of three daughters, shamed spirits, broken dreams. Each portrait had a heavy gold frame, overbearing and ornate. Nick urged me to toss them. He dismissed them as bad art, tacky clutter. D.O.M. agreed: "They're depressing, all busted up; you don't need them. That one of your mother doesn't even look like her." So out they went, along with Betty Bradley's tattered custom-made suits from Hollywood, Herbie's ties, and the sweaters from Mr. Gaines; the moth-eaten clothes of all my dead parents, remnants of lives left unfulfilled. I sold all my furniture, gave away my plants, and scattered the ashes of my beloved Sarah-Ann, the Burmese cat who'd died that spring. It was the end of an era.

By 1996, youth homicide rates had upstaged suicide. Raves, hip-hop, and alternative had inherited the earth. Metal was forced out of the marketplace again, banished underground. For better or for worse, the life I loved for so many years slowly slipped out of my hands. I couldn't hold on to anything or anyone. But all was not lost. I still had Professor Aloysius.

Professor Gaines (center) after hours with her teaching assistants.

14

53RD & 3RD

Sometimes we have to be dragged kicking and screaming into a better life. In my darkest hour, the Panel of Experts came to my rescue, setting me up with a rent-controlled apartment on the Upper East Side. I had never been above East 14th Street until the day I signed the lease. Now I lived down off Swing Street, where small clubs like Jimmy Ryan's once hosted interracial jams, where my parents had hung out. I had a doorman, an all-night Korean deli, and neighbors like Henry Kissinger and Raoul Felder. I walked around in a fog. Most everything I knew about my new neighborhood I'd heard from the Ramones. According to Dee Dee's song, East 53rd and 3rd was a favorite chicken-hawking spot, quick-fix employment for a strung-out Queens kid. A corner that promised redemption but delivered misery, false images, and self-betrayal. I guess this was providence, because 53rd and 3rd was now my subway stop.

Beyond the downtown punk palaces like Continental, Coney Island High, CBGB's, and Don Hill's, I didn't have a clue how to negotiate anything in the big city. The high-rise building had an army of maintenance workers. When I needed things fixed, I kept asking, but nothing happened. After a while the porters gave me the skinny: "Donna, you're too nice. You gotta raise hell or they'll ignore you." In New York City, you have to be a cunt. Everything must be an emergency, and you cannot relent; you threaten, nag, and bully your way through the most mundane interactions. Fending off interlopers at the checkout at D'Agostino's, queuing at the ATM machine, even hailing a cab. On Long Island, the guy who fixes your car is someone's brother. Your bartender's wife sends you Christmas cards. The manager of the deli knows your boyfriend from high school. It's all interconnected, local, personal. Here, everything was formal, professional. The doormen called me Miss Gaines. From Delancey Street to Sutton Place. If my snooty relatives the Cretins could have seen this, they'd have shit the bed.

Actually, New York City on early Giuliani time was a lot like Republican suburbia. Everywhere, full cop: young, handsome police standing guard, looking ever so manly. Third Avenue was evolving into a strip mall peppered with Gaps, Starbuckses, a Kmart right there off St. Mark's. There was even a McDonald's right next door to the Continental. The boho purists at the *Voice* hated that Kmart, but I was grateful. Before it arrived, it took me days to figure out where to get planters, lightbulbs, and batteries.

Nothing in Manhattan made sense. I kept tripping on the sidewalk because I wasn't used to walking on streets. Nobody walks on Long Island, even the DWI outlaws take the car service to the bar. The urban service economy broke down along strict racial lines. If people spoke Spanish here they were probably workers, not neighbors. The only black people were the African diplomats from the United Nations. On Long Island, we had de facto apartheid. Fear of a black planet was rampant. You only saw people of color if you went to buy drugs. "They" never came near our towns, not even for work. Consult with Chuck D, if you don't believe me.

On top of all this, I didn't like city guys. The only hot ones were the police or the pumped-up Chelsea boys. I had never dated anyone except macho rock & roll guys from suburbia. Yuppies, art-boy types, Sutton Place gentry: Would they know the difference between Johnny

Thunders and Tom Petty? Uh-uh. When I was younger I froze in terror whenever I walked by a group of horny construction workers. Now, if I walked by and no sexual innuendo was offered, I panicked. I felt ugly and old. The tables had turned, I was almost forty-five, and I found myself *leering at them*—more likely, at their nephews and sons. Everyone knows you have to be born into that union. Thankfully, there's always a lot of construction going in Manhattan. Otherwise my sex mind would have atrophied.

When I did date, I drew from the same gene pool I'd left behind—cute guys from Long Island. What was I supposed to do? Give up rock & roll for performance art? Groove with nicotine-stained Eurotrash at stiff SoHo dinner parties? Sip wine and discuss the stock market at some stale cigar bar? No, thank you. I preferred to import my dates from Jersey, to meet them on the street or at downtown punk strongholds. By night I favored miniskirts, faux fur jackets, and slinky blond wigs I bought down on West 14th Street. When a guy at Coney Island High asked me if I was a transvestite, I almost threw my drink in his face. I thought I looked smashing, like Tina Turner, but I was Maggie May, a dirty old lady, D.O.L. Poised at the edge of the mosh pit, on the threshold of menopause, holding some guy's leather jacket, watching Murphy's Law. I wasn't aging well, but I was moving up.

Ironically, as my freewheeling suburban soul withered in New York City, my career flourished. Like everyone, I had to increase and accelerate my workload to meet my burgeoning expenses. I had never seriously considered a career in academe. I preferred the glamorous life of the freelance writer—another oxymoron. In my crusades on behalf of our nation's youth, I had visited many colleges and communed with colleagues. I loved being around students; it energized me. Whether at universities or conferences, from Florida to Iowa, in Ottawa or San Francisco, who else is willing to listen to endless, detailed discussions of Durkheim, Marx, and Weber? Students are a captive audience. Without them, we'd be writing sitcoms about social theory.

By now *Teenage Wasteland* had become a staple on college reading lists, including Columbia's. One day the chair of the sociology department at Barnard asked me to develop a course. I agreed and embarked upon a journey of discovery. Barnard is a women's college of Columbia University, so classes are open to everyone, net of gender. Still, my students were predominantly female, hailing from elite Manhattan private schools like Dalton, Chapin, Brearley, and Spence, from boarding schools in New England and abroad.

Many were children of high-powered two-career couples—parents were doctors, artists, diplomats, celebrities, wealthy businessmen. Once upon a time, being an only child was an anomaly, a stigmatizing condition. A generation later, careers, single parenting, delayed childbearing, affluent urban life, and adoption have increased the number of sibling-free offspring. Membership in the Only Child Club brings with it subtle changes in peer relations and identity formation. An only child typically suffers more loneliness and parental hovering, in inverse proportion to the enjoyment of greater individuality and more resources. As the norm bends toward more single childbearing, so must our understanding of the experience of solo childhood. We can expect the social interaction between four of five sibling-free children in a play group to be different from existing models. The burden for learning cooperation, sharing, and tolerance is no longer on the solo child. Now it's a shared adult concern.

Several of my Asian students were first generation, marginalized, negotiating traditional Korean, Chinese, or Vietnamese family values with American culture. So I assigned Maria Hong's book of essays, *Growing Up Asian American.* Teen depression had been steadily rising, and students were fascinated and sometimes familiar with Elizabeth Wurtzel's *Prozac Nation* and her experience of growing up depressed, medicated, and in therapy.

I figured someday maybe I'd end up teaching at a community college, go back to my roots, give something back. Yet here I was, teaching at a private college for *women.* I knew very little about being a woman or growing up elite. The only upper-middle-class experience I had was with the Cretin family and the snobs of Belle Harbor. Anything I understood about the ruling class was based on what I'd read of Marx. All I knew about Columbia was that my great-grandpa Moses Cretin de Incesticide had gotten his medical degree here. Now I was a professor, standing in a lecture hall across the street, on the northwest side of Broadway, assigning *Reviving Ophelia* to my students. I felt protective, ready to teach them firearms assembly if necessary.

The Sociology of Youth (SOY) course explored the various institutions that impact upon young people's lives: the schools, family, legal system, the economy. I designed another course, Worlds of Youth (WOY), to investigate the inner and outer experiences of young people in their own voices—through the study of youth subculture and memoir. It is old social work practice wisdom to "start where the client is at," and there is no better way to teach the sociology of culture, organization, music, or religion than acknowledging and utilizing students' own lived experience. Students periodically brought their mothers to class; sometimes friends and lovers came, too.

At the end of every semester I organized a WOY Youth Subcultures Day. Students volunteered for show-and-tell performances and presented materials, artifacts, and ethnographies from their respective scenes and subcultures. We heard the inside scoop from cheerleaders, Pakistani-American hip-hop crews, working-class kids on sports scholarships, Goth outlaws, techno DJs, and gay club kids. Subcultures Day was a multimedia extravaganza. It was also the only time I abandoned my professorial garb—dark, formal Simone de Beauvoir dress suits and elegant silk blouses—for my scuzzy rocker rags.

Students saw *The Blackboard Jungle* and read Dick Hebdige's classic *Subculture: The Meaning of Style.* They read *The "Girl Problem"* about class, race, and female delinquency in the nineteenth century. I also assigned journalist Kathy Dobie's articles about being a slut in high school, about squatter kids and teenage Latina hookers in Williamsburg. Over the years I imported a series of guest speakers—guitarist Chris Stein of Blondie lectured on the rise of punk in New York City, journalist Jim Farber spoke about growing up gay, listening to glitter.

At one point I orchestrated an invasion of the Modern Times Collective, a Long Island–based radical contingent of boys from the hardcore scene. The antiracist skins spoke about workers' rights and local youth disenfranchisement. Then they fell in love with some of my students, and I suspect serious dating ensued. I'd worked on several assignments with *Village Voice* ace photographers Teru Kuwayama and Andrew Goldberg. The Gen X camera crew came to class, presenting powerful slide shows of offbeat subcultures here and abroad. Teru and Andrew were alumni of state universities; scrappy, cool, and very cute. More phone numbers were exchanged, and I decided there were too many boys visiting the class. When it came to "my girls," I found myself becoming uncharacteristically puritanical.

Realizing my students needed good female role models and job contacts, I brought in music critic Evelyn McDonnell to speak about the riot grrrl movement in Olympia, Washington, and the rise of women in rock. Former bass player and publisher Carla DeSantis sent us several gift cartons of *Rockrgrl,* a music magazine for women with the motto, "No Beauty Tips or Guilt Trips." *Rockrgrl* features include strategies for buying equipment as well as rocker "mom talk." A large percentage of the class grew up reading *Sassy,* so former editor Kathy Rich came to class to discuss the rise, fall, and reconfiguration of the magazine. Some professors do use teaching as an opportunity to proselytize, so I tormented the class with '60s girl groups, the Ramones, and heavy metal. Education is a dialogue, not a monologue. I understood that my feminist frame of reference was somewhat archaic, dated. I needed a crash course in contemporary girlcult, and my students provided it.

At one point, the Sociology of Youth course enrollment peaked at 267; the lecture hall was full, a nation-state of kids sitting cross-legged in the aisles. I had to divide the class into two separate rooms just to administer exams. Nineties youth subcultures were fragmented, with musical tastes so diverse I found it nearly impossible to locate one recording artist uniformly loved or hated by the class; I even had one devoted Celine Dion fan on my roster. Only in Alanis Morissette did I find unanimous animosity. In a moment of haste, I revealed a deep personal dislike of Madonna's music, only to receive a flurry of angry e-mails from a generation of loyalists. Even though I explained that it was an ancient paradigm war from the days of punk and hardcore, I got no mercy. Many Barnard students have revered Ms. Ciccone since the fourth grade. They adored her like I worshiped Ronnie Spector. When I realized how rude I'd been, I formally apologized to my class. I'll never insult another person's hero again. Yea, I repent, so rock on, Backstreet Boys, Blink-182, Britney, and Beyoncé. It's all good (please kill me).

Barnard provided me with an army of sharp, stylish graduate-student teaching assistants. Skank (her stage name) was a statistician, a chanteuse in the neo-glam scene. Sarasvati Jen was a yoga teacher, a lotus flower in combat boots with roots in classic 1980s hardcore. GiGi was a maniacal Janis Joplin fan, a Greek-American classic-rock fan born a generation too late. I couldn't have survived without them. The population of SOY was so huge, sometimes I couldn't match students' names to faces. We communicated after class, during breaks, and mostly by e-mail. It was a twenty-four-hour proposition. During office hours the lines outside my door looked like the methadone clinic at six A.M. Intellectual discussion could take place at anytime, anywhere. Social theory fused with popular culture and everyday life, in the women's bathroom, the library, or the snack bar. The students viewed intellectual process as pleasure. They were playful and serious about ideas. There is no finer combination.

SOY soon became famous, generating a buzz across campus, even the deans heard about it on parents' day. In March 1998, the nation-state earned a writeup in the *Spectator,* Columbia University's school newspaper. As I galloped across the lecture hall stage, headlines read BARNARD'S BOLD, "POSTMODERN" SOCIOLOGIST. The article discussed my philosophy of teaching—bringing social theory alive by drawing from students' lived experience. My risqué linguistic style and periodic references to Led Zeppelin and Metallica were mentioned, too. But it didn't matter if I said "fuck." By now I walked on water.

The summer before I started at Barnard, I had interviewed almost thirty female musicians for a feature about sexuality and women in rock. My hit list included Tori Amos, Luscious Jackson, Lil' Kim, Sleater-Kinney, Aliyah, Tribe 8, and Liz Phair. The article appeared in *Rolling Stone's* thirtieth anniversary issue. These were my students' heroes, but I also got to interview some of my own: Marianne Faithfull, Janis Ian, Pat Benatar, Deborah Harry, Joan Jett, Chrissie Hynde, and Ronnie Spector. These early women in rock fought off demeaning stereotypes with faith, irony, and compromise. They had to negotiate the tits & ass attitude of old-boy record companies, managers, radio programmers, and fans. They kicked down the doors by playing both sides.

For many years, Marianne Faithfull was known as "Mick's girlfriend." Her snarling 1979 masterpiece *Broken English* changed that. At fifteen, Janis Ian wrote "Society's Child," boldly challenging America's interracial dating taboos. The song prompted death threats. But another kind of love would remain off limits to the young lesbian songwriter. For too long, the early women in rock were viewed as puppets, under the sway of Svengali record companies and managers. Pat Benatar had to shoot down accusations that flaunting her sexuality onstage was anyone's idea but hers. Chrissie Hynde also took complete control of her presentation of self: "I just looked like any skanky chick from the bowling alley. If someone had come to me when we were doing our first album cover and suggested we use a stylist, that guy would have gone home with a black eye."

When Joan Jett toured with the Go-Go's, people threw garbage at her. They dismissed the clever, quirky Debbie Harry as just another dumb blonde. The early women in rock had to figure out how to play guitar without getting their nipples caught in the strings. For role models, the early women in rock looked at Keith Richards, now young girls looked at them. Even though some reactionaries thought Biggie Smalls penned Lil' Kim's rhymes and Kurt wrote Courtney's songs, things were changing. In and out of my classroom were members of all-girl bands who cited L7, Elastica, and Hole as their influences. They never even mentioned the boys.

Teaching women, interviewing them, listening critically to their music, I discovered something about myself, too. I couldn't relate to the humorless Rusty Nuts of academe or their daughters-in-arms, the new wave of angry women in rock. Was I supposed to trade my Ozzfest tickets for the Lilith Fair? Sell off my Danzig CDs and replace them with Fiona Apple? Whenever my female editors mentioned women's bands they liked, I'd puke, "Ugh! Courtney Love is the only one who even knows how to hold a guitar!!" With such a piss-poor attitude toward women in rock, how could I teach female students anything? I was supposed to be a positive role model, not the anti-Christ.

How do these things happen to us? By virtue of my credentials I was now an upper-middle-class feminist. Was I somehow an unwitting collaborator in my own oppression? My students opened my eyes to the future. Bikini Kill didn't *want* to play guitar like Eric Clapton. L7 didn't fret over "Aunt Flo." They tossed dirty tampons into the mosh pit. Lil' Kim declared, "I don't need dick tonight, eat my pussy right." The females in my classroom grew up as Title IX girls—strong, smart, and compassionate. They played sports, made documentaries, wrote software, applied to medical school, and got their nails done, too. Sometimes they fell in love with Mr. Wrong, drank too much, obsessed over having perfect bodies, and getting top grades.

I was descended from two generations of Cretin incest, born free, the first in a long line of female slaves and serfs. Nothing could repair the damage done to my mother, my grandma, and my great-aunts. My position as a Barnard professor seemed a vindication, reparations for war crimes against defeated Cretin daughters. My mother protected me, my students restored me. Like Sleater-Kinney, my students were busting through the gender barrier at a hundred miles an hour, first goddesses of the millennium.

As most professors know, the best stuff usually happens after class. When I went to college, giving your professor a joint was considered good form. My students made me tapes, burned CDs of favorite bands and their own music, too. Korean-American kids with strict parents pondered the relationship of prefigurative cultures and contemporary family life. Others considered Midwestern girl gangs in terms of Robert Merton's theories of anomie and opportunity structures. Then, out of nowhere they'd say, "Dr. Gaines, I love your eyeshadow!" They would ask about my tattoos or where I got my boots. Some were body modified with tribal ink, multicolored dreadlocks, and piercing. Others were '90s yoga chicks who drove me nuts talking about the healing properties of echinacea and green tea.

When I taught sociology at Big Science in 1984, one of my students confided his homosexuality. Discreetly, I lent him all my books by my cousin Karla Jay—*After You're Out, Lavender Culture, The Gay Report.* He carted them off in a plain brown paper bag and hid them under his bed all semester so his parents didn't see. We'd discuss the readings privately during my office hours. He submitted his term paper surreptitiously. Now, the entire class was reading Ann Heron's cross-generational collection *Two Teenagers in Twenty: Writings by Gay and Lesbian Youth,* writing papers, reading them in class, examining homophobia on campus, politicizing the personal, and personalizing the political. Baby lesbians stood at the edge of the closet door, poised to come out, lipstick in hand.

Today my former students have jobs in publishing, as photographers; others are finishing law school or working on doctoral degrees. A few are traveling around the world, studying culture informally, indefinitely. They sometimes e-mail their crotchety old sociology professor with news about births or upcoming gigs, or seeking advice about careers. Sometimes I'll be at a show and I'll hear "Professor Gaines!!" and it's one of my students. We'll discuss housing, jobs, lovers, creative projects. Scene makers, creators of culture, sometimes I'd see them at shows, spinning at clubs, planning parties. Some play in garage pop bands like Racquet, others dance at clubs like Don Hill's, bad little go-go girls.

Although a smaller demographic, SOY boys were as diverse as the girls. Journalists, entrepreneurs, Cali surfers, rockers, hackers, club kids, sons of great patriarchal capitalists like the men who built Columbia University. Some were athletes, stars of their teams, willing to rethink their socialization after reading books like Bernard Lefkowitz's *Our Guys: The Glen Ridge Rape and the Secret Life of the Perfect Suburb.* They, too, want whole lives—to fall in love, become fathers, make money, or find truth and light. To make films, write, paint, and never settle down. Or any combination of the above.

For some reason, my courses were very popular among Greeks. Not Hellenic Americans like GiGi; I mean sorority and fraternity kids. Ironically, the Greeks at Columbia constituted an abject minority, especially the sororities. According to local Greek mythologies, Margaret

Mead adjudicated them elitist and exclusionary in the 1960s and they were subsequently banned. Students who typically would have been the teachers' pets now reported feeling like outcasts, ostracized by radical faculty. They were afraid to wear their Greek colors to class, fearing the affiliation might affect their grade. Ironically, this *perception* of minority persecution among traditionally more conforming and culturally mainstream youth illuminated their understanding of outlaw subcultures.

Professor Aloysius, too, was indirectly responsible for the popularity of my courses among the Greeks. At one point I was an invited guest at the sorority houses. My students prepared a dinner party for me and answered my questions about Greek life. I explained that in the 1960s Greeks were outlawed at my school. It was considered way too hegemonic, like the prom or Nixon's daughters' hairdos. I was curious about Greek life. I had no frame of reference. I had been to Athens, but 1990s sororities were Greek to me. I approached it like I was conducting a study. But I was also becoming concerned about high national rates of college drinking, especially at fraternity houses.

Like any American college, Columbia was a high-pressure environment. Ivy League students especially strive for academic excellence, cram hard for exams. Many overbook activities and course schedules against the advice of faculty. After exams, once papers were submitted, it is typical for binge drinking to begin at most colleges. Rates of drinking at Columbia University were no higher than at any other school. In fact, statistically, they were somewhat lower. But concern over college student alcohol consumption had been growing nationally. I was starting to explore how dangerous patterns of heavy social drinking can take root in college, often the result of manic cramming and then bingeing.

When the State of New York raised the drinking age from eighteen to twenty-one, it created a brand-new subclass of lawbreakers. Some kids wanted to protect their right to party, so they went Greek, joining frats and sororities, because drinking at house parties was a way around the law. Naively, I brought in experts to talk to the class about drinking on campus, as well as suicide. But the students hated it. It reminded them of high school, of adult hysteria and hypocritical preaching: "Do as I say, not as I do." By the end of the lecture, my classroom was almost empty. However, reading and discussing *Drinking: A Love Story,* Caroline Knapp's memoir of young, upper-middle-class female alcoholism, hit closer to home.

Some of my students had parents in recovery; a few were in recovery themselves. I never discussed my own debauchery. I figured if they read my stuff in the *Voice,* they knew enough. I don't think anyone at Barnard knew that during my first semester there I was bottoming out.

Professor Gaines by day, Professor Aloysius by night. It took me a total of about six months living in New York City to hit the brick wall. Maybe it was clinical depression, alienation, and anomie. I might have smothered my raging anxieties in food, sex, or pills. But it was booze that came to my emotional rescue in the final days. I was teaching at Barnard, helping to set up the ill-fated *Long Island Voice,* and freelancing as a journalist. I continued to do Dr. Gaines's business, speaking out internationally on behalf of youth. I had a nice apartment, went to book parties and rock & roll shows, and had distinguished dinner dates. Everything looked just fine. Outside, life kept getting better—career, finances, power, and prestige. Inside, I was disintegrating.

By the end of 1996 I had perfected my chosen method of destruction. One night I found myself at the Continental. Somebody put something in my drink and I passed out. Somehow I ended up downstairs puking my guts out. Drinking water to clear out my system, I was afraid I'd die. Drink, binge, and purge. As usual, I was surrounded by the ex-boyfriend club, a collection of guitarists and lead singers, fine gentlemen I'd dated over the years. Unless you've cheated on them, ex-boyfriends will stay loyal forever. They become like brothers, a mutual aid society. Their new loves become your friends, too. If the ex-boyfriends were around, I was safe. If not, I had another strategy.

Under escort I was free to drink to oblivion. So I did most of my serious damage undercover—on dates, with a lover, secretly. I drank in between deadlines, like I always had. To calm down, I told myself, like Keith Richards coming off a tour. But something was changing; I could feel it. At some point, partying became heavy social drinking. After a while, and I'm not sure exactly when, I started to cross over, to make that final transition into alcoholism.

Mostly, there was a shift in focus. My thinking slowly began to revolve around the drink; cocktails. When I was a kid, it was the obsession for candy. As a teenager, it was that guy. Later, the deadline. Now I really *needed* that shot of Sambuca in my coffee. Walk across town? Had to have a dark Beck's beer in a brown paper bag. The glass of red wine at the dinner party probably wasn't gonna be the last. It ended hours later, stomach blown out, retching in the kitchen sink. Then came the dry heaves. Why am I gagging while brushing my teeth? The first drink now punctuated the day. Even music sounded better with a boost. Sometimes my hands shook in the morning. I didn't drink every day, but eventually I would have. I could see where it was heading, but I couldn't stop it.

Then one day it happened. Professor Aloysius whispered in my ear, *"I'm always there for you, baby girl. Nobody will ever love you, and anyone you love will die. Your career? It doesn't mean shit. You'll always be alone, unloved and unlovable. Life sucks, so fuck it, you might as well drink."*

I was always careful not to drink on the job—that included book parties, power lunches with editors, even shows I was covering. I knew my concentration would be lost, my personality would get stupid, sloppy, even mean. Now I didn't care. By the second drink, I was an asshole. Fuck it. So what? In New York City I had friends and colleagues, but nobody really close. I didn't have Anthony or Nick to cover my back. Nobody except the Professor. Without him, I felt raw. First sip, instant calm.

My mood swings were becoming so severe that Nick was sure I'd started menopause, but my hormones tested fine. Neptune had been transiting my sixth house since 1989. Neptune is the planet of dreams, idealism and fantasy, inspiration and delusion. The sixth house is the area of the horoscope that deals with work and health. Such a transit can be a time when miracles are experienced through spiritual healing. If misused, it can mean slipping into darkness. We are especially prone to toxicity at this time. We must avoid drugs, alcohol, and all negative forms of escapism; they only make matters worse. And they sure did. That Neptune transit was full speed ahead and I'd been at it for years. Now I was losing my grip—tumbling dice, falling stars.

The first time I actually saw the Professor taking over, I was in bed with a much younger man, a musician who should have just stayed a friend. I remember lying there with him, our reflections in the mirror. Sex was new, thrilling, all-consuming. Lit candles, "Kashmir" on rotation, scent of Shalimar and liquor mixed with sex juice on pale satin sheets. Moist, bodies opening. On one side of the bed I had a pint of Jack Daniel's. On the other side, I had him. We were on the threshold, the prelude to an endless kiss. But I didn't reach for him. I didn't see him at all. I went straight for that bottle. Jack was my baby now.

I got into fights everywhere, even at staid and sedate Barnard. I instigated illogical disputes with the most pleasant people. I had temper tantrums, my makeup was caked, I had a bad haircut, my hair color was oxidizing, my skin was turning gray. Like most binges, the last one (please God) began around Thanksgiving and went on for eight weeks.

First, Nick and I got totally blasted at the family dinner, in front of the loved ones. We'd never done that before. The script was changing. Now I drank hard with anyone I knew. I was losing my dignity, day by day. By New Year's Eve I was still wasted. Nick and I started with a cocktail at dusk. Sea Monster was playing, the house was packed. By five in the morning, after a long night of dark liquor and white powder, we were still at Coney Island High, blasted. And then it happened. I crossed the line. *I said mean things to Nick.*

Nick is the one person in the whole world that mattered, the only person I loved unconditionally. I placed him above everything and everyone. He was my sweetheart, husband, father, best friend, junko partner, muse, and coconspirator. And he loved me too, always, no matter what. He never once said one mean word to me. I considered him a higher life form, an enlightened soul. Kindness is one of the great spiritual values—it *actualizes* compassion, mercy, grace, and empathy. Nick is the kindest human being I have ever known. But that didn't stop me.

Whatever I said, I hurt him so bad that witnesses to the crime recall him turning white. *And I didn't remember.* And then he never even mentioned it. A month went by before I heard about it from a mutual friend. It floored me. I asked Nick about it over dinner and he confirmed it. In a blackout, I had accused him of being bossy and domineering, of always criticizing me. But worst of all, *I told him he ruined my life.* In reality, the opposite was true. Nick accepted me completely, gave me room to breathe, inspired my creativity and my individuality. He was always there for me, tolerant, patient, and protective. How could I say those things, blame Nick for my misery and shortcomings? Like a drunk driver who kills a pedestrian, like a mother who beats her baby to death in a crack rage, I had fallen as low as I could go, violated the most precious love in my life. I could never take back those hurtful words, but I would make sure it never, ever happened again.

The last Merlot at dinner that night with Nick was my last drink. It was January 26, 1997. I remembered the date because it was two days after D.O.M.'s birthday, ten days after the anniversary of Betty's death. As I emerged from a lifelong coma, an old spiritual advisor leaped out of my dreams and into my life—Joey Ramone, incarnate.

With my spiritual advisor, Joey Ramone.

15

LIFE IN THE POST-RAMONES EMPIRE OF NYC

Do it from the heart, follow your instincts . . .

uh, excuse me, is the sushi fresh?

—JOEY RAMONE

One day I went to the *Voice* to pick up my hate mail. The music editor asked if I wanted to interview the Ramones. After twenty-two years of service my boyz were retiring. Although they were my heroes, I'd never been interested in actually meeting them. I felt I already knew them, especially Joey. I'd rarely missed a show. The band lived inside my stereo speakers and my head. Joey was in my dreams. But I did need to get some quotes.

It was widely known that the Ramones were one of rock's most dysfunctional families, venomous intrigues and endless back-stabbing. Johnny married Joey's fiancée, CJ married Marky's niece, and everyone was in love with CJ's sisters. At any given time, Dee Dee hated Joey or Marky. Or Joey was pissed off at Dee Dee. Or Johnny said something about Joey. The next week they were busy collaborating, setting up deals. Together, they were even more fucked up than the Cretins. Alone, they were the sweetest men in the world. Still, if you hung out with one, you didn't mention that you'd seen the others.

By now I'd done my share of wacko interviews—Howard Stern, Mister Rogers, Eric Bogosian, even Nick's precious Steve Malkmus (Pavement). But interviewing the Ramones would take all my social work skills. And when it was over, my life would never be the same. Original drummer Tommy Erdelyi had retired years ago, Marky was out of the country, and nobody could find Dee Dee. Everyone warned me that Johnny told each reporter the same thing and that Joey would make me interview him twice. From what I gathered, CJ—the bass player who replaced Dee Dee—was the only normal one.

Johnny met me at the Empire Diner, exactly on time like everyone said. He showed up wearing a KILL A COMMIE FOR MOMMY T-shirt and wanted to make sure Ramones fans knew he didn't read the *Voice*. I explained I was from Long Island, how my dad banned that filthy commie rag from the house for years. Like me, Johnny was an only child, very close with his father, too. I flashed the DEATH FROM AFAR Marines shirt under my jacket, and we had a bond. Merciless, Johnny described Joey as a "bleeding heart" and Marky as a "socialist," viciously dismissing them both as "a pair of old hippies." There had been long-standing rumors of Johnny all douched up in the '60s with love beads, a headband, and bell-bottoms, but I said nothing.

Johnny had been known to play with such fierce determination that once his white guitar turned red from blood that spurted from fingers shredded by strings, raw to the bone. The last time I saw the Ramones play was at the Academy—their last New York show. By the end of "53rd & 3rd," they had soared past Ramones toward speed of light. And now it was over. According to Johnny, the Ramones story is a tale of innovation born of incompetence. "We didn't realize we were doing something so different. We were just trying to be like other people, writing normal songs, and we couldn't. This was the best we could do." This accidental discovery sparked a cultural revolution in music. Still, Johnny kept it simple: "This ain't art, it's entertainment. It's a great job, but it's a silly job. I jump around playing silly songs, and I can see in the kids' faces that they are having a good time. I'm playing from the heart. I love rock & roll and just want the kids to have fun and be happy." I was always a little afraid of Johnny. I thought he was mean looking. But he was very nice to me, a real professional.

Unlike the other band members, Johnny had no plans to do anything after retirement. He had been a construction worker before the Ramones. "Work is bad," he said. Besides, he figured, what could he do that would ever top the Ramones? It was time to retire before the band sucked, quit while they're ahead. He had royalties coming in, a collection of baseball player autographs, horror movies, sports, his wife, the gym. There was plenty of stuff to keep him busy. After the interview I asked Johnny to sign an autograph for my friend's kid, a nine-year-old fan on dialysis. Ramones adored their fans, especially the little ones. He smiled and obliged.

Dialing that 516 area code made me really homesick. CJ replaced Dee Dee on bass when he quit the band in 1989. CJ was a U.S. Marine but he went AWOL for personal reasons. Post-Ramones it's all about engines and ink. When I called for the interview, CJ was busy building a custom EVO and a Shovelhead. He also had a '70 Nova with a 350-cubic-inch engine. He was friends with Mr. Bonge. CJ is a life member of the NRA who enjoys hunting and target shooting at Calverton. For his sixteenth birthday his dad got him a Marlin rifle. CJ loved his Mossberg 590 assault shotgun so much he wrote a song about it— "Scattergun." Neither right-wing like Dee Dee or Johnny or liberal-lefty like Joey and Marky, CJ was more Long Island, like Howard Stern, wack-libertarian-populist. He was registered to vote as an Independent, like me.

Meeting Johnny and talking to CJ was fun, but Joey? That was a whole other story. I couldn't believe I was actually going to meet my spiritual guide in person. It seemed so anticlimactic I almost didn't want to do it. Like what would happen if we finally saw God? Really knew the meaning of life? Then what? Without our fantasies, hopes, and dreams, all the magic in the world would disappear and we'd be lost, out in the cold. I couldn't bear the thought. On top of all this existential terror, my girlfriends were urging me to try and date Joey. "He's sooo cool! I love him, tell him I said hello!" I was furious. Didn't they realize how serious this was? Dating him was trivial in comparison to this—a sacred audience with my personal bodhisattva.

Besides, I never went for rock stars. Why bother? There were always enough great guys on the local scene to meet my needs. In addition, Betty Bradley had warned me (in vain) to steer clear of musicians. "A full-time baby-sitting job," she said. Male musicians were big trouble, bad news. Always sucking off Big Mama, real charmers, she warned, typically dopers, drunks, and womanizers. Still, three great rock stars did stand out as spectacular. Lemmy was in England with Motorhead, James Hetfield was out in California with Metallica, and there I was, ringing Joey's bell.

I had to stay calm, I had an agenda. Now that the Ramones were retiring, Joey planned to put out a solo album, gathering his closest pals: longtime Ramones collaborator, songwriter-producer Daniel Rey on guitar, Dictators' bass player Andy "Adny" Shernoff, and Cracker drummer Frank Funaro. Of course, Joey wanted Daniel to produce it. Rey is known as a musician's musician, producing such bands as Gluecifer, death metal godz Entombed, Richard Hell, Circus of Power, and the soundtrack to the film *Welcome to the Dollhouse*. Girls like to watch Daniel play guitar; he's cute, he grew up in Jersey, he surfs.

Johnny had tipped me off that Joey liked oldies. So I brought him a tape of my favorite doo-wop songs hoping he'd cover them. After producing the Ramones in the '80s, Phil Spector approached Joey to do a solo album; his voice reminded the tycoon of teen of Ronnie herself. Maybe I had a shot. Imagine Joey Ramone singing the Chantels, Skyliners, Moonglows, and Penguins. I boned up for the interview by eating pizza, the ritual bread of our homeland, Queens.

I rode the elevator up to the tenth floor of Joey's East Village highrise. By the time he came to the door, I was so nervous, the cheesy grease had my stomach in knots. But the moment the door opened, everything was purple. Once inside, I felt completely relaxed and calm. "Purple is for healing," Joey says in a soothing tone, his voice rich and lush like when he sings a ballad. Without saying a word, I presented him with the tape, my humble sacrifice. "This is a good tape," he says. Yes, I was thinking, I have found favor, he is pleased.

He was so tall, you had to look up. Standing there, I wondered, what color are his eyes? I didn't know, he was always wearing rose-colored shades. He took them off, revealing big, beautiful, soulful brown eyes. The sun was shining, streaming in across his shoulders. I saw rainbows, needles and pins of light bursting all around. Was this really happening? My head was swirling, I wanted to dance with him. But I got hold of myself and started futzing with the tape recorder. I had a job to do.

Joey's mystic purple emporium was also very high-tech, replete with all the essential gear of a rocker lifestyle. Endless piles of magazines, videotapes, and CDs, computers, framed collectors' series Fillmore East posters, monitors, huge speakers, plastic dinosaurs, and Ramones memorabilia, including the band's one gold album, *Ramonesmania.* Meeting your hero can be very disconcerting. You want to blurt out every thought and feeling you've ever had, all the esoteric, brain-damaged reasons you and he have this immortal bond. Ultimately, those feelings are best left unsaid. You are better off *not* reciting back all the lyrics he's ever written or offering lengthy treatises on what he said onstage at the Roxy in 1976. Just be yourself and go with the flow. It took me another six months to get over the fact that *he was Joey Ramone.*

Some years prior, Joey had an accident that led to a revelation about the meaning of life. He got sober, health conscious; he even deleted pizza from his food file. "This was a reawakening, a spiritual rebirth," he explained. His whole worldview changed, no more resentment or anger, no cynicism or tired urban sarcasm. Now Joey wrote songs filled with joyful optimism, uplifting, proclaiming "Life's a Gas." In the months that followed, Joey's power of example helped me embrace sobriety. He filled my head with positive energy. At shows, he steered me toward bottled water and club soda. Proving to me that I didn't need Professor Aloysius to have fun. In fact, the opposite was true: The Professor was really a drag.

I felt comfortable with Joey, so I told him my secret—that I'd been a fat girl in high school. I didn't have to say much. He understood my pain instantly and offered solace: "The Ramones are there for all the outcasts. Alienation was definitely a feeling we went through in the early stages of the band. We were outsiders, loners. Okay, this is me, I'm myself. I'm an individual. I don't want to be like you, I wanna be who I am." Joey had found the courage to be himself, to transform the pain he knew as the misfit Jeff Hyman into the hero Joey Ramone. Joey meant what he said, he was who he claimed to be.

Like all fans who use music to soothe personal agony, in the Ramones I'd found something to believe in. Still, fans must be careful never to confuse the artist with the art. Sometimes rock stars—like authors or actors—can be real assholes. But Joey kept the promise. He was true blue, neither a poser nor an imposter. He epitomized it all— struggle, triumph, and truth. On top of that, he was so cool, so funny and smart. He never ducked the tough questions. He spoke out on all the issues without ever subordinating his art. Regardless of who wrote the lyrics, Joey was the symbol of everything the Ramones stood for. In a seamless transition he became the friend in real life he had been in dreams and songs.

The week my article came out in *The Village Voice,* Joey was onstage at Continental hosting one of many awesome shows he would organize during his reign as local scene patriarch. Flashing a copy of "My Life with the Ramones," he told the audience, "This article is one of the best fuckin' things ever written about my band. I wanna dedicate this song to Donna Gaines and *The Village Voice, 1-2-3-4 now I wanna sniff some glue. . . ."*

On that night I was anointed, granted a permanent position in the Post-Ramones Empire of New York City. I devoted myself completely to my new local scene. Sartre was right about engagement; nothing feels better than belonging to something you really believe in and working hard to move it forward. To walk into a room and see people who share your worldview, who accept you and include you. I've always been a little phobic about too much group involvement, but this was loosely organized, haphazard, and voluntary—no smothering. Once I was immersed in the Post-Ramones Empire I'd found a new reason to live—another Slugland, my next Pyrexia.

Most of the Ramones were also clean and sober. In the Post-Ramones Empire I started learning how to love rock & roll without killing myself. From the time I stopped drinking to the time I surrendered to AA, these were the people who helped me stay sober. All the bands were different and there was always something going on. I rarely missed a gig. My service to the community was to list upcoming shows in the *Voice*. The Ramones were the founding fathers of the DIY subculture I came out of, where everybody contributes whatever they can to make the scene what it is. The Post-Ramones Empire already had plenty of photographers, hairdressers, and managers, so I served as a scribe. No conflict of interest, when it came to the Ramones, everyone knew I was a fan, not a critic.

Life in the Post-Ramones Empire of New York City was a full-time commitment that included not only da bruddahs but their parents, step-parents, siblings, aunts, uncles, wives, ex-girlfriends, and all the people who ever managed, produced, or handled them. Then there were all the post-Ramones bands, each member had several projects that required my attention. When Dee Dee first quit the Ramones in 1989 he went hip-hop, recording as Dee Dee King. Then he wrote *Lobotomy: Surviving the Ramones,* a vitriolic memoir of life with the Ramones, and later a deranged novel, *Chelsea Horror Hotel.* Dee Dee was the ultimate punk who hated everyone and everything (but not really). At one point, I interviewed Dee Dee at the Chelsea Hotel for an insider documentary, but I'll spare you the details of a four-hour seminar about Judas Iscariot and Kessie, our childhood pets. Kessie was later featured in "Dee Dee and Kessie's Adventures" a comic strip in *Taking Dope,* a punk art collaboration with Paul Kostabi.

Germany! Glue! Queens! Dachshunds! While the ferocious intensity of each Ramone exploded into the glorious whole we knew and loved since 1976, Dee Dee was at the core of the band's genius. He was at once demonic, a scumbag, pop savvy, feral, and silly. He was also sensitive and kind, fun and totally fucked up. He either loved you or hated you. Absolute childlike trust or total paranoia. As far as I was concerned, Dee Dee wrote the best Ramones songs, heartfelt quasi-autobiographical lamentations like "Born to Die in Berlin" (with John Carco) or "Poison Heart" (with Daniel Rey). Then he turned out lunatic rants like "Cretin Family," then prayerful homilies like "I Believe in Miracles" (both also with Rey). Like all Ramones, Dee Dee was an American patriot, an original, a populist, and an artist. He was passionate about his rock & roll, his hair, and deeply in love with his young wife, whom he'd met on tour in Argentina.

Once when I ran into Dee Dee at a New York club, he seemed out of sorts, upset. He complained he didn't fit in anywhere, he felt like a misfit. Dee Dee had lived in Germany, New York, Argentina. He'd traveled around the world, but where did he actually belong? Astonished that one so beloved, so revered, would still feel so alienated, I said, "Dee Dee, you don't *have* to fit in. We all fit in with you!" Weren't millions of fans worldwide proof enough that he was wrong? The Post-Ramones Empire included generations of fans, family, and friends, crossed all boundaries of race, religion, sex, nation, and age. We were straight, gay, transsexual, Christian, Jew, pagan, Muslim, Hindu, and godless, too. Right wing, left wing, and didn't give a shit. But even this was not enough to convince him.

Dee Dee's post-Ramones bands have included Dee Dee Ramone and the Chinese Dragons and Dee Dee Ramone ICLC (Inter-Celestial Light Commune). But everyone loved the Remainz—Dee Dee on vocals and guitar, his wife Barbara Zampini on bass and additional vocals. If they were all getting along, Marky played drums and periodically Joey and CJ sat in, too.

CJ's Los Gusanos (the Worms) were a Long Island–based road crew that featured sizzling metal chops by guitarist "Dirty" Ed Lynch. In true Long Island tradition, CJ's mom baked chocolate chip cookies for backstage. His sisters were cosmetologists, great rock & roll girls like the Mordreds. They did everyone's hair and extolled the virtues of deep conditioning with Climatress by Redken. CJ usually booked with bands like Zeke and Reo Speedealer, generating a gritty bass sound he called "motor rock." Their original material shrieked of white-line fever, odes to the road and automotive engineering. This was the music of the turnpike, an indigenous sound. When Los Gusanos broke up in March 2000, I was devastated. But CJ formed the Warm Jets, then Bad Chopper, and kept on playing.

Meantime, Marky Ramone and the Intruders featured hard-driving post-punk hardcore, pounding Ramones for a new century. Marky favored young musicians like Ben Troken and Johnny "Fingers" Pisano. For a while, Todd Youth of Murphy's Law fronted with guitar and vocals. Marky filmed and produced the *Ramones Around the World,* a documentary of the band's travel footage, a real tribute to the fans. Later a spoken-word tour put him back on the road.

To this day, Marky lives in Brooklyn, the land of his birth. He was proud to say he was still married to Marion, his childhood sweetheart. Marky's wife is a tall blonde, some of her family lives in Rockaway Beach. Her nephews surf where I once caught my first waves.

At one point I interviewed Marky at home for *Details.* The Brooklyn apartment was a swirl of pop culture, toys, science fiction and horror movie posters, electric model cars, robots, and a jukebox. When I mentioned that I needed a bicycle, Marky and Marion gave me a 1947 Sears Roebuck original, a red steel Pee-Wee Herman job with shock absorbers, a rearview mirror, and foot brakes. It's a girl's bike, it weighs a ton, and I'm still riding it today. But Marky's gift to me that day was not just the bicycle. After my editor quit, *Details* killed my story, but that was meaningless, because what happened that day was a miracle: I hadn't been back to Belle Harbor for many years. And now I was returning under a Ramones paramilitary escort.

Marky decided we should have lunch in Rockaway, so we drove east, across the Marine Park Bridge to Belle Harbor. Riding down Twennyninth in Marky's vintage Cadillac, I looked at the Irish faces, hoping to see traces of past acquaintances. Groups of sun-streaked surfy kids hung around the stores like they always did. But these were different kids and newer stores. The Magnet, more formally known as the Belle Harbor Tavern, was now called Jamesons. The Newport Inn, where

Pablo and I once prowled for cigarettes, was now the Harbor Light. The pizza place near the gas station was gone, so we ate Italian food at Plum Tomatoes, right where the old grocery store used to be. Like many places, Twennyninth had yuppified. But it was still turf.

I showed Marky and Marion the immortal school yard, the place where I first saw Tommy. We made a visit to the holy shrine behind the old drugstore, where I drank my first beers and made out with boys. To consecrate my pilgrimage to Twennyninth, we posed for photos, right there on the street corner, in the place where it all began—sex, drugs, rock & roll, and sociology.

On the way home we stopped by my old house on Beach 139th. I felt that old familiar ache in my solar plexus. I dreaded coming back to this house with all the sadness, the fear, and loneliness. All the ghosts of all my dead parents and friends. By now the original neighbors were gone, new families had taken over, remodeled, modernized. The air was fresh and clean. The trees seemed so tall, swaying gracefully in the warm sea breeze. We stood there, right in front of my house. I asked Marion to take a photograph to document my triumphant return. Marky put his arm around me, protective like a big brother. Nobody could hurt me now. My house looked so much older and smaller than I remembered. For the first time, I noticed how beautiful Belle Harbor was. Sunshine, clear skies, so calming and serene. Maybe it always was. Maybe Rockaway hadn't changed that much, but I had.

As our scene patriarch, Joey kept hope alive for NYC punks. Although CBGB's was more famous, the Continental, at 25 3rd Avenue, between St. Mark's and East 9th Street, was always my home. The club was originally called the Continental Divide. In 1990, a guy named Trigger bought the club and dropped the *Divide*. He took out the kitchen, moved back the stage, cleaned up the bathrooms, and relocated them downstairs, bomb-shelter style, concrete and steel. Trigger met Joey Ramone in the late 1980s on a spiritual retreat. Joey lived diagonally across the street from the Continental, in a high-rise. Once Trigger took over Joey began booking shows. He said the club had the same vibe as CBGB's in the 1970s.

With over one hundred photos on the wall, including everyone from Guns n' Roses to local favorites like Sea Monster, the Continental is more like a local venue than an industry place like Brownie's or the Mercury Lounge. It's got the look, but it still has an underground innocence, the indigenous scene credibility that made New York punk what it is. Iggy Pop liked the Continental because it reminded him of upstairs at Max's Kansas City. The first time he visited, Iggy told Trigger, "This is a really cool place to do a show." Kidding around, Trigger said, "Okay, bring me a demo." The humble Stooge replied, "Sure, I'll drop one off tomorrow." Stunned, Trigger stammered, "I have every one of your records. You can play here anytime, anytime."

Like many bridge-and-tunnel marauders, I spent years foraging the backrooms of the Continental for free lines and pirate love, puking in the basement surrounded by the ex-boyfriend club. Dee Dee had consecrated the black space with graffiti, a whimsical chalk tribute to Kessie, Über Dachshund of Berlin. Over my period of residence, the Continental has booked local and touring bands about to break, as well as scene dignitaries like Patti Smith, Ronnie Spector, and Sebastian Bach. I've gladly sacrificed chucks of brain matter to bands like Raging Slab, PCP Highway, Nashville Pussy, and Felonious Punk. Of course, Long Island's finest have gigged here, too—the CorpseGrinders, Slugs, Nihilistics, NutJob, and Graveyard Slut. My best nights were spent with Nick, watching Thunders and the Waldos.

Guitarist Walter Lure was Johnny's longtime consort in the Heartbreakers. A stoic survivor of too much junkie business, Walter's lost his bandmates, Johnny, Jerry, and later, bass player Tony C. Sadly, he even outlived his younger brother, Sea Monster's bassist Richie Lure. But he kept on playing, cranking Heartbreakers classics, a defiant wank in the face of loss. Ferocious sets dedicated to the fallen souls that once filled the Continental with wrenching power chords, magicians who fired up the stage like the Cosa Nostra, dressed to kill, guitars pointed at you like Uzis. Fans crowd the stage in tribute, including rabid fans too young to have seen Johnny play. Everyone knew that by day Walter was a successful stockbroker. Sounding as tough as ever, even now, when

Walter plays, the Saints come moshing in, departed spirits return home to the Continental. I once told Walter if he ever stopped playing, I'd leave New York City for good. He replied, "If I ever stop playing, I'll die."

In addition to their own bands, each Ramone produced or supported several others. When the Bullys met Marky at a studio in Brooklyn in 1998, they were too scared to talk to him. But he liked them so much he produced their first album, *Stomposition*. Feral as Deadboys, polished as Professionals, pure bridge-and-tunnel like the Ramones, the Bullys mixed old-school punk with a Gen X face and a strong left hook. Because three of the original members grew up in my hometown, Rockaway Beach, Marky introduced us. Johnny Heff, the principal Bully, lived right near Sixteenth, a tough St. Camillus boy who came up stomping. The rhythm guitarist sang backups, wrote most of the material, set up their website, fronted cash for recording, and booked shows.

The Bullys' songs were heartfelt tales of life on mean suburban streets. "Still My Home" was an oath of bloody loyalty, a Celtic warrior's do-or-die pledge to love and defend his turf. Pumped and inked for the 1990s, the Bullys were direct descendents of the Magicians, my Celtic teenage heartthrobs from Twennyninth. Unlike most leatherette punks on the scene, the Bullys could back it up. The fearless "Tonite We Fight Again!" wasn't a pose, it was autobiographical. I always enjoyed hanging out with them at shows. If some guy walked by and accidentally brushed my arm, the Bullys went into full alert. Full of scrappy tough-guy attitude, they were secretly very good boys.

Like Marky, CJ had his bands, too. He met the members of Blackfire while on tour with the Ramones. A Navajo punk band from Arizona, the sibling trio incorporated grassroots activism with traditional Native American chanting. CJ produced their first album, and Joey liked them enough to do vocals on subsequent recordings. Their father, Jones Benally, is Diné (Navajo) and their mother, Bertha, comes from Far Rockaway. During the hippie years, Bertha split for the coast and fell in love with the handsome Navajo medicine man. As children, Blackfire traveled with their father as the Jones Benally Family, bringing the old ways back to the people, performing ceremonial dances, demonstrating rituals, and healing. Nominated for several Grammy awards, today Blackfire tours worldwide and is known internationally for their music as well as their politics.

As more Native Americans assimilate and reservation poverty forces young people into the mainstream of America, Blackfire works to help them walk in both worlds. When Bertha read my book, she organized a speaking tour that took me to northern Arizona. I talked with Navajo community leaders, social workers, and teachers. Reservations are desolate lands with high rates of alcoholism, suicide, and gang violence. Hopelessness, hunger, and isolation have left kids feeling defeated. I met with kids at a high school in Kayenta. We swam near the Utah border and ate mutton in Tuba City. Touring the local hardcore scene with Blackfire, watching them perform at the high school, it was so obvious: Everywhere in America, music kept so many kids alive.

A highlight of my life in the Post-Ramones Empire involved a collaboration between my teen idol Ronnie Spector and Joey Ramone, with all their "Oh ye-ah's" and "Bay-beee-oooo's." By now they actually looked alike, hair in thick pageboys, dressed in matching black, with leather gloves, packing New York attitude. Ronnie was usually chaperoned into the club Vegas-style by her manager and devoted husband Jonathan Greenfield. Sometimes their two teenaged sons, hip-hop fans, were in the audience, too. Backed by a full constellation of scene stalwarts like Daniel Rey and Joe McGinty, Ronnie's band always packs the house. Joey wrote "Bye Bye Baby" for her and sang on her 1999 EP, which he and Daniel Rey coproduced. In the U.K., *She Talks to Rainbows* was released on Creation, Oasis's label. In America it was issued on Kill Rock Stars, the same label as Sleater-Kinney.

At the Continental and Coney Island High, fans span two generations. Westbury Music Fair patrons—doo-wop nostalgia fiends—sway to the songs we first heard dry humping under the boardwalk. At the foot of the stage adoring young gay boys reach up to touch the Diva. They bring her roses and poems. Punks whip out tributary Bic lighters as "rock's original bad girl" torches Johnny Thunders's ballad "You Can't Put Your Arms Around a Memory." The house explodes as Joey joins her onstage for "Bye Bye Baby." Everywhere, alternative nation's neopunks are dancing, grrrls are celebrating the great *her*storical lineage that links Spector to her Kill Rock Stars labelmates. This connection alone says everything we need to know about women in rock.

In every life there are regrets, but I have only this: I fell asleep on the night Keith Richards joined Ronnie onstage at Life. In an interview I did for *Rolling Stone,* Ronnie described their relationship in the early 1960s, when the Ronettes toured with the Stones. Keith was polite, an earnest Britboy who confessed his undying love. Sweet as he was, Ronnie declined his advances; she was already seeing Phil. "I'm a one-man woman," she explained. When I heard this I was elated; again, my faith had not been betrayed. Like Joey, Ronnie was true blue, from the Ronettes to Eddie Money, she never lied to us, it was all the truth, just like Ronnie said.

Joey spent most days watching CNBC, especially *Squawk Box,* a daily financial analysis program featuring Maria Bartiromo. Joey fell in love with her, describing the market floor reporter as "hot and fiesty." He even wrote a song about her. *I watch her every day, I watch her every night / She's really out of sight / Maria Bartiromo.* The network had actually invited him to perform the song on the floor of the New York Stock Exchange, but Joey declined. An acoustic set just wouldn't cut it.

At one point Joey's success in the market earned him a two-page feature in *Smart Money* magazine. It seemed bizarre for the King of Punk to be so engaged in a corporate capitalist venture, but Joey explained, "When I stopped drinking, I started getting into the stock market because it's sort of a mosh pit down there." Counterintuitively, Joey Ramone loved Starbucks Frappuccinos. The company has been derided as a yuppie scum sellout. But Joey thought it was really cool, like some democratized version of a bohemian pleasure. He loved to stroll along East 9th Street enjoying a coffee, grabbing cookies at the Blackhound bakery, scarfing down luscious pumpkin ravioli at Danal. He favored vegan meals at the Angelica Kitchen and sushi at Hisaki.

The East Village was Joey's neighborhood and it had endless culinary delights for the man with Venus in Cancer. He was a big food enabler, not that I needed much prompting. Once we went out for pasta and ordered a sick dessert called the fonduta. It was fresh fruit you'd dip into a chocolate sauce, like fondue. We had to order it because it was so go-go boots and *Laugh-In*. It was totally gross; we could barely swallow it. But I couldn't stop saying "Fonduta! Fonduta!" I drove him insane with my high-pitched bleating. Joey could be extremely good-natured. He'd just laugh and call me "a nut job."

Like me, Joey didn't cook. He also had a wicked sweet tooth, so we often got into trouble together, especially at the movies. We ate too much candy, and if Joey liked the film, we'd have to see the movie twice. Joey gave me advice about dealing with an explosive but loving father. Joey's dad also taught him how to shoot, just like mine. Whenever I broke up with a boyfriend, Joey offered pep talks. He was as unlucky in love as I was, but Joey adored kids and wanted to get married. There were always girls around, but his illness had become a full-time job, he didn't want to drag anyone into it.

A simple phone call with Joey could easily turn into a seven-hour marathon because he had call waiting. You'd be deep into it, and then his broker would call. Or his lawyer, Daniel Rey, his mother, or some girl he met in Japan. He would ask you to please hold, and then he'd forget. So you'd call back, and he'd do the exact same thing to the other person. It was easy to spend a whole day on the phone with Joey. A fiend for details, he knew the answer to any obscure pop culture question you could dream up. Like, Who wrote that song on which label? Who did backup vocals? And what style of clothes were we wearing when the song hit the charts? Then he correlated all this with our favorite TV shows for that year and what drugs we were taking. And then he'd rattle off his five stock picks of the week. Early in our friendship, Joey urged me to buy Iomega, a tech stock that's crashed through the killing floor. He probably made a fortune on it, but I still can't sell it, for sentimental reasons.

For years, Joey had kept the local punk scene alive by putting together a series of quirky, cool, sold-out extravaganzas. After Ramones retirement, he devoted himself to it wholeheartedly. Unlike most promoters, according to club owners, Joey was unconcerned with making money himself. "Make sure the bands get paid," he'd say. For him, the scene was all about supporting new bands, making sure they got a decent cut and some media attention. Each show had a festive moniker, like "Joey Ramone's Cyber Bash 1999 at Don Hill's" and featured local darlings like the Prissteens, Electric Frankenstein, and Furious George. If Blackfire or the Independents were in town, they played too. Sometimes Dee Dee's Remainz would headline or other "special guests" showed up, like Lenny Kaye from the Patti Smith Group, Joan Jett, Deborah Harry and Christ Stein of Blondie. Then there were appearances by assorted members of Green Day and Rancid.

The Dictators, a legendary pre-punk band from the Bronx, were also major players in all this. Joey's mother, Charlotte Lesher, a.k.a. Mama Ramone, was another scene stalwart, with her entourage of family and friends from Forest Hills. Some nights the club looked like a hip Bar Mitzvah. After so many years of Roman Catholics, lapsed Protestants, and Satanic suburbanites, here I was among a nation of Jewish rockers. Dictator's kosher frontman Dick Manitoba affectionately called this lineup the "Jew parade."

Situated in the center of St. Mark's Place, Coney Island High was a bilevel asylum for New York's indigenous punks; youngsters as well as those barely alive and kicking from 1977 showed up. "Coney" evolved out of GreenDoor parties organized by a hardcore kid from Brooklyn named Jesse Malin. At thirteen, he fronted Heart Attack. Jesse in dreadlocks later became the charismatic singer of the now defunct D-Generation—one of the scene's most celebrated punk ensembles. After D-Gen broke up, some members went off to Los Angeles to play in Danzig, and Jesse formed PCP Highway, then Bellvue, then he went solo.

Loyalty to the local scene was Jesse's calling, his hardcore roots. His contribution to keeping NYC music alive was immeasurable. Articulate and politically minded, he's defended our civil and cultural liberties for over a decade. Thanks to Mayor Giuliani's wacko "quality of life" crackdowns, old statutes stagnating on the books from before Prohibition were now being enforced, and dancing was outlawed at Coney. You had to stand at the foot of the stage and not move. Maybe you could sway, but if your feet moved, you were breaking the law. Eventually the club did shut down, but Jesse didn't miss a beat. Nearby, Niagara and Dictators' stronghold, Manitoba's, quickly picked up the slack.

Joey's post-Ramones activities included showcasing and producing the Independents. The funeral funboy horror-ska punks from Florence, South Carolina, had an eclectic mix Joey loved. The singer, Evil Presley, had a voice like Elvis and a swagger like Glen Danzig. Joey and Daniel Rey produced them, and Joey sang with them live and on their album *Back from the Grave*. Evil, a.k.a. Chris Snypse, was one of Joey's closest friends. They played video games together, watched dopey movies, and Joey got the young Chris hooked on sushi. When Joey got really sick in early 2001, Chris rarely left the hospital room. Dressed in regulation raunchy leather and chains, menacing in fierce metal spikes, Chris advocated for his best bud and gently nursed him, making sure his leg brace didn't cut his flesh, that his meals were hot. In addition to family, close friends like Daniel Rey, Dictators' bassman Andy Shernoff, and Jesse Malin rarely left his side. These were the Apostles.

My years in the Post-Ramones Empire had elevated me to a favored scribe. I covered anything new coming out of the scene. I thought of it as community service, something I had to do as a good citizen. On Joey's advice, Rhino hired me to do the liner notes on the reissues of the first two Ramones albums, *Ramones* and *Leave Home*. I listed the shows and album release parties. As always, *Voice* editors indulged my obsession. I covered the release of Ronnie Spector's EP and anything Jayne County was doing. *The Village Voice* is like a bad ex-boyfriend who treats you like shit, but the sex is hot so you always go back for more.

So when *No Exit* was released in 1999, the *Voice* asked me to interview Blondie, New York punk's most commercially successful band. *Almost famous, I'm with the band*, I rode in the limo with Blondie out to Massapequa, Long Island, for the *No Exit* in-store signing at Tower Records. By midday, the mall was overrun by obsessive fans who were children when the band crumbled years ago, the result of infighting, mysterious illness, and bad business. Suburban moms in parkas and black leggings, banana-clipped bi-level cuts, brought in their daughters, six- and nine-year-olds in full parochial school outfits. With their best manners, the beaming kids asked Ms. Harry for her autograph. They grew up hearing the music; they knew exactly who she was.

Body-modified kids mixed it up in raggy NIN T-shirts, green spikes, dog collars. Ravers, jocks, even two members of the North Massapequa Fire Department were making the scene. Cookie from West Babylon told me "Heart of Glass" was her first 45, back in seventh grade; she was the only punk in the dark ages, when the hair bands ruled Long Island. Most of the fans were in their mid- to late twenties, but Brankita, a Lunachicks fan with a Rancid patch, was only fourteen. She and her seventeen-year-old sister, Michelle, were two Croatian teens from Astoria who cut out from Cathedral High to see their idols. They stuck around for the whole four hours. I milled around, taking snapshots, running into old friends.

I'd spent the earlier part of the morning trying to get my hair like Clem Burke's, but it didn't quite work out—I looked like Janet Reno. I needed more body, and my color was off. Sympathetic, Clem advised, "Try Herbatint. It's natural, no ammonia or peroxide." The handsome drummer was wearing a navy blue suit, black shirt, maroon tie, black flat boots. The band was dressed in total Hilfiger, even their shoes. Burke said, "We told Hilfiger we wanted a Rat Pack look. Our biggest score was getting all these clothes from him for free."

Nobody had looked this cool since the Majestic Lords of Coats and Boots (Johnny Thunders and Jerry Nolan) had departed the earth. Chris Stein's silver sharkskin suit matched his hair. For almost a decade, the asexual, loose-fitting "alternative" regalia of grunge culture and hip-hop's droopy drawers had cast a dull cloud over American fashion. Back to the body, I wanted to see boys in tight black leathers again, Jimmy Destri style. Faux skins were even better—thanks to Chrissie Hynde, PETA was now rock & roll. Debbie Harry's elegant black-on-red diva-slut getup knocked everyone out. She was over fifty and stunning as ever. There was hope for humankind. Like Tina Turner, Ronnie, and Keith, Debbie Harry was proof to all aging rockers that we would never have to surrender, never become frumpy, boring, and lame. Think of the future: geriatric rockers in skintight pants, thigh-high boots, eyeliner on everyone, mascara, too. Sterling silver canes, gold-encrusted wheelchairs, fringed enema bags. And imagine what we'll do with a little Crazy Color on silver-white hair.

On the way home from Massapequa I conned Chris Stein into speaking to my Worlds of Youth class at Barnard. Deborah Harry, as she prefers to be called, gave me a Jazz Passengers tape. I gave her a gift, too: a bottle of No Miss nail polish, Florida Orange. I heard that's where she was born. Jimmy Destri and I bonded for life reminiscing over the hitters. His rapturous hit song "Maria" brought me back to the days of *West Side Story,* of forbidden love, race, class, and ethnicity. Destri and I had family ties, too. He'd met Nick's brother at a wedding.

To this day, the Post-Ramones Empire is huge, worldwide. This local scene crossed generations and geographic boundaries, transcending time and space. It was a cretin family of kindred spirits. When I needed a new car, Monte Melnick, the Ramones' longtime road and tour manager, acted as my consultant, helping me to cut a hot deal on a teal blue Toyota Corolla christened the *Mystic Monte.* The Queens-based Monte is a cult figure in his own right, the subject of several tribute bands, including the Melnicks and Monte's Revenge. When I needed a camera for quick stage shots, pioneer punk photographer Bob Gruen flashed his cool Olympus and I was sold. Ida Langsam was the band's longtime publicist. She looks like she just walked out of Carnaby Street. Sometimes we'd meet for kosher sushi, discuss Talmud, cats, and secret strategies for hair care.

Art director Arturo Vega's innovations in band merchandising and on their official website has kept fans connected worldwide. Most crucial, though, are the Ramones legions from Queens to Queensland, people who have tribute 'zines, organize fan clubs, and keep the faith from Hong Kong to Argentina. The multitudes of the Post-Ramones Empire cannot really be measured, but a quick cruise down the information superhighway will give you some idea of the scope.

The people I met backstage with Joey were there for all the shows, for all projects that followed the breakup in 1996, and they were there again at Joey's funeral, at his burial, and at all the postmortem events that have followed his death on April 15, 2001. As sick as he was, Joey put on a great show December 11, 2000, at the Continental. Joey and Marky were backed by Arno Heckt of Uptown Horns, Daniel Rey, Andy Shernoff, Jesse Malin, and Joe McGinty (keyboards). The party continued into the next day at Manitoba's. It was a birthday bash in honor of Evil Presley. It was the last dance.

Woke up thinking 'bout you today, sad and lonely. . . . A few weeks later, on New Year's Eve day, Manhattan was covered with fresh snow. It was risky for Joey to be walking around, but he had cabin fever and refused to let cancer get the best of him. Diagnosed with lymphoma in 1995, Joey fought back, stayed sober, ate health foods; he kept on being Joey Ramone. He was determined to keep his illness a private matter. Friends and family guarded his privacy, and Joey made sure the illness never intruded into his fundamental conviction that "life's a gas." But Joey's bones were brittle from all the years of powerful medications. That day he slipped, fell down, and busted his hip. As he recovered in the New York-Presbyterian Hospital, the lymphoma came raging back from remission. He went into the hospital at the end of December, but for a brief reprieve in February, he never got out. To make matters worse, his father, Noel Hyman, had died just a few months earlier, and Joey was still shattered.

I had spent long afternoons with the two poolside in East Hampton at Nancy's condo. Nancy was Noel's longtime girlfriend. Dressed in our ratty surf-rocker clothes, situated among the demure senior citizens, we felt like retirees in Miami Beach in the 1950s. We ate deli while Noel and Joey fought ruthless games of checkers. Noel always won, Joey always demanded a rematch. Once when we went to Gosman's to pig out on lobsters, some kids slipped out of the kitchen and followed us out. Accelerating their pace, gaining momentum, they caught up to us. I got edgy; we were alone, it was dark, isolated. I had no weapons. But I'd forgotten *who he was*—the kids just wanted his autograph. Driving home on Montauk Highway, "Stairway to Heaven" came on the radio and we harmonized. Well, Joey did. I squawked along.

Sometimes, Joey visited me up in Springs. Mornings we'd scarf down homemade blueberry muffins and coffee, making the scene at the Springs General Store. Evenings we'd stroll through the town of East Hampton searching in vain for decent cappuccinos, stopping in at Alex Echo's art gallery, watching people, checking the movies. We'd hang at Main Beach and scope out the surfers or swim in Bonac Creek (Accabonac Harbor). Once, I was underwater, diving for good mudpack material when I heard Joey's voice. "Uh, Donna, I'm stuck. I can't get my foot out of the mud." We were boroughs kids, terrified of the elements. Rats and roaches we could handle, but oozing gypsy moth carcasses splattered on the sun deck? Forget about it. When Joey finally wrestled free, his sand sock was gone, buried deep in the muck. I tried to retrieve it, snorkeling the creek for hours, but it had disappeared. That night it mysteriously washed up on shore, and there it was, under a tree. My neighbor, a bayman, had fished it out.

Springs was once the bohemian land of De Kooning and Pollock, where local fishermen still sell the fresh catch of the day from their yards, and the light is so breathtaking you have to stop and praise God for such a beautiful world. Once I got sober, I realized there was more to life than deadlines and after-hours bars. My idea of sports was watching Nick shoot pool while I fed the jukebox. I hadn't been out in the sun in almost twenty years. Most arty types go to Woodstock, with its ashrams, recording studios, and covens. East Hampton was the land of Donna Karan and Steven Gaines, not Donna Gaines. Joey had Nancy and Noel, but what the hell was I doing there?

Because of my asthma, I needed to vacate Manhattan during smoggy summers. So I started renting in East Hampton with two friends from the *Voice,* writer Kathy Dobie and photographer James Hamilton. At first I was reluctant, but Kathy drove me out there for the first time in her vintage gray Camaro. We blasted Led Zeppelin on the Long Island Expressway, scarfing cherry Slurpees from the 7-Eleven. I trusted Kathy with my life; I figured if she liked East Hampton, I'd give it a try.

Kathy and James lived in Springs, "north of the highway." Though gentrifying rapidly, for years, the rural enclave was home to a collection of surfers, fishermen, carpenters, healers, skate punk kids, bikers, and animal activists. A little funk in the center of so much soulless materialism. Here, locals (Bonackers), retired dope smugglers, full-moon drummers, people in recovery, and visual artists chilled out, far from the glitz of "Citiots" (local lexicon for urban intruders) with their Range Rovers, cell phones, and bad manners. But Joey Ramone loved it all—the arty funk, the celebrity glamour, the new money and the old, the woods, the deer, and the ocean. Yet even on a sunny day, when the waves were really good, he preferred sitting inside, checking his e-mail, watching Maria on CNBC.

Except for local Bonac Rock City bands like Chum and Mantra, the Hamptons are about as rock & roll as an LL Bean catalogue. Stiff as a Stewart 9′6″ longboard. You might as well be living on Plymouth Rock with the Puritans. But once or twice we did get lucky. When Jonathan Richman played at the Talkhouse in nearby Amagansett, Joey was visiting and Deborah Harry joined the party, too. She had a house in Southampton that year. Another time Joey's brother's band, the Rattlers, did a reunion show at the Maidstone Pavilion. On the beach, under a full moon, the raw sounds of early punk battered the misty sea air. Nineteen seventy-seven revisited, but with monster trucks and fierce-looking mongrel dogs, frosty beer kegs, rock lobsters, and fresh clams. Joey's father, Noel, came, too.

For Sunday afternoon kicks we'd cruise down Lily Pond Lane in Noel and Nancy's Cadillac, checking out the stars' homes. If security stopped us we'd just say Joey was meeting some record company guy and oh gosh, sorry, we must be lost. Then we'd go check the waves at Georgica Beach. The Ramones revered surfing like pizza, TV, and comic books. They even did a benefit for the Surfrider Foundation, a nonprofit worldwide organization that works to keep oceans clean. They contributed a cover of "California Sun" to the first *Surfrider MOM (Music for Our Mother Ocean)* compilation CD. Life in the Post-Ramones Empire had brought me full circle, home to the source, back to Rockaway, surfing, the Beach Boys, glue, and Ronnie

Spector. And now, five years after I met Joey in all his purple glory, he was dying.

Though he had been sick for a long time, Joey always rebounded. After he fell in the snow, though, everything changed. Each week brought new triumphs and defeats. When you visited Joey in the hospital, you never knew if he'd be wiped out in pain, asleep, or laughing on the phone. By Good Friday, April 13, loved ones prepared for the worst. Joey was moved to the intensive care unit, hooked up to a morphine drip. He had a blood infection that wasn't responding to antibiotics, but there was one last round to try, one final hope that things would turn around. With Joey, anything was possible. Bono had called him that day, and although Joey was out of it, hearing from the longtime Ramones admirer made him very happy.

But by Sunday, all hope faded. Friends and family gathered bedside, including Joey's brother, guitarist Mickey Leigh, and their mother, Charlotte. Joey kept a boom box next to his bed, and when he nodded, Mickey played him the U2 song "In a Little While." *In a little while, this will hurt no more. I'll be home, love, in a little while.* When the song ended, Joey was gone.

On Easter Sunday I took the Long Island Railroad out to see Nick and spend the holiday with his family, like I always did. I kept thinking about Joey. I could feel it like I felt it when Betty Bradley was slipping away. I touched her hand and I knew it was time. That year, both Passover and Easter Sunday fell on April 15. It was the Beast's birthday. I imagined Joey crossing over into the great cosmos, with the Beast reaching down for him. As the Long Island Railroad pulled out of Jamaica, I asked the Beast to help lift Joey up. That day, I felt him go. He was forty-nine.

When I first visited Joey at the hospital, I panicked. I felt helpless and useless like I had around my dying parents. I'd witnessed most of life and death from behind a Plexiglas wall. But now all I had to do was show up, just be there, hold his hand. Amuse him with my nonsense. Sit with him while he relished *Spin*'s "25 Years of Punk" issue—he was on the cover. Help figure out what he could eat. Concoct lies for the press. For the first time, I didn't run or hide or seek out Professor Aloy-sius. I stayed right there.

I'd never actually experienced mourning before Joey Ramone died. After Betty, I iced myself with work and chemicals and worrying about D.O.M. Same thing when Mr. Gaines died. I shifted my concern to the surviving parent. I never even considered Herbie a personal loss—that was Betty's, not mine. Swytie, Pablo, Lizzie, Beast—all my grief came flooding up when Joey died. He was a double loss, a cultural hero and a personal friend. He was part of my inner life and my outer experience, a critical link between sacred and profane worlds.

The funeral at Schwartz Brothers Memorial Chapel on Queens Boulevard brought Joey back home to Queens, where the Ramones had formed in 1974. It was a very personal tribute to a public hero. Jewish aunts and uncles grieved along with rock stars, a shattered spectrum of ex-bandmates, DJs, VJs, journalists, club owners, record company ex-ecutives, former girlfriends, and fans. Photographs of Joey from child-hood to fame adorned the closed casket, chronicling his journey from gawky, skinny outcast to punk icon. Sobbing, we sat around swapping Joey stories. How he could answer any obscure rock question in a flash, how he liked toys and Italian girls and sweets and anything Japanese. How generous he was, how he doted on his two young goddaughters, Raven and Millie. How he could make you feel like a little kid, open-ing your heart, giggling and playful. What a dick he could be if you crossed him, and how he always forgave you. A week before he died, he was busy planning a huge fiftieth birthday bash for May 19, coordinat-ing the gig from his hospital room. I was half-waiting for Joey to crash his own funeral, grab the mike, and greet the crowd with a hearty "Hey ho, let's go!"

At the funeral I sat quietly in the back row next to Mr. Bonge. Sur-real, all these people from backstage, from the hospital, sitting in disbe-lief. Vin Scelsa, the first DJ to break the Ramones on New York radio, gave the opening eulogy. He acknowledged Joey Ramone the legend, frontman of the band that ignited punk around the world. Brother Mickey spoke of Jeff Hyman, the man, the shy, sickly son of an artist mother who was constantly picked on in school. Like me, Jeff Hyman had three different fathers—divorce and death whisked them away. Friends recounted how an early life of pain and humiliation was transformed by the love of rock & roll. Rabbi Stephan Roberts described a deeply spiritual man who considered music a miracle of life. Indeed, for twenty-five years Joey walked me through broken hearts and shattered dreams, first from my turntable and later as a friend.

Lord and ruler of the Post-Ramones Empire, Joey would saunter down St. Mark's Place signing autographs for anyone who asked. "I remember meeting certain artists I admired, and them being real obnoxious," Joey told me. "That wasn't how I wanted to be." He never missed a gig either, even when he was sick, exhausted, and hurting. Commando Joe was the spiritual leader of all proud social rejects, warthogs, cretins, and pinheads. But some scars take a lifetime to heal. He was rich and famous, but in his heart Joey Ramone still understood the misfit's suffering, the festering rage that drives kids to self-destruction from Bergenfield to Brownsville, from Compton to Columbine.

May 19, 2001, would have been Joey's fiftieth birthday. In his honor, Charlotte and Mickey organized a huge "Life's a Gas" birthday party for him at the Hammerstein Ballroom. Thirty-five hundred people who loved Joey also attended. Everyone was there. All Joey's favorite bands played, including Blondie, the Damned, and Cheap Trick. Metallica and Bono piped in on video, Steven Van Zandt was master of ceremonies. Jerry Only from the Misfits distributed thousands of Ring-Dings and Devil Dogs, Joey's birthday cake for the masses. Populism from beyond the grave.

At the end of the party, U.S. Representative Gary Ackerman (D-Queens/LI) paid tribute to Joey by presenting Charlotte with an American flag he'd had flown at half-staff over the United States Capitol in memory of Joey Ramone. Ackerman presented the Post-Ramones Empire with a formal proclamation, citing Joey Ramone's "voyage to rock & roll stardom, thrusted from gigs at the New York club CBGB to critical acclaim throughout the world." How Joey "created a musical and cultural revolution by rebelling against mainstream music and pioneering punk rock." How "his leather jacket image and fast three-chord songs influenced the lives of millions of fans while providing the musical formula for countless bands that followed in his footsteps." The congressional proclamation declared May 19 Joey Ramone Day. Joey's minions will celebrate this national holiday forevermore.

Elvis is the King of Rock, Michael Jackson is the King of Pop. Upon his death, Joey Ramone became the King of Punk. All night long at the Hammerstein, kids came over to thank Joey's mother for such a great show, for the opportunity to mourn, for giving the world her son, Joey Ramone. People flew in from Los Angeles, Germany, Tokyo, and Brazil. NutJob flew in from Long Island, and my Barnard students showed up, too. Two generations of Ramones fans, everyone there in a spirit of unity. Joey's fiftieth-birthday jubilee was a night of miracles and rejoicing.

At four A.M., as we stood outside, a lone girl approached me and asked if the slender lady with the piercing eyes and dark pixie bob was in fact Charlotte Lesher. The girl began sobbing, trying to explain to Joey's mom how she had been an outcast, an alien in her small Ohio town, how Joey's music saved her, how she'd be dead without him. Charlotte was overwhelmed. She knew Joey had devoted fans, that he was a world-famous rock star. But I doubt even Joey himself could fathom how much he meant to us. Joey was our leper messiah, our Savior. By simply being himself, he stuck up for all of us. All the kids who don't fit in, who feel shut out, put down, and alone. He's there for us all. Some people have a friend in Jesus. We have one in Joey Ramone—eternal, immortal, forever, *oh ye-ah, oh ye-ah, oh ye-ah.*

JOEY RAMONE
1951–2001

In the mid-'70s, the Ramones changed the sound of rock music forever. Punk rock was born. Since then, whether playing a small club like this one or stadiums, Joey always stayed true to his roots, his fans, and the music. Joey never turned down an autograph request, and no one has ever supported a local scene more than Joey and his beloved New York City. New York and especially the Lower East Side loved him right back. It's hard to imagine the future without him. Thank God we've got the music to listen to whenever we want to, especially when we need to. Joey's last show was here at the Continental, December 11, 2000. His spirit will live on here and all over the world forever.

Trigger's memorial plaque, the Continental, NYC

Johnny Bully (right) and his bandmates, NYC, 2000.

16

MY BEST-KEPT SECRETS

The day is thine, the night also is thine;
thou hast prepared the light and the sun.

—PSALMS 74:16

One night I had a vision. It came to me in a dream state, though I think I was actually awake. On the wood floor, a mass of hot pink ooze appeared. A luminous blob, shimmering, glowing, pulsating with light. I knew it to be *pure love.* A gentle voice spoke to me, "Everything you need is in your heart. All the answers to the universe are there. Just go inside." In that moment, eternal truth blasted me out of one life and into another. Almost twenty years had passed since that long night in San Francisco, when I cried out for God and Jesus came to comfort me. But this was different; God came to me *uncalled.* From that day on, I was born again, though not specifically in Jesus Christ.

It happened shortly after I'd moved to New York City. Who knows how or why? By then, I'd accomplished my life's goal—to be free. I had no family, no religion, no fixed occupation, no connection. I was an

itinerant soul, a subcontractor on the astral plane. Smug in my alienation, I had a critical edge, the outsider's advantage. I had built a career
on it. I wasn't looking for anything. I thought I had it all, moving mer-
rily along, still drinking too much, working too hard, boy-toying,
nightclubbing, popping an occasional rooster for Thunderella. I had no
thoughts of redemption. And yet God came.

Spiritual awakening is a lifelong journey, an ongoing process we can
accelerate or suppress. For some people, it happens gradually, as a result
of structured spiritual practice—meditation, prayer. For others, it is the
result of bottoming out on an addiction, of working the Twelve Steps
of Alcoholics, Narcotics, Overeaters, or Gamblers Anonymous. Some
people stumble upon God in a psychotic break, as a revelation in a pey-
ote dream, or at the bottom of a K-hole. When it happened, I wasn't
doing anything unusual. I was just minding my own business and God
appeared.

Psychics say some souls do reincarnate within the same lifetime.
One dies, another is reborn. Maybe I got lucky, maybe God got tired of
bailing me out. It was like, *Okay, sweetie, the party's over. I want you
back.* Maybe this blip in my spiritual condition occurred as the result of
an extra teaspoon of sugar in my morning coffee. A norepinephrine
rush, the hormonal imbalances associated with perimenopause, a
midlife crisis or postmillennial ennui. I still don't know what really happened, maybe I never will. But suddenly, I needed new answers to the
Old Big Ones: Who am I? What am I doing here? What is the meaning of life? Beavis and Butt-head on air guitar, live at the Ashram,
AAAUUUMMM!

The night the big pink blob appeared, I experienced a transformative leap to a higher consciousness. Gradually, everything began to
change. William James writes in *The Varieties of Religious Experience*
that without hopelessness, great spiritual awakening is unlikely. Usually, at the end of their rope, tormented souls are famous for finding
God. Bottoming out, AA founder Bill W. experienced a spiritual awakening, which he described in the "Big Book," *Alcoholics Anonymous:* "I
was soon to be catapulted into what I like to call the fourth dimension
of existence. I was to know happiness, peace, and usefulness, in a way

of life that is incredibly more wonderful as time passes." For me, it was more like, *Yikes!! I've had a fucking God experience!!!*

Nobody cared if I drank too much. It was expected. It made great copy and situated me among a long tradition of literary drunks and cultural outlaws. By now, even going to AA meetings was considered rock & roll. Sobriety was the final rite of passage, proof that you'd lived on the edge. Everyone knew Ozzy, Alice Cooper, Lou Reed, Eric Clapton, and most Ramones were sober. When Aerosmith's Steven Tyler got a Grammy, he publicly thanked his "higher power." But Big Pink came to me *before* I stopped drinking, *before* I ever surrendered to Alcoholics Anonymous.

And it happened in Manhattan, a landscape dressed in black. Rude, aggressive, cynical, urban chic, I was an intellectual, a woman of science, an antipatriarchal feminist. Now I had a real problem. How would I "come out" about God? It seemed so tacky. Imagine, even now, telling my colleagues at the university, at the *Voice,* at the Continental *that I pray every day?* That now I *know* every love song is secretly about God? And what about D.O.M. and Nick? Would they think I was some New Age crackpot, or worse, an airhead? I didn't care. I wanted that light.

I have Plutonian willpower, so breaking another bad habit was no big deal. It didn't matter if I was clinically alcoholic or if booze was the liquid form of my lifelong sugar addiction. I was messed up. I needed a new structure, guidelines for managing my overwhelming obsessions and compulsions. I quit drinking on January 26, 1997, on a promise to Nick. I understood, too, that that was also a promise to God, an unspoken pact. I knew if I broke it, I'd lose contact forever. I'd be hurled back into the old life with no chance of a return. Resolute, absolute, I journeyed forth.

The Post-Ramones Empire offered temporary shelter, but by June, I realized it would take more than club soda and iron will to stay sober. So I found myself a spiritual community. My new street-smart, worldwide Fellowship of men and women didn't care whether I thought God was a snapping turtle, a vintage Harley, or an oozing pink blob on my floor. Maybe this God thing didn't have to make any sense.

And now, after all these years, I belonged to a congregation again. But unlike Beth-El, my church basement meetings occasionally featured some very attractive Celtic-American gentlemen. They say once you've gone over, you never come back. By the grace of God, many women can recover from alcoholism, but few will return from a taste of the Blarney. Hmmm, maybe I was really in heaven!

Anonymity is the cornerstone of Twelve Step spirituality. It encourages a humility that allows people to bypass social differences like race, class, sex, and gender preference. The focus shifts to what we human beings have in common. People from all walks of life belong—celebrities, housewives, cross-addicted jocks, artists, crack whores, surfers, investment bankers, dykes, priests, leather queens, and rabbis. Nobody there knew much about my outside life. The person I brought into the rooms of AA was not Tessa on the guest list or Dr. Donna Gaines who wrote a book. It was the little fat kid, the trembling, dysfunctional mess I'd buried in all my accomplishments and personae.

On spiritual grounds, members of Twelve Step programs are discouraged from promoting or discussing the Fellowship in public forums. So let me simply say this: Whether I went to meetings in East Hampton, New York City, San Diego, or South Florida, people there embraced the little fat kid unconditionally. She cried, ranted, and raved, talked trash, and she was still welcomed.

In *The Elementary Forms of Religious Life*, published in 1912, sociologist Emile Durkheim distinguishes between the sacred and the profane. The profane world is empirically knowable, experienced directly through the senses. This is the "natural" world we grasp with varying degrees of comprehension. The sacred exists above and beyond the sensate world; it is unknowable. It fills us with awe; it cannot be fully understood, measured, or proved. It creates fear, terror, a relentless desire to dominate and control. The sacred world requires our surrender and faith. It is larger than anything we are, everything we comprehend. The most we can hope for is a fleeting glimpse. Gradually, my sense of God was ever-present. I couldn't explain it, I refused to defend it.

They say religion is for people who are afraid of going to hell and spirituality is for the ones who've already been there. While I do respect the spiritual foundations of all religions, my experience had little to do with organized religion. My understanding of God was not the abstract, angry, judging deity imagined in my childhood, the wrathful ruler who made my loved ones suffer and die, condemning me to a life of loneliness and self-hatred. The God of my spiritual awakening was neither a big butch sky god nor a flowery granola goddess of unconditional acceptance and love. This universal force had no name or face. It came unmediated, as a direct contact, a Great Spirit found in nature, fleeting yet undeniable, present in all living things yet invisible. I couldn't touch it or taste it, but it connected everyone and everything, inside and out, everywhere, at all times.

Geneticists and family therapists can tell us why we become addicts. Sociologists and psychologists can tell us what causes self-alienation, what obscures our connection to our own truth. But only metaphysics can begin to explain why some of us are called back. Why do some of us survive, even against our own will? Why am I here now, happy, healthy, and safe while so many of my friends and family are dead, casualties of the life? Warriors who died trying to find God in endless elixirs, powders, tonics, and nights of pirate love. There had to be a rational explanation.

According to my astrologer, the gloomy planet Saturn was transiting my natal sun in the Ninth House—the sphere of activity that governs the higher mind, philosophical and religious experience. Saturn passed over my sparkling Aries sun from November 1996 to January 1997—*exactly when I was bottoming out.* Saturn is known as the Lord of Karma, whose energy clears away whatever is outworn and useless to our spiritual path. A challenging Saturn transit will break down any obsolete structure or belief system blocking our journey. Marriages, jobs, and faith systems will collapse in its wake and we will be forced to confront reality. Alternatively, if the soul is traveling the right path, things will stabilize. Either way, a Saturn transit is a sobering experience, and mine was literally.

As my old life died, a new one replaced it. Heeding Saturn's call, I wanted to eliminate anything that separated me from this purified sense of God. There can be great transformative healing power at the bottom of our deepest wounds, so that's where I was headed. I had to rethink everything. When I was bottoming out, I wrote some lyrics that were later incorporated into "Rock and Roll Is Dead," a Brain Surgeons song on their *Piece of Work* album: *I hate everything, I hate everyone, there is no god, and rock and roll is dead.* But this wasn't just an attitude or a pose. I really did hate everything—most of all, myself. And that was a secret, even to me.

At one point I drifted into a New Age Expo. Sleepwalking through the arena, I stumbled upon a healer. It was so arbitrary and random, I have no idea what spiritual tradition or religion she represented. As the healer's hands scanned over my body, she stopped abruptly at the center of my chest. Chakras are energy centers in the body, places where we receive, process, and transmit life energies. According to the Legion of Light, "The heart chakra anchors the life-force from the Higher Self. Energizes the blood and physical body with the life-force, blood circulation." It rules the heart, thymus gland, circulatory system, arms, hands, and lungs.

I had been recently diagnosed with asthma and thyroid dysfunction. I could barely breathe, like I had barbells on my chest. I was always tired, sluggish. I had poor circulation, too. I would wake up each morning with no sensation in my hands; they were dead, numb. My nose and feet were always cold. I usually attributed such symptoms to bad genes or hangovers. There were occupational hazards, too: long nights in smoky clubs, too much hair spray, sitting at the keyboard too long. But there was more to it.

"There is no energy coming from your fourth chakra. It's completely black," the healer explained. Then she asked me to close my eyes, go inside myself, and quiet the mind. To visualize my poisoned heart. "Talk to it," she suggested. I described what I saw; I was a bystander, utterly powerless against human misery, loss, and sorrow. Dead loved ones rotting away from cancer, AIDS, and addiction. All the war crimes of humanity against itself: the Holocaust, the Crucifixion, queer-bashing, homelessness, high school, rape, animal medical experiments, child abuse. As the story in my heart unfolded, I jumped the track. I became more theoretical, displacing my sorrow. How can we do these things? Why do we allow them? She stopped me cold. "Okay, now you're getting away from it, you're moving from the source. Try to keep it personal."

When I finished, she asked me to repeat an affirmation, "I believe that the world is a safe place. I believe there is love for me in this world." I just said the words. I didn't believe them or even understand them. The healer explained that my heart had shut down from grief and if I didn't open it, I would die. My prana was jammed, I had to learn how to breathe, how to love, how to trust life. I had to find faith. I didn't have a clue where to begin, I barely grasped her message. The shimmering pink blob had instructed me to look inside. Now it was time to start. The healer said, "You've been hiding in a bunker, you're beginning to peek out, you're slowly looking around."

As a child, I'd often wake up terrified. Sometimes it just happened for no reason at all. Hours before dawn, my heart racing, my breathing so shallow, I saw dots. Cramps in my sacral plexus, spasms. Then my stomach exploded, waves of panic expelled into the polished suburban toilet bowl. Over and over, four, five times until it was light out and I finally passed out, exhausted. I never told anyone, not even my mother. I assumed this was normal, my private hell, my punishment for being. By the time I was an adult, the panic attacks were no longer nocturnal. They happened anytime, anywhere. Sometimes I'd double up in spasms, I'd have to call in sick, call an ambulance, grab quick for my medication. Drinking, too, calmed the crippling anxiety. A quick shot and I felt warm and safe.

Our bodies speak truth when we cannot. The third chakra is the solar plexus, above the navel, below the chest. It governs the sympathetic nervous system, digestive processes, the emotions, the stomach, and muscles. It's the energy center of personal power, of the will. Like me, my mother and grandmother experienced dread in the belly. Powerless against fear, both needed medication for nervous stomachs, digestive disorders.

Imagine growing up wondering which of four sisters is Daddy's favorite lover? Who is most beautiful, most charming, the smartest? You don't really exist. Serving *him* is all that matters. Your will negated, your power usurped for his sake. My grandmother, Miriam the Cow, retreated into a fantasy world of ceramic animals and costume jewelry. Then she looked the other way while her own daughter was sacrificed. She lived out her life as a shadow being, narcissistic and vindictive.

My mother was Betty Bradley, glamorous star, Hollywood's Lush Thrush, Cinderella standing in the spotlight of Cretin jealousy. In the Ulanovs' comprehensive study *Cinderella and Her Sisters* we see how envy spoils goodness, devastates and disintegrates the psyche of both the envied and envious. The Cretin death gaze was all about envy—the negation of empathy, of subjective experience, the absence of mercy. Poisoned by envy, punished by life, toxic with grief, at sixty-eight the center of her belly exploded, and my mother died of stomach cancer.

II

Over the years I had accumulated knowledge—metaphysics, politics, cultural analysis, feminism, and organized religion. I'd gathered tools for understanding the social world. Sex, drugs, and rock & roll also helped open the doors of perception. I'd spent a lifetime studying alienation, mastering it, lamenting it, all the while steering clear of people. Watching life from behind a Plexiglas wall.

If I had attempted this inquiry any sooner, I wouldn't have had the courage or strength to face what I saw. I would have run away, hidden from it, mocked it with sarcasm and irony. Inside was a sad little fat girl in orthopedic shoes and oversized clothes, sitting alone, waiting. Afraid to make waves, ashamed to ask for anything, stuffing, swallowing instead. I'd iced her out years ago. Now she was back, issuing ultimatums, *If you don't let me live, I'm taking you down with me.* My entire presentation of self was predicated on being cool, above it all. I gagged at the thought of dealing with my fucked-up "inner child." Ugh! How could I be reduced to such a stupid cliché? And yet, I was terrified of facing her.

After Betty Bradley died, D.O.M. went on a tear. He ripped up all my "fat pictures." He wanted no reminders. It had been his military victory to make me normal, thin, to have rescued me from a childhood of neglect, trauma, and shame. He called me his "champion," a survivor who walked away from a bad beginning and emerged victorious. The fat-kid photo album was evidence of the damage done, a dirty secret to be kept to myself. Like my dad, the world now saw me as smart, beautiful, and successful. One doting boyfriend actually imagined me growing up as a pretty girl-child with long dark braids, sitting at her coloring book, dainty, her tongue slightly curled over her top lip in concentration. Oh, if he only knew. D.O.M. was the lone remaining witness to my years of humiliation and he wanted them destroyed.

Luckily, after the bonfire, a few photos survived. I took one out and engaged the little fat kid, talking to her like she was my daughter, like one of my students. Someone young, filled with hope and optimism, dreams and plans. I saw all the good in her, told her I was proud of her, proud to *be* her. I walked with her to the mirror, I showed the little fat kid who she'd become, who I am today. I thanked her for keeping the faith, for waiting until I could come back for her. I would give everything to her that my mother could not give me. What her mother couldn't give to her, what her mother's mother couldn't, all the way back to the original wounded mother. I'd protect and guide her, love her like I loved my students. I'd instruct her, root for her. I was on her side, no matter what.

Over time, I aborted the hurtful voices that told her she was a fat piece of shit, that nobody would ever love her, that she deserved to be alone and unhappy. There is a lethal gaze that every shamed child feels. It tells you there is something essentially wrong with you. This stain on your being can never be cleansed. It marks you for life as unlovable, worthless, and undeserving of joy. Loving my students helped me to reverse that.

I never wanted children, not born in my heart or my belly. Damaged people generally fear passing on their disease. I was afraid of failing, of hurting them like I'd hurt Nick. And then, what if I lost them, if they died? I knew I couldn't survive that.

I also feared losing myself. I enjoy solitude and freedom. My idea of a perfect moment was sitting alone quietly at my desk, just thinking. To achieve this simple state of grace had taken a lifetime of planning. I cherished what I had. Like everyone who makes a choice, at the end of my childbearing years I reflected back on my decision to remain un-married and childless. I wondered if I'd missed something. What was it like, that overwhelming feeling parents describe when they first hold their baby? When their child looks up at them so completely trusting, innocent, and vulnerable?

In 1995, when I wrote "Jews in Cyberspace," the *Voice* article about the Lubavitchers online, I met with Rabbi Anschelle Perl, the dynamic head of Congregation Beth Shalom, the Chabad House in Mineola. He called me Devorah Leah, my Hebrew name, never Donna Louise. Jew-ish law does not recognize conversion out—whether to sociology, rock & roll, or a big pink oozing blob. Even an armful of tattoos cannot nul-lify *neshuma*—a Jewish soul. Once a Jew, always a Jew. "No, Rabbi," I explained, "I'm not married, and I don't have children. In fact, I haven't been to shul since the 1970s. No, I don't observe *Shabbas* or keep kosher." Then there were the Catholic boys, the tattoos, the penta-grams, and my relationship with Jesus. But by not having children, I'd defied a central mandate of Judaism: "Be fruitful and multiply." The rabbi reassured me with a loophole: If I taught the law to children, that was a great *mitzvah*—a righteous deed, a fulfillment of obligation, ser-vice to G-d and Israel.

My Barnard students were, of course, not my own children. And most of them were not Jewish. Although Durkheim, the father of soci-ology, was descended from French rabbis, much of what I passed on to young people had little to do with *Yiddishkeit.* Reflecting back on my conversation with Rabbi Perl, I now realized how blessed I'd been. I'd fulfilled my promise to myself and to the greater good. I'd tended to young people on the streets, in the courtroom, and in the classroom. If I had been a man I might have become a rabbi. But I was born a woman, so I followed Durkheim's path instead. A generation later, for-mal sociology kept its promise, and so had the feminist movement.

III

To the world I was a sociologist who studied human behavior, under-stood the motivations of the social actor, the relationship between structure and agency—individual action in the context of social order. But offstage, Dr. Donna Gaines had no clue how to actually get along with people. In fact, all the skills that made a rigorous scholar—scientific objectivity, critical distance, intellectual detachment—reinforced the Plexiglas wall that separated me from other humans. I had unconsciously self-selected into an occupation that offered me an emotionally sheltered life, that kept me feeling safe.

By now, my idea of a "relationship" was something to kill time between deadlines. Friends, too, were kept at a distance, a Panel of Experts in cyberspace carefully regulated in time and space. Yes, I was there for them, available for emergencies, crisis intervention, and pep talks. But I rarely spent "quality time" with anyone, just kicking back, chilling. I was too busy working, comatose, or trancing out at the foot of the stage. Social integration is the antithesis of alienation. But integration means engagement, and that threw me into a real quagmire.

When I saw how I hurt Nick, I realized what love was for the first time. It wasn't sexual or even romantic. I had an awareness of another person, separate from my bottomless pit of need and dependency. There was more to loving than shooting someone up my arm. More than lyrics, Hallmark cards, or multiple orgasms. In trying to repair the harm I'd done to Nick, I understood that my capacity to love was stronger than my addiction. But only if I was willing to believe it.

As I migrated away from the hidden injuries of my youth, my life was changing so drastically. Strangers embraced me with open, loving arms. I found a world of people who were nice to me, unconditionally accepting, inclusive. I had no reason to run. I've had opportunities all along the way to belong, and still I pulled away, I declined. Mostly, I fled in terror.

In his classic work *Suicide*, Durkheim demonstrated how suicide rates varied inversely with the degree of social integration. The greater the degree of disengagement, the higher the risk. When a society is strongly integrated, when people feel strongly "a part of," they are held in check, cushioned from the impact of frustrations and tragedies that can wipe us out. We're less likely to resort to suicide when we feel a sense of belonging. As horrible as it is, *we need other people*. Interaction, participation in rituals, shared values and beliefs and work activities that foster cooperation keep us connected. Without some common faith, a *conscience collective,* we are doomed. It doesn't matter if it's a Twelve Step Fellowship, a religion, or a subculture. If it happens when you're singing "Amazing Grace" in a church choir or pumping your fist at a Slayer show, without it, we're lost. Too much personal autonomy from the group, too much isolation, can lead to a suicide solution.

The higher the level of individualism, the greater the risk of alienation and suicide. Johnny Thunders's misanthropic masterpiece "So Alone" expresses that feeling of abject, solitary suffering. From Durkheim to Thunders, this truth permeates all our societal institutions—integrate or isolate, live together or die alone.

To my dismay, I often found social interaction excruciating, tedious, and intrusive. Social groups were greedy and possessive. I couldn't win, according to Durkheim, I was doomed or damned. By nature, I'm a loner, I "need space," I think more clearly without the imposition of other people. Sometimes after prolonged human interaction, I feel like my brains are being sucked out of my ears. It's like my friend Anthony says, "Being around other people can be very stressful." I enjoy solitude. Creativity would be impossible without it.

But solitude and loneliness are not the same. Solitude is healthy. It allows a meditative state, the quietude needed for communing with a higher power, for accomplishing serious works of art or science. It is essential to human existence. Loneliness is deadly. It tells me I am unwanted and unnecessary. It makes me feel ashamed and pathetic. I felt that way for most of my life. I assumed it was normal.

When asked why he did sociology, Max Weber once commented, "To see how much I can take." The more clearly I grasped the social world and its processes, the creepier I felt. Why was I at once obsessed with community yet repulsed by it? Simultaneously filled with remorse yet joyous that after a lifetime, I was still free, still on the road, searching. I lived in America like I was down in the jungles of Brazil with Lévi-Strauss. A psychotherapist once attributed my behavior to an "inability to commit," a "fear of intimacy," and "terror of rejection," the result of an overbearing, devouring mother and dead, disappearing, distant fathers. These are universal themes, challenges that many humans face. It is in the nature of nurture to be caught short, needing something more. Unfortunately, I got slammed too soon, too hard, too often, and without explanation.

The shrink made good sense, up to a point. Psychoanalysis generally proceeds from a gloomy assumption of individual pathology, and I sure had my share. Alcoholics, too, are people who like to "isolate," who often feel "less than" and apart from other people. We take special pride in being different, "terminally unique," a huge ego coupled with low self-esteem. But what if my social distortion was also rooted in something else?

I needed a macro-theory, so I hit up an astrologer for a metaphysical fix on my existential dilemma. He studied the aspects and placements in my natal horoscope and concluded, "Horseshit! You have no problems with intimacy or commitment. It's fear of losing your freedom that keeps you on guard." I longed for community and connection but when I got it, I couldn't breathe, had no room to move. Like a moth to the flame, we crave the very thing what will destroy us. Community meant a gradual surrendering of individuality. This paradox is one of the greatest challenges of the Aquarian Age—to experience the integrity of one's own individuality within community, to belong without being swallowed, dominated, and controlled. Cooperation without subordination to collective will.

According to sociologist Bennett Berger, "Every soul understands the yearning for community, but we also know that being a central member carries a very high price: *They own you.*" He explains, "Compliance is the price of membership, and that perspective transforms our alienation from a vice to a virtue." Forging a new paradigm for our age, Berger argues, "In the postmodern world, we all have multiple identities, we establish ties with other people, with people like us." We have fractured memberships. He says, "It all depends on how we see ourselves at the moment. Whatever draws you closer to yourself." According to Berger, our marginality as sociologists is "both a sadness and a strength."

For me, alienation has been a double-edged sword, at once a gift and an albatross. Berger and my astrologer concurred. I wasn't afraid of commitment, I had no problem being devoted, intimate, or loyal. I was afraid of being hijacked, taken hostage. At any moment, I could run screaming into the night, cringing, queasy, compelled to resist. I couldn't risk getting caught, being stuck, fixed in any one time or place. All growth would end, all possibility would cease. Apparently, I wasn't the only one caught in the quagmire.

For Durkheim, altruistic suicide was the opposite of egoistic suicide. In an egoistic suicide, we are insufficiently integrated, we're loners, serial killers cut off from the group. So alone, tattooed Jews, scavengers without roots or relations. Where lack of social integration can be fatal, overintegration can be equally deadly, leading to suicide. Once a community owns you, they'll peel off your identity, smother you in a web of affiliation, and gradually displace your goals with theirs. We are enriched by membership in the group as we are depleted. Cults, therapeutic communities, professions, congregations, complex organizations, small towns—they're all needy, greedy institutions. The pressure to cooperate, to conform, is relentless, to subordinate self-interest for the "good of the group." The individual is sucked into a vortex, trapped behind the Berlin Wall, locked in an iron cage, no exit. Engagement always carries the risk of entrapment. Sartre understood it well; hell is other people.

Just as excessive individualism leads the lone wolf to suicide, *insufficient individualism* produces the same effect. In essence, the lack of individuality is caused by total absorption into the group. Altruistic suicide is the most extreme form of self-sacrifice, as in the case of the martyr or the kamikaze. Self-sacrifice becomes a duty, an obligation to the group. Durkheim noted that altruistic suicides were rare in contemporary societies because, he argued, the "individual personality is increasingly freed from the collective personality." That leaves us sitting on a fence, somewhere between the Son of Sam and Jesus the Martyr.

Participation in group consciousness was as alien to my nature as sex without alcohol. But according to astrologer Liz Greene in her book *Saturn,* "Group consciousness is not mass consciousness, for with the former the contribution is voluntary and the worth of the individual is not lost." So I decided to give it a try. Just to see, like Max Weber, how much I could stand.

Being an only child can be a great asset for a writer. I could spend weeks alone, weaving narratives, enjoying my own company. But when I did go out, I had to be larger than life, cranked up to ten, performing like my showbiz mom. Professor Gaines had to be "on" or absent—there was nothing in between. Directing the narrative or watching it. I couldn't just be part of it. I had street wisdom, but no basic social skills. I could handle the world as a hostile enemy to be conquered, but I had no clue how to *just be,* how to go with the flow. The basic process of human cooperation and quotidian interdependence completely eluded me. Anyone who grows up in a family, around people, intuitively understands this stuff. For me it was like some great mystery.

In time, God would restore everything I'd lost and give me many things I'd never had. For some people, the talking cure goes just so far. I wasn't going to learn about human interaction from reading about it in books, or hearing about it in songs, church basements, ashrams, or synagogues. I would only discover it first person, in *relationships*—a thought that repelled and frightened me. I would have to learn life's lessons the way I did sociology; through lived experience, out in the field, out in the street. So I took a stage dive out of the books, out of my head and into real time.

The simplest things terrified me, like cooking dinner or making percolated coffee for thirty people. I cringed at the idea. But it was okay to be inept and clueless, we all start out that way. Had I grown up around siblings, I might have known about such mysteries. But there was no shame, I could learn. Sharing the summer house with Kathy Dobie and James Hamilton in East Hampton was a first big step. There, with other writers, artists, and misfits in the quasi-bohemian stronghold of Springs, I had started practicing normal human interaction. Over the years I spent with them, their idyllic country setting became my halfway house, a personal training school for participation in the human race.

I had no frame of reference for activities that most people took for granted. Hell-bent for leather, I'd never bothered with dinner parties, b-o-r-i-n-g! Nick and I barely ate, not until we were blasted. And then it was just a slice of pizza at four A.M. But at the Springs house, I'd watch James cooking, chopping herbs, carefully selecting ingredients. It never occurred to me that food was anything more than a tranquilizer I shoved into my face until I relaxed. I sat for hours transfixed by the sight of people milling around, helping out in the kitchen, mowing the lawn, sweeping the deck; Kathy tending her garden, James framing photos for the upstairs hall. They'd come and go, attending to their tasks, exchanging pleasantries. At first it baffled me. I wasn't used to prolonged exposure to large groups of people. Like how do they know what to say?

So I studied my housemates like an anthropologist, an outsider trying to understand an alien culture. Kathy grew up in a big family, the oldest girl. Sometimes she coached me gently, quietly, like she was teaching me how to kayak or garden. Joining in, I slowed down, gradually lowered the volume. It didn't matter if I had nothing to say; it was okay. I didn't have to be fabulous, perform slick tricks to be noticed or to convince myself that I existed. I could just be there and that was *enough*.

Like the Springs summer house, life in the Post-Ramones Empire had imparted some useful social skills. But both were intentional communities, not blood relations. I wondered what was it like to belong to a large group of people who looked just like you, backed you up, hung in during the bad times? To just go with the flow around a dinner table, to wake up, day after day and still see them there. I've never been afraid of death, but I was petrified of being sick, alone with nobody to watch out for me. I would rather be dead then defenseless.

Terror of abandonment in the hour of final agony was why I'd salvaged my mother's Dilaudids after she died. It wasn't to get high. I was hoarding them for my eventual suicide. I thought of it as auto-euthanasia, self-empowerment. Given my gene pool, cancer seemed inevitable. I had seen the horror. When my time came, I didn't want to be caught short, forced to depend on some merciless hospital regime. Hedging my bets, I joined the Hemlock Society, an organization dedicated to helping people die with dignity, on their own terms. Live free and die proud. Civil liberties from cradle to grave.

D.O.M. and Aunt Rose loved me like I was their own. They treated me like blood. For over twenty years, Nick's big Italian family included me in every holiday. They never forgot my birthday; they called if I was sick. They considered me kin. I had deep and meaningful connections, but that taken-for-granted genetic link still eluded me. True, I had never known my biological father, but most of my Denmark cousins were still alive. Why couldn't I reach out to them? I didn't have to sit around feeling sorry for myself, *nobody loves me, poor me.* So I took action, I did an Internet search and located Mort, the oldest of fifteen first cousins.

Twenty years my senior, Mort moved to California when I was a kid. I barely remembered meeting him. He said he'd been trying to locate me for years, but of course I had an unlisted number. Mort sent me our family tree, photos of my parents, and eventually he organized a family reunion. Herbie was one of eight, the youngest male. In addition to all my first cousins, there were second, third, and fourth cousins. They lived all over the country. A few were therapists, one was a rabbi, there were homemakers, writers, radio hosts, captains of industry, and artists, too. We rallied at a hotel in San Diego, all these people who looked like me. Together we represented a spectrum of social class and political opinion. Three cousins were named in memory of my father—one Joan and two Herberts.

The Denmarks were very animated people, always laughing, hugging, and touching, warm-hearted like Italians. Most of us love to eat, especially rich, creamy foods. Among us were a few sugar fiends, some addicts, too. In my cousins I recognized the faces of all my aunts and uncles. My favorite cousin, Bobby, was also at the reunion. Looking at him now, I realized how much he looked like Herbie. Bonding over food like we did as children at the Park Manor, oldest cousins recalled the catering hall in its entire splendor, a prominent Brooklyn Jewish family with influence and clout. The youngest mainly remembered the funerals. But there we were together in San Diego, joyful, celebrating life.

As we gathered around platters of fried wontons, shrimp quesadillas, and cold sesame noodles, I learned I wasn't the only one with lifelong body dysmorphia. Other female cousins had "body issues," too. In fact, one became an expert on eating disorders. Since we all grew up going to funerals, watching our parents wiped out by cancer, I wasn't the only one who pushed people away, fearful of loss and inevitable abandonment. Some of my cousins also lived behind the Plexiglas wall. Families are the keepers of our secret histories, a critical link to the collective guts and glory. I always thought it was "just me." Now I know whatever it is, it's never "just me."

On the second day of the Denmark reunion a miracle happened. Nobody called to get together. I felt a little sad, but I figured my cousins were busy with their own kids and grandchildren. I accepted my fate and organized my day. Summertime, the surf in San Diego sucks, something about the Gulf of Mexico and winds from Canada. Surfers can get picky about the waves, when they're too messy or small they'll pass. But I'm a lowly, smurf-riding, grommet sponge monkey—a novice bodyboarder, so I'll jump anything. Six inches of white foam if I have to. I rented a car and drove north to La Jolla, praying for swells.

On the way up, I stopped off to visit with the distinguished Professor Bennett Berger. He had saved my ass years ago when, like most college students, I struggled with an identity crisis. Now I needed a critical theory for surviving middle age. By thirty, society expects you to be set on who you are, to know where you belong. Social order depends upon individual stability and predictability. In an essay published in 1968 titled "The Identity Myth," Berger observed that society tolerates the "search for identity" in younger people because we view it as an age-graded, not a general cultural value. "Finding yourself" is considered an indulgence of youth, not a necessary lifelong spiritual quest.

In exposing the identity myth, Berger challenged social psychologist Erik Erikson's normative stage theory of identity formation. Where Erikson believed all humans must go through fixed stages of development, Berger leaned toward "flexible psyches" that would undergo on-going transformations throughout the life cycle. Berger's theory liberated me from feeling like a loser because I kept switching careers. At Barnard I assigned "The Identity Myth" to my students so they could survive parental interrogation at holiday break: "So Missy, what are you going to be when you grow up?" I had built my empire on a flexible psyche. By now it permeated everything—jobs, paradigms, god concepts, food choices, scenes, subcults. A generation later, my life had substantiated Berger's theory. In turn, his perspectives made me feel good about myself. So I wanted to thank him personally.

The professor and I chomped on hefty chicken burritos in a nearby strip mall and posed for photos near the Mormon Temple, a breathtaking palace that glistened like the lost city of Atlantis. As we sat ringside at the suburban parking lot, we pondered the current condition of sociology, humanity, and coastal variations in guacamole. When I left, Berger gave me a big hug and said, "Visit me anytime, Donna. You're one of my people."

Yes, these were my people now—American scholars, social critics like Berger, the Binary Boy, Barbara Ehrenreich, Ellen Willis, and Stanley Aronowitz. They navigated the social world, sharing their findings with joy and sorrow. When I was lost or troubled about anything from the personal to the sociological, these were the people I turned to. They had answers, they knew me, accepted me, and loved me too.

After lunch, I hit the beach and spent the day communing with the water people of the earth. *Surfinbrrrds*—longboarders, shortboarders, bodyboarders, and bodysurfers. I borrowed a Wave Rebel board off some guys I met at Cardiff and got some of the best rides of my life. Stoked, on the way back to the reunion I hit the surf shops, pricing SoCal's finest bodyboards. I picked up a silver toe ring for Cousin Doris, a Hawaiian shirt for Nick, and a slick black Xcel UV Ultra-stretch neoprene-laminated rash guard. That shirt would keep me warm in New York waters and protect me from burns if I skidded into sand. The world was wide open. Yes, my cousins had their lives, but hey, I had mine too.

When I came back to the hotel that evening, my cousins rushed over excitedly. "Donna, where have you been?" They'd tried calling me all morning, hoping to invite me to brunch, to the beach, shopping, sightseeing. Three or four clusters of cousins were looking for me, wanting to hang out. I forgot that I'd asked the front desk to block my calls. Jetlagged, I wanted to sleep in that morning. Unfortunately the hotel operator never removed the block. Nobody could get through. Self-pity ablaze, I assumed my cousins forgot about me, that I was still the outsider, marginal, superfluous. It was my lot in life, my fate to walk alone. But it *wasn't*. It was all in my head. I was the one making myself miserable. My cousins had been looking for me all morning. They assumed I was off by myself, surfing. After all, they said, "You're very independent."

IV

A s I was finishing this book, two men proud to be different were formally honored as American heroes. After months of petitions, community letters, and testimonies, the Public Safety and Transportation Committee of Manhattan's Community Board 3 unanimously approved Joey Ramone Place at the corner of East 2nd Street and the Bowery, near CBGB's. It was the first step toward memorializing the King of Punk on his own turf. The idea of a street sign for Joey came from Maureen Wojciechowski, a twenty-year-old college student from Staten Island. After Joey died, Maureen didn't want people to forget about her hero. She said, "Growing up, Joey's music was all I had. I was a misfit, I never felt welcomed. I guess I was a typical Ramones fan." By just being himself, Joey Ramone rescued Maureen just like he saved millions of fans, two generations, worldwide.

Then, when our city was attacked on September 11, the Post-Ramones Empire lost another hero, a great warrior. Johnny Heff of the Bullys was the Rockaway punk I'd met through Marky Ramone. He died when the World Trade Center collapsed. By day, the pumped up, inked-out, leather-clad guitarist we knew as Johnny Bully was John Heffernan, a fireman with Engine 28–Ladder 11 on East 2nd Street, eight years on the job. He transferred there from Midtown to be closer to the scene, near clubs like CBGB's and the Continental. Onstage, Johnny and voxman Joey Lanz boasted of bad-boy brawling, boozing, and womanizing. Offstage, Johnny didn't drink; he said he gave it up for rock & roll. A devoted son, his heart belonged to his wife, Laurie, and nine-year-old daughter, Samantha.

On September 11, Firefighter John Heffernan had the day off but decided to go in for the overtime. He rode into town from Queens on his Harley. By the second alarm, John's truck was headed out toward the WTC. All six members of his company, Ladder 11, went MIA. On September 11, Johnny walked into hell, in full stomp position. Whether you were his friend, his blood, bandmate, neighbor, or FF brother, Johnny had you covered. That day, homeboy showed the real bullies what our Bullys were made of.

They found Johnny's body in the rubble about two weeks later. His funeral at St. Camillus in Rockaway was a full Mass, outside engines, brass, bagpipes—complete firefighter's honors. The Continental hosted several memorial benefits for Johnny Bully. Shows were jammed with New York's finest bands, friends, family, fans, firefighters, police, and music critics. His funeral service was attended by over a thousand people, including state officials, reps from New York governor George Pataki's office, and uniformed persons. Mayor Giuliani visited the wake as well as the cemetery. John Heffernan was an honorable man, a *mensch* in every aspect of his life, worthy of a Congressional Medal of Honor. Like Joey, he died an American hero.

Two months after the attack on the World Trade Center, on Veterans Day, an American Airlines jet crashed into a small town on the South Shore of Queens killing over two hundred and fifty people, mostly Dominican. The plane crashed in Rockaway, in Belle Harbor, *right on Twennyninth,* the place where I first discovered the pleasures of street life, the art of hanging out so crucial to my emergent sociological imagination.

In Belle Harbor surfers often grew up to be lifeguards and eventually firemen. My hometown had been hit hard on September 11—many police officers, firefighters, finance workers, executives, secretaries, and stock boys were lost. This double death whammy made residents wonder if they were cursed. But the opposite was true. Having attended so many funerals at St. Francis, Mayor Giuliani said, "They're such beautiful people, such strong, strong people." On the TV news, U.S. Senator Charles Schumer described Rockaway as one of the toughest parts of New York. "They'll get through it," he said. "They're a hearty lot." They were right. If any place in America could survive two such heavy hits, it was that tough little town.

After September 11, people in New York City thought twice about making fun of "the bridge and tunnel set."

V

God grant me the serenity to accept the things I cannot change, the courage to change the things I can, and the wisdom to know the difference. After Big Pink I wanted to make it right, be part of a world where God could live. I decided to curtail a lifelong family tradition of petty pilfering. Unfortunately, I never got to tell Betty Bradley that so far, I've not stolen even one roll of toilet paper from Columbia University, *The Montel Williams Show, Rolling Stone,* or Random House. I was born again by the time I got to those places.

For many years I understood my life as a veritable Book of the Dead, an ongoing series of losses and sorrows beginning at birth. The original wound, the nuclear core of pain, the bottom of my prayer. Betty and Herbie loved life and they lived it fully, they had it all, and then "God" took it away. So I hated God, and I knew He hated me. I understood from the get-go; joy is fleeting, sorrow relentless. Maybe we broke the glass at the Jewish wedding to remember that, ultimately, life is a bummer, that God just wants to fuck you up. Even if you do the right thing, live right, uphold all of His 613 laws, you're still gonna get hosed. Convinced that this was the existential truth, I'd spent my life obliterating, filling the hole, plugging up the gaping emptiness, distracting the sorrow with food, sex, drugs, booze, always wanting more.

My biological father, Herbie Denmark, has been dead almost as long as I've been alive. I didn't even realize how much I missed him until I felt a suspicious lump in my left tit. In the days before my biopsy result redeemed me, I was convinced I was terminal. I found myself oddly comforted at the thought of dying. I imagined that in death, I would finally get to meet him, see him, hear his voice. Would he like me? I would have traded ten years of my life just to talk to him for ten minutes, to be near him, to know him. He held me once, and then he disappeared.

Why was I singled out, targeted to suffer loss? I believed that for most of my life. But I began to view things differently. Depression is a chemically based disease that causes us to shut out the world through negative self-absorption. But sorrow is an integral part of our humanity; it is all-inclusive. Sorrow and death offer a key to life's mystery. To let go, to accept the impermanence, the constant flux of energy, is to grasp the flow of life. Inherent in the art of loving is the risk of profound loss. All life ends in death. Or, following San Francisco's noise godz Flipper, "That's the Way of the World."

Participate joyfully in the sorrows of the world. An interest in Buddhism developed from my desire to explore and transcend sorrow. Death and loss were such persistent themes in my life, but why? Was it karmic residue, unfinished business from a previous incarnation? My friend Mitch is a lapsed Episcopalian. Like me, he's had trouble accepting organized religion's tradition of intolerance toward homosexuals and women. There's homophobia and sexism lurking in all religions, including Buddhism. God is perfect. We are not.

Mitch invited me to the Tibet Center to hear lectures. He gave me prayer beads and instructed me to read *Awakening the Buddha Within* by Lama Surya Das. The Eight Steps to Enlightenment correlated with the Twelve Steps of Alcoholics Anonymous. Although AA has strong Judeo-Christian underpinnings, Bill W. and cofounder Dr. Bob also drew heavily from Buddhist traditions, often conferring with Carl Jung.

The term *Buddha* refers to an enlightened being, one freed from the cycle of rebirth through his or her own insight. We long to be free from this cycle, because it carries with it such sorrow and loss, all the misery of human existence. Freedom comes in learning detachment, in letting go of our addictions, ego needs, and desires. Sorrow was at the center of my spiritual journey, the seed of my enlightenment. Presented to me shortly after my birth, it has taken a lifetime to comprehend. Herbie died so young, a vibrant life cruelly aborted, a promise broken. His death shattered my mother's heart and wounded me deeply. Devastating, profoundly tragic, this was the first lesson: Herbie's Hebrew name was Chaim—it means "life."

In simplest terms, the path to enlightenment begins with a search inward, to discover our own perfection, our Buddha nature. As Lama Surya Das points out, one can be a Buddha without becoming a Buddhist. Jesus was a Buddha, so was the Seventh Lubavitcher Rebbe, Rabbi Menachem Schneerson. Maybe John Lennon was, too, and for some of us, Johnny Thunders and Joey Ramone. A bodhisattva is a being who has partly or completely attained a state of enlightenment. Buddha Gautama called himself a bodhisattva, a searcher for enlightenment, before he attained Buddhahood. Next to my bed I have Green Tara, a female bodhisattva who represents the maternal aspect of compassion. She protects people against danger as they cross over the Ocean of Existence. Pink and green were the colors of my mother's bedroom. They're the colors of the fourth chakra, the energy center of the heart. So I try to keep it pink and green.

When I need balance, I turn to the Virgin Mary. Her open arms remind me of the fullness of the universe, its infinite generosity and grace. The ancient Virgin Goddesses were self-possessed, independent, beholden to no man. Mary is a gateway to the Goddesses of old, to the feminine principle, to life itself. Quan Yin, the Chinese Great Mother Goddess of Mercy, is the embodiment of loving kindness, the bodhisattva of compassion. Her symbol is a vase containing the water of life. Mary, Tara, and Quan Yin embody spiritual values so absent now in the material world. They are my guides in meditation and prayer.

For so long I was unable to fathom my mother's suffering. Her sorrow was so vast, her strong body and bright spirit so relentlessly tortured. She loved me deeply, but sometimes she hurt me, and that confused me. Sometimes I go to St. Patrick's Cathedral and sit quietly, meditating in the Lady Chapel. Forgiving our mutual trespasses helps me to make peace. Sometimes Betty Bradley comes to me in dreams.

Whenever I'm singing along to Laura Nyro's earthy spirituals, my mother seems especially close. Through music, I'll always feel her presence. In those moments we cease to be mother and daughter. We're released, free souls dancing.

As she lay dying, Betty Bradley asked of D.O.M., "Please be kind to Donna," and he has tried. D.O.M. never remarried; some people only love once and it's for life. At eighty-five, he's still a devoted *salsero*. Bored during a recent MRI exam, he asked the technician, "Can you please put on some Latin music?" He still has a loaded rifle and a jack-knife next to his bed. D.O.M. still claims he doesn't believe in God, but he's the most godly, righteous person I've ever met. He remains the father of my heart, the one I've loved the most, the one I've trusted. He appreciated and understood me. D.O.M. found me in the world, cared about me, and to my amazement, he stuck around.

Meanness is the defect of character that caused me to hurt Nick, it was final proof of my spiritual disease. Kindness is the opposite of meanness. It is a powerful spiritual virtue I saw in my mother and my father, it transcended all their *mishegas*. When we feel afraid, angry, hurt, or disrespected, we lash out. We use harsh words that injure the soul. Kindness is mercy, compassion, empathy, and love *in action*. It is the active, dynamic manifestation of spiritual love.

Nick is still making music. His new material is silky, sophisticated, more Sinatra than CorpseGrinder. Although he still hates my "goon" bands, in a conciliatory gesture Nick got me an AC/DC action figure for Christmas. Angus Young on guitar, on my shelf, right next to the Limoges collection. Nick has been the primary bond of my adult life. More than twenty-five years later, our relationship still defies conventional labels, but who cares? Like God, love may never make any logical sense. Learning to accept that possibility has been the greatest intellectual challenge of all.

A favorite spiritual muse is the Laughing Buddha often seen in Chinese restaurants. The happy fat Buddha is the Chinese master of Zen, Poe-Tai Ho Shang, who lived sometime between the sixth and tenth centuries and discovered the Buddha within himself. Carefree, always surrounded by children, he became a popular hero, a god of good fortune, symbol of luck. According to *The Book of Buddhas,* "He is still wandering all over the world as a tangible expression of unconcerned beatitude which can be attained by anyone when he finds his own true nature, the 'Buddha within himself.' "

Today the god of my understanding is a Great Spirit, all-knowing and all-seeing, ever-present and unknowable. Simultaneously abstract and universal, yet personal, internal, mine. Inside, outside, upside down. In our fractured, fragmented, multicultural, global, postmodern world, we're scavengers constructing our truths across paradigms, cutting and pasting bits and pieces to grasp at Divinity. I figure if metal, hardcore, and hip-hop cross-pollinated to produce bands like Korn and Slipknot, why can't we mix it up for the love of God?

God works in us, and we work in God. It doesn't matter how or where. Dogma is coherent, ordered, rational. Faith is not. It is our individual quest and collective project, the bringing together of the sacred and the profane, left brain, right brain. We do it in a variety of ways— through music, surfing, addiction, and true love. Religion is a discipline, a system, a means to an end. But it cannot be an end in itself. According to Max Weber, when we replace ends with means as our ultimate goal, that's irrationality. Then we're riding the crazy train.

One misty spring afternoon, I was walking on the beach, enjoying the silence of East Hampton off-season. I felt suddenly sick with panic. I'd lost my bearings. Terrified by the endless sea and sky, I stood alone, nameless, faceless in a timeless chasm. Unlike Rockaway, the beach at Indian Wells had no rocks or jetties, no familiar markings to situate me in my journey. In the past, this feeling of complete abandonment, of existential angst, would have been incapacitating. I would have run off to Nick, to a drink, to the radio, grabbed on to someone, something, anything to rescue me. But not this time.

Salvation came softly, like the whispering tide. *Don't be afraid, you're not alone, you're in God's world, like the sand and sea, the piping plover shorebirds, striped bass, and dune grass.* Now I understood. Like all life forms, I was unique but not other. Individual but not separate. Neither alien nor misfit nor abject. That day, the gnawing hunger that had always propelled me subsided, and I surrendered: Only God's love can fill the gaping hole, mend the addict's heart, heal the unloved child, soothe the outcast's weary soul.

Then, a few days later, I actually saw it. It happened just after sunset. *Crimson ball sinks from view.* I was riding my red steel vintage Marky Ramone bike up in Clearwater, north of Springs. As the summer clouds in East Hampton raced toward magenta, a silver cast off Gardiner's Bay reflected a magnificent shimmer, *color sky rose carmethene.* I turned around and there it was. Glowing, bilious, and bold, Big Pink splashed across the sky. It only lasted a second, then it was gone. Now I had proof: Big Pink was God, and God was everywhere. Inside me and out in the world, alive in my heart, pulsating in the clouds, in each breath, then released in death, *wear your love like heaven.* . . .

Does it really matter if we invented God or God invented us? Or if Johnny Rotten was right and *God is a bitch, spelled backwards is dog?* Who cares if meditation is a post-yuppie fad, a by-product of our vapid hypermaterialism? The gateway to Nirvana or a physiological state endemic to our biology? Who knows if the human experience of "God" is simply a neuro-fiction, a high-voltage chemical surge? And who is to say what is sacred and what is profane?

Life is a land of a thousand dances, and God's the DJ. All faith systems serve a common purpose, to help us access the Ultimate, organize and interpret the sacred. From the Ramones to the Church of Mormon, it's that connection we're after. As Patti Smith chanted, in words by Allen Ginsberg, *everything is holy, everything is holy, everything is holy.*

A few years after I bottomed out, after Big Pink, I felt strong and ready enough to face my worst fears, accept my losses, acknowledge my shortcomings, and celebrate my strengths. Eventually, I was able to experience a deepening connection to myself, to other people and a glorious world. For so long, I preferred living in cool, darkened rooms. I lived like a vampire. I hated the light, slept days and worked nights. Now I walked out into the blazing midday sun. I swam in the ocean, and I could breathe again. I slowed down, I stopped talking so fast. Unwinding, defrosting, I saw that the world was a safe place, and there was love for me, everywhere.

And everywhere, I saw miracles, in acts of kindness as well as in guitar hooks. I saw a magnificent light shining in people's eyes and in great ideas. Comatose or blinded by the light, sometimes a spiritual journey is little more than mastering the art of muddling through. I came to believe that this consciousness had always been in me. I heard it pounding in the music, saw it shimmering in the waves, felt it in the first rush, and in his kiss. I know now that God is always present, called or uncalled.

For a long time, rage and fear were my survival tools. I took abuse and I dished it out. I carried my weapons—the knife in my boot, a bad attitude in my back pocket, and a mega-chip on my shoulder. I viewed the world as a hateful, unloving place where people were out to demolish me. I wasn't giving them any advantages. My life was a series of crash-burns, exaltation then defeat, punishment then salvation. Through it all, a thread of mercy ran through my life, peeking out at me, calling me home, smiling. When I finally looked up and saw it, I was free. As God reopened my heart, my capacity for joy, my ability to love myself and to feel part of the world were restored. And then I could really dance.

After they were married, Betty and Herbie spent their first summer in Belle Harbor, renting an apartment near the beach. According to Mom, on one unusually hot night in 1950, that's where I was conceived. And so, like all great warriors of Xanthos, it was my destiny to return to the ocean, for I was born with it in my heart.

As a teenager I was a passionate bodysurfer. I rode the waves on my belly all day, sat by the shore till sunset, then waited for the dawn. Awed by the beauty, the magnitude, I was a child of the sea. And then it was over. I went indoors, underground, spent my life in clubs, after-hours bars, and libraries. Up all night, sleeping all day, always working, always running. Emotionally comatose, I never looked up. I'd grown afraid of life, of the sun, unable to breathe, indifferent to the sea, the clouds, and the birds. Numbed to the wonderment of God's world. Now, so many years later I returned. I came back to life, to the beach, to what surfers call the Church of the Blue Sky.

Today I have a bodyboard of my own. A magenta and turquoise

Wave Rebel GT 500 Tamega 42″ stringer—special edition, in honor of Brazilian champ Guilherme Tamega. I have MCD board shorts and mix-and-match rash guards. Sometimes liberation comes down to the clothes on our backs. I'm emancipated in a sleek women's Rip Curl Classic, 3/2-weight black neoprene wetsuit, trimmed in pale magenta. It matches my board, my sunglasses, and the Crazy Colored rose-tinted tips of my hair. Magenta is as close to Big Pink as it gets. It's somewhere under the blue sky, between God and purple, between my heart and Joey's aura.

A pair of O'Neill 3mm snakeskin gloves and my ankle booties will keep me cozy in New York waters from April through October. From Breezy Point to Montauk, I'll wake up and call the local surfline. Then I'll go check the waves myself, to be sure I'm not missing anything. My skills suck, but there's a saying: "The best surfer in the water is the one having the most fun," so, dude, I rule. Surfing is as addictive as everything else, but it leaves me feeling refreshed and sublime.

Maybe all knowledge is like the ocean—here today, gone tomorrow. In the morning, the waves are awesome. You're walking on water, gliding along. An hour later, they suck, they're messy, breaking into each other, dissolving into chaotic smurf and foam. But as long as there are waves, there's hope.

The waves are full of metaphors, ironies, Zen riddles, and assorted cosmic truths. The ocean has taught me to accept life on life's terms. Sometimes the waves are so big, they just keep coming and I can't catch my breath. I try to fight them back, but I can't beat them. So I wait them out, I let them wash over me, and eventually the water gets calmer. The sea teaches me to have patience, faith in the future, that nothing is forever. The tides change by the hour, the wind, storms come and go. Whatever it is, I know it will pass.

I am a mighty swimmer from Xanthos, but even I can't control the ocean. It is a power so much greater than me. Tides and currents are things I can't change. So when the sea is flat and I can't get a ride, I find other things to do. I swim or float, do laps, invent quirky water calisthenics. If it's too fierce, too volatile, I'll stage dive into crashing waves and let myself be carried. I've learned to accept what I get, to make the most of what I have, and to walk away when it's impossible. When a beautiful hollow wave breaks close to shore, I'll steer clear; shorebreakers can be backbreakers. If I get caught up in a rip, and the water carries me too far, I'll panic. I'll start thrashing around, swimming against the undertow. That only makes it worse. But if I calm down and swim sideways, one stroke at a time, I'll get back to shore.

Every surfer dreams of the perfect wave. Sometimes, there it is, rolling right at you. Jump too soon, you won't get far. Wait too long, you'll get slammed. Sometimes you grab a killer wave only to realize the one behind it was better. Or you skip a wave because the next one is "it." Then you realize you blew it, you missed the ride of your life. You can't be too sure what's coming next, but you always know something's coming. It's never too late to catch another wave.

There are many spiritual journeys to be had. Some sacred, some profane. If the path to enlightenment is so many rivers converging into one great sea, then the Ultimate Truth must be somewhere out in the ocean. If I ever figure it out, I'll let you know.

Meantime, see ya in the water.

ACKNOWLEDGMENTS

Although this book is about me, it includes other people, too. To protect their privacy, names, places, and other identifying details have been altered. To everyone mentioned in my journey, whether interviewed, quoted, or otherwise identified by name or pseudonym, dead or alive, you have made this a book of gratitude. Special thanks to Nina Antonia, Anna Crane, Ellen Carbone, and Jean Morrissey for providing important materials. To Alan "Skip" Weinstock and Carol Marston for re-creating a lost community in cyberspace—www.farrockaway.com.

Telling a story involves taking three vows of fidelity: one to the narrative, another to the reader, a third to the heart. A great editor helps the writer keep all three. To Jon Karp of Random House, for his insight, support, and steadfast commitment to this work. Special thanks to Ann Godoff, Janet Wygal, Patty Romanowski, Janelle Duryea, and Jake Greenberg. Bruce Tracy of Villard provided pep talks, Greek food, and guidance at a crucial time. To my agent, Susan Ramer of Don Congdon Associates, for her faith, integrity, and keen Virgo eye.

To the people who nourished me while I was writing this book; The Cuz, Rachel Felder, Howie Weinberg and Millie, Dorris Lang,

Monyaka, Aunt Rose and Charlotte Lesher. To Cherie Sperber and family, Cat Rebennack, Alex Echo, Kathy Dobie, Ellen Watson, Bobby and Raina Turano, and Patrick Christiano. To Greg Simmons and Sons, Kevin Ahearn, John Kowalenko, Steve Haweeli, Steve White, Raymond DeMarco, Cherie Butler, and the Associates. To Ryan Van Meter and Ryan Crozier; Graham Hawks and John Marchesella. Thanks to rock & roll girls Holly George-Warren and Barbara O'Dair. Special love to Susie and the Witches of the North.

To my cousins on all four sides. To a generation rising—to my students and the amazing children of all my friends—you make everything matter so much more.

Following his death, Joey Ramone's solo album, *Don't Worry About Me,* was released to both critical and popular acclaim. The songs, even those written from his hospital bed, were amazingly upbeat and life affirming. I am forever indebted to him for showing me that in spite of everything, it's a wonderful world.

In an ultimate, ironic triumph for punks and misfits everywhere, on March 19, 2002, the Ramones were formally inducted into the Rock and Roll Hall of Fame. I had the honor of writing the Ramones induction essay and attending the ceremony at the Waldorf-Astoria. Accepting his award in his sharp burgundy sharkskin jacket and cool black shades, Dee Dee Ramone said, "I'd like to congratulate myself, and thank myself, and give myself a big pat on the back." It was like he was saying, "I did it my way, fuck you." He had followed his heart and found his place.

On June 5, 2002, eleven weeks later, barely a year after Joey, Dee Dee died in Los Angeles. Early reports listed the cause of death as drug related. *Sometimes I feelin' my soul is as restless as the wind . . . maybe I was born to die in Berlin.* A few weeks later, Trigger and some surviving Ramones organized a memorial show at the Continental with many special guests, friends, family, and bands. Like Joey, Dee Dee Ramone is a national treasure, *too tough to die.* God bless America, God bless the Ramones and their mighty legions. *Today your love, tomorrow the world.*

To Betty Bradley, D.O.M, Nick, and all musicians; to all my bands past and present, signed and unsigned, God's love you do deliver.

Above all, I am grateful to Big Pink.

Make a joyful noise unto God, all ye lands;

Sing forth the honor of His name:

Make His praise glorious.

—PSALMS 66:1–2

ABOUT THE AUTHOR

DONNA GAINES has written for *Rolling Stone, Ms., The Village Voice, Spin, Newsday,* and *Salon.* She's been published in underground fanzines, numerous trade and scholarly collections, professional journals, and textbooks. Her photographs, liner notes, lyrics, and poetry have been published or shown as well. A sociologist, journalist, and New York State certified social worker, Dr. Gaines grew up hanging out in Rockaway Beach, Queens, a surf town made famous by the Ramones.

Gaines received a Ph.D. in sociology, and a master's degree in social work. Her first book, *Teenage Wasteland: Suburbia's Dead End Kids,* was published by Pantheon Books in 1991. An international expert on youth violence and culture, Dr. Gaines has been interviewed extensively in newspapers, for documentaries, and on radio and television. She has provided consulting services to attorneys defending young people in death penalty trials, as well as to community leaders, school administrators, clergy, and producers and reporters in the print and broadcast media in the United States, Canada, and Europe. Professor Gaines has taught sociology at Barnard College of Columbia University and at the Graduate Faculty of Political and Social Science at New School University. Donna Gaines lives in New York City and online at www.donnagaines.com.